Studies in Eighteenth-Century Culture

Volume 50

Studies in Eighteenth-Century Culture

Volume 50

Editor

David A. Brewer
The Ohio State University

Associate Editor

Crystal B. Lake
Wright State University

Editorial Board

Theresa Gaul
Texas Christian University

Robert Griffin
Texas A&M University

Michael B. Guenther
Grinnell College

Gabe Paquette
University of Oregon

Wendy Wassyng Roworth
University of Rhode Island

Amy S. Wyngaard
Syracuse University

Published by Johns Hopkins University Press for the
American Society for Eighteenth-Century Studies

Johns Hopkins University Press
Baltimore and London
2021

Johns Hopkins University Press
2715 North Charles Street
Baltimore, Maryland 21218-4363
www.press.jhu.edu

ISBN 978-1-4214-4010-1
ISSN 0360-2370

Articles appearing in this annual series are abstracted and
indexed in *America: History and Life, Current Abstracts, Historical
Abstracts, MLA International Bibliography, Poetry and Short Story
Reference Center, and RILM Abstracts of Music Literature*

Contents

Presidential Lecture

Clifford Lecture

CONSUMPTION AND REMEDIATION

Cluster: Consuming Foreign Music and Theater in Eighteenth-Century Britain

Cluster: Remediating Eighteenth-Century Texts

Cluster: Teaching Tough Texts

ASECS Affiliate and Regional Societies

American Antiquarian Society
Aphra Behn Society
Bibliographical Society of America
British Society for Eighteenth-Century Studies
Burney Society of North America
Canadian Society for Eighteenth-Century Studies
Daniel Defoe Society
Early Caribbean Society
East-Central ASECS
Eighteenth-Century Scottish Studies Society
German Society for Eighteenth-Century Studies
Goethe Society of North America
Historians of Eighteenth-Century Art and Architecture
Ibero-American Society for Eighteenth-Century Studies
International Adam Smith Society
International Herder Society
Johnson Society of the Central Region
Lessing Society
Midwestern ASECS
Mozart Society of America
North American British Music Studies Association
Northeast ASECS
North American Kant Society
Rousseau Association
Samuel Johnson Society of the West
Samuel Richardson Society
Society of Early Americanists
Society for Eighteenth-Century French Studies
Society for Eighteenth-Century Music
Society for the History of Authorship, Reading and Publishing
South Central Society for Eighteenth-Century Studies
Southeast Asian Society for Eighteenth-Century Studies
Southeastern ASECS
Voltaire Foundation
Voltaire Society of America
Western Society for Eighteenth-Century Studies

A Note from the Editors

This 50th volume of *Studies in Eighteenth-Century Culture* also marks the 50th anniversary of the founding of the American Society for Eighteenth-Century Studies (ASECS). As is usual on such occasions, the Society took some time to reflect upon its past. Three of those reflections are included here. But most of the attention at ASECS's 50th Annual Meeting in March 2019 and at the meetings of its affiliate and regional societies that academic year (during which the original versions of all of the contributions to this volume were presented) was devoted to considering the present and future of eighteenth-century studies. That present and that future certainly have their challenges, and those challenges have only been amplified by recent events: this volume went into production amidst a global pandemic (which has claimed the life of one of our contributors), the world's accompanying slide into severe economic recession, and the most far-reaching—and we hope, effective—campaign for racial justice in a generation, which has prompted some necessary and overdue self-scrutiny among humanists about their relation to structural inequities. The economic, environmental, and political difficulties facing us are considerable.

However, as the contents of this volume amply demonstrate, this is nonetheless an exciting time for scholarship. New questions are being asked; new methods are being developed; new archives are being explored. At the same time, old questions and familiar texts are being revisited in ways that productively unsettle what we thought we knew. Our task is to press still harder and push still further. What the next half century will hold is, of course, unknown. But if we can build upon and extend the kinds of important, often exhilarating scholarship on offer here, then the future of eighteenth-century studies is secure, at least as an intellectual enterprise, and that, in turn, might yet help repair the world. We've been warned many times about overestimating the social utility of our work. In moments of crisis like the present, it's perhaps equally important that we not underestimate it.

This volume also marks a change in the editorial personnel of *Studies in Eighteenth-Century Culture*. The contents and arrangement of this volume reflect the insight and judgment of Eve Tavor Bannet. We have merely shepherded her vision into production. We would like to thank Eve and her Associate Editor, Roxann Wheeler, for their service to the field and for their generosity and guidance in the transition. Whatever further advances we are able to make will be profoundly indebted to what they have passed on to us.

Here's to another fifty years!

David A. Brewer
The Ohio State University

Crystal B. Lake
Wright State University

ASECS AT 50

Past

Genesis: Donald J. Greene and the Founding of the American Society for Eighteenth-Century Studies

HOWARD D. WEINBROT

Donald Greene was teaching at the University of California, Riverside, in 1966–67. Probably late in 1967, he asked his three eighteenth-century junior colleagues if they were interested in forming a national eighteenth-century society. We were. Enthusiastically. Greene, after all, studied the relationships between religion, literature, and politics and had written a major revisionist book on Samuel Johnson and eighteenth-century politics. He was among the most eminent students of eighteenth-century British culture. He embodied multidisciplinary scholarship. Greene never was awed by the Great and the Good because he was among them.

A few days after the invitation, John Norton, David Hansen, and I joined Greene for lunch at a local restaurant and discussed possibilities. The interdisciplinary society would of course encourage research areas other than literature. Its official journal would reflect such breadth of interest. The society would be North American and encourage regional branches. It would have geographical and disciplinary representation. When occasion allowed it would be more broadly international. It would have an elected executive board and secretary as cementing forces. My own efforts were to begin by organizing a western and, for the time being, largely Californian regional society for eighteenth-century studies. The talk was good and the options many. In the event, Messrs. Norton and Hansen soon left the Riverside English Department, and in the summer of 1969 I departed for the University of Wisconsin, Madison.

After I arrived in Wisconsin, I continued to exercise Greene's vision of supporting regional eighteenth-century societies. He saw these as a way of furthering eighteenth-century studies locally in order to expand them nationally. On 28 July 1970, he told Peter Stanlis that five regional societies had been established: "All to the good, I'm convinced—the wider the 'grass roots' are extended, the stronger and healthier the whole organization will be, I'm sure."[1] I hoped to put that concept into practice. I paid special attention to the Johnson Society of the Central Region, which soon was invited to become an affiliate of the American Society for Eighteenth-Century Studies (ASECS) and is now a thriving sixty-one-year-old scholarly enterprise. I encouraged the University of Wisconsin Press to offer a three-year contract for *Studies in Eighteenth-Century Culture*. I attended several regional ASECS meetings during my amiably long tenure in Madison. As President of the Midwestern American Society for Eighteenth-Century Studies in 1979–80, I hosted a large conference in Madison. I also served on two national meeting planning committees, presented a plenary paper and thereafter the Clifford Lecture for the national conference, and had the pleasure of serving on the Editorial Board of *Eighteenth-Century Studies* (1977–80) and on the Executive Committee (1996–99). Greene's vision of international affiliations never left my mind. I was part of the joint exchange committee for ASECS and the British Society for Eighteenth-Century Studies (1999–2000) and the International Society for Eighteenth-Century Studies (ISECS)'s planning committee for the wonderfully successful 2003 meeting in Los Angeles. That happy conclave exemplified Greene's concept of regional, national, and international eighteenth-century societies as a unified and unifying intellectual and social force. I confess to special delight in returning to the fledgling ASECS's founding and to Donald Greene's seminal role during those years.

I now write with a combination of always unreliable memories and the more reliable ASECS archives. Paul Alkon, Greene's successor as Leo S. Bing Professor at the University of Southern California, wisely arranged to have these moved to the William Andrews Clark Memorial Library at UCLA, where they have been stored since 1994. The volunteer archivist Ann Soady expertly sorted them into useful preliminary files. The Society owes thanks to each helpful individual as well as the Clark Library. Some of the information I cite below comes from my own experience. Most of the narrative, however, draws upon the Clark's ASECS archives. They demonstrate our founder's extraordinary vision and manifold generosities. Predicting the past is almost as foolish as predicting the future, but those of us present at the creation nonetheless are likely to agree on one absolute: without Donald J. Greene's commitment the American Society for Eighteenth-Century Studies would not exist in its present form, and perhaps not exist at all.

Greene had splendid allies, especially Stanlis, Lester Crocker, and James Clifford, but Greene himself always was the moving force. He originated discussion, selected the Society's first provisional president and provisional officers, wrote the constitution, revised the constitution, financed many expenses, and persuaded the University of Southern California to support the endeavor. He established *Eighteenth-Century Studies* as the Society's official journal and was its first Book Review Editor. He helped to create *Studies in Eighteenth-Century Culture* and, through Crocker, built its early home at Case Western Reserve University. He encouraged the expansion of *Philological Quarterly*'s eighteenth-century bibliography and supported its brief stay at USC. He organized several interdisciplinary units within ASECS and saw to its affiliation with ISECS, which he also helped found. He was instrumental in designating Yale University as the site for ISECS in 1976, the first time that group convened in North America. His immediate allies and other colleagues clearly helped and deserve enduring gratitude, but Greene's letters make plain that he became the dominant force because many others in authority preferred the safe sidelines. For example, on 14 November 1969, Greene informed Crocker and Stanlis that the three of them needed to be a steering committee: "I think we may as well give up hope of getting much in the way of work out of most of the other members of the executive board unless we take the initiative firmly." That was a familiar condition. On 13 January 1971, Greene wrote to Provisional Treasurer Stanlis: "I keep extremely busy with ASECS affairs, among others. The problem is mainly to find people who will do some work—not just talk about—and what a chore that is! But we'll get there eventually."

"Eventually" was only one of the words with which Greene had to cope. "A slight headache … has developed," he laments to the Executive Board on 12 May 1972. "Problems, problems!" he repeats to Stanlis on 22 May 1972. Arranging to fund *Eighteenth-Century Studies* as the official Society publication, ongoing difficulties with efforts to continue publishing *Studies in Eighteenth-Century Culture,* further complications with subsidizing and transferring publication of *The Eighteenth Century: A Current Bibliography* from *Philological Quarterly* to USC—all these would take their toll, but not before Greene established the Society as a perceived functioning force. On 18 March 1970, he advised Crocker and Stanlis regarding a committee on prizes. Perhaps, he says, it is best to make appointments to the committee and provide its guidelines before the Cleveland meeting. "The more we can give the impression of concrete activity on the part of the Society, the better it will be for general morale (and increased membership)."

Interdisciplinary scholarship is chief among the Society's native "concrete activities." On 17 June 1970, Greene compliments Stanlis for an article that had appeared in the journal he edited, *Studies in Burke and his Time*:

> I meant to tell you earlier how much I admired the article about recent studies of the French Revolution in the last number of *Studies in Burke*. It is exactly the kind of thing we should have (in many fields) in *Eighteenth-Century Studies*—something that intelligently brings students in other disciplines up to date in what is being done in an area of scholarship. I'm almost prepared to ask permission to reprint it in *ECS* or have copies of it made to send to potential reviewers and contributors as a model.

That emphasis remains in the Society today in large part because Greene established a framework of representation for several disciplines other than British literature, including various national histories, Art History, and French. Greene recognized that an emphasis on interdisciplinarity would also increase attendance at Society meetings. On 14 November 1969, Greene reported a problem to Crocker and Stanlis. Several colleagues could not attend the national meeting without the support of their home institutions, support that was available only if they were on the program. "These are the terms of academic life," Greene noted, and then added what he thought a good way to solve the problem:

> the society should have sections devoted to the various disciplines—a music section, a visual section, an English literature section, British history section, and so on. Each could have a steering committee, with a chairman, and this would provide a lot of members with transportation to the meeting. Each section could have a bibliographer, or bibliographical sub-committee, to help with the (eventual) annual interdisciplinary bibliography. One half-day during each of the future annual meetings could be devoted to section meetings, handling their own programs and business.

Greene is aware of the potential splintering effect inherent in the proposal, but suggests that his idea could avoid "vague, wooly, dilettantish discourse that will repel the really serious scholars." Fortunately, ASECS clearly established different sections but without the complex bureaucratic procedures that Greene suggested. The problem of attendance largely has been resolved by expanding the program and thereby accommodating numerous disciplinary interests.

Greene's response nonetheless reflects his insistence that the Executive Board and major Society committees include both geographic and disciplinary diversity. On 19 May 1973, Greene alerted the Executive Board to a glitch in the election process: "we seem to have goofed." The Board should not give the impression that it is "attempting to load the dice in favor of Sections A [English] and B [Other Modern Languages]." Since members tend to vote for those in their own disciplines, "disciplines with a small representation in the membership (e.g., music, art, history of science) are unlikely to elect an executive board member. It is to be hoped that our new constitutional committee will eventually come up with a means of overcoming this difficulty."

That desirable diversity also extended to younger colleagues, and to Canadians in particular, lest the "American" portion of the Society's name be reduced to the United States rather than North America. On 26 June 1970, Greene wrote to Members of the Executive Board that James A. Leith would be an excellent Chair of Section D, History. "We were all impressed with young ... Leith's performance at the annual meeting—as well as youth, energy, and initiative, we should have a Canadian as chairman of at least one important section." He then adds another characteristic trait: the Secretary's submission to the Executive Board. "Of course," he writes, "we would like the approval of the historians on the Board (Gottschalk, Ritcheson, Neatby) before proceeding with this."

The respect Greene displays here for proper administrative procedures was not unusual. Messrs. Crocker, Stanlis, and Greene himself were almost always referred to as the "Provisional" officers, whose titles could change only when so voted by the membership. Greene was equally sensitive to the need for clean hands and for the appearance of clean hands. On 29 July 1969, he advises the Provisional Executive Board that it "probably would not be wise" for the unelected body to nominate candidates for President or First Vice President. That could provoke accusations "of trying to shape the course of the Society too far in advance." Moreover, the Society now had a budget and consequent temptations to use it. On 20 July 1970 he tells a colleague how concerned he is not to run up significant administrative costs before the Society is financially secure: "With all due respect to your daughter, I would suggest that if we need to hire clerical assistance, we make it a firm rule not to hire members of our own families." Once such hiring is known, it "will cause some justified lifting of eyebrows among the membership."

Nor was the encouragement of junior scholars unusual. On 14 September 1970, Greene asked Stanlis to invite George Jones from Eastern Illinois "to come to Rockford" and the Midwestern ASECS: "send him a special invitation" to attend so that he can present his work. Some academics think themselves too important to attend putatively less important venues. Greene did his best to correct that error, too. On 9 October 1970, he told Crocker and Stanlis that Reynolds McLeod was organizing a regional conference in Morgantown, West Virginia. McLeod tried and failed to get distinguished speakers from "the national executive" to attend. He asked Greene to come, but Greene's exhausting travel schedule for five consecutive weekends, and the budgetary expenses thereof, made his appearance difficult. So Greene then asked Owen Aldridge at the University of Illinois if he could help. "Owen has very kindly replied that, although he has to attend the Midwest meeting at Milwaukee the same weekend, he would be willing to take my place—the program contains papers on two of his interests, Tom Paine and Hispanic literature, and by people he knows." Greene also arranged for Aldridge's travel expenses.

On 14 November 1969, Greene told Crocker and Stanlis that he has "been thinking that after a few years, when the Society gets really established, I might retire as Secretary—I am basically not very fond of administrative work." The vast amount of such work indeed soon established the Society as a young, but flourishing scholarly entourage. On 24 October 1972, Greene thus wrote to the Executive Board that "I have decided to give up the secretaryship of the ASECS when my three-year term expires next spring." There was much to be done to continue the Society's growth, and "I simply no longer have the energy" to complete that work successfully. He hoped to serve the Society in other ways. On 5 February 1973, Greene informed the Board "of my own wish not to continue as Secretary, and that Paul Korshin (English, University of Pennsylvania) has kindly agreed to take over, for at least the next three-year period, and has secured financial support from his university for the office." He added that Stanlis was willing to step down as Treasurer and that Jean Perkins (French, Swarthmore) would replace him. Perkins "did an excellent job in getting our Section B (foreign languages and literatures)" functioning and was treasurer of the Northeast Modern Language Association. Greene clearly recognized and welcomed generational change.

The Donald Greene I have described was meticulous regarding respect for boundaries and for individuals within those boundaries. He could be stern when others crossed those boundaries: no family members should be employed with ASECS money, for example. He also felt strongly about ASECS's unified continental structure. Unfortunately, it seemed to him that at points each of those Society-givens were violated by his successors. Anger from some members of the Society already had been growing because the (significantly enlarged) eighteenth-century bibliography had moved from *Philological Quarterly* at the University of Iowa to USC. On 19 April 1973, Greene wrote to Hoyt Trowbridge, lamenting the extensive work that move had entailed and the consequent absorption of most of his own time. But "to make this a viable operation is going to take plenty of effort, and I understand that the move has given rise to a good deal of (completely unjustified) hostility toward me in various quarters, particularly in the East." Greene insists that he is not trying to enlarge his involvement, since he wants to return to his own research and writing, "but when it's a matter of rescuing an important project like this that seems to be on the point of collapse, I feel a sense of responsibility."

He soon felt that responsibility was not shared in the Society's executive office. During the summer of 1976 the Executive Secretary Paul Korshin advised the Executive Board that mailing costs for *Eighteenth-Century Studies* had increased. There now should be a surcharge for foreign members, including Canadians. Greene was outraged. On 1 November 1976, he wrote to then-President Gwin Kolb: "as a Canadian, I am now classified as a 'foreign member' ... and required to pay the Society dues of $2 more than 'regular members' are." The money was insignificant. The principle was not. Canadians and Americans, he wrote, struggled together to found the Society whose constitution clearly states that "American" means North American: "Now that most of those [original] difficulties have been surmounted and the Society is prospering, we are demoted ... and penalized for our 'foreignness.'" Greene planned to resign. The conflict was, it seems, resolved, and Greene would be elected Second Vice President in 1978, with a scheduled ascent to the presidency to follow two years later.

Bad blood nonetheless had been flowing. In 1979 Greene objected to apparent irregularities in the recent election. There were angry words during the Executive Board meeting at the Atlanta conference that year; the Board denied reimbursement for Greene's expenses; each side hardened its positions behind shields of impregnable High Virtue. In Atlanta on 18 April 1979, Greene verbally resigned from the Society he founded. On 19 June he wrote to then-Executive Secretary Ronald Rosbottom as "Dear Sir" and resigned as First Vice President and from the Executive Board, but agreed to remain temporarily a member of the Society. He hoped to "make some effort to try to render the Executive Board more answerable to the wishes of the membership of the Society." Harsh letters to and from members of the Board ensued, together with more harsh words not put on the record. The Board nonetheless sought amelioration. On 6 September 1979, Rosbottom sent Greene a friendly letter and a check for his expenses, to which on 31 October Greene responded with thanks, returned the check, and asked that it be used for Society needs. He also made plain that he would advise other members of the Society why he had resigned from the Board. Rosbottom's humanely softened words to Greene deserve quotation:

> Don, there is no other person to whom ASECS owes more as
> an institution than to you … you were instrumental in the very
> founding of this society. The next issue of the News Circular will
> have a column by Art McGuinness on ECS in which he mentions
> that you single-handedly and unselfishly saved that journal from
> expiring in its early years (a fact of which I was unaware). Your
> estrangement from ASECS and your resignation from the Board
> have caused consternation among our members.

He concluded with a request for Greene's support and trust: "I regret the present status of our relationship very much; the Society can only suffer should it continue."

Rosbottom's wisdom, however, did not wash away much resentment. Some years ago I recommended that the Society create an award in Greene's name. It was promptly rejected. Someone who had resigned from the Executive Board and the Society would not be so honored. The 2018–19 Executive Board has generously reversed that decision and thereby respected ASECS's origins.

In so doing, the Board also implicitly followed its predecessors' better angels. On 30 June 1989, then Executive Secretary Richard Peterson wrote his last official letter—to Donald Greene. He was pleased to "be the one welcoming you as the Society's only honorary life member. The Executive Board was happy to approve a resolution making this tribute to the one person most responsible for the flourishing organizational and intellectual state of eighteenth-century studies in North America." Henceforth Greene will be listed with "this unique designation and you will receive all our publications." Copies of the letter were sent to Isaac Kramnick, Paul Alkon, and E. P. Harris, no doubt friendly guides who encouraged the cause. It is fitting to conclude with Greene's own gracious response to a graciously offered, and well deserved, award:

> It is indeed a great honor the Society is conferring on me, and I
> am deeply grateful to you and the Executive Board for it. When
> twenty years ago, the ASECS was only a gleam in my eye (and
> those of Jim Clifford, Lester Crocker, and Peter Gay), it was not
> easy to foresee that, thanks to the devoted efforts of you and
> other leaders of the Society, it would develop into the flourishing
> organization it has become. Please convey my sense of gratitude
> to the Executive Board.
>
> *Esto Perpetua*.[2]

Notes

1. All quotations from dated letters are taken from the American Society for Eighteenth-Century Studies archives at the William Andrews Clark Memorial Library of UCLA. It is a pleasure to thank Helen Deutsch, Rebecca Marschall Fenning, Maria Ortiz, and especially Scott Jacobs for helping to arrange my visit, housing, and necessary photocopying. Ronald Rosbottom and Richard Peterson have granted permission to quote from their letters. ASECS has granted permission to quote from the Society's archives.

2. Paul K. Alkon read an earlier version of this essay and verified the circumstances within his experience. Paul passed away on 13 January 2020. He was a founding member of ASECS, convened the Annual Meeting at the University of Maryland in 1971, and was instrumental in preserving the Society's archives at the Clark Library. He was a distinguished husband, father, scholar, teacher, colleague, and dear friend. He is missed.

Women in the Archives

FELICITY A. NUSSBAUM

Recently I spent a strangely interesting day at the splendid William Andrews Clark Memorial Library in Los Angeles: the very rare red-flanked bluetail bird, which usually spends its winters in Asia, had flocked to the Clark grounds. As a result, the grounds were crowded with hordes of dedicated ornithologists and amateur birdwatchers carrying fancy cameras, tiptoeing very slowly and very softly, hoping to catch a glimpse. But I contented myself with a beautiful picture of said bird displayed in an encyclopedia entry within the Clark as I tore myself away to read through several boxes of the archives of the American Society for Eighteenth-Century Studies (ASECS) where I discovered, among other things, what I had forgotten—that my first talk was entitled "The Better Women" at the ninth Annual Meeting, hosted by the University of Chicago in April 1978.

As I understand my task here, it is to say a few words about the formation of the Society, its initial meetings, and the role of women in those early days.

The founders of our Society were extremely ambitious and well organized. They made immediate plans to sponsor an annual meeting, an annual volume, and a bibliography and to award prizes and to produce a journal, a news circular, and a directory. An organizing meeting took place at the Conrad Hilton Hotel in Chicago on 6 September 1969, the founders having met earlier in New York City. A provisional Executive Board was appointed—all male. The Program Committee for the conference had seven members, one of whom was a woman, Mary Kay Howard, who taught history at John Carroll University. The Nominating Committee consisted of three men. Lester Crocker, Peter Stanlis, and Donald Greene formed the Steering Committee. There was considerable debate about whether the Society should be broken up into disciplines and much worry over how to make the Society interdisciplinary. The various correspondences were painstakingly typed, often along with carbon or mimeographed copies. Dues for the Charter and Regular Members were a staggering $7.00, $2.00 of which went to the International Society.

To provide a bit of historical context: in 1969 a woman could legally be fired when she became pregnant. A single, divorced, or widowed woman had difficulty gaining a credit card in her own name without a male co-signer until 1974 when the Equal Credit Opportunity Act was passed. A woman could legally be given a lesser pay than a man for performing the same job. Women could not serve on juries in all fifty states until 1973. A wife could not refuse to have sex with her husband. Women could not have a legal abortion in most states, and abortion was legal on request in only four states: Washington, New York, Alaska, and Hawaii. Roe v. Wade was not law until 1973.

By 16 April 1970, there were believed to be 588 paid members of ASECS, with 250 attending the first Annual Meeting at Case Western Reserve in Cleveland. Eleven men constituted the first Provisional Executive Board. When one of the men resigned (R. M. Wiles), he was replaced by Hilda Neatby, a Canadian historian who taught at the University of Saskatchewan and at Minnesota. Lester Crocker provides a quaint comment regarding the April 1970 meeting of the Provisional Board. He writes, "I am reserving my own office for the meeting of the Executive Board on the afternoon of April 16th. I thought it would be better for us to meet here since the dinner at my home will probably be graced by the presence of several wives."[1]

By 2 February 1970, the Board had agreed to establish *Eighteenth-Century Studies* as the official journal of the Society, and they worried mightily about the preponderance of English literary studies, a problem that persists. Their notes indicate that "the journal, with the best will in the world, finds it difficult to balance its present overwhelmingly English literary content with contributions of good scholarship quality from other disciplines."

At the second annual meeting on 22 April 1971, at the University of Maryland, College Park, Beatrice Fink was the sole woman on the eight-member Program Committee, but in the next few years, both Adrienne D. Hytier (French, Vassar) and Renée Waldinger (Romance Languages, City College of New York) served on the Executive Board. By 1974 Jean Perkins was appointed Treasurer of the organization. In 1978 three women were nominated to the Board, but only one was elected. By the fifth Annual

Meeting (25–27 April 1974, at the University of Pennsylvania), the program had expanded to eleven pages. A sea change had begun. Seventeen women presented, including a session on "Women in the Eighteenth Century" headed by Patricia Meyer Spacks, Professor of English Literature at Wellesley College. It is now hard to imagine that only one session was devoted to what has proliferated into a central topic and multiple sessions at subsequent conferences. Further, Yvonne Noble recently reminded me that after the 1975 roster for the International Society for Eighteenth-Century Studies had no women nominees from ASECS, the Women's Caucus was formed.

In 1975 the Executive Secretary enjoined the Society to become more inclusive, saying, "There are still areas where we have not by any means reached everybody, especially among women professionals, historians, art historians, and historians of science." Finally, in 1975 Elizabeth Eisenstein (History, University of Michigan) was elected First Vice President, but the following year she withdrew from becoming the President of the Society. By April 1976 the membership had risen to a staggering 2,400 people, at least by some counts. There were twenty-three seminars and five plenary sessions at that year's Annual Meeting.

In 1978, to my great surprise as a newly tenured Associate Professor, I was elected to the Executive Board to be a member-at-large—the result, as I recall, of a motion from the Society's members for better representation of its junior members. This surely had something to do with my being a woman. After my three-year term had ended, I was appointed as the delegate from ASECS to the American Council of Learned Societies (ACLS) for two terms until 1989. There too I was pushed forward, again, I think, because of the women's movement. I was made Chairperson of the Executive Committee of Delegates to ACLS (1986–88), whose duties included serving as the Standing Committee on Admissions to ACLS and choosing the topic for the annual meeting of the Delegates.

These were heady experiences for a young associate professor. My position also meant that I sat on the Board of Directors for the ACLS. This allowed me to have an expense-paid annual trip to New York City for the meetings. Of course, I was thrilled, since I then lived in snowy upstate New York. But for me personally, these appointments provided invaluable training in learning what to say and not to say in a meeting, and watching the inner workings of two very important scholarly societies. After ascertaining that there was no rule preventing a person from serving twice on the Executive Board, I was again elected in 2005, and I had the honor of rotating into the position of President of the Society. I tell you all of this because I want to emphasize that I was treated extremely well by ASECS in its early days by the Board and by the members of the Society, who were overwhelmingly male. I attribute this in large part to the considerable power of the women's movement of the mid–1970s and 1980s.

I do remember rather vividly that I was a nursing mother—my daughter had just been born in May 1978—when I attended one of the Executive Committee meetings of the ASECS Board at The Ohio State University, which meant that I had to excuse myself to pump. This was all done very quietly and without incident.

In 1976, at the Annual Meeting hosted by the University of Virginia, the Board included Eisenstein, Jean Perkins, and Madeleine Therrien. At the 1977 Annual Meeting it was voiced that one of the prime considerations was "to see that the plenary sessions give some representation to women speakers." Happily, the first Louis Gottschalk Prize in 1976 went to Margaret Jacob (who later became a president of the Society) for her book *The Newtonians and the English Revolution 1689–1720*, a prize awarded by four male scholars who made up the committee.

There's much more to tell, but let me limit my comments to one important historical issue found in the archives. The 1979 Annual Meeting was planned for Atlanta, Georgia. The women's historian Barbara Schnorrenberg introduced a resolution: "Resolved, that after 1979, no annual meeting will be held in those states of the United States which have not ratified the Equal Rights Amendment (ERA), until the matter of said amendment is resolved." She wrote: "For the second year in a row, the ASECS has clumsily and embarrassingly chosen to meet in states that have rejected the Equal Rights Amendment." You will remember that the Equal Rights Amendment is a proposed amendment to the Constitution designed to guarantee equal legal rights for all American citizens regardless of sex, including in the realms of divorce, property, and employment. By 1977, thirty-five states had ratified the ERA but Georgia was not among them. Four states later retracted their ratifications. Two more, Nevada and Illinois, have since ratified the amendment.

But there was opposition to the proposal, voiced most forcefully by Jeanette Lee Atkinson, who wrote from Comer, Georgia, "I would like to register strong opposition to such acquiescence to the demands of whatever pressure group may happen to be popular at the moment. ... Although as a youngish female I allegedly stand to benefit in the short run from passage of this amendment and its enforcement by zealous minions of the HEW, in the long run I sincerely believe that scholarship and the democratic process—what is left of it—will sustain grave, if not irreparable, damage from the principle that the end, however dubious, justifies the means." Such a move would "gratify the desires and egos of the most strident pressure groups." Nevertheless, the measure introduced by Schnorrenberg passed in the Society, but the question was moot since the meetings after the Atlanta meeting were already planned for Washington, DC, and in states that had ratified the ERA: California and Texas.

The 1979 Atlanta meeting was held in the Sheraton Biltmore, where one paid $25 for a single, $32 for a double. Remarkably, there was considerable irony in holding the tenth Annual Meeting in a state where the ERA had not been approved but when, at long last, the Society was headed by its first woman president, Madeleine Therrien! Since then, twenty other eighteenth-century women scholars have followed her in becoming President of the Society.

Notes

1. All quotations are from the ASECS archives housed at the William Andrews Clark Memorial Library at UCLA. ASECS has granted permission to quote from the Society's archives.

50 Years of Women at ASECS

HEATHER McPHERSON

My personal history with the American Society for Eighteenth-Century Studies (ASECS) has coincided with the growing prominence of women in the organization and the emergence of a strong coterie of art historians. The first ASECS Annual Meeting that I attended was in 1983 in New York. Although ASECS was conceived as an interdisciplinary society and art historian Barbara Stafford was on the Executive Board, Art History was virtually non-existent at the Society's meetings. My name does not appear in the program for that year because I was a late addition to a two-part interdisciplinary panel on "Visitors to Eighteenth-Century Rome." My paper on "Greuze's Italian Sojourn, 1755–57" was published in expanded form in Volume 14 of *Studies in Eighteenth-Century Culture* (1985). There were fifty-two panels in 1983, as opposed to almost two hundred in 2019. Art History was a bit better represented at the 1984 ASECS Annual Meeting in Boston where Kim Sloan, Barbara Stafford, Robert Neuman, and I presented papers, and Tom Crow chaired a session on "Uses of Antiquity."

The mid–1980s were watershed years when ASECS began to diversify and take a more visual and theoretical turn, reflecting the expanding field of eighteenth-century studies. At the 1985 Annual Meeting in Toronto, there were multiple sessions devoted to the visual arts: "French Prints," "Cityscapes," "Social Ideals and Criticism in the Visual Arts," "Walpole and the Gothic Revival," and a plenary lecture on the gardens at Stowe—as well as musical and theatrical divertissements. I participated in a panel on

"Jacques-Louis David and Parallels with the *Oath of the Horatii,*" with James Leith as commentator. Having the opportunity to present my research in that venue with senior scholars was an important academic milestone for me. The 1986 Annual Meeting in Williamsburg included special visits and workshops and a rich array of interdisciplinary panels on topics including "Prisons and Asylums," "Images of Madness in Arts and Letters," "Baroque Art and Literature in the Hispanic World," "Visual Interpretations of Eighteenth-Century Life," "Images of Women in French Art," and "Automata," with many more art historians (primarily women) participating, including Pat Crown, Elise Goodman-Soelner, Reed Benhamou, Barbara Stafford, Jane Kromm, Judith Stanton, and myself. I presented a paper on the "Rococo Revisited through Postmodern Eyes" in a cross-disciplinary session, "The Tie that Binds: Eighteenth-Century Arts Alive Today," that critically reconsidered eighteenth-century art, music, and literature in relation to the present, indicative of a growing interest in demarginalizing and revitalizing the eighteenth century by recognizing its continuing influence.

ASECS continued to expand its offerings, as evidenced in the splendid 1989 New Orleans Annual Meeting, which had ninety-six seminars. The meeting's theme, "Reflections on the Revolution," was prominent in a wealth of offerings on topics ranging from Revolutionary dress to medicine during the Revolution, to the Clifford Lecture on "The Literary Revolution of 1789," delivered by Robert Darnton. Art History was much in evidence, including sessions on "The Artist as Hero," "The Political Unconscious and Revolutionary Imagery," "Portraiture and Ideology," "Gendering Art: Rococo and the Feminine," and "Culture and Cataclysm in the Late Eighteenth Century." Although many different factors undoubtedly played a role in the expansion and diversification of ASECS, the prominence of women, from the outset—on the Executive Board, as officers, and in the Women's Caucus—has been essential in fostering the Society's mission of interdisciplinary scholarship and inclusiveness.

At the beginning of my academic career, ASECS played a crucial role in introducing me to eighteenth-century scholars across the disciplines, and the Society became a sounding board and key arena for presenting my research and networking. With a heavy teaching load focusing primarily on modern and contemporary art, in a predominantly studio department, the Society was vital to my continuing engagement with eighteenth-century studies. ASECS itself continued to evolve in the late 1980s and 1990s, becoming more open and inclusive and expanding its scope through the addition of affiliates and new members working in diverse areas, including theater and performance studies, race and empire, and gender studies. Art History's profile within ASECS continued to rise, notably with the founding of the Historians of

Eighteenth-Century Art and Architecture in 1993, which became an affiliate and recently marked its 25ᵗʰ anniversary with a spectacular conference in Dallas.

When I became Affiliates Coordinator in 1998, my engagement with ASECS intensified and was greatly enriched. As I traveled across the country and occasionally abroad to report on the conferences I attended, I came to more fully appreciate and treasure the breadth and scholarly dedication of the regional and affiliate societies. "The Eighteenth-Century Tourist," the quarterly newsletter that I penned, was a welcome antidote to the pressures of academic publishing. I also had the pleasure and satisfaction of assisting scholarly organizations in applying for affiliate status and seeing them become integral parts of ASECS.

After I stepped down as Affiliates Coordinator, my leadership role in ASECS entered a new phase. I was elected Second Vice President in 2008, and went on to serve as First Vice President the following year and as President in 2010–11, a great honor and one of the highlights of my career. But my path was paved by the many other admirable women who had preceded me as President, beginning with Madeleine Therrien (1979–80). Therrien and others served as leadership models to whom I could look for inspiration and advice, most notably, Barbara Stafford (the first art historian to serve as President), Jane Perry-Camp, Joan Landes, Felicity Nussbaum, and Bernadette Fort. Those years also led to my active involvement with the International Society for Eighteenth-Century Studies, where I was initially an ASECS delegate and was later elected to the Executive Committee (2011–15). That, too, was a wonderful experience that brought new friendships and international contacts and expanded my horizons. It was rewarding to play a role in planning the Graz and Rotterdam conferences and in selecting Edinburgh as the 2019 site.

ASECS has played a central role in my academic development and scholarship. It has also been tremendously important on a personal level, enriching my life immeasurably with wonderful friends and colleagues across North America and beyond from whom I have learned a great deal. It has been an honor and a pleasure to have the opportunity to play a leadership role as Affiliates Coordinator and as President of the Society. The program for the 50ᵗʰ Annual Meeting in Denver is an indication of the vitality of ASECS and its continuing journey as a scholarly organization devoted to exploring the long and deep eighteenth century across the disciplines. To all the women who have played a leadership role and participated actively in ASECS over five decades I would like to send a collective *"Brava!,"* and, as the French say, wish them *"Bonne continuation!"*

ASECS AT 50

Cluster: Scholarship across the Aisle (Establishing Meaningful Scholarly Relationships Outside of One's Linguistic/Cultural Tradition)

Introduction: Scholarship across the Aisle (Establishing Meaningful Scholarly Relationships Outside of One's Linguistic/Cultural Tradition)[1]

LOGAN J. CONNORS AND JASON H. PEARL

It has been fifteen years since *The Global Eighteenth Century*—a landmark collection of essays, edited by Felicity Nussbaum—called on specialists in the long eighteenth century to consider as their purview a "wide" eighteenth century, one that stretched across national and natural borders to the Earth's farthest corners.[2] Many have heeded the call, transforming the way we think about everything from the history of science to literary history. And yet much of this work is confined to a single imperial power and its colonies. Much of it is focused on a single linguistic or cultural tradition. Much is addressed to members of a single discipline. Much, in other words, remains to be done.

We can start with our major conference, the annual meeting of the American Society for Eighteenth-Century Studies (ASECS), where panels on British literature outnumber all other fields combined—a problem invisible to most British literature specialists but obvious to everyone else. Entire disciplines and subdisciplines are absent or troublingly underrepresented. At several of the "ASECS at 50" Presidential Sessions at the 2019 meeting in Denver participants wondered: where are the historians? The economists? The political theorists? Where are the specialists in eastern Europe? Of Asia and South America? And this is to say nothing of the racial and cultural diversity of the participants themselves. Whatever their field, regular participants at ASECS go to similar panels year after year, interacting with the same colleagues, ensconcing themselves from everyone else to talk about research on the same places, authors, and texts. This type of scholarship will always receive support from ASECS, and it probably should. Yet the Society and its members can and should do more to bring underrepresented scholars into the fold and to catalyze broader interdisciplinary conversations across its ranks.

That is why we proposed, for the 2019 meeting, the roundtable, "Scholarship across the Aisle: Establishing Meaningful Scholarly Relationships Outside of One's Linguistic/Cultural Tradition," an attempt to reflect on disciplinary divides and posit new methods for crossing them. In our call for papers, we asked, "What can we do to make ASECS more welcoming to people working in areas outside British literature? What can we do to facilitate more interaction among scholars of different fields? What would it take for us to work beyond those boundaries and create meaningful interactions that would allow us to learn more from each other?" At a time when the humanities are under siege—under threat from even universities themselves—we need to support smaller disciplines most at risk, from French and German to Dance and Music. One of the ways to do this is to imagine and establish new opportunities for dialogue based on topics that transcend the specializations in which we feel the most comfortable.

What emerged from the roundtable was a conversation about not only eighteenth-century places (England, France, Italy, Russia, North America, the Caribbean, and more) but also the place of eighteenth-century scholars. We need to enable scholars from outside the usual Europe-North America axis to engage with ASECS. A litany of new questions ensues: what structures—ideological, financial, and linguistic—enable the continuation of the Anglo-ASECS paradigm? What can ASECS do to encourage scholars from the global south, geographically distant nations, and other underrepresented zones to attend its annual meeting, regional conferences, and other programs? How can new technologies help to create a more robust intellectual network of eighteenth-century studies around the globe? These questions demand research, resources, and commitment. We hope that the cluster of essays here is a helpful step towards democratizing and decolonizing the tools and opportunities that help eighteenth-century scholars research, collaborate, publish, and teach.

Participants in the roundtable spoke about the content of eighteenth-century studies—what we study and why—as well as the formal norms of scholarship and scholarly communication. If several subdisciplines lack a critical mass of scholars for a stand-alone panel on Russian folk singing, Japanese painting, or French rural policy, what other models of collaboration, session design, and panel constitution could bring this type of scholarship to more (or at the very least, some) ASECS participants? Could shorter sessions, theme-based topics ("singing," "printing," and "things," for example)—or even deliberate attempts by the ASECS program committee to mix and match scholars—help catalyze cross-disciplinary conversations and give a voice to less commonly taught languages and other underrepresented groups? What responsibility do panel organizers have in ensuring variety in the composition of their meeting sessions? Should ASECS encourage or require, as one of our participants suggested, "blind" submission of paper proposals?

Thought provoking but far from conclusive, the roundtable produced more questions than answers. Nevertheless, each of the following four essays describes how ASECS can welcome more scholars into its ranks, generate broader interest in the yearly meeting and in its publications, and maintain the Society's role as one of the world's preeminent learned organizations dedicated to the study of the eighteenth century. For example, in "Scholarship from the Periphery: An Israeli Perspective," Jessica Zimble writes about the institutional and logistical difficulties faced by scholars in Israel and other locations outside of the Anglo-American sphere. Zimble details the challenges of conducting basic research for her dissertation on eighteenth-century British literature owing to the small number of period experts in Israel and the modest holdings of its academic libraries. She then proposes several ways for ASECS to better support academics "from isolated communities." These include mentorship programs, a caucus for graduate students living outside of North America, and new mobility scholarships to enable graduate students and independent researchers from abroad to attend ASECS events.

In "ASECS beyond Borders," Adam Schoene argues that the organization should spotlight research from less-commonly taught languages and cultures through incremental changes to its session formats. Schoene, a scholar of Romance Studies, argues that ASECS must "create multiple spaces ... for those of different cultural traditions or disciplines to have occasions to express themselves as unique, as well as part of a broader community," which, he admits, is no easy task. Schoene describes several recent initiatives that attempt to bring scholars together from diverse geographies, professional ranks, and academic disciplines, such as Valentina Denzel and Tracy Rutler's *Legacies of Enlightenment* website and a 2019 conference at UCLA on early modern migrants, refugees, and asylum seekers. [3] Shifting the focus from the Executive Committee of ASECS to the session organizers at the yearly meeting, Schoene encourages us all to leave our comfort zones by assembling panels with scholars from different and diverse backgrounds—

an act of scholarly courage that would honor both the uniqueness and the interconnectedness of cultures and disciplines.

Rebecca Messbarger, who was elected Second Vice President of ASECS in 2019, argues in her essay that the organization should look to existing programs such as Washington University's Eighteenth-Century Interdisciplinary Salon to increase cross-disciplinarity, intellectual inclusivity, and professional collaboration. In "Twenty-First Century Salon/Salotto Culture for ASECS after 50," she draws from several decades of experience co-directing Washington University's Salon and attending yearly ASECS meetings. Messbarger recounts an electric session in 1998 during which Roy Porter antagonized continental European scholars with a lecture on English Enlightenment exceptionalism. More interested in that speech's form and its powerful effect on the audience than in its explicit content, Messbarger proposes a salon structure for at least part of the ASECS meeting sessions. These mini-symposia or salons of 90 to 120 minutes, Messbarger argues, would catalyze "moments of constructive contest" around critical debates in eighteenth-century studies that are often "tacit or argued neatly and without challenge in published scholarship."

In the final essay of the group, Morgan Vanek recounts a fascinating interdisciplinary methods course in northern Iceland and argues that disciplines and localities should work together to achieve a common goal. Vanek, a specialist in Restoration and eighteenth-century British literature, was embedded with a diverse team of climate scientists, biologists, and experts on environmental humanities in an effort to study the precarity and resilience of the human and non-human inhabitants of the Lake Myvatn region—a small community that has withstood plague and environmental disasters for hundreds of years. The diversity of data and approaches that she witnessed in Iceland was a source of intellectual stimulation and community-anchoring for Vanek, who proposes that eighteenth-century scholars could "reimagine the field's current focus and objectives" by looking at local examples, and especially the communities in which they live, to find new scholarly directions, collaborations, and research opportunities.

All four of these essays acknowledge that research in eighteenth-century studies cannot be taken for granted. At a time when humanities scholarship is undervalued and often denigrated, ASECS must adapt to a complex and changing environment in order to foster the work of the next generation of scholars. The road ahead is filled with challenges—but also opportunities. In the short term, researchers in the humanities can count on less funding for conferences and research trips. Many of us will likely retire without replacements. As a result, ASECS could get smaller, a dispiriting prospect. But as the field adjusts and evolves, maybe we can rethink the parameters of specialization as well as the ways in which we communicate our research to colleagues and the public. With fewer specialists, maybe there will be less specialization, making it necessary for all of us to expand our areas of expertise and engage with a more diverse range of colleagues. Some of us may look forward or backward in time, connecting the eighteenth century with traditionally separate periods. Others may look across borders, languages, and cultures. Maybe we can foster bigger conversations that reach beyond subfields, beyond the field itself, beyond even the boundaries of academia. Maybe then we will attract the economists, the political theorists, the specialists in Asia and South America, ultimately making common cause. The field should not need a crisis in order to effect change, but with forethought and decisiveness, perhaps we can bring about a positive result. The two of us remain cautiously optimistic. Three of the essays in this section were written by early-career researchers, tomorrow's leaders of ASECS; the other, by a current member of the organization's Executive Committee. Their shared vision of a more diverse and interdisciplinary body of scholars—this collusion between present and future—gives us hope.

Notes

1. The following essays were written before the outbreak of COVID-19, which has threatened not just disciplinary diversity—the topic of this cluster—but also the ability of anyone at all to gather for our yearly conference. We believe these circumstances, which are sure to have lasting effects, will make the issue of inclusivity all the more pressing. The essays here begin a conversation that will have to address new issues, from the availability of travel funding to the logistics of online conferences. We look forward to continuing this discussion and hope these essays will remain a useful starting point.

2. Felicity A. Nussbaum, ed. *The Global Eighteenth Century* (Baltimore: Johns Hopkins University Press, 2005).

3. Valentina Denzel and Tracy Rutler, eds. *Legacies of the Enlightenment*, *https://legaciesoftheenlightenment.hcommons.org*.

Scholarship from the Periphery: An Israeli Perspective

JESSICA ZIMBLE

When I read the call for papers for "Scholarship across the Aisle," I was unsure if my own experiences would be relevant. The roundtable would focus on encouraging interdisciplinary approaches and collaborations within eighteenth-century studies. My research, however, is very much within the dominant cultural tradition of the American Society for Eighteenth-Century Studies (ASECS): I study British literature, and I focus on Samuel Richardson. Further, I am a graduate student, and this would be my first ASECS conference. Who am I, I wondered, to participate in a Presidential session that will advocate for new directions in the organization and, possibly, in the discipline?

Nonetheless, I decided my perspective is important. I approached this roundtable not as a scholar who breaks disciplinary boundaries, but as a scholar who works beyond geographic ones. I am an advanced doctoral student at Bar Ilan University, which is one of five research universities in Israel. I moved to Israel seven years ago, having completed my M.A. at the University of Pennsylvania. My experience has been unique as an *Israeli* eighteenth-century scholar. I'd like to suggest that beyond recognizing the theoretical and content-driven divides that characterize eighteenth-century studies, it is worth considering other boundaries that prevent engagement with scholars who work outside of North America and Europe. In this short essay I describe some of the challenges that Israeli scholars face in studying

English literature on the periphery of the English-speaking world. I also hope to describe some of the innovative solutions they have come up with and to pose some suggestions of my own.

The first challenge is the small number of people in the country who specialize in the eighteenth century. While eighteenth-century literary studies is, by comparison, a relatively popular field in American academia, this is far from the case in Israel. At the University of Pennsylvania, I took courses with eight to ten other graduate students working on the eighteenth century, but at Bar Ilan there are fewer graduate students overall. As far as I know, there are two professors in Israel who specialize in eighteenth-century British literature, and I am the sole doctoral student in this specialty. This means that we lack a local community of scholars to learn from, collaborate with, and share our ideas with. I fondly remember my days as an M.A. student when I took a course on Samuel Richardson with a sizable group of eighteenth-century specialists. I took a different graduate course on the 1680s, and the next year a course was offered on the 1790s. No such courses would be taught at an Israeli university; nor would such students be found. While my peers can provide me with general feedback, I lack peers who specialize in my field and who can relate to my work in a specific, knowledgeable way. Beyond a lack of a peer group within my specialty, the demographics of most graduate students in Israel also impacts the overall student experience. Students tend to be older—I'm the youngest at thirty-two, with the next in age at forty. The other students are in their forties and fifties. We almost all have children, and those without a fellowship work full time. This demographic has its advantages. The students have more life experiences and are genuinely committed to their research, often sacrificing a lot amidst their busy schedules with work and family to devote time to writing. However, since there are few course requirements and almost no one lives on campus, there is a much greater feeling of isolation.

Other challenges result from limited institutional funding, particularly in our libraries. My campus library has a surprising inventory of scholarship, and what I cannot find there I can likely order from Hebrew University, Tel Aviv, Haifa, or Ben Gurion. However, logistical issues make the process of basic research fairly complicated. Like most graduate students, I do not live on campus. Any time I want to check out a book, I need to travel by car, bus, or train for almost an hour. Merely procuring the research materials that I need takes the better part of a morning. Additionally, there is no scanner or copy machine in the departmental library at my university. These are very basic research tools that I took for granted at my American research university. There I could request articles to be scanned and emailed to me. In Israel, the librarian has no assistant and no document scanner. That said, more crucial than the travel time and lack of basic copying technology is the lack of access to databases. Because the number of potential users for the databases on which our work is dependent is so small in Israel, our libraries cannot justify the expense of subscribing to them. My university does not have access to Eighteenth-Century Collections Online, so I have to travel to the National Library in Jerusalem any time I want to use it. No university in Israel has access to Proquest British periodicals. The lack of immediate accessibility to all of the primary sources we might need informs and potentially limits our projects.

Finally, scholars without a faculty position struggle to receive funding for international conferences. Participation in conferences such as ASECS is incredibly important because we get to meet other scholars in our field and be a part of a community. Due to the challenges I have already described, participation in conferences is even more vital for scholars outside of North America or Europe because it provides a kind of camaraderie that we lack in our home institutions. Conferences also provide us with a sense of what people are interested in and thinking about. But international travel is extremely expensive, and funding for graduate students is quite limited. Thus, to a certain extent, institutional budgets and the sheer distance of travel limit our participation in these events, even though that participation is crucial. This challenge is even greater for scholars who have completed their Ph.D.s but are unaffiliated with a research university. I will likely lose my affiliation with Bar Ilan when I graduate. In Israel, like North America, academic positions are scarce. I anticipate that I will need to continue my research as an independent scholar, which means that I will not have funding available to participate in conferences like ASECS.

In spite of the challenges eighteenth-century scholars encounter in Israel, there are some surprising benefits to our marginality. Most significantly, because the number of overall scholars is few, there is more dialogue between specialties. Being at an Israeli university puts me in cross-period, even cross-national conversations. I'll give you two examples.

My first example relates to the Israeli community of scholars who research literatures in English. A few years ago, four professors from different universities founded the Study of English Literatures in Israel (SELI) in an effort to create a cohesive sense of community for Israeli scholars, and the Society has hosted an annual conference ever since. Organizing a successful conference on English literature that gathers participants based on location, rather than specialty, is a challenge. How much can an audience really relate to endless papers that may have little to do with their specialized field of study? To address this challenge, the planning committee has begun structuring the conference around "keywords." Each session had a keyword, and the participants had to respond to it through the context of their research. Some examples of keywords they used include "memory," "relatable," and "reception." One excellent session with the keyword "archive" joined scholars of queer theory, Native American and indigenous studies, the U.S. Civil War, and Victorian literature. Some of the intersections between their presentations were surprising and also incredibly fascinating. This conference format was an innovative tool for bridging the gap between specialties.

I also experience these cross-period conversations within my institution as a doctoral student. Since 2018, the department chair has formally organized a Ph.D. group that meets twice a semester to share writing, ideas, and professional development tips. The cohort of students is diverse. Some of the students are American, others are English, and others are Israeli. Some speak English as a first language, others Hebrew, and others Arabic. We also study different periods and focus on different cultures. Although I lack a group of knowledgeable peers in my specialty, this level of diversity in such a small group affords exposure to wide-ranging research interests.

Given all of these considerations, I propose the following to facilitate more interaction with scholars who work outside of the Anglo-American academic context. The International Society for Eighteenth-Century Studies (ISECS) is crucial in its facilitation of an exchange of ideas between eighteenth-century specialists from all countries. However, ISECS meets only once every four years. A doctoral student might miss this conference, depending upon when the conference occurs in relation to how far along she is in her degree. ASECS is valuable as an annual conference, and because of this regularity, I propose a roundtable or a caucus for doctoral students who work outside of North America. I also propose the creation of two new grants to support travel to the conference for scholars who work from the margins: one for scholars who live outside of North America and another for independent scholars who lack access to institutional resources.

Beyond the annual conference, I also propose more extended engagement programs within the organization. "The Doctor Is In" provides valuable resources and mentoring and offers useful workshops at the annual conference. However, this service focuses more on professional development and the job market than on specific research interests. Additionally, this program is not featured on the ASECS website. Most members learn about it from the annual conference. Perhaps "The Doctor Is In" can be featured on the ASECS website and create a bigger presence beyond the annual conference, so that ASECS members who cannot attend the conference can also benefit from its services. Perhaps, too, "The Doctor Is In" can coordinate a mentor program, one allowing doctoral students to reach out for guidance to ASECS members who specialize in their field, if such mentorship is unavailable in their home country. Finally, I would suggest that ASECS create a listserv for graduate students who would like to participate in an online reading group. I think some of these actions would encourage interdisciplinary dialogue. I also think they would help break down the boundaries that constrain scholars who work in isolated academic communities.

ASECS beyond Borders

ADAM SCHOENE

In contemplating one of the central questions of our "Scholarship across the Aisle" roundtable about what structures prevent us from engaging with those beyond our own national, linguistic, or disciplinary traditions, I began by thinking broadly about the varied composition of different academic divisions. The study of languages, literatures, and cultures is often divided into separate departments based on geographic regions, although they are also now increasingly merging. While cross-cultural collaboration may occur in departments that are home to multiple national or cultural groups—such as Departments of Modern Languages, Romance Studies, or Literatures, Cultures, and Languages, as well as in places where languages and literatures are separate—there is also frequently a desire from these different groups to maintain a degree of distinctiveness and specificity. This creates a challenge as to how best to create multiple spaces for those of different cultural traditions or disciplines to have occasions to express themselves as unique, as well as part of a broader community. Extending this challenge to the American Society for Eighteenth-Century Studies (ASECS), I reflected upon the ways by which many are currently working to create such spaces and how we might do even more to overcome the related barriers, both of which I will briefly sketch in what follows.

From its inception, ASECS has been characterized by its interdisciplinary spirit, yet it has also encountered moments of tension between languages and disciplines, times that call for patience, diplomacy, and creativity. The establishment of regional and other affiliate societies is one significant way that ASECS members have responded to this challenge, setting up unique realms of focus and collaboration within the larger society. Important connections around specific areas of interest are often fostered within these smaller or regional subgroups, such as the Aphra Behn Society or the Northeast American Society for Eighteenth-Century Studies, which are conducive to building ties that may be more difficult to construct in a larger or more distant setting. New affiliate societies such as the recently established Southeast Asian Society for Eighteenth-Century Studies might also address underrepresented or less prominent areas of focus within ASECS, helping to further expand the interdisciplinary character of the society and to attract and build greater diversity.

In his remarks during the Q&A of the "ASECS Past and Present" 2019 Presidential Session, Logan Connors offered another example of what a space that might nurture cultural diversity as well as cross-disciplinary borders could look like in the setting of an annual meeting: he suggested the idea of organizing linked double sessions around a theme where participants could consider an issue from one cultural perspective on one panel and from another cultural perspective on another panel, which would bring people together around this common theme in both separate and shared spaces. For example, a double session on the theme of "Actresses" or "Cities" might offer one Anglophone panel, while another panel could be focused on Africa, Asia, or continental Europe, but the fact that they are considered a double session and are centered around the same theme could entice scholars to attend both sessions. Constructing such sessions around themes with each part of the double session focusing on one region or linguistic tradition would offer people the space to pursue their own specialized interests and allow them to come together in a broader context. This need not apply to all panels, as some would, of course, still represent a variety of perspectives, as many already do.

Extending beyond the context of the annual meeting, another potential method for bridging linguistic, cultural, and disciplinary divides both within and beyond ASECS is by designing conferences or working groups around texts or themes that serve to enact this interconnected form of movement and dialogue. One such point of entry is through travel narratives. The eighteenth century is particularly rich in the genre of travel writing. This area of exploration can open the door to discussion and collaboration across cultures and disciplines, allowing for consideration by specialists from each of the different backgrounds raised in the texts and by those interested in broader global issues. Travel narratives often use what is foreign to critique what is familiar, albeit with a varying degree of attention to accurate depiction of the other culture, as at times the foreign may be used more as a means to shine the spotlight upon problems within one's own society. Even if this is the case, such narratives may reveal the existence of misconceptions or prejudice while addressing alterity and underscoring the ongoing relevance of Montesquieu's famous formulation in the *Lettres persanes*: "How can one be Persian?" (translation mine).[1] In travel literature from the period, there is also much contemporary resonance with migration, which may attract scholars from a range of different fields, as occurred with the 2019 conference on "Exodus and Exile: Migrants, Refugees and Asylum Seekers 1750–1850" hosted by the UCLA Center for 17th- and 18th-Century Studies.

Another initiative that leverages the contemporary context as a way to bring eighteenth-century specialists together across cultures and disciplines is the *Legacies of the Enlightenment* project, developed jointly by scholars at Michigan State University and Pennsylvania State University. The *Legacies* project is funded by the Mellon Foundation's "Humanities Without Walls" program, which aims to bring together cross-institutional teams of faculty and graduate students to collaboratively pursue research related to "The Work of the Humanities in a Changing Climate." "Humanities Without Walls" funds "applied humanities" projects on issues such as political and cultural divides, environmental challenges, and the ethics surrounding technology. In addition to this research component, "The Humanities Without Walls" program also supports workshops and events for graduate students aimed at illustrating how doctoral-level study of the humanities can be applied to careers beyond academia. The *Legacies of the Enlightenment* project is led by Tracy Rutler and Valentina Denzel, both in French, along with scholars of English, History, Philosophy, Spanish, Women's Studies, and other disciplines, with the aim of exploring how the Enlightenment informs—and haunts—our current worldviews. This team created a website containing a database of teaching and research materials as a tool for students, teachers, and researchers, with topics organized around five groups: Disciplines, Climates, Materialism, The In-between, and Upheavals. Each of these different groups addresses the enduring impact of the Enlightenment, featuring curated research materials (such as books, articles, plays, works of art, and online resources) related to its area of focus in order to foster in-depth analyses of how the Enlightenment continues to shape our ways of thinking and perceiving the world. As with the other "Humanities Without Walls" initiatives, an important element of the *Legacies* project is its dedication to mentoring graduate students. As such, Rutler and Denzel held a conference in 2018 that brought together graduate students and faculty working across cultures and disciplines, with a format that combined presentations and paper workshops with mentoring sessions.

Other similar initiatives also exist within the global network of eighteenth-century studies societies, such as the International Society for Eighteenth-Century Studies's meetings and Early Career Seminars that bring together young scholars and faculty from around the world. Indeed, much is being done in the field of eighteenth-century studies as a whole to cross boundaries and borders. The 2019 ASECS meeting program revealed that members are by and large thinking this way, with sessions such as "Diversity, Differences, and Dilemmas"; "Imagining Exile"; "The Planetary Turn"; "Women in the Early Caribbean"; "Subaltern Archives"; "The Animal and the Human in the Anthropocene"; "Refugees and Emigrés"; "The Time of Slavery"; "Absence in the Archives: New Methods for Representing Exclusion"; "Questioning the Canon: Unfinished Revolutions in the Caribbean"; and "The Digital Humanities and the Global Eighteenth Century." While there is great diversity across and within these and numerous other panels, one area for us as an ASECS community to continue to pursue is how to develop our own membership to represent the diversity that much of this research emphasizes. In conceptualizing and organizing panels and events, we might also question our own rationales for how we construct them, with an aim to balance the honoring of what makes different cultures or fields unique and their broader interconnectedness with other regions and disciplines. It may be difficult to strike a perfect balance between these tensions, but we should definitely keep trying.

Notes

1. "Comment peut-on être Persan?" Charles-Louis de Secondat, Baron de la Brède et de Montesquieu, *Lettres persanes*, in *Œuvres complètes de Montesquieu*, ed. Roger Caillois, 2 vols. (Paris: Gallimard, 1949), 1:177.

Twenty-First-Century Salon/Salotto Culture for ASECS after 50

REBECCA MESSBARGER

The late historian of medicine Roy Porter's plenary address at the 1998 Annual Meeting at Notre Dame would appear the exact wrong example to mine as a model for mitigating British ascendancy and fostering greater interaction among scholars in different disciplines within the American Society for Eighteenth-Century Studies (ASECS). Yet, his defiantly Brito-centric lecture incited an intensity and scope of scholarly debate at the conference extraordinary in my experience as a member of ASECS. I was a newly minted assistant professor and had joined several of my junior colleagues in the last row of a large, dark auditorium to hear Porter's preview of his forthcoming book, *Enlightenment: Britain and the Creation of the Modern World*. He proved his reputation as an "intellectual anarchist" with a spectacularly confrontational defense of what he called "the British Enlightenment project."[1] He reveled in playing the provocateur, looming on stage, calling out by name leading scholars, some of whom were present in the packed room, not merely to refute but gleefully to rebuke their arguments against the notion of a coherent, self-conscious British Enlightenment movement that gave birth to modernity. Porter's baiting worked. Scholars he had contested on stage hastened for microphones dotted across the auditorium to make their reply. This ardent academic exchange would continue beyond the bounds of the auditorium. That year, by accident or design, two of the three plenary talks and the presidential address—by Porter, J. G. A. Pocock, and Margaret Jacobs—sought to define the Enlightenment, its history, and its social, cultural, and intellectual significance. The Enlightenment itself thus became the unifying Big Question of the conference, one debated relentlessly among the membership over the course of the rest of the meeting.

To be clear, my aim is neither to endorse Porter's triumphalist thesis, nor to propose a revamping of the annual conference into an academic version of the British Parliament in the throes of Brexit. The civil exchange of ideas has rarely been more important. But I do see the benefits of a thematic organizing structure for the annual conference that would bring people of diverse disciplinary, cultural, and linguistic specializations and from different professional echelons and interest groups into the same orbit to debate robustly a common question. These mini-symposia or salons, as I propose to define them, of 90–120 minutes could conceivably constitute 20 to 30 percent of the total sessions and would receive special billing, much as the 50th anniversary this past year gave special status to panels concerning the history and future of the Society. They offer more time to delve, to discuss, more time to profess, to defend, and to counter critical claims that are often tacit or argued neatly and without challenge in published scholarship. It is in those moments of constructive contest that the opportunity resides for us to revise our thinking and learn something new, both individually and more broadly as a discipline. Thematic rule need not tame radical and defiant discourse, but would situate discrete disputations within a larger conceptual framework that would allow for a more serious and layered examination of new ideas as well as the greater circulation of them.

This kind of thematic approach has worked for the regional and international (ISECS) affiliate conferences. I have also experienced the benefits firsthand at my home institution of Washington University, where my colleague in French, Tili Boon Cuille, and I co-convene the Eighteenth-Century Interdisciplinary Salon, whose tenure-track and non-tenure-track faculty and graduate students are affiliated with our institution and several neighboring universities. During its twenty-three-year existence, the Salon has been the most active, the most cross-disciplinary, and the most productive (in terms of publication) scholarly workshop on campus. I believe this is largely due to its ethos of professional and intellectual inclusivity and collaboration. Two decades ago, I chose the name *Salon* to underscore a distinct model of leadership and cultural practice reminiscent of our eighteenth-century forebears, one that would, in the ideal, supplant standard hierarchies based on academic rank, discipline, and, indeed, gender for the greater promotion of egalitarian, reciprocal, and constructive scholarly exchange. The salon model has worked well for us, as evidenced by the hundreds of articles and scores of books written by our members that have come through it en route to publication and by the robust community it has built across our local landscape and the country. I think it also holds promise for a renewal of ASECS.

As Dena Goodman has shown in her ground-breaking studies of the cultural power of the salon in France in the eighteenth century, what distinguished this institution from the traditional all-male, socially elite academies were women insiders.[2] The salon signified the real embodiment of the ideal Republic of Letters, and these establishments served as crucial, if often highly imperfect, instantiations of those Enlightenment principles of egalitarian social exchange credited with fostering modern subjectivity.[3]

In eighteenth-century Italy, the focus of my studies, the cultural sway and production of the *salotti* and salon-esque literary and scientific academies peppered across the peninsula frequently went further than their French counterparts in challenging traditional social and cultural hierarchies, and the effect was more broadly transformative. As Paola Giuli, Irene Zanini Cordi, Elisabetta Graziosi, Paula Findlen, Susan Dalton, Elena Brambilla, and others have shown, women frequented, sometimes governed, and even founded not only eighteenth-century Italian salons but also literary and scientific academies, including the many "colonies" of the national literary Academy of Arcadia that sprouted in cities and villages throughout Italy over the century.[4] Women's public presence was often more conspicuous and enjoyed greater official sanction than elsewhere in Europe.[5] There was, of course, no actual Republic of Italy at the time, nor would there be for more than a century and a half from Arcadia's founding in 1690. Arcadia, together with the proliferation of "inter-class, inter-gender," and international (comprising citizens from other countries and other Italian states) salons and household academies thus constituted in real time and space a yearned-for modern Republic dedicated to cultural renewal and the production and circulation of knowledge.[6] These highly varied assemblies drew men and women not only of the upper but also of the middling classes: clergy—including cardinals and future popes—alongside libertines, natural philosophers and artists, medical lights, and improvisational poets. They showcased new erudite and popular writing; musical, theatrical, and visual works; and scientific experiments. And they served as forums for philosophical and political debate, including debates about the merits of women's new cultural authority.[7] While words were the currency of the *conversazioni* of the *salotti* and *accademie*, as well as the expansive epistolary networks, periodicals, and literary anthologies they produced, cultural progress was ideally measured by *Cose non parole*— "Things not words"—an influential motto of this worldly (*read* practical and socially mixed) Age of *Illuminismo*, which aspired above all to advance the *pubblico bene* or public good.

How might ASECS develop a twenty-first-century model of salon/salotto culture, particularly at its annual conference? How might we shake off at the session door the hold of hierarchies of academic, institutional, and disciplinary rank and not only bring those on the outside in, but also create a wider proscenium for scholarly exchange and collaboration among more of our members, one that seeks to amplify new and previously unheeded voices?[8]

To return to the model of the Eighteenth-Century Interdisciplinary Salon at Washington University, it is organized annually around an overarching theme that also serves as the focus of our symposium. These themes are elastic, have resonance across an array of disciplines, and speak to the influence of the period across time and place. For example, a recent theme was Eighteenth-Century Economies of Exchange. Our *conversazione* over the course of the academic year among our members and invited outside speakers included scholars of all ranks, working in history, art history, the history of theater, French, Italian, Spanish, German, and English, who presented on such topics as the gift economy of the Qing Dynasty, paper money in England, slavery at sea, the trade in commodities, and culture and religious belief at the Port of Livorno. At the start of the year, members and invited scholars with a critical stake in the proposed question engage in a great debate, which has proven boisterous, polemical, and edifying. These debates have upturned assumptions many of us have held too casually, not only about what took place during the eighteenth century and what it means, but also about how we theorize, study, and teach this period.

Beyond the Salon, my experience as a member of the small but dynamic cohort of scholars in eighteenth-century Italian Studies has long been marked by the challenges of moving from the wings to the mainstage of ASECS. After many years of vigorous collaborative outreach, my fellow Italianists have gained visibility and official recognition by the Society. We now have an Italian Caucus with a markedly interdisciplinary membership and increasing numbers at our sessions. To raise the stature of our Caucus, we have also found value in framing our sessions with broad but magnetizing themes that have drawn into our fold a number of art historians, historians of science and medicine, digital humanities specialists, and scholars in other national and cultural traditions.

ASECS as an institution must do more to bring those on the outside in and to fulfill its stated aim to "welcome scholars pursuing all aspects of eighteenth-century studies and in all careers and career stages."[9] I believe that we must actively recruit from the widest spectrum of disciplines and research foci through membership incentives, fee waivers, and guest plenary talks. We must pragmatically remedy the cronyism and segregation by discipline and rank that inevitably take hold in a long-standing organization. Blind submissions of paper abstracts for themed sessions would undoubtedly thwart some of this favoritism and enhance the range and novelty of arguments presented on panels, while also bringing scholars from different linguistic and cultural specializations as well as different professional statuses into conversation.

Finally, eighteenth-century salons met frequently and via sociable and scholarly exchange nurtured a sense of community, long-term relationships, and artistic and scholarly collaboration, including co-authored or collective works.[10] At the annual conference, the Society, the caucuses, and various interest groups sponsor convivial events, such as the memorable Masquerade Balls, which build a sense of unity among our members. While sociable gatherings are vitally important today, as they were in the eighteenth century, for developing a communal identity and personal relationships, how might we, as a Society, also provide support for enduring scholarly relationships that extend beyond a single session or conference? I propose the sponsorship of follow-up in-person or virtual workshops of select session panels with the ideal outcome of a collaborative publication, conference, or creative/ performance piece.

It is the spirit both of the *querelle* and of collaboration in the eighteenth-century salon/salotto that I hope we might nurture in ASECS going forward. The Italian Enlightenment journal *Il Caffè* perhaps best captures its promise: "You cannot call the true spirit of society that which consists of nothing other than the continual dispersion of ourselves, but instead has the aim of honest communication among [us]."[11]

Notes

I am grateful to Irene Zanini Cordi and Paola Giuli for their invaluable assistance with key aspects of this essay, including the sharing of work in progress. I would also like to thank Logan Connors and Jason Pearl for their careful editing of this piece.

1. Roy Porter, *Enlightenment: Britain and the Creation of the Modern World* (London: Allen Lane, 2000).

2. Dena Goodman, *The Republic of Letters: A Cultural History of the French Enlightenment* (Ithaca: Cornell University Press, 1994).

3. Goodman, *Republic of Letters*, 5.

4. Paola Giuli, Elisabetta Graziosi, Susan Dalton, and Irene Zanini Cordi have written extensively on eighteenth-century Italian salon culture. See especially, Giuli, "Prospero Lambertini and the Accademia degli Arcadi," in *Benedict XIV and the Enlightenment: Art, Science, and Spirituality*, edited by Rebecca Messbarger, Christopher Johns, and Philip Gavitt (Toronto: University of Toronto Press, 2016), 315–40; Elisabetta Graziosi, "Presenze femminili: Fuori e dentro l'Arcadia," in *Salotti e ruolo femminile in Italia fra Seicento e Primo Novecento*, ed. Maria Luisa

Berti and Elena Brambilla (Venice: Marsili, 2004), 67–96; among Paula Findlen's numerous articles on the influence of Italian salonnières, two of note are, "Becoming a Scientist: Gender and Knowledge in Eighteenth-Century Italy," *Science in Context* 16 (2003): 59-87, and "Founding a Scientific Academy: Gender, Patronage and Knowledge in Early Eighteenth-Century Milan," *Republics of Letters* 1, no. 1 (2009): 1-43; Susan Dalton, *Engendering the Republic of Letters: Reconnecting Public and Private Spheres in Eighteenth-Century Europe* (Montreal: McGill University Press, 2004); and Irene Zanini Cordi, "Botteghe da Caffè, Sociability and Gender in Eighteenth-Century Venice," in "New Perspectives on Veneto," special issue, *NeMla Italian Studies* 35 (2012–13): 26–50.

5. For an in-depth overview of this transformation, see Luciano Guerci, *La discussion sulla donna nell'Italia del Settecento. Aspetti e problem* (Turin: Terrenia, 1987–88); Rebecca Messbarger, *The Century of Women: The Representation of Women in Eighteenth-Century Italian Public Discourse* (Toronto: University of Toronto Press, 2003); Messbarger, "The Enlightenment Reform of the Querelle des Femmes," in *The Contest for Knowledge: Debates Over Women's Learning in Eighteenth-Century Italy*, ed. and trans. Rebecca Messbarger and Paula Findlen (Chicago: University of Chicago Press, 2005).

6. For example, the Swiss painter Angelika Kauffmann hosted an important international salon in Rome. See Wendy Roworth, "Painting for Pleasure and Profit: Angelica Kauffman and the Art Business in Rome," *Eighteenth-Century Studies* 29, no. 2 (1995): 225–28. For other, anti-conformist salons hosted by foreigners in Italy, see Alessandra Contini, "La memoria femminile negli archivi: I salotti attraverso i carteggi (secolo XVIII)," in *Salotti e ruolo femminile in Italia,* 29–64.

7. On women's authority in scientific academies in the Italian eighteenth century, see Paula Findlen, "Founding a Scientific Academy: Gender, Patronage and Knowledge in Early Eighteenth-Century Milan," *Republic of Letters: A Journal for the Study of Knowledge, Politics, and the Arts*, 1, no. 1 (May 2009), *https://arcade. stanford.edu/rofl/founding-scientific-academy-gender-patronage-and-knowledge-early-eighteenth-century-milan.*

8. Numerous scholars, including myself, have noted, of course, that even the most self-consciously modernizing salons and academies of the eighteenth century were far from class and gender blind and often inclined to conformity. Nevertheless, the eighteenth-century salon/salotto epitomized a sea change in the expansion and diversity of both cultural authorities and consumers, as well as the greater circulation of ideas, and are thus worthy of emulation. As E. Graziosi has observed, the salons, "constituted alternative circles where minority ideas could be cultivated." See Graziosi, "Presenze femminili," 92.

9. Who We Are and What We Do, ASECS, *https://www.asecs.org/who-we-are-what-we-do.*

10. Zanini-Cordi discusses Italian salons' collaborative literary publication in her forthcoming book, *Women before the Facebook Nation: Salons, Social Networking, and Italian Identity.*

11. Alessandro Verri, "Lo spirito di società," in *Il Caffè, Ossia Brevi Discorsi Distribuiti in Fogli Periodici*, vol. 2 (Venice: Pietro Pizzolato, 1766), 506–7.

Closer to Home: Towards a Local Eighteenth Century

MORGAN VANEK

As specialists in the eighteenth century, our research is often defined by its focus on this period of time—but as this article aims to demonstrate, this expertise can also make an important contribution to interdisciplinary studies defined by other principles, including studies of place. By engaging in this type of interdisciplinary research, furthermore, we, as members of the American Society for Eighteenth-Century Studies (ASECS), might also come to think differently about the boundaries and obligations of our scholarly community—or to whom, and for what, we imagine our scholarly work should be held accountable. Taking a wide view of these obligations, I am especially curious about how our typical subjects and methods might relate to the present climate crisis and, specifically, how they may contribute to the widening inequity this crisis will bring to the various places we teach and work. In what follows, I want first to examine a model of the type of transhistorical scholarship that could help us tell this story, and then to argue that experimenting with new approaches to interdisciplinary research is especially urgent now.

As many scholars across the environmental humanities have observed, the problems of both the climate crisis and the inequities it exacerbates are dense, nearly impossible to see in their entirety from any one angle. It now appears, however, that one significant challenge of this crisis is representational, a difficulty in narrating both the many commitments of modern life, anthropogenic but not individual, that have brought us to this point and any consequences beyond what can be measured with empirical methods.[1] In this context, any scholarship that can illuminate the influences, priorities, and quirks of perspective that make up this crisis's historical context is well situated to help researchers trained in more empirical methods see what exclusively material analyses cannot—and scholars with a special expertise in the period often identified as the origin of our current myopia are especially well equipped to help denaturalize the conditions of this crisis.[2] To date, however, successful models for interdisciplinary scholarship that incorporates both of these types of evidence remain relatively rare—and so to this end, I want to present here as an exemplar an Icelandic research team I encountered during a 2018 summer course on new research methods in the environmental humanities.[3] Because their project, MYBIT, has a narrow geographical focus and a wide historical reach, spanning eight hundred years, this team includes no scholars with particular expertise in the long eighteenth century—but it does include a literary historian (Viðar Hreinsson), a historian (Árni Daníel Júlíusson), a biologist (Ragnhildur Sigurðardóttir), a climate historian (Astrid Ogilvie), and two archaeologists (Megan Hicks and Thomas McGovern), as well as a farmer in the Bárðardalur valley (Guðrún Tryggvadóttir), each with different expertise in dimensions of environmental sustainability and resilience. Together they aim to explain why the population of Lake Mývatn, a small region in northern Iceland, has consistently rebounded during the periods of encroaching sea ice or ovine plague that starved out many others—and in the interdisciplinary method they have developed for this work, I would argue, we can find a suggestive model for other studies of a single (and seemingly familiar) place over time.[4] Attending specifically to the status of historical knowledge in the MYBIT project, we also find a number of opportunities for eighteenth-century scholars in particular: opportunities, mostly positive, to expand the range of our objects of study to include more material traces of eighteenth-century ideas in the present, but also opportunities to better account for the absences—material, intellectual, and human—that our methods and archives have often helped to justify.

To date, the MYBIT team has identified a number of different aspects of both local geography and land management practices in the Lake Mývatn region that appear to have contributed to its resilience, publishing the results of these collaborative investigations in a range of discipline-specific journals. In each publication, the lead author appears to have interpreted the evidence of the soil and rock record differently from the others—but taken together, the team's body of work makes it clear that these individual findings are interconnected. According to Sigurðardóttir, the team's biologist, for instance, "what made the Mývatn region different from the other early settled mountainous regions of Iceland was undoubtedly its water"; the temperature and insulation of the water supports an unusual amount of algae, she explains, which supports a huge number of flies (Lake Mývatn means "Midge Lake"), which in turn make the lake home to a large number of water birds, especially ducks.[5] According to one of the team's zooarcheologists, however, there's also a social story in the bones of these birds, a trace of the land management practices that have helped to maintain these ecological conditions. It is true, Hicks argues, that the ducks have significantly contributed to the survival of this community. The key, however, to the region's resilience is not the ducks alone (as a source of food), but rather the ways the northern Icelanders harvested the duck eggs to make sure the ducks would come back.[6] These ecological and social dimensions of resilience are interdependent: the ducks have to be there in order for the harvesting practice to work, but the fact that the ducks are there has as much to do with the harvesting practice as it does to do with the flies. What these findings suggest, furthermore, is that even limited resources can be leveraged to sustainably support a human population over a long period of time; in other words, as McGovern, also one of the team's archaeologists, explains, "despite climate fluctuation and severe economic hardship ... [l]ong-term sustainability is possible."[7]

As Jonathan Kramnick has observed, it is not unusual, on an interdisciplinary research team, to find a hierarchical relationship between the data gathered by team members trained in the life and physical sciences and the interpretations "layered" on top of this data by social scientists and humanists.[8] This is not the arrangement of the MYBIT team's analyses. In fact, even more striking than the optimism of their projections about long-term sustainability among small-scale, non-state societies is how the research team suggests that ideas—about land, risk, and trade—have contributed to this resilience. Both in their publications and throughout the 2018 course the team co-facilitated to introduce international scholars to their research methods, the MYBIT team positions these ideas—traces of which they explicate in the region's storytelling and folk traditions, as well as in the forms of historical records of trade in local archives—as no less significant a factor in developing that long-term resilience than the geographical features of the region that attract so many water birds. Alongside the duck bones, for instance, the archaeologists found the bodies of many marine fish—and in the archives, the presence of these fish is explained by evidence of "the most advanced trade [network] of any Icelandic communities during the 18th century."[9] That trade, Hreinsson argues, was itself sustained by a view of environmental "resources," reinforced throughout the corpus of Icelandic literature, that lends itself to conservation and freeholding rather than exploitation over time.[10] (We could call this view "pragmatic but superstitious," presuming both that the environmental conditions necessary to support human life are limited and prone to change without warning, yet also imagining that the way these conditions will change depends, to some extent, on small matters of human behavior, including the maintenance of particular beliefs.) As in the case of the ducks and the harvesting practice, however, the team argues that the trade network and this view of resources are interconnected pillars of resilience; like the duck eggs, the trade network helps to mitigate scarcity, but it is there in part because of this storytelling tradition that emphasizes the cultivation of relationships, both local and far-flung, as a buffer against unpredictable environmental change. If we are curious, then, about how we might export even some of these conditions at this moment of widespread ecological crisis, the particular approach the MYBIT team has developed to track the influence of these intellectual commitments may help identify the cultural resources needed to protect natural resources—and help affirm that these intangible conditions are as significant a dimension of regional resilience as anything in the water.

This kind of interdisciplinary work also has the potential to open up new ways of conceiving of the conditions that comprise an environment itself, and thereby to help answer a now-longstanding call from scholars of the Anthropocene for new approaches to narrating this crisis. According to Rob Nixon, for instance, representing the climate crisis is so difficult in part because neither the scope nor the speed of its worst outcomes lend themselves to narration in the terms we recognize as references to an emergency; likewise, as writers from Dipesh Chakrabarty and Jason Moore to Amitav Ghosh and Christina Sharpe have argued, the persistence of an overwhelmingly material definition of climate has made it difficult to acknowledge the many unseen operations of the global political order—of capitalism, colonialism, or democracy—that entrench environmental injustice.[11] Under these circumstances, many have called for new approaches to narrating both the history and the present of this crisis, as well as new approaches to describing the immaterial forces, including ideas, operating in any given environment to promote or erode its resilience.[12] As a methodological model, the MYBIT project illustrates one way that those trained in the humanities can help bring some of these immaterial but environmental conditions into focus, and the project as a whole demonstrates how this information can be productively interpreted on the same plane as more empirical data.

What is most suggestive, however, is the project's scope. MYBIT is a transhistorical project, but it is focused on a single place—and for the most part, this is the place where the research team lives and works. On its own, of course, the first of these features would not be a novel turn for research in the humanities. From "translocal" studies to global studies in the long eighteenth century, we already have many good models for developing nuanced and intersectional analyses of the many avenues of circulation that connect any one place to the wider world.[13] Yet what makes the MYBIT project unusual, even in this context, is its focus on a place where most of the research team lives. Among North American scholars working in the long eighteenth century, this is atypical. There are exceptions, but largely as a consequence of the structure of the academic job market, there is often not a strong connection between the places featured in the texts we study and the places we live and work.[14] In the space remaining, then, the rest of this piece will explore some of the opportunities and challenges that might be opened to eighteenth-century scholars if we more often focused, after MYBIT's example, on the eighteenth century of the places we do live, and what new forms of collaboration and accountability this shift could make possible.

Like every place, the city where I work, Calgary, has an eighteenth century. Every dimension of its present—from its architecture to its demographics to its relationship to the First Nations of what is now called Treaty 7 territory— has been shaped by eighteenth-century activities, and as in the model above, these activities range from approaches to land management adapted to the unique geographical features of the region to the introduction of particular ideas, germs, and modes of social organization at a particular time.[15] Arguably, even the depth and rigidity of the province's economic dependence on a single industry (fossil fuels) has its origins in the eighteenth century and, specifically, in the westward movement of a particular way of looking at a landscape as a collection of resources, or material forms of capital more and less available for extraction. As I have started, however, to develop a project to identify these eighteenth-century influences—or, more precisely, to identify where in the economic and political order of present-day Alberta we can see the trace of, say, the particular form of record-keeping popular among the Hudson's Bay Company representatives during this period of westward expansion—the obligations of an interdisciplinary approach have become both clear and complicated. As an eighteenth-century scholar, I can form preliminary research questions about the possible significance of these formal changes in Company record-keeping, but my next step must be collaborative, reaching out both to other researchers based in the same region with expertise in the intellectual currents that might have carried these changes across the Atlantic and also to colleagues contributing to the archaeological work already underway on Cree and Company land management practices in what is now western Canada.[16] To date, fortunately, this project has been supported by the Calgary Institute for the Humanities, an institution committed both to cultivating interdisciplinary scholarly community across Calgary and to funding time for collaborative work. Even in this supportive context, however, and in the project's preliminary stages, the local focus of this study has raised logistical and ethical questions.

Many of these questions are about accountability: how we imagine ourselves to be accountable to the communities that have helped to hold and now uncover the information we study, wherever we work, and how the practice of that accountability changes if the places we study are no longer quite so distant from the location where we do this work. A greater commitment to local scholarship has the potential to help to facilitate new forms of community-building. In addition to encouraging new forms of collaboration with other scholars who study the same region, for instance, and perhaps widening our existing networks of scholars who study the same period of time, research grounded closer to home may also motivate those working within traditional academic structures, like colleges and universities, to build stronger connections with local archives and public libraries—and in this way, more local studies could even help to counter some of the displacement that has, over the last several decades, become part of the high price of entry to the academic job market. Both for those who have moved far from their roots or community for a job and for those who cannot, developing studies of a local eighteenth century could also make some aspects of academic work somewhat more accessible than resource-intensive work in distant archives—and could, particularly for those who move often, help to motivate more finely grained comparative studies or research on how the same phenomena unfold differently in different places.

In addition to these opportunities for new forms of collaboration and inquiry, however, a shift to research more focused on explicating a local eighteenth century also comes with charges to the field. To examine the eighteenth-century history of any place, particularly in North America, is to look directly at the work of English, as both a literature and a field of study, to displace, appropriate, or otherwise contort the lifeways of that place as part of an ongoing process of settlement. There is always a risk, as decades of postcolonial scholars have now observed, that any close study of the archives of this moment will reproduce these erasures, the methods that the discipline has naturalized further obscuring the dimensions of a local eighteenth century that was never written (or never written in English), as well as the perspectives of any communities that did not ever acknowledge the "Enlightenment" project. More recently, a rising call to decolonize higher education has amplified this imperative to reconsider how our disciplinary practices and legitimation strategies still prop up a contemporary colonial order.[17] In this context, then, a shift to more local research projects could also motivate eighteenth-century scholars to reimagine the field's current focus and objectives. In the project here presented as a model, the characteristic that identified the Mývatn region as a productive object for interdisciplinary study was its resilience—but if we narrow our focus to the eighteenth century of any particular place in North America, a closer study of how this past has shaped the present is equally likely to turn up a pivotal moment in the development of the ideas, practices, and values that have, according to many ecocritics, significantly contributed to the local shape of the climate crisis. This would be challenging work, of course, because it demands that we begin to account for how the terms of literary studies (and wider research in the humanities) have contributed to the ossification of the categories—nature and history, for instance—that now make climate change so hard for some to see. Arguably, however, this effort—to try, through more local research and other methods, to make the enduring influence and operations of these eighteenth-century ideas visible in the present—is also an imperative and urgent response to this crisis. That project is necessarily interdisciplinary, well beyond the scope of any study specific to one period (or region, or linguistic tradition), but it is necessary everywhere—and the particular history that we are, as eighteenth-century scholars, best equipped to explicate is already there, waiting to be drawn into the narrative of the present crisis, wherever we happen to live.

Notes

1. See, among many others, Ian Baucom, "History 4˙: Postcolonial Method and Anthropocene Time," *Cambridge Journal Of Postcolonial Literary Inquiry* 1, no. 1 (2014): 123–42; Jason W. Moore, *Capitalism in the Web of Life: Ecology and the Accumulation of Capital* (London: Verso Books, 2015), 51–74; see also note 11.

2. See, among others, Paul J. Crutzen, "Geology of Mankind," *Nature* 415, no. 23 (2002): 23; Andreas Malm, *Fossil Capital: The Rise of Steam Power and the Roots of Global Warming* (London: Verso, 2016), 1–36; and Alan Mikhail, "Enlightenment Anthropocene," *Eighteenth-Century Studies* 49, no. 2 (2016): 211–31.

3. This course was called *Svartárkot, Culture—Nature: Human Ecology and Culture at Lake Mývatn*; for more, see *https://svartarkot.is/past-courses/*.

4. MYBIT (or Mýbit) refers to an ongoing research program focused on the sustainability of the Lake Mývatn district. To date, this research has been supported by a 2014 National Science Foundation Award (project title: Investigations of the Long-Term Sustainability of Human Ecodynamic Systems in Northern Iceland, or

MYCHANGE) and a 2016 Rannís award from the Icelandic Centre for Research (project title: The Mývatn District of Iceland: Sustainability, Environment and Change, ca. AD 1700 to 1950, or MYSEAC).

5. R. Sigurðardóttir, A. E. J. Oglivie, A. D. Júlíusson, V. Hreinsson, and M. T. Hicks, "Water and Sustainability in the Lake Mývatn Region of Iceland: Historical Perspectives and Current Concerns," *Mountain Ice and Water: Investigations of the Hydrologic Cycle in Alpine Environments*, ed. Gregory B. Greenwood and J. F. Scroder Jr. (Amsterdam: Elsevier, 2016): 158.

6. Megan Hicks, "The Historical Archaeology of Rural Subsistence and Trade in Mývatn, 1703–1910" (lecture, Svartárkot, Culture—Nature: Human Ecology and Culture at Lake Mývatn, Bárðardalur, Iceland, 23 August 2018); see also Seth Brewington, et al., "Islands of Change vs. Islands of Disaster: Managing Pigs and Birds in the Anthropocene of the North Atlantic," in "The Anthropocene in the Longue Durée," special issue, *The Holocene* 25, no. 10 (2015): 1,676–84.

7. Thomas H. McGovern, et al., "Landscapes of Settlement in Northern Iceland: Historical Ecology of Human Impact and Climate Fluctuation on the Millennial Scale," *American Anthropologist* 109, no. 1 (2007): 46.

8. Jonathan Kramnick, "The Interdisciplinary Fallacy," *Representations* 140 (2017): 69–70.

9. "MYBIT," *Svartárkot, Culture—Nature, https://svartarkot.is/mybit/*.

10. Viðar Hreinsson, "Heath Settlements and the Local Historian Helgi Jonsson: Glimpses of Environmental and Literary History," (lecture, Svartárkot, Culture—Nature: Human Ecology and Culture at Lake Mývatn, Bárðardalur, Iceland, 22 August 2018); Viðar Hreinsson, "Manuscripts and Literatures of Mývatn, Stories and Poetry," (lecture, Svartárkot, Culture—Nature: Human Ecology and Culture at Lake Mývatn, Bárðardalur, Iceland, 25 August 2018).

11. Dipesh Chakrabarty, "The Climate of History: Four Theses," *Critical Inquiry* 35, no. 2 (2009): 197–222; Rob Nixon, *Slow Violence and the Environmentalism of the Poor* (Cambridge: Harvard University Press, 2011), 2–3; Amitav Ghosh, *The Great Derangement: Climate Change and the Unthinkable* (Chicago: University of Chicago Press, 2016), 9–11; Christina Sharpe, *In the Wake: On Blackness and Being* (Durham: Duke University Press, 2016), 111–12; see also Baucom, "History 4ʹ," 123; and Moore, *Capitalism in the Web of Life*, 51–74.

12. For more, see Clark A. Miller and Paul N. Edwards, eds., "Introduction: The Globalization of Climate Science and Climate Politics," in *Changing the Atmosphere: Expert Knowledge and Environmental Governance* (Cambridge: MIT Press, 2001), 1–30; and Mike Hulme, *Why We Disagree about Climate Change: Understanding Controversy, Inaction, and Opportunity* (Cambridge: Cambridge University Press, 2009), 1–34.

13. For more, see Ann Cvetkovich and Douglas Kellner, eds., "Introduction: Thinking Global and Local," in *Articulating the Global and the Local: Globalization and Cultural Studies* (New York: Routledge, 1997), 1–32; Felicity A. Nussbaum, introduction to *The Global Eighteenth Century* (Baltimore: Johns Hopkins University Press, 2003), 1–20; as well as the essays collected in Miles Ogborn and Charles W. J. Withers, eds*., Georgian Geographies: Essays on Space, Place, and Landscape in the Eighteenth Century* (Manchester: Manchester University Press, 2004).

14. This is perhaps more true north of the forty-ninth parallel than south of it, as American studies much more often include an American eighteenth century than Canadian studies include a Canadian eighteenth century; it is perhaps also more true in the western states and provinces of the continent than in the east, if only as a consequence of settlement patterns (and their influence on the methods and objectives of academic research in English).

15. Treaty 7 was signed by the Siksika (Blackfoot), Kainai (Blood), Piikani (Peigan), Stoney-Nakoda and Tsuut'ina (Sarcee) First Nations and the Canadian Crown in September 1877. Since 1928, this region has also been identified as Region 3 of the Métis Nation of Alberta. For more on the settlement of this region, see James Daschuk, *Clearing the Plains: Disease, Politics of Starvation, and the Loss of Aboriginal Life* (Regina: University of Regina Press, 2013), 27–40.

16. See, for instance, Gerald Anthony Oetelaar, "Better Homes and Pastures: Human Agency and the Construction of Place in Communal Bison Hunting on the Northern Plains," *Plains Anthropologist* 59, no. 229 (2014): 9–37; and David Meyer and Dale Russell, "'So Fine and Pleasant, Beyond Description': The Lands and Lives of the Pegogamaw Crees," *Plains Anthropologist* 49, no. 191 (2004): 217–52.

17. See, for instance, Eve Tuck and K. Wayne Yang, "Decolonization is Not a Metaphor," *Decolonization: Indigeneity, Education, and Society* 1, no. 1 (2012): 1–40.

ASECS AT 50

Presidential Lecture

Ambitions, Modest and Otherwise of Two Parisian Painters: Marie-Anne Loir and Catherine Lusurier

MELISSA HYDE

Ambition. The laudable daughter of emulation, who gives birth to the desire to distinguish oneself in a career of talent and genius.
C-N Cochin, "Ambition," *Iconologie par figures* (1791)

What is the ambition of a woman? To be likeable and to be loved.
J-F Marmontel, "Le Misanthrope corrigé,"
Contes moraux (1765)

How brave, how energetic, or how ambitious must be the woman who would win the title Artist.
Léonce Bénédite, "Of Women Painters in France" (1905)[1]

Around 1710, a Lyonais print seller by the name of Balthazar Gentot published a print that humorously depicts a well-dressed man in a domestic interior, brandishing a cudgel and shouting at his wife (see fig. 1). She returns the favor, armed with a distaff. Between them, suspended in a tug-of-war, is the object of their dispute: a pair of the husband's breeches, a metonymical sign of his masculinity and authority. The theme of the battle over the *culottes* was nothing new.[2] But this particular engraving caught my attention because it bears a title that attributes the quarrel over the breeches to a specific cause: female ambition, as indicated by the inscription on a petticoat-shaped cartouche at the top of the composition, "Ambition of the Wife to Achieve Mastery by Means of the Breeches." Defining female ambition in terms of an unruly wife's struggle for authority at home is a striking conceit, given that the print was made at a time when in actuality, women's ambitions extended to domains—intellectual, artistic, political— that were decidedly beyond the purview of the domestic sphere. The print, though humorous, offers a fair idea of how the ambitious woman was conceived in the popular imaginary of France: she was both unruly and the object of ridicule. This image is also tacitly predicated on the normative view that wives (and women in general) are supposed to be submissive, obedient, and faithful, with no ambition to rule. However, like other treatments of the subject, the print can also be read in another way, against the grain, as articulating and thereby normalizing an alternative vision of the world in which women do not adhere to the notional norms, and spouses are equal in strength and independence.[3] As such, it calls to mind the assertion by Janet Burke and Margaret Jacob that "women have been (and remain) able to act independently even when living in societies that wish to imagine them as subordinate or to reaffirm traditional gender relations."[4]

This essay focuses on two women whose artistic ambitions enabled them to find ways to work successfully within systems that were legally, socially, and institutionally structured not to include them. My central protagonists, Catherine Lusurier (1752–81) and Marie-Anne Loir (1705–83), were both painters who went after their ambitions by quietly breaking the rules, both out of necessity and as a professional strategy. They operated almost exclusively in the domain of the social and in "the Republic of Painting," rather than that of official art institutions or the open art market.[5] Their modus operandi contrasts markedly with that of two other women, the marquise Du Châtelet and Madame Du Bocage, whom I will have occasion to discuss because, as it happens, both of these *femmes savantes* sat to Loir for their portraits. Both pursued their intellectual ambitions as notable figures in Parisian society and as members of the Republic of Letters, but also, in a more highly public way, as published authors. Drawing on these examples, I mean to complicate the notion of ambition as traditionally applied to women and to show that there were many different ways to be an *ambitieuse*.

Ideas of "female ambition" as they appear in the dominant discourses and visual cultures of the eighteenth century have little to do with "ambition" as it was defined in sources such as the *Encyclopédie* and the *Dictionnaire Trevoux*. Without the qualifier, ambition both implicitly and explicitly

Figure 1. Balthazar Gentot, *Ambition de la femme*, ca. 1712. Copper engraving, 59.4 cm x 43.1 cm. Cabinet des estampes de la Bibliothèque nationale de France.

concerned only men. Ambition could have positive meanings—as in the noble ambition to be of service to one's fellow citizens—but was often discussed in negative terms as an unchecked desire for glory and fortune, as an excessive passion for self-aggrandizement, or as an ardent desire to surpass others in merit and glory. It is almost impossible to read about ambition without also encountering the term "glory." Though itself not a stable uncontested concept, glory was often identified with military achievements or with other more abstract forms of mastery.[6] Voltaire described glory as a matter of brilliant actions, dazzling virtues, talents, great difficulties surmounted.[7] However construed, glory, like fame, was the province of men. This is assuredly the position taken in the *Encyclopédie*'s entry on *Femme*, which presents the desire for public recognition as foreign to women's nature: "The happy woman's glory is to be ignored. Enclosed in the virtues of wife and mother, she devotes her days to the practice of obscure virtues."[8] By this account, glory for women means the opposite of what it is for men; it is to be virtuously enclosed, private and un-famous. By implication, men's glory is defined by its expansive publicness and its close ties to fame.

Émilie Le Tonnelier de Breteuil, Marquise du Châtelet—Voltaire's intellectual consort and, for a time, mistress—offered her own reflections on ambition and glory in her *Discourse on Happiness*. Surprisingly, given how intellectually ambitious she was herself, Du Châtelet advised her readers (particularly women of the privileged classes) to distance themselves from ambition because "it makes our happiness dependent on others" and was therefore inimical to happiness.[9] At the same time, in a refreshing departure from most of her contemporaries, she observed that men *and* women are animated by a desire for glory. But, noting that men had many more means to attain it, the marquise opined that women could only achieve glory (and happiness) through love of study.

Du Châtelet was far from alone in thinking that a passion for study could bring a woman happiness and that it was essential to her sense of self.[10] Almost a century later, the artist Stéphanie de Virieu (1785–1873) said much the same thing, when she wrote that the "duty [of women] is to study and to instruct themselves." The form of study in which she herself was most invested was the study of art, as De Virieu recalled in her souvenirs:

> I did not simply have a taste for drawing, it was a dominant, singular absorbing passion; it endured with an intensity beyond many other passions and to the point that disappointments, continual worries forced me to tear myself away; and then when I was a little more calm, drawing again became almost my sole occupation and the source of all my joy.[11]

From this account of De Virieu's passionate drive to be an artist, it is clear that art making was her raison d'être. Her "incessant ardor" for the study of art took her to Paris and the orbit of Jacques Louis David for several rounds of lessons (the first in 1798, when she was just 13, and "hoping to become Raphael").[12] De Virieu sounds as ambitious and obsessed as another ardent young artist a generation before her who belonged to the inner circle of the Davidian school. Working day and night with an intensity that worried his family, the young man declared that he would "Conquer or Die. I must be a painter or nothing." This was Jean-Germain Drouais (1763–88), who would become David's star pupil in the 1780s, playing an important role in the making of David's famous *Oath of the Horatii* (1784, Musée du Louvre). His prize-winning student work would be permanently on exhibit in the Academy's rooms in the Louvre.[13] By contrast, De Virieu, who was born into the oldest noble family of the Dauphiné region, never exhibited or sold a work. Family tradition has it that David was one of her teachers also and that he said of her: "If she had remained poor [in the wake of the Revolution], she would have become famous."[14] Instead, despite being "young, rich and charming," as her brother's close friend, Alphonse Lamartine, put it, she "renounced the world in order to devote herself entirely to her family *and to painting, for which she had a genius*" (emphasis mine).[15] If De Virieu was satisfied with the (woman's) glory of being ignored and practicing the obscure virtues of a devoted daughter, she nonetheless devoted herself also to painting. Her example makes clear that a woman of talent did not necessarily have to be a professional, or go public, to be ambitious. What is more, ambition need not spring from a desire for fame and glory, but rather from something fundamentally human: for one's existence to be remembered.[16] Here again, Du Châtelet's words are apposite: "One does not always acknowledge the enjoyment of the ill-defined desire to be spoken of after one has passed out of existence, but it always stays deep in our heart."[17]

Voltaire famously said that Madame Du Châtelet "was a great man whose only fault was being a woman."[18] However, the ambitious women under discussion here did not seek to be men. Rather, as Elisabeth Badinter put it in her foundational book, *Emilie, Emilie ou l'ambition feminine au XVIIIe siècle*, to be an ambitieuse was to be "a woman who refused the limits assigned to her sex and gender, and even wished for liberty."[19] Following Badinter, I understand as ambitious any woman who sought to succeed by and for herself; any woman who sought to change her condition, and to have power (or at least volition and agency) in the world. Considered from this perspective, ambition is a personal matter, deeply bound up with notions of the self and a person's status as an individual. Recasting ambition in these terms separates it from the public (and "masculine") values of fame and glory. By this definition, many women were ambitious, including artists like Stéphanie de Virieu, as my brief account of her shows. While in general women's ambition to study and create art can be understood as an expression of agency or as an assertion of their very existence, the drive of eighteenth-century artists to make art in their own name might also be understood with more historical specificity, as a means for women to insist on their status as individuals at a time when they had few civil rights and were beginning to lay claim to them.[20]

Léonce Bénédite observed, in the 1905 passage quoted as one of my epigraphs, that the woman who would win the title of artist had to be brave, energetic, and ambitious. This was no less true in the eighteenth century when Marie-Anne Loir and Catherine Lusurier built their successful, independent careers. Though neither had a highly public career, both won the recognition of important patrons and collectors. Both were able to work in their own names and did so outside of any institutional framework. That they found ways to realize their professional aspirations without going public demonstrates that ambition could be manifest in a variety of forms, some of them publicly visible and others much less so. As we will see, the life and work of these two artists are connected both directly and indirectly in a number of ways that are revealing about how women functioned in the art world.

Lusurier and Loir have remained almost totally beyond the view of art history, though both painted portraits of illustrious people that are remembered, even when those depicting them are not (see fig. 6 and fig. 8).[21] The history of French art (and beyond) has not yet fully undertaken its own version of the "great work of recovery" of women writers that has so enriched the study of French literature in recent decades.[22] I am introducing Lusurier and Loir as new protagonists in an art historical narrative that has largely been defined by the Académie royale de peinture et de sculpture and its pedagogies, its exhibitions in the Salon du Louvre, and its philosophical and political engagements. Though this was the only royal academy in Paris to admit women to its ranks, by the eighteenth century women were understood to be foreign to the nature of the institution and were allowed admission only as exceptions to the rule. In much the same way, women have been regarded more broadly as exceptions to the traditional rule of art history. Rather than treating Lusurier and Loir as exceptions that existed in isolation, I am considering them in the context in which they worked: a world that extended beyond the Académie and was inhabited by women as well as men, one deeply shaped by social connections, and one in which women were present and active. The careers of these two artists attest that in eighteenth-century France women were fully embedded in artistic practice on a variety of levels. They were not merely marginal to the traditional story of masculine creation and triumph that remains central to art history. My discussion of Marie-Anne Loir also challenges the received wisdom that there were no professional women artists to speak of before the 1780s, though that period did see a marked increase in the visibility of women artists, if not necessarily an increase in the actual number of artists themselves.[23]

Mademoiselle Lusurier

I want to turn first to Catherine Lusurier, who was some fifty years younger than Marie-Anne Loir, but died before her. A contemporary of renowned *académiciennes* Elisabeth Louise Vigée Le Brun and Adélaïde Labille-Guiard, Lusurier's career ended just as theirs were beginning. She died at the age of 28, two years before the election of the other two women to the Académie royale in 1783. Unlike them, Lusurier was not a member of the guild (then known as the Académie de Saint Luc). She never exhibited at its Salon. She never participated in the Exposition de la Jeunesse, a one-day exhibition that took place annually in the Place Dauphine and was already an important venue for aspiring young women artists when Lusurier arrived in Paris in the mid–1760s. Unlike quite a few other women of her generation, her name does not appear in any of the almanacs listing the addresses of professional artists. These facts have given rise to the supposition that Lusurier only worked behind the scenes as an assistant in the studio of her cousin, François-Hubert Drouais (father of Germain Drouais), who was her teacher, along with the family patriarch, Hubert Drouais. Like Drouais père, François-Hubert Drouais was a portraitist and a member of the Académie royale. He was much sought after by the courtiers of Versailles and wealthy Parisians for his uncanny ability to make almost anyone look like fashionable and perfectly doll-like versions of themselves (and each other). He was often criticized by forward-thinking critics, such as Denis Diderot, who liked their art with a lot less rococo polish and artifice. It has been supposed too that Lusurier had no independent existence of her own as an artist, but that, like the other women in the Drouais family who were artists, Lusurier operated completely within the collective logic of the family studio, assisting her cousin and making copies after his works.[24] That notion is roundly contradicted by several portraits that Lusurier signed, two of which are widely reproduced because they depict important sitters, and the paintings have ended up in major museums. The one is of d'Alembert, the other, of the youngest Drouais, Germain—he of the "Painter or nothing" cri de coeur (see fig. 6 and fig. 2).

In her admirable book, *La Griffe du Peintre*, Charlotte Guichard analyzes artist's signatures as a means of establishing authorship. She discusses Lusurier as an example of a woman's use of this "authorial strategy." Guichard argues that when women signed their names to their works it enabled them to navigate their legally subordinate status in significant ways.[25] I would add that the act of self-naming, the assertion of authorship, the very fact of the signature itself, is in a quite literal sense a mark of ambition. There is, of course, a practical wisdom to signing one's work, especially for women whose authorship was so often called into doubt. Lusurier was wise to put her name on her two best known works—had she not, they would surely have been attributed to a man, a fate that has befallen many of her paintings, to say nothing of the vast majority of unsigned works by other women.[26] The prominence of Lusurier's signature in her portrait of Germain Drouais is noteworthy in this regard because her image of a "young draftsman" (*un petit ecolier*) belongs to a genre made famous by François-Hubert Drouais and by Nicolas-Bernard Lépicié, probably another of her mentors. Both men made a veritable industry of depicting adorably roguish apprentice artists. It is a genre that Lusurier nonetheless managed to make her own in how she reconceived it (see fig. 2). This is clear if we compare her portrait of Germain Drouais to her copy of the painting that became famous when the elder Drouais showed it at the Salon of 1761 (see fig. 3). Diderot rhapsodized about Drouais's mischievous "little rascal," whom he imagined to be on his way to a drawing class at the Académie.[27] Lusurier transforms Drouais' generic social type into a portrait of a specific individual. Rather than the cherubic child who looks out impishly as he poses with his portefeuille tucked under his arm, Lusurier gives us Germain Drouais, seated in three-quarter length, in the act of drawing. He looks up momentarily, and gazes at the viewer with a forthrightness that is uncharacteristic of figures by Lusurier's mentors.[28] Though a smile plays at the boy's lips, there is nothing here of Drouais's "little rascal." Germain Drouais is older and engages seriously in the practice of art, much as Lusurier herself practiced art seriously. What is more, the intent look and staging of the body reminds one of the pictorial rhetoric of a self-portrait, such as that adopted by Gabrielle Capet in her stunning self-portrayal from the 1790s (see fig. 4). Lusurier portrays the young Drouais as if he were looking in a mirror, making a self-portrait—a possibility evoked by the fact that we do not see what he is drawing.[29] A further possibility comes to mind. Perhaps what is implied here is an act of reciprocal portrayal. Is he drawing Lusurier painting him? This suggests a certain reciprocity between the two artists and a world in which men and women practice art in the same place, sometimes collaboratively and intersubjectively.[30] The whole tenor of Lusurier's picture suggests the young Germain's seriousness of purpose, his intensity and ambition. That seriousness is absent in other works in this genre.[31]

Lusurier also produced one of the very few representations of the apprentice artist as a girl (see fig. 5).[32] Without the slightest trace of coquetry in her expression or attire, this girl gazes out fixedly and unsmilingly at the viewer. The picture lacks the sentimentality or nascent eroticism that is usual in eighteenth-century images of girls (one need only think of Jean-Baptiste Greuze). Sitting in a simple wooden chair, with her uncoiffed hair, black pinafore apron, a simple dress and neckerchief, she is actually dressed for work—something virtually unprecedented in representations of women artists. The features of Lusurier's girl are also so distinctive that they insist we understand this painting as a portrait of a specific individual, one that Lusurier refused to idealize. Instead she presents us with a sitter who, though not a beauty, has an expression that suggests interiority, subjecthood. The picture comes across as a representation of an actual person who has thoughts, and even ambition, to judge by the intensity of her gaze. If Lusurier's portrait of Germain Drouais evokes associations with the self-portrait, this picture could actually be one. The girl's unwavering gaze suggests the possibility, though her youth makes it seem doubtful.[33] Whether or not Lusurier's picture is a self-portrait, the sensibility of the picture and Lusurier's decision to depict the apprentice artist type as a girl make it entirely her own, even without the autographic signature. As such, it functions as an expression of herself as an artist—and of her ambition to be recognized as an individual.

As is true of some of her other portraits, Lusurier's *Young Draftswoman* also markedly differentiates her from Drouais on the level of style. When Lusurier chose to do so, she could readily perform in the Drouais mode, as exemplified by her signed *Portrait of Charlotte-Françoise De Bure* (Milwaukee Museum of Art, 1776), which until recently was attributed to Drouais.[34] In Lusurier's other works in her signature style, she rejects the éclat, the polish, the delicacy and frothy beauty of Drouais's rococo. Her vision of childhood is also quite different from her cousin's. Where Drouais's children are all effervescent innocence and playful mischief, Lusurier's are more sober and restrained, evincing a vivid sense of character and presence.[35]

When Lusurier painted in her own idiom, she avoided the "feminine" "made up" character that critics often objected to in Drouais's portraits.[36] An example of that is her *Portrait of Jean Le Rond d'Alembert* (see fig. 6). As Helen Ashmore has rightly pointed out, Lusurier's rendering of d'Alembert has vitality, dignity, and force and is at the same time psychologically revealing. It attests that painting mature male sitters was another of Lusurier's strengths. She painted the philosophe in 1777, the year after the death of Julie de Lespinasse, the object of his passionate, unrequited love. The portrait is

Figure 2. Catherine Lusurier, *The Painter Jean-Germain Drouais at the Age of Fifteen*, 1778. Oil on canvas, 80 x 64 cm, inv6406. Photo: René-Gabriel Ojéda. Musée du Louvre, Paris, France, ©RMN-Grand Palais/Art Resource, New York.

Figure 3. Catherine Lusurier, after F-H Drouais, *The Young Scholar*, ca. 1770-1780. Oil on canvas, 51.1 x 38.4 cm. Courtesy of the Huntington Art Collections, San Marino, California.

composed in penumbral tonalities of black and umber, punctuated by warm reds, golds, and accents of white. Depicted in three-quarter view, d'Alembert is shown working, seated at a Louis XV desk of ebony trimmed with gilt, quill pen in hand. The subtle articulation of different textures and shades of white on the lace on his sleeve, the paper, the quill, and the serviette d'Alembert holds in his hand are a virtuoso display of Lusurier's painterly talents. Pausing from his writing, d'Alembert looks up. He is dressed with elegant nonchalance in a red *robe de chambre* lined with green, his shirt collar open. Illuminated by an unseen light source outside the frame, the right side of the philosophe's body stands out against the gloom of the background; his left side is cast in shadow. The raking light, which draws particular attention to his writing hand and his face, makes visible the lines on his brow and deep creases along the nasolabial fold. D'Alembert's expression is at once careworn, slightly quizzical, and in perfect harmony with the melancholic sensibility of the portrait. Lusurier did d'Alembert justice as a brilliant thinker and a man of feeling.[37] D'Alembert evidently prized the portrait—at the time of his death in 1783, it was hanging in the

Figure 4. Marie-Gabrielle Capet, *Self-Portrait*, 1790. Trois crayons on tan antique laid paper, 34 cm x 29.4 cm. The Horwitz Collection, Wilmington, Delaware.

bedchamber of his Louvre apartment, along with Quentin de la Tour's 1753 pastel portrait of the philosophe (Paris, Musée du Louvre).[38]

My argument that Lusurier worked to create an independent artistic identity for herself is based on visual evidence. It has lately found confirmation in an archival discovery, made by Guichard, of the inventory detailing Lusurier's estate at the time of her death in 1781. The document clearly shows that Lusurier had her own residence, her own studio and clients, and was making enough money to provide modest support for an unmarried sister. It shows

Figure 5. Catherine Lusurier, *The Young Draftswoman (Self-Portrait?)*, before 1751. Oil on canvas, 32 x 26.7 cm. Kunsthalle Bremen, ©Lars Lohrisch/Artothek.

Figure 6. Catherine Lusurier, *Portrait of Jean Le Rond d'Alembert*, 1778. Oil on canvas, 96 x 76 cm. Musée Carnavalet, photo: Roger-Viollet.

in material terms that Lusurier was quietly "making a name for herself," as Guichard has put it.[39] In producing works that never went public, Lusurier nonetheless had the ambition to succeed by and for herself. Lusurier's was an unobtrusive, perhaps even modest, ambition, but it enabled her to practice professionally and independently from the family studio. And, as we will see, it won her recognition from at least one important member of the Académie royale outside of her family.

Just how quiet Lusurier was in making a name for herself is forcefully apparent when compared to other women who strove (some quite desperately) to draw public attention to themselves as artists. One tactic of striving artists was to put announcements in gazettes, periodicals, and daily newspapers.[40] This stratagem was adopted by Geneviève Brossard de Beaulieu (1755–c. 1835), a particularly poignant case of unquiet female artistic ambition. A student of Greuze, Mademoiselle Beaulieu belonged to the same generation as Lusurier and Vigée Le Brun. She followed the enterprising example of her teacher by organizing exhibitions of her work in her studio. These were announced and received positive notice in the *Mercure de France* and the *Journal de Paris*, and they garnered additional attention as well.[41] Inspired by the recent admissions of Vigée Le Brun and Labille-Guiard into the Académie royale, Brossard de Beaulieu tried valiantly to gain election herself. Like others who had tried and failed earlier in the century, the doors of the Académie royale remained obdurately closed to her. Brossard de Beaulieu continued to exhibit publicly wherever she could, and petitioned French fine arts administrations for decades to come. When considered beside Beaulieu's pertinacious attempts to ally herself with esteemed art institutions and to have a highly visible career, Lusurier's nearly total absence from the public sphere of the art world (the press and art exhibitions) make evident that she was able to adopt different career strategies and, being well connected professionally and socially, had different opportunities open to her.[42]

Lusurier's name appeared in the French press on just one occasion before her death: this was in connection with the engraving by Pierre Savart, after her *Portrait of d'Alembert*. Announcements about the availability of the print for sale were published in the *Mercure de France* and the *Journal Encyclopédique*.[43] This was the only one of Lusurier's paintings to be engraved and made publicly visible in this way. The next time that Lusurier's name got a public exposure was in an article that appeared on the occasion of her death. Published anonymously in the *Journal de Paris*, the essay is now attributed to Charles-Nicolas Cochin, who had been secretary of the Académie royale under Louis XV, as well as an important art critic.[44] In January of 1781, the *Journal de Paris* had published a one-line notice about Lusurier's funeral, identifying her as a "peintresse."[45] Given her low profile, that short notice and the recognition of her profession are surprising. More unexpected, however, is the Cochin essay that followed the next month. For a man such as Cochin to write a public tribute to the artistic talents and potential of a young woman who was just starting to build an independent, but decidedly un-public, professional career is already extraordinary. That Cochin's text takes the form of a semi-official eulogy of the kind usually reserved for famous men was virtually unprecedented.[46] Cochin lauds Lusurier for her skill as a portraitist. Comparing her to painters Anne Vallayer-Coster, Élisabeth Vigée Le Brun, and Rosalie Filleul, he comments that if Mademoiselle Lusurier had lived, she might have one day been their "émule." Cochin cites these women as if his readers can be expected to know who they are. This is not surprising in Vallayer-Coster's case, given her status as académicienne, but that Cochin also described Vigée Le Brun as famous for her historical and allegorical subjects, even though she had not yet been admitted to the Académie royale, is noteworthy.[47] That Rosalie Filleul (née Bocquet), another quiet ambitieuse, should be mentioned at all, is even more so.[48] It suggests that there is much to learn about how artistic reputations and careers operated outside of the official sphere of the Académie royale and the Salon.

Perhaps most remarkable of all is that Cochin used the occasion of his éloge to Lusurier to make an apologia for women artists in general in which he calls for opportunities to be opened to them and for them to be recognized and remembered. Noting how France has seemed to refuse to recognize that women are capable of artistic talents of the first order, Cochin says that it will be left to his own century to be distinguished by women who are "truly artists" and whose names will be remembered. He laments that to attain the status of true artists women "will go through a thousand travails, be without encouragement, and deprived, for the most part, of the help necessary for the study of Nature; study that so often in vain is lavished on men."[49] He does not actually use the term ambition, but makes it clear that no woman could be an artist without it.

Mademoiselle Loir

A small irony of Cochin's calling out France's Lethean failure to recognize women of talent is that in his short précis about women artists, he himself gives no indication of any awareness of Marie-Anne Loir.[50] She was elderly by that time and had given up painting. But that did not prevent another author from noting two years earlier, in 1779, that Mademoiselle Loir "is still living and has acquired a great reputation in painting."[51] Cochin's omission of Loir is curious as the two had too many shared colleagues and connections for him not to have known her (or at least known of her). Cochin would have known Loir's brother, Alexis. The two were contemporaries and *agrées* in the Académie within five years of one another.[52] Cochin would have been similarly acquainted with Hubert Drouais, the teacher and uncle of Catherine Lusurier, with whom Loir herself had professional connections.

Though her career spanned some forty years, from the 1730s to the 1770s, until recently little was known about Marie-Anne Loir, not even the correct spelling of her name or the dates of her birth and death. In 1976, Anne Sutherland Harris established a basic narrative about Loir in the famous *Women Artists* catalog.[53] The essentials of this pioneering account are as follows: Loir came from a family of goldsmiths and artists, was active around mid-century, and was a portraitist working in the vein of Pierre Gobert and Jean-Marc Nattier. Loir had an older brother: Alexis III (1712–85), a member of the Académie royale, a sculptor and also a portraitist, who specialized in pastels, and fostered her career. She had ties to Jean-François de Troy, who remembered her in his will. Like her brother, she is supposed to have lived a peripatetic existence for years, traveling to Italy with him and painting portraits of provincial nobility all over France. Loir was admitted to the Académie de peinture et de sculpture of Marseille in 1762. Only a handful of works are securely attributed to her.

Thanks to the scholarly diligence of Catherine Voiriot and others, new facts have lately come to light that have advanced our understanding of Loir's career and her body of work. Voiriot has firmly established that Loir was born in 1705, not 1715, making her seven years older than Alexis.[54] Voiriot has also established that Loir was living on her own as early as 1740 in the rue Neuve des Petits Champs, a street on which many artists resided.[55] This adds to information Sutherland Harris gleaned from a notarial document of 1746 that gave the same address and listed Loir as "peintre, fille majeure," living with her sister, also a *fille majeure* (a single woman who enjoyed the rights and legal status of an adult). The landscape painter, Joseph Vernet listed Loir in his address book of 1764–73 as still living on the same street. For decades, then, Loir had her own residence and lived independently as a professional painter. In 1783, the year of her death, she was prosperous enough to name Alexis and three of her sisters as her heirs.[56] There is no evidence that Marie-Anne Loir ever left Paris for any length of time. She did not even go to Marseille for her admission to the Académie there. It is thus unlikely that Loir traveled to Italy, even though her brother seems to have been there in 1738, and Jean-François de Troy was the Director of the French Academy in Rome.[57] A cache of Loir's letters written to her colleagues in Marseille dating from 1762–81 reveal crucial details about her training, her personality, and her attitudes towards her work. I will discuss some of these details in due course.[58]

As to reconstituting the body of her work, scholars are steadily adding to Loir's oeuvre.[59] Despite her long and productive career, few of her paintings can be identified definitively, as most are unsigned. This includes the Du Châtelet portrait now in Bordeaux, whose attribution at times has been doubted (see fig. 8).[60] However, the inscription of Loir's name on eighteenth-century engravings of the Bordeaux portrait confirms Loir's authorship of that painting.[61] It is also thanks to prints that some additional works can now safely be attributed to her. Other prints attest to the existence of lost works by Loir.

One striking thing about Loir's portraits of known sitters is how many of her clients came from the upper reaches of society—especially early in her career, when her sitters included members of the highest nobility. Loir never became a portraitist for the immediate family of the king, as other women would later do, but her first recorded commissions were portraits (untraced) painted for the duc de Bourbon, *prince du sang* and scion of the Bourbon-Condés.[62] Other sitters included Princes of Monaco; members of the family of the cardinal de Fleury; Pierre Mayeur, the abbot of Clairvaux; provincial Parliamentary nobility; and wealthy non-nobles such as the famous collector, Jean de Julienne.[63] Besides the Marquise Du Châtelet, Loir also did portraits of women of high intellectual and artistic ambition, such as the author Madame Du Bocage (see fig. 9, original painting untraced) and the composer and musician Madame Brillon de Jouy (1763, private collection).[64] Loir is also the author of a portrait plausibly identified as Madame Geoffrin (National Museum of Women in the Arts, Washington, D.C.). More unexpectedly, Loir painted military heroes—the Maréchal de Saxe, posed next to a cannon (1749, Chambord) and Victor-François de Broglie, also a Marshal of France, in a full-length equestrian portrait, now known only through an engraving (see fig. 7).[65] In its deft mastery of the conventions of heroic military portraits, that picture bespeaks abilities and ambitions in Loir that extended beyond those of a peintresse of modestly scaled portraits for the familiars of her sitters. Similarly, a lost gouache depicting *Diana and Endymion* points to other unexpected aspects of Loir's oeuvre.[66] The subject matter is noteworthy for a woman artist: drawn from Ovid, it centers on the beautiful male body. Through the figure of the goddess Diana, who gazes amorously at the sleeping Endymion, the painting thematizes the pleasures of female spectatorship. These facts complicate the notion—still prevalent today—that propriety confined women to genres that ranked below history painting according to academic doctrine: portraiture, generally of children and other women, and still life. This is at best an oversimplification and at worst is a stereotype. Like women before and after her, Loir ventured into the more ambitious, notionally masculine genres.

Figure 7. Bugey, after Marie-Anne Loir, *Victor-François, duc de Broglie, Prince de St Empire, Maréchal de France*, 1761. Copper engraving, 32.5 x 49.5 cm. Prints, Drawings and Watercolors from the Anne S. K. Brown Military Collection. Brown Digital Repository. Brown University Library.

We can only surmise how Loir became one of the preferred portraitists of so many elite patrons and did so without any official affiliations with the Académie royale or the guild. Her family connections to François de Troy (1645–1730), one of the leading portrait painters of the late seventeenth and early eighteenth centuries, likely played a role.[67] Dezallier d'Argenville, a period authority who seems to have been overlooked by modern scholars, noted in 1745 that Mademoiselle Loir "is the student of François de Troy, as well as that of M. Drouais peintre de l'Académie."[68] The Drouais in question here is Hubert Drouais, who was himself a de Troy pupil. As noted earlier, it has long been recognized that Loir had a personal connection to François de Troy's son, Jean-François (1679–1752), a history painter, but her status as a student of de Troy père is usually not noted. What is more, Loir's letters make plain that her association with de Troy fils also had a professional dimension to it; she mentions that she frequented his studio, where she and Michel Dandré-Bardon (J-F de Troy's student) were "comrades of the eye."[69] Decades later, Dandré-Bardon and Loir were still friends. It was he, as Director of the Académie de peinture et de sculpture in Marseille, who secured her admission there in 1762 and whose portrait (untraced) she painted as one of her reception pieces.

Despite her connection with the de Troys, Loir's work generally bears little resemblance to either of theirs. However, her portraits often have been identified with (or been mistaken for) those of Pierre Gobert (1662–1744) and Jean-Marc Nattier (1686–1766).[70] Yet, stylistically, her paintings, especially from the 1730s, are closest to Hubert Drouais, who she is likely to have first known during her time with François de Troy, which could have begun as early as her teens.[71] Drouais entered de Troy père's studio around 1717 and worked under his protection—i.e., as a copyist or an assistant—until the latter's death in 1730. Within two months of de Troy's demise, Drouais sought and won preliminary admission to the Académie, an achievement that allowed him to shed his journeyman status and establish his own studio.[72] At what point Loir became Drouais's student is uncertain, but given the similarities between their works in the 1730s we can speculate that their association dates to that period.[73] However, *student* ought to be understood here as a qualified term. Drouais was only six years Loir's senior, and by 1730, at age twenty-five, she would have been a fully trained artist, or very nearly so. Her reference to her early friendship with Dandré-Bardon firmly establishes that she was already painting by 1723. By 1737 Loir had made enough of a reputation for herself to have received her first paid commissions. It is probable that, like Drouais, Loir worked as a protégé of François de Troy well after she was his student properly speaking. Shifting her affiliation after her kinsman's death to Drouais, a new member of the Académie, must have enabled Loir to practice her art professionally without being licensed by the guild (until 1776 the Académie de Saint Luc had legal jurisdiction over all forms of painting and sculpture, except for those produced by members of the Académie).[74] An expanded understanding of what it meant to be a student helps to explain why, in a letter written some fifteen or twenty years later, Jean-François de Troy was still referring to Loir as Drouais's élève.[75] In fact, by that point (c. 1745–50) she had, as Dezallier d'Argenville put it at the time, "distinguished herself in portraiture."[76]

Connections, then, were essential to Loir's success in "the Republic of Painting," a term used by Dandré-Bardon.[77] Presumably, word-of-mouth recommendations from well-placed patrons and influential artists meant that, like Lusurier, Loir had no need to advertise her talents in newspapers, journals, and almanacs in order to attract clients. But connections cannot explain everything about the success of these two artists. To make a living at it, a portraitist had to have the right skills, both socially and artistically—a point made in the *nécrologe* of the artist Françoise Basseporte, who died in 1780, three years before Loir. Basseporte's eulogist, Charles Palissot de Montenoy, noted that despite her great talent as a portraitist, she turned to botanical illustration for "fear of a lack of work, the trouble of endlessly having to make new acquaintances and other inconveniences."[78] Loir and Lusurier fully embraced the risks, trouble, and inconveniences of being portraitists. Loir, of course, had a much longer time to establish herself than Lusurier, who did not make it to thirty. Given the longevity of Loir's career, it is safe to assume that she had the requisite social skills and that her patrons liked her. We get an inkling of why from her note to the secretary of Jacques I, Duc de Valentois and Prince of Monaco, concerning payment for his portrait and that of his two sons. It shows Loir to have been not only an efficient business woman, but also a person of tact and, thanks to a little witty flourish at the end, possessed of a certain esprit.[79] Clients must also have liked the signature traits of Loir's portraits, which tend to be flattering but not overly idealized. The faces of her sitters are enlivened by a distinctive half-smile; the head usually given an engaging turn; the bodies arranged in slightly stilted poses. Then there was Loir's mastery of what was fashionable in portraiture: her evocative, often quite painterly, treatment of luxurious dress and accoutrements, and her admirable ability to capture the luster of pearls and watered silk, the delicate intricacies of lace and flowers, the contrasting textures of fur trim, brocade, and velvet, as well as her attention to the sheen of a silver tea pot, polished armor, or the gilt trim of a chair.

Portraying Madame Du Châtelet and Madame Du Bocage

Loir's *Portrait of the Marquise Du Châtelet*, painted around 1745, is the work of a fully mature, even brilliant, artist at the height of her abilities (see fig. 8). We know nothing about how Loir came to paint the portrait of Émilie Du Châtelet. Loir portrayed many people of the marquise's class, so she was not an unusual choice of portraitist in that sense. Du Châtelet's turn to Loir is nonetheless notable on several counts. The marquise might have sat to Loir for practical and/or financial reasons. Loir was surely more available than the ferociously popular Nattier. Du Châtelet had sat for him in 1743, describing him as "the best for portraiture."[80] Loir certainly was considerably less expensive than Nattier, which could have been a factor for Du Châtelet, who was often pressed for lucre.[81] However, more interesting possibilities may have inspired the choice. Around the time that Loir painted the Bordeaux portrait, the marquise declared herself to have a particular "interest in the glory of her sex." Might her taste for "rendering us justice" have factored into her decision to entrust Loir with this commission?[82] Perhaps the marquise shared the attitude of Madame Alissan de La Tour, who wrote to Jean-Jacques Rousseau of her preference for a talented woman who would paint her truthfully, even though a man might have flattered her more.[83]

In truth, Loir did flatter her sitter a bit—she made Du Châtelet look younger than her fortyish years—but Loir also painted in a more naturalistic idiom than Nattier. She did not idealize the marquise's features and costume, as he had done in his portrait of 1743.[84] Instead, Loir depicted the marquise frankly, as an intellectual who was also a woman of fashion. In terms of the setting and the accouterments, the portrait of the marquise more closely aligns with portraits of lettered men than it does with conventional portraits of women (at that time often depicted in the guise of wood nymphs and goddesses). Loir would make something of a specialty of portraying urbane men sitting at their desks (usually a large *bureau plat*) with books and papers at hand.[85] So perhaps it is no coincidence that Du Châtelet commissioned Loir to picture her in a way that evokes the iconography of Loir's portraits of men, while still keeping the accent very much on "the feminine" (both in terms of the artist and the details of dress and toilette). Whatever the case, this is evidently the portrait that Du Châtelet considered to be most successful—it is the one that is engraved most often and the one that exists in multiple copies.

Almost certainly one version of the painting belonged to another ambitieuse, the salonnière and author, Madame de Bocage. Anne Marie Le Page, Madame Fiquet Du Bocage (1710–1802) was a member of the haute-bourgeoisie from Rouen, who, with her husband, divided her time

Figure 8. Marie-Anne Loir, *Portrait of Gabrielle-Emilie Le Tonnelier de Breteuil, marquise Du Châtelet*. Oil on canvas, 118 x 96 cm. Photo: A. Danvers, Musée des Beaux-Arts, Bordeaux, ©RMN-Grand Palais/Art Resource, New York.

between Paris and Rouen. Beginning in the 1730s, she held a Salon that was regularly frequented by men of letters such as Fontenelle, Marivaux, and Condorcet, and men of science, such as Alexis Clairaut and Jérôme Lalande. In the 1740s, Du Bocage began to pursue her own literary aspirations, which were rewarded in 1746 with a prize from the Académie des sciences, belles-lettres et arts of Rouen, and published under its auspices. It was in connection with this prize that Madame Du Châtelet had written in 1746, "I am far too interested in the glory of my sex not to have been very much in favor of hers. I am delighted that an academy founded in a country so full of talents and *esprit* has begun its career by rendering us justice."[86] For some years to come Du Bocage would be a literary figure of note, though for some—particularly Melchior Grimm—she was a figure of ridicule and scorn, not least of all because of her literary ambition.[87]

Du Bocage published *Le Paradis terrestre* (1748), a prose imitation or paraphrase of Milton's *Paradise Lost* that won praise from the likes of Voltaire and Fontenelle and garnered a good deal of public attention. The author sent a inscribed copy of her work (now in the Bibliothèque nationale) to Madame Du Châtelet, who chose to spend some of the last days of her fateful pregnancy reading it with Voltaire. The philosophe recounted this to Madame Du Bocage in a mournful letter written just after Du Châtelet's death in childbed, mentioning that the two of them had also reread Du Bocage's tragedy, *Les Amazones*, adding, "You would regret her yet more if you had been present at this reading. She rendered you justice: you had no more sincere admirer.[88]

For her part, Du Bocage was evidently an admirer of Du Châtelet, later paying homage to her as "Uranie" in an epic poem, *La Colombiade, ou la foi portée au nouveau monde* (1756). The author's esteem for Du Châtelet was emphatically declared by the presence of the marquise's portrait in her Paris home. In 1788, Jérôme Lalande mentioned this detail in connection with a portrait of his friend and fellow astronomer, Nicole-Reine Lepaute, painted by Guillaume Voiriot. Lalande described that portrait, which adorned his own cabinet, as a depiction of Madame Lepaute "tracing the figure of the eclipse of 1764 ... and with a globe next to her." Lalande noted that his Voiriot portrait "resembles a bit" the portrait of the marquise Du Châtelet belonging to Madame Du Bocage.[89] Guillaume Voiriot has been identified as the author of a portrait in the château de Breteuil, Chevreuse, which shows a woman seated at a desk with a globe on it, with a compass in her hand. This picture has been widely reproduced and discussed as a likeness of Emilie Du Châtelet. The identification is understandable, given Du Châtelet's fame and the relative obscurity of Lepaute. However, Lalande's description of his Voiriot portrait strongly suggests that the woman in the château de Breteuil is not Émilie Du Châtelet, but Madame Lepaute.[90] In view of Lalande's observation of the similarities between the portraits of Lepaute and Du Châtelet, it is not much of a leap to surmise that the portrait of the marquise that Lalande saw chez Du Bocage was a version of Loir's celebrated picture, even though Lalande does not mention the artist.

This surmise seems all the more probable when one considers who Madame Du Bocage chose to produce the portrait that would represent her for posterity: none other than Marie-Anne Loir.[91] Loir's portrait (untraced), immediately became Du Bocage's public face, for although the painting could not be shown at the Salon, an engraving of it could (see fig. 9).[92] Jacques-Nicolas Tardieu fils included it amongst the several engravings he exhibited for his debut at the Salon of 1748. The Salon livret noted that it was made "after the picture painted by Mademoiselle Loir."[93] Tardieu's engraving itself clearly credited Loir with authorship of the painting on which the engraving is based with the inscription "Peint par Mlle Loir."[94]

The image received a wider and more durable airing in 1748, when it was included as the new frontispiece for the second of many editions of Du Bocage's *Le Paradis terrestre*. Eight years later, Tardieu's engraving featured as the frontispiece for *La Colombiade*.[95] In 1762, the first of a three-volume *Receuil* of Du Bocage's collected works appeared, adorned with the same engraving. Madame Du Bocage did her part to celebrate and publicize Loir's talents as a painter: the 1762 *Receuil* includes a verse entitled "To Mademoiselle Loir, Who Painted the Portrait of the Author." It is an encomium to Loir's "supreme" painterly talents, which "animate the enchanted canvas."[96] Du Bocage's praise for Loir seems a bit extravagant and perhaps more than a little self-serving, as the author's extolling of the portrait's beauty can scarcely be separated from that of Du Bocage herself. At the same time, the poem very publicly insists upon Mademoiselle Loir's status as an artist and generously lauds the genius and talent of a woman who received no other public encouragement. If Loir was not publicly ambitious, Du Bocage seems to have been publicly ambitious for her.[97]

Du Bocage's poetic homage to Loir and the credit given to the painter in Tardieu's engraving prevented Loir from falling into anonymity as its author—something that does seem to have happened with Loir's *Portrait of Madame Du Châtelet*. In all the contemporary textual references to the portrait of the marquise, I have not yet found one that notes the artist's name. Lalande's mention of the portrait of the Marquise without any reference to the portrait's maker follows a pattern that is typical for portraits of famous sitters, especially when the work is unsigned and/or by a painter who is not so famous. Loir's *Portrait of Madame Du Châtelet* is another case in which her authorship has only been definitively established thanks to eighteenth-century engravings that credit her.[98]

Figure 9. Jacques-Nicolas Tardieu fils, after Marie-Anne Loir, *Portrait of Madame Du Bocage*, 1746. Engraving, 14 x 9 cm. Cabinet des estampes de la Bibliothèque nationale de France.

Mary Terrall has addressed the uses of anonymity in scientific writing and how "institutions and individuals, in fact, manipulated invisibility for a variety of purposes."[99] Terrall counts the marquise Du Châtelet as one of those individuals and has shown that Du Châtelet was able to use anonymity to her particular advantage as a woman when she made her first published contributions to scientific debates. In the case of Marie-Anne Loir, and Catherine Lusurier after her, it is difficult to know whether anonymity or near-anonymity was a chosen strategy or a fact of life. Their low public profiles gave them some advantages: it allowed them to avoid the controversy, criticism, and ridicule faced by other women who publicly pursued their ambitions. It enabled them to have independent careers outside (or at least on the fringes) of the official art world and its institutions. At the same time, the status of these two artists as professional painters was public knowledge. This is particularly true of Loir, who had such a long career. Loir welcomed the public honor of her admission to the Marseille Academy. Like Catherine Lusurier, she did sometimes sign and date her pictures (especially in the 1750s and 60s). These facts suggest that neither artist sought anonymity. Rather, the works of Loir and Lusurier, and the archival traces we have of their lives, show that both women found ways to make virtues out of necessity and were able to work successfully as professional artists, even if they never quite attained public glory.

Quietly Ambitieuse

Marie-Anne Loir and Catherine Lusurier were both talented artists who worked in their own names and were professionally successful enough to live and work independently as filles majeures. Never having advertised or exhibited work, they seem not to have been driven to seek recognition in the various public spheres.[100] Yet despite connections and talent, their success must have been hard won. Surely neither Loir nor Lusurier could have been exempt from the travails that Cochin lamented as the lot of women artists. Living in a culture that often scorned and dismissed women's aspirations when they went beyond being likeable and loved, both women had to have a certain gumptious ambition to become professional artists at all. Catherine Voiriot has rightly noted that Loir was "undoubtedly endowed with a strong personality and had a true need to create."[101] The point is attested by the letter Loir sent to the academicians of Marseille in 1774, when she was almost seventy. She wrote that she had, at last, put aside her palette for health reasons, but she had done so regretfully and at the insistence of her sisters and her friends. She plaintively remarked upon the sense of deep deprivation she experienced daily since she had given up painting.[102] In writing to her fellow academicians, Loir was writing to them as professional colleagues who could be expected to understand the strength of her attachment to her vocation and to sympathize with her sense of loss. All of the evidence we have about Lusurier indicates that, like Loir, she too felt "the desire to distinguish oneself in a career of talent and genius," the very definition of ambition itself in Cochin's *Iconologie*. In sum, although Loir, Lusurier, and so many other women did not achieve (or maybe even seek) glory, they were ambitious in the expanded sense I have tried to sketch out in this essay. They went about realizing their ambitions, modest and otherwise, in ways that have been far too easy to overlook.

Notes

I wish to extend warmest thanks to my dear colleagues, Mechthild Fend, Paris Spies-Gans, and Katharine Jensen, who so kindly read and made very helpful comments on various drafts of this essay.

1. "On ne parle point ici de cette Ambition louable, fille de l'émulation, qui fait naître le desir de se distinguer dans la carrière des talens & du génie." Charles-Nicolas Cochin, Hubert Gravelot, and Charles Etienne Gaucher, *Iconologie par figures, ou Traité complet des Allégories, Emblèmes, etc. à L'Usage des Artistes,* 4 vols. (Paris: Le Pan, 1791), 4:103. Jean-François Marmontel, "Quelle est l'ambition d'une femme? D'être aimable, & d'être aimée," in *Contes moraux,* 3 vols. (Paris: Chez Merlin, 1765), 3:283; Léonce Bénedite, "Of Women Painters in France," in *Women Painters of the World,* ed. Walter Shaw Sparrow (New York: Frederick A. Stokes Company, 1905), 169.

2. See Christiane Klapisch-Zuber, "La lutte pour la culotte, un topos iconographique des rapports conjugaux (XVe-XIX siècles)." *Clio. Femmes, Genre, Histoire* 34 (2011), *http://journals.openedition.org/clio/10331.*

3. Patricia Mainardi, *Husbands, Wives, and Lovers: Marriage and Its Discontents in Nineteenth-Century France* (New Haven: Yale University Press, 2003), 83–84.

4. Janet M. Burke and Margaret C. Jacob, "French Freemasonry, Women, and Feminist Scholarship," *Journal of Modern History* 68 (September 1996): 17. On "strategic reinterpretation" and oppositional reading as interpretive strategies, see Mary D. Sheriff, "Seeing Beyond the Norm: Interpreting Gender in the Visual Arts," in *The Question of Gender*, ed. Judith Butler and Elizabeth Weed (Bloomington: Indiana University Press, 2011), 161–86.

5. For the "République de la Peinture," see note 77.

6. See Valerie Mainz, "Gloire, subversively," in *The Saint-Aubin "Livre de caricatures": Drawing Satire in Eighteenth-century Paris*, ed. Colin Jones (Oxford: Voltaire Foundation, 2012), 151.

7. Voltaire, "Gloire, Glorieux, Glorieusement," in *Encyclopédie, ou dictionnaire raisonné des sciences, des arts et des métiers, etc.,* ed. Denis Diderot and Jean le Rond d'Alembert (1757). University of Chicago: ARTFL Encyclopédie Project (Autumn 2017 Edition), ed. Robert Morrissey and Glenn Roe, *http://encyclopedie. uchicago.edu/*, 7:716.

8. Quoted in Mary Terrall, "Émilie Du Châtelet and the Gendering of Science," *History of Science* 33 (1995): 299. See this article for further discussions of women and glory.

9. Du Châtelet wrote the essay over the course of the 1730s and 1740s. It was published posthumously in 1779. See *Discourse on Happiness,* in *Selected Philosophical and Scientific Writings,* ed. Judith P. Zinsser, trans. Isabelle Bour and Judith P. Zinsser (Chicago: University of Chicago Press, 2009), 357.

10. For other examples, see Mary S. Trouille, *Sexual Politics of the Enlightenment: Women Writers Read Rousseau* (Albany: SUNY Press, 1997).

11. "Le dessin n'était pas un simple goût chez moi, c'était une passion dominante, unique, absorbante, et elle m'a duré avec une intensité au-delà de bien d'autres passions et jusqu'à ce que les chagrins, des inquiétudes continuelles, soient venus m'en arracher, et encore dès que j'étais un peu tranquille, le dessin redevenait presque ma seule occupation et faisait toute ma joie." Stéphanie de Virieu, *Souvenirs inédits,* quoted in *Une artiste en Italie: Correspondance de Stéphanie et Aymon de Virieu (1823–1824) et Récit du voyage en Italie par S. de Virieu,* ed. Marie-Renée Morin. *Cahiers d'études sur les correspondances du XIXe siècle,* vol. 3 (Paris: Nizet, 1993), v.

12. Morin, *Une artiste en Italie,* vii.

13. On the Drouais anecdote, see the entry on Jean-Germain Drouais in *Encyclopédie des gens du monde,* 8 vols (Paris: Treuttel et Würtz, 1837), 8:599. For Drouais's relationship with David, see Thomas Crow, *Emulation: Making Artists for Revolutionary France* (New Haven: Yale University Press, 1995).

14. Louis Fournier, "Stéphanie de Virieu, Artiste de Son Temps," *L'Essor* 42 (16 March 2015), *https://www.lessor42.fr/stephanie-de-virieu-artiste-de-son-temps-9414.html.* For Virieu's account of her later study in Paris and her travel to Italy for further study, see *Une artiste en Italie.*

15. Alphonse de Lamartine, *Oeuvres de Lamartine,* 13 vols. (Paris: L. Hachette, 1866), 7:266.

16. A sentiment that was poignantly expressed in a letter written during the Revolution by the sculptor Louis-Pierre Deseine, who wrote "J'ai l'ambition de la gloire, je l'avoue franchement et je quitterais la vie sans regret, si j'étais sûr de laisser après mois quelques ouvrages capables d'honorer mon pays et rappeler à mes concitoyens que j'ai existé." Louis-Pierre Deseine, letter of 9 fructidor, an IV, in Georges Le Chatellier, *Louis-Pierre Deseine: statuaire (1749–1822) Sa Vie et ses oeuvres* (Paris: Librairies-Imprimerie Réunies, 1905), n.p.

17. Du Châtelet, *Discourse on Happiness,* 358.

18. The flip side of such compliments was that ambitious women could be condemned as unwomanly, as having unsexed themselves. Such was the case when Louise Vigée Le Brun, having aspired to the noble genre of history painting, was labeled a monstrous, unnatural creature: an *homme-femme.* The subject was brilliantly

analyzed by Mary D. Sheriff in *The Exceptional Woman: Elisabeth Vigée-Lebrun and the Cultural Politics of Art* (Chicago: University of Chicago Press, 1996).

19. See Elisabeth Badinter, *Emilie, Emilie ou l'ambition feminine au XVIIIe siècle* (Paris: Flammarion, 1983), 28. Taking a page out of Joan Rivière's famous 1929 essay, "Womanliness as Masquerade," Badinter here discusses briefly the hyperfeminine excesses of Du Châtelet's toilette that perhaps were intended to make up for the marquise's perceived masculinity. In Abbé Gabriel-François Coyer's *L'Année merveilleuse* (n.p., 1748), Madame Du Châtelet, Madame Du Bocage, and Madame de Graffigny figure (without being named) as women who have transformed themselves into men, while men have transformed into women.

20. For women authors and their "capacity for self-constitution and for participation in public reasoning" through writing and publishing under their own names, see Carla Hesse, *The Other Enlightenment: How French Women Became Modern* (Princeton: Princeton University Press, 2001), xii.

21. Already by the nineteenth century Loir was so much beyond the view of art history that Louvre curator Louis Clément de Ris could doubt that a portrait so worthy of attention as this one could have been by an artist as obscure as Marie-Anne Loir, whose existence he also doubted. This despite the fact that it was attributed to Marie-Anne Loir from the time it came into state hands during the Revolution and was transferred under her name to the fine arts museum in Bordeaux in 1802. Clément de Ris, *Les Musées de Province*, 2 vols. (Paris: Ve. Jules Renouard, 1861), 2: 355–56. On how the painting came to be in Bordeaux, see Henri La Ville de Mirmont, *Histoire du Musée de Bordeaux*, 2 vols. (Bordeaux: Feret & Fils, 1899), 2:120–21.

22. Julie Candler Hayes, Introduction to *Marie-Geneviève Charlotte Theroux d'Arconville. Selected Philosophical, Scientific, and Autobiographical Writings* (Toronto: Iter Press, 2018), 11.

23. Séverine Sofio, *Artistes femmes—La parenthèse enchantée, XVIII-XIXe siècles* (Paris: CNRS Éditions, 2016); and Paris Spies-Gans, "Exceptional, but not Exceptions: Public Exhibitions and the Rise of the Woman Artist in London and Paris, 1760–1803," *Eighteenth-Century Studies* 51 (2018): 393–416.

24. François-Hubert's wife, Anne-Françoise Doré and her sister, Marie-Jeanne Doré, were both artists. Mademoiselle Doré exhibited *A Girl Holding a Rose* at the Exposition de la Jeunesse in 1769. The painting of that title in the Victoria and Albert Museum can be attributed to her, thanks to the inscription of "Mlle Doré" on the parapet on which the girl holding a rose rests her arms. According to F-H Drouais's eulogist, his fourteen-year-old daughter, Marie-Anne-Louise (1762–76), and his twelve-year-old son (Jean-Germain) both showed great promise as artists. "Éloge de Monsieur Drouais," in *Le Nécrologe des hommes célèbres de France, par une société de gens de lettres*, 17 vols. (Maestricht: Chez J. E. Dufour, 1776), 6:122.

25. Charlotte Guichard, *La Griffe du peintre* (Paris: Seuil, 2018), 188.

26. See note 34 below.

27. Drouais's first "petit polisson" of 1755 was in the famous collection of Lalive de Jully. The version shown at the Salon of 1761 belonged to the marquis de Marigny.

Diderot sang the praises of this work, commenting on the luminous treatment of the boy's face, but also the gentillesse, finesse, and maliciousness of his expression. See Prosper Dorbec, "Les Drouais. II," *Revue de l'Art ancien et moderne* 94 (January 1905): 54.

28. Helen Ashmore, "Catherine Lusurier (1752–81): A Woman Painter in Eighteenth-Century Paris," *Apollo Magazine* (May 2001): 34–40.

29. For comparison, see Antoine Vestier's *Allegory of the Arts*, 1788 (Horvitz Collection), a portrait of Vestier's daughter drawing a bust, *https://commons. wikimedia.org/wiki/File:Allegory_of_the_Arts_by_Antoine_Vestier.jpg*.

30. For a discussion of intersubjective exchange between artist and sitter, see Angela Rosenthal, "She's got the look! Eighteenth-Century Female Portrait Painters and the Psychology of a Potentially 'Dangerous Employment,'" in *Portraiture: Facing the Subject,* ed. Joanna Woodall (Manchester: Manchester University Press, 1997), 147–66.

31. See also Lusurier's *Portrait of the Young Carle Vernet*, an artist who would become a prominent figure in the early nineteenth century. That portrait has much the same sensibility as her portrait of Germain Drouais, *https://evbaeyer.com/catalogues/ Master-Drawings-and-selected-Paintings/lusurier/*.

32. It is worth noting here that one of the few treatments of this subject to be exhibited publicly was by another woman, Sophie Chéron, whose contributions to the Salon of 1704 included a girl drawing.

33. This possibility is raised by Ashmore, "Catherine Lusurier," 39.

34. Lusurier's signature of "Cne Lusurier, 1776" on the *Portrait of Charlotte-Françoise DeBure* was painted over sometime between 1927 and 1934 to read "F-H Drouais/1776." See Catherine Sawinksi, "From the Collection–Charlotte-Françoise DeBure by Catherine Lusurier," *https://blog.mam.org/2011/06/21/from-the-collection-charlotte-francoise-debure-by-catherine-lusurier/*.

35. See, for example, Lusurier's *Little Girl with a White Cat*, High Museum, Atlanta.

36. About Drouais, Diderot remarked in his Salon of 1765, "All the faces of that man's painting are nothing but the costliest rouge artistically spread over the finest and whitest of chalk." Cited in Melissa Hyde, *Making Up the Rococo: Boucher and his Critics* (Los Angeles: Getty Research Institute: 2006), 87. For further discussion see Hyde, *Making Up the Rococo*, 83–106.

37. A month after Lespinasse's death, D'Alembert wrote to Voltaire of "cet affreux malheur" as virtually all-consuming. Quoted in *Les registres de l'Académie françoise 1672–1793*, 3 vols. (Paris: Firmin-Didot, 1895), 3:395, note 2.

38. Inventaire après décès de Jean Le Rond D'Alembert, secrétaire perpétuel de l'Académie française, membre de l'Académie des sciences. 1 December 1783, Archives nationales, Paris, MC/RS//505, *https://www.siv.archives-nationales. culture.gouv.fr/siv/rechercheconsultation/consultation/ir/consultationIR. action?irId=FRAN_IR_042787&udId=c1p72eys6l4b--1ce0892daxhh4&details=tru e&gotoArchivesNums=false&auSeinIR=true*. D'Alembert bequeathed the Lusurier to his longtime friend, Alexandre Remy, maître en les chambre des comptes. On Remy see François Launay, "D'Alembert réveillé par l'astronome Lalande," *Recherches*

sur Diderot et sur l'Encylopédie 50 (2015): 335–46. Like the will, the inventory after d'Alembert's death specifically names "Mlle Luzuriez" as the author of the painting. This is a surprising detail because the inventory values the pastel by Quentin de la Tour (then as now, the much more famous artist), together with an undescribed oil painting, and does not name the author of either one.

39. Charlotte Guichard, "Se faire un nom. Catherine Lusurier (1752–81), une carrière feminine à la veille de la Révolution," unpublished paper, presented at the Louvre conference, "Femmes artistes à l'âge Classique," 20 May–1 June 2018. My sincere thanks to Charlotte Guichard for sharing the manuscript of her talk with me.

40. Short notices about the work of Madame Vien (Marie Thérèse Reboul) and Madame Roslin (Marie Suzanne Giroust) appeared in the press during the 1750s and 1760s in the *Feuille nécessaire, L'Avant-coureur,* and the *Mercure de France.* For other examples, see Jean Chatelus, *Peindre à Paris au XVIIIe siècle* (Paris: Jacqueline Chambon, 1991), 51–52.

41. Brossard de Beaulieu's first exhibition, in 1785, featured an allegorical painting, *Poetry Mourning the Loss of Voltaire* (1785, Musée Rupert-de Chièveres, Poitiers). The picture aroused a certain amount of interest and was acquired for the collection of Catherine the Great by 1788. Brossard de Beaulieu's second exhibition was a more elaborate affair. It included a painting of Andromache (untraced), which prompted the short-story writer, Madame Marie Monnet (née Moreau) to compose a verse dedicated to Mademoiselle de Beaulieu, which appeared in a collection of Monnet's writings in 1788. For more, see Fortunée Briquet, *Dictionnaire historique, littéraire et bibliographique des Françaises et des étrangères naturalisée en France* (Paris: L'Imprimerie de Gillé, 1804), 357. On Brossard de Beaulieu, see Pierre Moisy, "A Pupil of Greuze: Geneviève Brossard de Beaulieu," *Gazette des Beaux-Arts* 32 (1947): 177–84; and Melissa Hyde, "Women and the Visual Arts in the Age of Marie-Antoinette," in Eik Kahng, et al, *Anne Vallayer Coster, Painter to the Court of Marie-Antoinette* (Dallas: Dallas Museum of Art, 2002), 79. For Beaulieu in the eighteenth-century press, see Chatelus, *Peindre à Paris*, 51–53.

42. One work by Lusurier was exhibited publicly in her lifetime. This was a copy after a painting by Fragonard, shown in 1779 in Toulouse. Pierre Sanchez, *Dictionnaire des artistes exposant dans les Salons des XVII et XVIIIeme siècles à Paris et en Province,* 3 vols. (Dijon: L'Echelle de Jacob, 2004), 2:1120.

43. *Mercure de France,* February 1780, 191; *Journal Encyclopédique* (1780) 2, part 3:528. In 1787 Savart's engraving would be used as the frontispiece for D'Alembert's *Histoire des membres de l'Académie française, morts depuis 1700 jusqu'en 1771,* 6 vols. (Paris: Moutard, 1787).

44. The article is attributed to Cochin by Christian Michel, *Charles-Nicolas Cochin et l'art des Lumières* (Rome: EFR, 1993), 607. Cochin (1715–90) was a prominent draughtsman and engraver whose parents were engravers and came from prominent families that practiced this art. He was *agrée* in 1741, *reçu* in 1751, and Secretary of the Académie royale from 1755 to 1771.

45. *Journal de Paris,* 12 January 1781.

46. Such eulogies were very rarely written for women, though one had been published that same year for Madeleine-Françoise Basseporte who died in her

eighties after having held her post at the Jardin du Roi for some fifty years. See *Nécrologe des hommes célèbres de France par une société de gens de lettres,* vol. 16 (Paris: Moutard, 1781). I owe the point about the exceptionality of the Basseporte éloge to Nina Ratner Gelbart, author of a much-anticipated book that discusses the artist. Working in a similar vein about an earlier moment, Anne Perrin Khelissa has recently published an essay entitled "L'hommage de Fermel'huis à Élisabeth-Sophie Chéron (1712). Le premier éloge académique dédié à une femme artiste en France: un événement historiographique resté sans suite?," *Revue de l'art* 204 (2019–20): 41–49.

47.   In this context there is special relevance in a letter D'Alembert wrote to Vigée Le Brun in 1775 to thank her for the gift of two portraits she made to adorn the walls of the Académie Française. In it, he declares that her talents were already well known to him before. See *Souvenirs de Madame Louise-Élisabeth Vigée Le Brun,* 2 vols. (Paris: Librarie de H. Fournier, 1835), 1:43–46.

48.   For information on Roslie Filleul (née Bocquet), see the entry in Neil Jeffares, *Dictionary of Pastelists, http://www.pastellists.com/Articles/Filleul.pdf.*

49.   "La France seule sembloit refuser les talens du premier ordre à ces exe fait pour réussir à tout ce qu'il entreprendra, lorsqui'il y apportera le courage et la ténacité nécessaires, et quand la route qui conduit aux grands talens pourra lui être ouverte. … C'est au siècle present que la France devra d'être illustrée par des femmes véritablement Artistes, et dont les noms vivront dans la mémoire des hommes." *Journal de Paris,* 8 February 1781. Cochin does mention seventeenth-century académiciennes Sophie Chéron and Claudine Bouzonnet-Stella, the latter an artist he remarked to the marquis de Marigny in 1766 as having studied the male nude in her father's (actually her uncle's) studio. "Correspondance avec Coypel, Lépicié et Cochin," ed. Marc Furcy-Raynaud, *Nouvelles archives de l'art français,* 3e series 20, année 1904, 2e partie (1905): 69. Strangely, Cochin insists that Chéron was only a miniature painter, even though she painted in oils—as attested by her reception piece, a self-portrait (Paris, Musée du Louvre), which hung in the Academy's rooms—and that Stella was only an engraver.

50.   In fact, Cochin claims that "dans la Peinture, le sexe paroissoit ne pouvoir embrasser que les genres en petit, ou ceux qui n'ont pas pour l'objet la nature vivante" (*Journal de Paris,* 8 February 1781), effectively forgetting or ignoring women like Loir.

51.   "Mlle Loir. … actuellement vivante, s'est acquise une grande reputation en peinture." Pahin de la Blancherie, *Nouvelles de la république des lettres et des arts,* 9 March 1770, 41.

52.   When, many years later, Alexis Loir was finally granted full admission to the Académie, one of his reception pieces was a portrait of Cochin's cousin, Clément Belle (1779, Musée du Louvre).

53.   Anne Sutherland Harris and Linda Nochlin, *Women Artists: 1550–1950* (Los Angeles: Los Angeles County Museum of Art, 1976, rpt. 1984), 167–68.

54.   Catherine Voiriot, "Marie-Anne Loir: une femme portraitiste sous le règne de Louis XV," *Revue de l'art* 204 (2019): 39–50. Perhaps she even supported her brother, as Sophie Chéron supported hers. See Fermel'huis, *Éloge funebre de Madame le Hay, connuë sous le nom de Mademoiselle Chéron* (Paris: François Fournier, 1712), 9–15.

55. Voiriot, "Marie-Anne Loir," 41. Hannah Williams's *Artists in Paris* open-access digital art history project is a tremendously helpful new tool in mapping the geography and demography of the Paris art world in the eighteenth century. See *https://www.artistsinparis.org/about.html.*

56. Sutherland Harris and Nochlin, *Women Artists*, 167. In a legal treatise of 1781 Jean-François Fournel defined the fille majeure as a girl or widow who has attained the age of twenty-five and as "maitresse absolue de sa personne et de ses biens." *Traité de la seduction considérée dans l'ordre judiciaire* (Paris: Demonville, 1781), 25. For the fille majeure in the context of the guild, see Séverine Sofio, *Artistes femmes*, 28–29. In 2014 Neil Jeffares published the Parisian notarial document of 1783 in the Archives Nationales, which named Loir's heirs. Jeffares, *Dictionary of Pastellists, http://www.pastellists.com/Articles/LOIRm.pdf.* For Vernet's address book, see Léon Lagrange, *Joseph Vernet et la peinture du XVIIIe siècle* (Paris: Didier et Ce, 1864), 441.

57. The theory about Loir's Italian sojourn seems to have been introduced by Ann Sutherland Harris, based on a label in Italian on the back of Loir's *Portrait of the Comte de Matignon Playing the Bagpipe,* now in Saint-Lô. The inscription is not mentioned by Léon-Honoré Labande, archivist of the Palace of Monaco in the early twentieth century, who stated that the portrait of the Comte de Matignon was painted in Paris. Léon-Honoré Labande, *Catalogue des peintures, miniatures, aquarelles & dessins formant la collection du palais du Monaco* (Monaco: Imprimerie de Monaco, 1919), 25. Presumably Labande's assertion was based on Loir's letter to the duke concerning payment for portraits of the prince and his sons. The letter must date from around 1739, when she painted the Monagasque princes. It clearly places the artist, her portraits, and her sitters in Paris, which was, in fact, the primary residence of the Prince of Monaco, Jacques 1er (the Duc de Valentinois), and his son Honoré III. See note 79 for text of the letter. In 1725 the duke purchased the Hotel Matignon on the rue de Varennes, where he and Honoré III moved permanently after 1732. In 1751 Loir's portraits of *Honoré III Playing the Hurdy-Gurdy* and the *Comte de Matignon Playing Bagpipes* were paired in the grand salon of the Hotel Matignon in Paris, suggesting they were intended to hang together in this space and casting further doubt on the idea that Loir painted the Comte de Matignon in Italy. For Loir's letter and the location of the two portraits in Paris in 1751, see Léon-Honoré Labande, *Les Portraits des princes et princesses de Monaco executés par le peintre Pierre Gobert* (Monaco: Imprimerie de Monaco, 1908), 25–26, 83. There is no evidence to support the idea sometimes advanced that Loir's portraits of provincial nobility, such as the Dulpàa and Bayard families who lived in Pau, suggest she was having trouble finding commissions in Paris. In fact, Loir's portrait of the young Antoine Duplàa bore the inscription: Peint le 1er septembre 1763 à Paris. Joconde database, *https://www.pop.culture.gouv.fr/notice/joconde/02650003028.*

58. Voiriot, "Marie-Anne Loir," usefully discusses several of Loir's letters, written annually to the Académie de peinture et de sculpture de Marseille. The letters first came to my attention through an article by Émilie Roffidal, "Marseille, contacts et relations inter-académiques: les liens entre l'Académie des sciences et belles-lettres et l'Académie de peinture et de sculpture," *Les papiers d'ACA-RES, Actes des journées d'étude, 29–30 November 2018, Rouen, Hôtel des Sociétés Savantes,*

https://hal.archives-ouvertes.fr/hal-02157598/document. Loir's letters, which are held by the Bibliothèque municipale à vocation régionale, are available online at *https://acares-archives.nakalona.fr/*.

59. Voiriot mentions a dozen or more works that can be safely attributed to Loir, five of which are signed. She acknowledges that the artist's oeuvre is undoubtedly much larger, but because Loir did not often sign her works, the process of establishing convincing attributions is challenging. Voiriot, "Marie-Anne Loir," 43–49. For other attributions to Loir, see Guillaume Faroult, *"La Vielleuse* par Marie-Anne Loir au musé de Riom: fortune iconographique savoyarde, entre peinture et littérature au XVIIIe siècle," *Bulletin de la Société de l'Histoire de l'art français année 2003* (2004): 241–56; and Jacques-Charles Gaffiot, *La Cour de Lorraine en ses meubles 1698–1766. Découvertes inédites* (Paris: Jacques-Chalres Gaffiot, 2008), 97–101.

60. On Clément de Ris, see note 21. Recently, Michelle Lespes has unconvincingly claimed that the Bordeaux portrait—by consensus the prime version— is but a copy (by Marie-Anne or even more improbably, Alexis Loir) of the original version, which she believes to be in the collection of the château de Breteuil. Lespes attributes the château de Breteuil portrait to Jacques-André-Joseph Aved. Michelle Lespes, "Le peintre Aved et la cour de Stanislas," *Le Pays lorrain* 86, no. 3 (September 2005): 171.

61. The earliest print based on the Bordeaux *Portrait of Madame Du Châtelet* dates from 1751 (Versailles, Châteaux de Versailles et de Trianon). Other prints that give Loir as author of the painting on which the engraving was based include Charles-Etienne Gaucher, *Comtesse de Carcado* (Paris, Bibliothèque nationale); Manuel Salvador Carmona, *Victor-François duc de Broglie*, 1760 (Paris, Bibliothèque nationale); Nicolas de Larmessin, *Pierre Mayeur, abbé de Clairvaux*, 1745 (Versailles, Châteaux de Versailles et de Trianon) exhibited at the Salon of 1745; and F. R. Ingouf, *J. N. Regnauld, docteur en Théologie, Curé de St. Etienne-Dumont*, 1754 (Versailles, Châteaux de Versailles et de Trianon).

62. Labille-Guiard was the official painter of Mesdames, the aunts of Louis XVI. Though Vigée Le Brun did not hold any official title of that kind, she was the de facto court painter of Marie-Antoinette. Around 1780 Rosalie Filleul obtained the title of "painter of the royal family," which entitled her to do portraits of the princes and princesses of the court. On Loir's earliest commissions, see Gustave Macon, *Les Arts dans la maison de Condé* (Paris: Librairie de l'art ancien et moderne, 1903), 72–73.

63. Between 1739–44 Loir painted the duc de Valentinois, Prince of Monaco, as well as three of his sons: a signed and dated portrait of *Prince Honoré III Playing a Hurdy-Gurdy* (1739, Monaco), and another of him "en montreur de marmotte"; a *Portrait of Marie-Charles-Auguste Grimaldi, Comte de Matignon and de Carladès Playing the Bagpipes* (c. 1739, St-Lô, Musée des Beaux-Arts and d'Histoire); and a portrait of the Chevalier de Monaco. Loir did copies of at least two of these: her portraits of Honoré III playing the hurdy-gurdy and the comte de Matignon playing the bagpipes hung at the Chateau de Torigni, hereditary estate of the Matignon family in Normandy. The St Lô portrait of the Comte de Matignon playing the bagpipes was one of these copies. Labande, *Les Portraits des princes et princesses de Monaco,*

26–27. See also Labande, *Catalogue des Peintures*, 24, 44, 82, 83. Loir did a portrait, signed and dated 1747, that may be of Jean de Julienne. The painting, which shows the sitter at half-length holding a fur muff, was reproduced in an announcement for the Gallerie Marcus, 20, rue Chauchat, Paris, 9e in 1965. It is listed by Isabelle Tillerot as part of the Julienne collection. See Isabelle Tillerot, *Jean de Jullienne et les collectionneurs de son temps* (Paris: Maison des sciences de l'homme, 2011), 177, 346 note 76. Other sitters included Jean Bonne de La Croix and his wife (Lyon, Musée des Arts décoratifs). Voiriot reproduces several of these and other examples in "Marie-Anne Loir."

64. For Madame Brillon de Jouy (née Anne-Louise Boyvin d'Hardancourt) and a reproduction of the portrait, see the entry in SEIFAR, *http://siefar.org/dictionnaire/fr/Anne-Louise_Boyvin_d%27Hardancourt*. There is another portrait attributed to Loir in Auxerre, which has also been said to depict Madame Du Bocage. Voiriot, Marie-Anne Loir," 48.

65. I thank Kristel Smentek and Elizabeth Rudy for their thoughtful advice concerning this engraving.

66. *Catalogue des tableaux, dessins, estampes, bronzes et porcelains du cabinet due M.***, 6 mars 1783, lot number 67. "Marianne Loir," Getty Provenance Index, *https://piprod.getty.edu/starweb/pi/servlet.starweb?path=pi/pi.web*.

67. François de Troy was the student of Marie-Anne Loir's great uncle, Nicolas Loir (1624–79). De Troy became Loir's brother-in-law when he married Madame Nicolas Loir's sister. Both women were daughters of the painter Jean II Cotelle (1646–1708). François de Troy made portraits for the Bourbon-Condé family and was perhaps one of the means through which Marie-Anne Loir came to the duke's attention. On de Troy, see Dominique Brême, *François de Troy* (Paris: Somogy, 1997).

68. "Mariane Loir petite niece [*sic*] de Nicolas Loir, et qui se distingue dans le portrait, est élève de François de Troy, ainsi que M. Drouais peintre de l'Académie." Antoine-Joseph Dezallier d'Argenville, *Abrégé de la vie des plus fameux peintres*, 3 vols. (Paris: De Bure l'Aîné, 1745–53), 2:360. More often cited is Joseph Vien's recollection of Jean-François de Troy's reference to Mademoiselle Loir as Drouais's student in "Les Mémoires de Joseph-Marie Vien," fol. 27, transcribed in Thomas Gaetghens and Jacques Lugand, *Joseph-Marie Vien peintre du roi* (Paris: Arthena, 1988), 294. On Hubert Drouais, see "Éloge Historique de Monsieur Drouais, Peintre," *Le Nécrologe des hommes célèbres de France, par une société de gens de lettres* (Paris: Deprez, 1768), 187–94; Prosper Dorbec, "Les Drouais. I," *Revue de l'art ancien et moderne* 16 (juillet-décembre 1904): 409–20; C. Gabillot, "Les trois Drouais," *Gazette des Beaux Arts* (1905): 182–87.

69. "Camarades d'oeuil." Lettre de Marie-Anne Loir à l'Académie de peinture de Marseille, Paris, 12 June 1762, Marseille, BMVR, Archives de l'Académie de peinture et de sculpture de Marseille, Ms 988, vol. 6, f 18, mis en ligne dans Les ressources d'ACA-RES, fonds d'archives, 24 June 2019, *https://acares-archives.nakalona.fr/items/show/921*. As Voiriot notes in "Marie-Anne Loir," 42, this detail places Loir in the studio of De Troy fils between 1723–25, *a minima*.

70. Loir did paint for some of the same clients as these two artists. Voiriot notes that Xavier Salmon habitually attributes to Loir works regarded as too weak to be by Nattier. Voiriot, "Marie-Anne Loir," 47.

71. Loir would have been fifteen in 1720. Loir and Hubert Drouais could have overlapped chez de Troy anytime between 1717 and 1730, when de Troy père died. Voiriot and Faroult have both noted stylistic similarities between Loir and Drouais. Farroult has pointed out the close affinities between Drouais's portrait of the singer Marie Pélissier (c. 1736, Louvre) and Loir's work from this period. Voiriot, "Marie-Anne Loir," 47; Faroult, *La Veilleuse*, 243–44.

72. Gabillot, "Les Trois Drouais," 187. After De Troy's death Drouais was successively employed by J.-B. Van Loo, Oudry, and Nattier. "Éloge Historique de Monsieur Drouais."

73. An idea forwarded by Voiriot, as well. See her "Marie-Anne Loir," 43.

74. A lesson Mademoiselle Vigée learned the hard way in 1774, when the bailiffs of the Châtelet sealed her studio and seized "the instruments of her art," because she was painting professionally without having been admitted to a guild. Joseph Baillio, et al. *Vigée Le Brun* (New York: Metropolitan Museum of Art, 2016), 67. For more on the Académie de Saint Luc's jurisdiction over the arts and its demise, see Katie Scott, "Hierarchy, Liberty, and Order: Languages of Art and Institutional Conflict in Paris (1766–76)," *Oxford Art Journal* 12, no. 2 (1989): 59–70; and Charlotte Guichard, "'Liberal Arts' and 'Free Arts'" in Paris in the Eighteenth Century: Artists between the Guild and the Royal Academy," *Revue d'histoire moderne et contemporaine* 49, no. 3 (2002–03): 54–68, *https://www.cairn-int.info/article-E_RHMC_493_0054--liberal-arts-and-free-arts-inparis.htm*.

75. "Les Mémoires de Joseph-Marie Vien," in Gaetghens and Lugand, *Joseph-Marie Vien*, 294.

76. Argenville, *Abrégé de la vie des plus fameux peintres*, 2:360.

77. "République de la Peinture" is an expression used by the painter Michel-François Dandré-Bardon. See "Traité de peinture, suivi d'un essai sur la sculpture et d'un catalogue des artistes les plus fameux de l'École française, morts jusqu'en 1764," in *Oeuvres de Dandré-Bardon, professeur de l'Académie de Peinture et de Sculpture*, 11 vols (1783). Manuscript, Bibliothèque nationale de France, Paris, 11:361, *http://archivesetmanuscrits.bnf.fr/ark:/12148/cc43963g/cd0e393*.

78. See *Nécrologe des hommes célèbres de France par une société de gens de lettres,* 26 (Paris: Moutard, 1781), cited in Neil Jeffares, "Basseporte, Madeleine-Françoise," *http://www.pastellists.com/Articles/Basseporte.pdf*.

79. Sometime between 1739–44, Loir wrote to Chabrol, the Prince's steward "J'apprand dans le moment, mon très chère Monsieur, que Mr le Duc part demain, voilà son portray que luy envoye, il y a un mois qu'il est fait et que j'attans sa bordure. … Si par hazard, Monsieur, il étoit question du prix, ayés la bonté pour moy de luy faire entandre que se portray doit se payer mieux que les Princes [who had also sat to her]; pour un particulier je ne le ferois a moins de 300 livres, ainsy proportionnés, cela a la grandeur de Monseigneur." Quoted in Labande, *Les Portraits des princes et princesses de Monaco*, 26.

80. "Je fais faire une copie de mon portrait que Natier [*sic*] qui est le meilleur pour le portrait, vien de finir." Gabrielle Émilie de Châtelet-Lomont d'Haraucourt, marquise Du Châtelet-Lomont, to Johann Bernoulli, Monday, 3 June 1743, *https:// doi.org/10.13051/ee:doc/voltfrVF0920368a1c.*

81. Ian Davidson characterizes Du Châtelet as "permanently penniless" due to her financial extravagance and love of gambling. Ian Davidson, *Voltaire: A Life* (New York: Pegasus Books, 2012), 192. Concerning the cost of a painting by Loir, relative to one by Nattier: in 1729, Mademoiselle de Clermont, one of the daughters of the duc de Bourbon, paid Nattier 1,800 *livres* for an allegorical portrait of herself. Loir was paid more modest sums by Mademoiselle de Clermont's father some ten years later for three portraits (510 livres, 242 livres, and 752 livres). This is comparable to what Mademoiselle Clermont paid to Gobert in 1722 (700 livres in 1722). Loir's letter to the Prince of Monaco in the 1730s indicates that she charged 300 livres for each of the portraits of the princes. On the Nattier portrait of Mademoiselle de Clermont, see Kathleen Nicholson, "Practicing Portraiture: Mademoiselle de Clermont and J.-M. Nattier," in Melissa Hyde and Jennifer Milam, *Women, Art, and the Politics of Identity* (Burlington: Ashgate, 2003), 73. On the Loir portraits, see Macon, *Les Arts dans la maison de Condé,* 72–73, and Labande, *Les Portraits des princes et princesses de Monaco,* 25–26.

82. For the full quotation, see note 86 below.

83. Mary McAlpin, *Gender, Authenticity, and the Missive Letter in Eighteenth-Century France: Marie-Anne de La Tour, Rousseau's Real-Life Julie* (Lewisburg: Bucknell University Press, 2006), 67–68.

84. Untraced. Reproduced in the catalogue for the Heim Gallery exhibition, *French Paintings and Sculptures of the 18th Century. Winter Exhibition, 10th January–15th March 1968* (London: Heim Gallery, 1968), 4.

85. See, for example, *Man at his Desk,* Portland Museum of Art. For the significance of the bureau plat, see Dena Goodman, *Becoming a Woman in the Age of Letters* (Ithaca: Cornell University Press, 2009), 229–34.

86. "J'ai bien des grâces à vous rendre, monsieur, de l'attention que vous avez eue de me procurer l'ouvrage de Mme Du Bocage. Je crois ne pouvoir choisir personne de plus propre que vous, monsieur, pour lui marquer combien j'en ai été contente et combien je suis reconnaissante de ce qu'elle a bien voulu m'en envoyer un exemplaire. Je m'intéresse trop à la gloire de mon sexe pour n'avoir pas pris beaucoup de part à la sienne. Je suis ravie qu'une académie fondée dans un pays si rempli de talents et d'esprit ait commencé sa carrière par nous rendre justice. Il faudrait que l'académie de Rouen fît pour Mme Du Bocage ce que l'institut de Bologne a bien voulu faire pour moi, qu'elle l'agrégeât à son corps, et assurément ce serait à bien meilleur titre." Quoted in François Bessire, "Une carrière exemplaire," in *Forma Venus, Arte Minerva. Sur l'oeuvre et la carrière d'Anne-Marie Du Bocage (1710–1802),* ed. François Bessire and Martine Reid (Rouen: Presses universitaires de Rouen et du Havre, 2017), 23.

87. She wrote a tragedy, *Les Amazones,* in 1749 and managed to get the play performed at the Comédie française, one of the few women ever to do so. On the performance of *Les Amazones* at the Comédie française, see English Showalter,

"Writing off the stage: Women Authors and Eighteenth-Century Theater," *Yale French Studies* 75 (1988): 95–111.

88. "Hélas! madame, il n'y avait pas quatre jours que j'avais relu votre tragédie avec elle. Nous avions lu ensemble votre Milton avec l'anglais. Vous la regretteriez bien davantage, si vous aviez été témoin de cette lecture. Elle vous rendait bien justice." Voltaire to Anne Marie Fiquet Du Boccage, 12 October 1749, *https://doi.org/10.13051/ee:doc/voltfrVF0950176a1c.*

89. Jérôme Lalande, *Bibliographie astronomique: avec l'histoire de l'astronomie depuis 1781 jusqu'à 1802* (Paris: Imprimerie de la République, 1803), 680. On Lepaute, see Meghan K. Roberts, "Learning and Loving: Representing Women Astronomers in Enlightenment France," *Journal of Women's History* 29, no. 1 (Spring 2017): 14–37.

90. Catherine Voiriot has attributed the chateau de Breteuil portrait to Voiriot and dates it to 1755–69, proposing that the Loir portrait was a model for that of Madame Lepaute. Given the similarities between the Loir and Voiriot portraits, it is also suggestive, as Voiriot notes in her recent article on Loir, that Guillaume Voiriot and Loir lived in the same building. Madame Voiriot is preparing an article on the de Breteuil portrait, which has traditionally been regarded as a copy after Quentin de la Tour. The publication of that article is eagerly awaited. Catherine Voiriot, "Guillaume Voiriot (1712–99), portraitiste de l'Académie royale de Peinture et de Sculpture," *Bulletin de la Société de l'Histoire de l'Art Français* (2004): 150, and Voiriot, "Marie-Anne Loir," 43.

91. The choice of Loir is all the more significant considering that artists such as Bouchardon, Carle Van Loo, and Joseph Vernet attended her salon. Grace Gill-Mark, *Une femme de lettres au XVIIIᵉ siècle, Anne-Marie Du Boccage* (Paris: Champion, 1927).

92. The lost painting *Du Bocage* is reproduced by Voiriot, who dates it on stylistic grounds to the 1730s (Voiriot, 46). Such dating would suggest that Du Bocage had a particular fondness for this portrait, since she preferred to have Tardieu engrave a picture that was some fifteen years old, rather than have another one made, which she could easily have done.

93. Loreline Pelletier has noted that there were at least three editions of the livret. The first included several works by Tardieu that were not in subsequent editions. See Loreline Pelletier, "Le Salon de 1748," *Mémoire de master, l'Université de Paris* 4 vols. (2011–12),1:12, 158.

94. Tardieu's mother Marie-Anne Horthemels was herself an artist and engraver.

95. For more on the editions of Du Bocage's work and her ambitious pursuit of the grand genres of poetry, see François Bessire, "Une carrière exemplaire," *https://hal-normandie-univ.archives-ouvertes.fr/hal-02320765.*

96. "A Mademoiselle Loir, qui a peint le Portrait de l'Auteur."

> O Loir! par ton talent suprême,
> Mes yeux parlent sous ton pinceau,
> Et le coloris du tableau
> Efface l'original même.

Je le vois, le don créateur,
Qui ravit au ciel Prométhée,
Est dans tes mains; ton art vainqueur
Anime la toile enchantée.
Le feu de ta pensée a passé dans mes traits;
Le Dieu qui t'inspira d'embellir mon image,
Accroît l'orgeuil de mes attraits,
Et la gloire de ton ouvrage.

Receuil des oeuvres de Madame Du Boccage, 3 vols. (Lyon: Freres Perisse, 1762), 1:259.

97. This would not be the only time that Du Bocage took up her pen to support other women who were authors or artists. Du Bocage's *Receuil* includes accolades for Louise La Daulceur and her engravings of the illustrations for *Le Paradis Terrestre*. That La Daulceur produced the engravings and that Loir painted Du Bocage's portrait suggests the author went out of her way to work with other women, even though the number of male artists she could have employed were legion. As Maria Isabel Corbi Saez has recently argued, Du Bocage adopted a courageous position in defending writing—and I would add art making—as a vocation for women. She took the side of the writer Jeanne-Marie Leprince de Beaumont, who in the 1750s claimed for herself the label of "female author" and declared her incapacity for the frivolous roles assigned to women by the society of her time. See María Isabel Corbí Sáez, "Enjeux de l'Éloge à Jeanne-Marie Leprince de Beaumont dans les *Lettres sur l'Angleterre, la Hollande et l'Italie* d'Anne-Marie du Bocage," *Cuadernos de Investigación Filológica* 43 (2017), *http://doi.org/10.18172/cif.2974.*

98. The first such engraving of the Du Châtelet portrait was produced by an anonymous engraver in 1751. Château de Versailles, INV.GRAV 529, *http://collections.chateauversailles.fr/#dd4961db-c3bd-4974-9006-3d3ae27b4cbc.*

99. Mary Terrall, "The Uses of Anonymity in the Age of Reason," *Scientific Authorship: Credit and Intellectual Property in Science*, ed. Mario Biagioli and Peter Galison (London: Routledge, 2003), 91.

100. Or, in Loir's case, almost never: one or two of her paintings received a public airing, and that was late in her life—in Toulouse in 1779. Her reception pieces, including her portrait of Dandré-Bardon (1762), were probably also exhibited in Marseille.

101. Voiriot, "Marie-Anne Loir," 49.

102. "J'ai enfin mis la Palette de costé, ce n'est pas sans regret, ma santée [*sic*] souffroit, j'ay sedé a la persecution de mes soeurs et de mes amies, mes yeux son tels qu'ils étoient a 40 ans, il n'i a point de jours où je ne souffre une vraye privation; je trouve Messieurs la consolation a vous en étourdir." Lettre de Marie-Anne Loir à l'Académie de peinture de Marseille, Paris, 7 janvier 1774, Marseille, BMVR, Archives de l'Académie de peinture et de sculpture de Marseille, Ms 988, vol. 6, f 18, mis en ligne dans Les ressources d'ACA-RES, fonds d'archives, 24 June 2019, *https://acares-archives.nakalona.fr/items/show/933.* Quoted also by Voiriot, "Marie-Anne Loir," 43.

ASECS AT 50

Clifford Lecture

Minette's Worlds: Theater and Revolution in Saint-Domingue

LAURENT DUBOIS

What is the relationship between theater and revolution? The history of Saint-Domingue, and of the Haitian Revolution, offer a particularly riveting space through which to explore this question. This essay offers a tentative answer, or at least a few paths for exploration, through three figures: Alzire, Zaïre, and Minette. The first exists just as a character in a play. The second as both a character in a play and a woman who lived in Saint-Domingue. And the third was an actress whose increasingly well-known story stretched into the early nineteenth century. Each of their stories is intertwined with those of the Haitian Revolution. Collectively, they allow us to think through the relationship between gender and sexuality and the political and cultural transformations of the era.

This essay is very much part of a constellation of work that has been deeply shaped by collaboration with two co-authors: Bernard Camier, the leading scholar of music and theater in Saint-Domingue, and Kaiama L. Glover, an eminent scholar of Haitian literature and translator of Marie Vieux-Chauvet's *Dance on the Volcano*, a twentieth-century novel about Minette. My findings are shot through with my ongoing conversations with both of them and refer to longer co-authored essays that explore some of the themes taken up here.[1]

This essay is also meant as an invitation for scholars to engage more deeply with the foundational work on theater in Saint-Domingue written by Haitian historian Jean Fouchard in the 1950s. Fouchard's most famous work, and the only one translated into English, presents an argument about the centrality of *marronage* in the creation of the Haitian Revolution. But most of the work published during his lifetime actually focused, interestingly, on the cultural history of colonial Saint-Domingue, particularly music, dance, and theater. Working in both Haitian and French collections, Fouchard was able to gather together a tremendous archive of material on theater during the period, producing a study of the topic and a repertoire of plays and actors. The latter helped lay the foundation for a current and more complete digital project by Julia Prest, itself part of a larger current flourishing of work on theater in Saint-Domingue.[2]

I came to study theater in Saint-Domingue as part of a project of trying to understand, interpret, and narrate the history of political thought and action on the part of people of African descent, particularly the enslaved, during the Enlightenment and Age of Revolution. As I sought to absorb prodigious and wide-ranging work on theater in eighteenth-century and revolutionary France, I came to understand the particular importance and richness of studying theater in the context of the plantation society of Saint-Domingue. In a place where a particularly small minority of the population had access to the reading and writing of texts, I came to believe, theater took on a notable role. The wide circulation of theater in the French Atlantic made it probably the most important vector of Enlightenment ideas about virtue, justice, freedom, and other themes that were at once literary and political.

The adaptability of theater, and particularly the fact that it always had to be performed by particular individuals, in particular spaces, with audiences that crystallized a broader community formation, meant that it could take on specific roles within a racialized plantation society. And the fact that theater opens itself up onto so many different interpretations and can be quoted and referred to, as well as re-performed informally, meant that phrases and plots could move into other realms of daily life, enabling a link between various sites of performance and self-presentation on and off stage.

Several recent scholars, particularly Camier, Lauren Clay, and David M. Powers, have documented the richness of theatrical life in the French Caribbean.[3] By the end of the eighteenth century, theatrical venues existed throughout Saint-Domingue, not just in the major port towns of Le Cap and Port-au-Prince but also in smaller ports such as Les Cayes, Léogane, and St. Marc. The well-known chronicler of life in Saint-Domingue, Louis-Médéric Moreau de Saint-Méry, wrote extensively about the theater in Le Cap, as well as in other parts of the colonies, in his detailed *Description* of the colony, published in Philadelphia in 1796. As he noted, governors, colonial administrators, and uniformed officers attended regularly. The Conseil du Cap, the island's equivalent to the French Parlements, rented the right balcony of the Le Cap theater with such consistency that it was named after them. The performances were an occasion to show off the latest fashions, to *rendez-vous* and flirt, to watch and hear plays, and to celebrate or excoriate those who performed them.[4]

Colonial Saint-Domingue was a society also marked deeply by the spectacle of violence and death. As many as a million Africans were brought to the colony over the course of the eighteenth century, and at the end of that time the enslaved population was about half a million. At one point in the 1770s, an anthrax epidemic spread through food given to the enslaved led to the deaths of as many as 30,000 in the course of six weeks. In the 1780s, while Minette was at the height of her theatrical career, earthquakes and hurricanes battered Port-au-Prince, and the enslaved were always the most vulnerable. Overall, Saint-Domingue was a place of remarkable contrasts: for example, in the 1770s in Le Cap, a port town surrounded by famously brutal sugar plantations, the average rent for a house was much higher than for similar lodgings in central Paris at the time. Slavery had produced remarkable wealth, spurring the expansion of the French economy in fundamental (if still largely unacknowledged) ways. It was this wealth that sustained the vibrant cultural life of the colony of Saint-Domingue.

Within this tightly controlled social and political order, theater became an important site for social struggle. Free people of African descent, who made up about 5 percent of the total population and played a vital economic role in the colony, asserted their cultural presence by pushing to attend performances. In Port-au-Prince, many free women of color owned real estate and lived on the profits from renting it; one free woman of color owned the Vauxhall of Port-au-Prince, a fashionable venue offering food, performances, and dancing.[5]

For people in the colony who were not literate, including both enslaved people and *affranchis* (emancipated former slaves and free Blacks), the theater was a particularly important cultural space. While free people of color and some enslaved people attended theatrical performances, this was not the only way to learn about plays, or to hear about their plots, themes, and lines, since those enthusiastic about attending the theater were also avid to speak about it elsewhere. People in the colony, writes Fouchard, "talked about theater as much as about the cost of sugar or politics."[6] The life of the theater intersected constantly with broader currents of urban life. For example, because the Port-au-Prince theater did not have dressing rooms until 1787, actors and actresses were often seen walking through the town in their costumes.

Though much of the repertoire, and many of the performers, had crossed the Atlantic from metropolitan France, the meaning and practice of theater was very much indigenous in its way. The experiences of plantation life in Saint-Domingue readily made their way onto the stage. There were a number of local dramaturges who produced popular plays, some of them in Creole—the first literary works produced in the language. One of them, *Jeannot et Thérèse*, was a reworking of Jean-Jacques Rousseau's blockbuster opera, *Le Devin du Village*. The play is a romantic comedy, and in the Saint-Domingue version the village is a plantation, the characters are enslaved and free people of African descent, and the magician who helps reunite lovers is an African-born healer named Papa Simon. Fouchard wrote about the play based on advertisements for it in the newspaper, but, more recently, Camier and Yvonne Fabella found full manuscripts of the play, first in the Public Record Office and later in the Library Company of Philadelphia. These manuscripts show us a play that was truly written in Haitian Creole—it would have been unintelligible for those who did not speak the language—and rich with symbols of Haiti's religious culture. First performed in 1758, it was a favorite among theatergoers in the colony for decades.[7]

As Fouchard emphasizes throughout his work, theater was just one part of a broader cultural matrix that also included forms of vernacular music and dance rooted in the culture of the enslaved. Understanding that particular intersection, however, is a complicated task. For what was the cultural space of Saint-Domingue in the late eighteenth century? How should we conceive of it?

It was, clearly, embedded in a rich circulation of French Atlantic culture, with plays, texts, troupes, and musicians moving frequently through the French Caribbean colonies. The vast majority of the population, however, was enslaved, and the majority of the population was also African-born. Their performance and cultural practices were not institutionally dominant, but they certainly dominated most of the space of the colony in terms of sonic and performative practice. In the years just before 1789, about 40,000 Africans a year were brought to the colony. When the 1791 revolution began, at least 100,000 and probably more individuals had spent very little time there. Their lives as enslaved people were a parenthesis within a much longer story that began in Africa and then stretched out into life in revolutionary and post-independence Haiti. They spoke a wide range of languages, and the most common languages in the colony were an already well-established Creole language and a range of Kikongo languages. Religious and musical cultures were also deeply involved with forms of performance and dance.

These forms made it onto the official stage as well in a few cases, most notably in *Jeannot et Thérèse* and other forms of blackface performance. The musicians who played in the theater were often enslaved themselves, and the advertisements for fugitives from slavery include many who played instruments, most commonly the violin, but also the mandolin and banza, or banjo.[8]

There is one particularly striking image from the period that allows us to catch a glimpse of these intersecting cultural spaces. It is the unfinished proof of an engraving (which does not seem to have ever been published), acquired by the John Carter Brown Library in 2009. A watercolor of the same image, likely the basis for the engraving, was recently sold by a private dealer to the Rubenstein Special Collections Library at Duke University. A short note about the piece by historian Jacques de Cauna commissioned by the dealer provides key information about the circumstances of the production of both images. According to de Cauna, the artist's full name was Pierre-Jean-Louis Bouquet, a painter who was part of the French navy and stationed in Saint-Domingue in 1793.[9] He also produced a much better-known engraving of the burning of Le Cap, seen from the harbor. He was part of a family that included Louis-René Bouquet, who designed costumes for the Opéra in Paris as well as for royal ceremonies, and Pierre-Louis, who painted sets and costumes at the Opéra, including for Rameau plays. This might explain why Pierre-Jean-Louis Bouquet took a particular interest in one feature of the 1793 events: the fact that the insurgents dressed themselves not only in clothes taken from the houses of the white inhabitants but also ones specifically taken from la Comédie du Cap. Indeed, the hand-written description at the foot of the proof notes that during the "massacre of a portion of the whites," Blacks had "clothed themselves in their clothes and those of the comedie."[10]

There are many stories being told in this engraving, and much to explore about it. In the bottom right, however, is a particularly rich condensation of the moment. A circle has formed around musicians. One is playing what is likely a banza, or banjo. Another is playing the drums. On the ground near them is a violin and a tambourine. A woman is dancing, another is clapping along, and in the center is a man dressed in what was likely a costume used in the theater for an indigenous character. He has feathers in his hair, is bare-chested, and has a necklace, a decorated belt, and a bow attached to his back. The moment captures a bit of the crossroads of cultural practices that would have shaped daily experience as well as broader political visions in Saint-Domingue. In the same way, the stories of the three women I explore in the remainder of this essay allow us to get a sense of the many layers and crossings between theater and politics before and during the Haitian Revolution.

Alzire

The repertoire in Saint-Domingue was largely made up of works by the reigning French playwrights of the era, most notably Rousseau and Voltaire. Somewhat surprisingly, one of the plays performed repeatedly over the course of the eighteenth century was Voltaire's *Alzire, ou les Américains*, a work with a strikingly anti-colonial message that celebrates an Inca revolt against the Spanish. Written after *Zaïre* and first performed in 1736, *Alzire* is partly about the conflict between Don Guzman, the Governor of Peru, a violent and haughty Spanish ruler, and his father, Don Alvarez, a Christian man who is gentle towards the Peruvians and laments that it is the Spanish who are the real "barbarians" in the New World.[11]

Alzire was not only a critique of European colonialism but also, of course, a product of it. It was written at the same time as, and probably inspired in part by, Jean-Philippe Rameau's extremely popular opera about the New World, *Les Indes Gallantes*, which was first performed in 1735 and became a sensation in Paris. Rameau's work, in turn, was partially inspired by the performance of two indigenous men from Louisiana who danced at the Théâtre Italian in Paris one night in 1725. Rameau was struck by the performance and sought to "characterize" their "song and dance" in a harpsichord piece called *Les Sauvages* that was later incorporated into *Les Indes Gallantes*.[12] According to one source, Rameau's work itself crossed the Atlantic some decades later when a French musician visiting the island of Dominica played *Les Sauvages* on a harpsichord to a group of Caribs, who responded with "surprise, joy, and admiration," dancing "according to their own rhythm" for a long while. Rameau, hearing of the incident, described it as the most "flattering" homage he had ever received.[13] Meanwhile, in making his own contribution to this vogue of plays about the Americas, Voltaire drew upon an earlier attempt both to comprehend and in some ways to confront European empire: Garcilaso de la Vega's descriptions of Inca civilization. The Peruvians are identified in the play as "Americans" and referred to as "children of the sun."[14]

The core plot of the play revolves around Alzire, the daughter of the "sovereign" of a part of Potosi called Montezuma, who is set to be married to Guzman. Previously, she had been the lover of an Inca man named Zamor, also a "sovereign" and leader of a recent uprising against the Spanish. Alzire believes Zamor to be dead. But after she marries Guzman, she discovers Zamor is still alive, jealousy and politics mingle in a toxic web, Zamor stabs Guzman, and he and Alzire are both condemned to death. But in a final act of redemption Guzman realizes that he has been wrong in his violent behavior and forgives them, allowing the two lovers to live together.

As both Fouchard and Camier have noted, the play was—somewhat surprisingly given its message—performed on a number of occasions in Saint-Domingue. This, along with other plays that included indigenous characters, would have brought the kind of costumes we see in the 1793 engraving to Saint-Domingue. In its Paris performances, the play presented "Americans" wearing "a breastplate ornamented with a sun" and a "plumed helmet," and in at least some of its performances in Saint-Domingue such costumes, described in newspapers as "Inca" costumes, were on display as well. In 1783, in Port-au-Prince, a performance of *Alzire* was organized as a benefit for an actor named Deauville who, it was noted, "was the only actor in the colony to have the true costume of an Inca Prince." His comrades, wishing to add to the "brilliance of the performance," had taken it upon themselves to procure themselves "appropriate" costumes to perform in.[15]

The presence of the play in Saint-Domingue may help to explain one of the most fascinating aspects of the symbolic politics of the war for Haitian independence. During the war of independence in Haiti in 1802 and 1803, the leaders of the revolution often made reference to indigenous peoples, notably through the recovery of the Taino name "Ayiti" for the nation that was eventually founded in 1804 and more broadly by calling themselves the "Armée Indigène." During the fighting, Jean-Jacques Dessalines also referred to his army briefly as the "Army of the Incas," and some soldiers apparently referred to themselves as the "Sons of the Sun." Several members of Dessalines's staff—including Louis Boisrond-Tonnerre, who wrote the Haitian Declaration of Independence—were literate and widely educated, and probably had read accounts of indigenous resistance in the Americas or heard about the Tupac Amaru revolts of the 1780s through the Spanish officers and soldiers many of them served with in 1792–94. And the landscape of the colony was literally littered with pottery, bones, and stone objects that recalled the decimated civilizations that had once occupied the land.[16]

Yet there is good reason to think that the theater, and particularly Voltaire's *Alzire*, had a particular impact on Dessalines's revolutionary discourse of 1804 and 1805. Theater remained popular in Saint-Domingue in the late 1790s when, under Toussaint Louverture's regime, theaters were re-opened—though the stage was occupied mostly by Black actors, among them (according to one early nineteenth-century French writer) several of "great talent."[17] Dessalines, or else members of his entourage, were familiar with and fans of this theater, for they chose the music from Rousseau's *Le Devin du Village* to be played at his coronation as emperor. Eighteenth-century French theater would remain popular in post-independence Haiti: as part of the celebration of the coronation of Henri Christophe as King in 1811, an opera and a play were performed. And in 1816, a "great theater" was built in Le Cap, and a "troupe of black actors" trained by a French actor prepared for their first performance on 1 January 1817 (to celebrate Haitian independence day), a performance that included Voltaire's *Zaïre*.[18]

There is another clear link that connects the theater to Dessalines's politics at this moment. In 1805, in a justification for the massacres he had carried out against whites, Dessalines announced: "Yes, we have paid back these true cannibals crime for crime, war for war, outrage for outrage. I have avenged America." The line seems to have been a reference to, and in a sense a direct quotation of, Voltaire's *Alzire*.[19] The character Zamor celebrates the virtues of his land in contrast to the barbarism of the Europeans and pursues the twin goals of love for Alzire and vengeance for his people. He is introduced by Alzire as "our state's avenger." After his first uprising is defeated, Zamor laments that he will "leave our bleeding country thus enslaved" to "European robbers." But as he plans once again for victory, one of his followers, an "American," encourages him to act by declaring of the other Americans that when they see their "avengers" rising up, they will join in the struggle. Zamor announces that his intention is to lead a "heroic crowd" that will either perish or will "avenge America."[20]

If this is indeed the case, then Dessalines had found in the theater something of value, not (or not only) because it represented "civilization" or the virtues of Europe, but rather because it could both inspire and be mobilized within a political project of liberation, resistance, and vengeance against Europe itself. Dessalines's Voltaire highlights the important ways in which the drama of colonial violence was rewritten by those who resisted it. For while Voltaire's *Alzire* ended with the redemption of the major Spanish character, who rejects colonial barbarism in favor of true Christian love and is forgiven and celebrated by his subjects, the ending in Dessalines's Haiti was considerably different. Of course, Dessalines wrote a conclusion to his play that was quite different from that of Voltaire; there was no redemption for the white colonizers in the version that unfolded in Haiti in 1804.

Zaïre

In 1793, a resident of St. Marc named Laurent Jolicoeur wrote a short petition requesting that a woman he owned as a slave, Zaïre, be freed. The petition read:

> Citizens:
> Citizen Laurent Jolicoeur, a merchant in St. Marc and a leading personality in that town, previously described as a citizen of color, although he is as black as the white is white, is honored to inform you that he owns a *négresse* named Zaïre, of the Ibo

nation, about 40 years old, who has rendered him great service since he has owned her. Zaïre is no ordinary individual; and if she were not enslaved, she would rival any female citizen in terms of her elevation of her sentiments; therefore her situation makes her suffer constantly; and several times the petitioner has said to her words from a tragedy that he has seen more than once: Ah! Zaïre, you are crying.

Yes, citizens, especially since the Revolution began, Zaïre is grief-stricken; and the petitioner requests your benevolence, or rather your justice, to help her escape a bondage that he has relaxed as much as he can. She is the mother of three children who have her color, which proves her wisdom and indeed her virtue. What female citizen could claim, like her, to have experienced only the caresses of those who resemble her? There are very few, if there are any. Zaïre is therefore a model of virtue, and if she reaches her goal, she will be able to claim to be the foremost of all female citizens. Zaïre's beautiful soul would not be satisfied if she had to enjoy the new existence she desires alone; she also requests it for her children.

It is therefore up to you, citizens, to bring happiness to four people, in granting to Zaïre and to Jean-Laurent, Jean-Paul and Jean-Marie, her sons, a state worthy of society.[21]

The petition spirals around a set of references to Voltaire's beloved blockbuster 1732 play *Zaïre*, a tragedy about a pair of star-crossed lovers in Jerusalem: Zaïre, a slave, and Orosmane, her Muslim master and the leader of Jerusalem, who hopes to free her and marry her.[22] The play was a huge success in France and was also performed consistently in the colony of Saint-Domingue throughout the eighteenth century. Its final performance in Saint-Domingue featured the French actress Julie Delavigne, who would go on to fame in Paris. It took place in Le Cap on 16 August 1791, during the same week when, south of the town, conspirators from various plantations gathered to finalize plans for—and to request divine assistance with—their imminent uprising.[23]

What are we to make of the way Jolicoeur mobilized Voltaire? The petition came at a particular moment in the history of the Haitian Revolution, in the midst of intense conflicts in the region of St. Marc between free people of color and white colonists, and just a few months before general emancipation was decreed in the colony by the French Republic's commissioner Léger-Félicité Sonthonax. Much about these dramatic transformations is refracted through the petition, but in curious ways. Jolicoeur rejects the terminology other free people of color had fought for intensely, explaining that he was "previously described as a citizen of color, although he is as black as the white is white." He was, perhaps, suggesting that the term "of color" was inappropriate, since it applied as well to him as to whites, or else simply seeking to distance himself from others of mixed European and African ancestry. In his description of Zaïre, Jolicoeur again emphasized the importance of color by pointing out that her children were of the same "color" as her and that she had therefore refused the "caresses" of white men.

Who was Laurent Jolicoeur? In an October 1793 document he was described as being sixty-five years old and sick. If the document is correct, he was born in 1728. And he was born not in Saint-Domingue, but in Africa.[24] When Jolicoeur was married in 1775, he described himself as being "of the Fond nation, in Guinea." The use of the term "Fon" or "Fond" was unusual in Saint-Domingue or generally among French slave traders, who more often used the term Arada to describe enslaved people from that region of West Africa.[25] That suggests that Jolicoeur had insisted the term be used in his marriage declaration. This connection to Africa, then, seems to have been important to him. And it makes the petition even more remarkable, for it was a document about the relationship between two West Africans, one a Fon and one an Ibo, mediated through a play by Voltaire.[26]

Jolicoeur's petition aimed at securing liberty for Zaïre was an act of literary invention and intervention. It was part of a longer tradition of notarial documents that transformed slaves into free men and women, but it creatively expanded beyond this tradition, improvising a text tailored to its revolutionary times. While emancipation documents traditionally listed the qualities and good services of the enslaved, the virtues attributed to Zaïre in Jolicoeur's petition presented slavery itself, at least in her case, as an unacceptable form of suffering. The references to the elevation of Zaïre's sentiments, to her sexual virtue, and to Voltaire all represented a dialogue with and contribution to the revolutionary changes in the colony.

Jolicoeur was making use of the play, and in a sense rewriting it, in pursuit of a very concrete goal. He assumed that his readers shared with him a knowledge of the play and would recognize the line he quoted: "Ah, Zaïre , you are crying!"[27] But Jolicoeur also seems to have expected them to understand the broader meaning of his allusion. Quoting from the play was a way of insisting on a shared set of principles of justice. Voltaire's Zaïre, a slave far from her homeland, was a model of virtue, seeking to balance her desire for freedom and love with her loyalty to her family in a difficult situation. Jolicoeur was suggesting that, like the famous heroine, his slave Zaïre deserved liberty and fulfillment. The play provided a larger reference point for his basic argument: that Zaïre's virtue and elevation made her enslavement a tragedy. But his petition left the ending of the story open, and in the hands of his interlocutors, in a potent way: they had the power to end this tragedy, to give the Zaïre in front of them a different life than the Zaïre they had watched die on stage.

Jolicoeur's use of the play may also have been a subtle way of indicating his own investment in the request he was making: Was he, like Voltaire's Orosmane, whose line to Zaïre he was quoting, a master seeking to free his slave in order to marry her? Were Zaïre's children also Jolicoeur's children? Was he, in taking pride in her sexual loyalty and virtue, speaking of her loyalty to him?

Historians of Caribbean slave societies are quite familiar with the many notarial records in which masters freed their enslaved sexual partners and children without explicitly recognizing the children as their own. Even though such family relationships were an open secret in the society itself, the vast majority of white masters chose not to register their paternity and legitimate their children, presumably to avoid the racial stigma and forms of discrimination they would suffer if they did. For Jolicoeur this would not have been an issue in the same way as for white planters, but it is possible that for some other reason he wished to avoid publicly acknowledging that Zaïre's children were his own. If so, his use of Voltaire's line may have been a creative way of saying nothing officially, while still indicating his link to Zaïre and his paternity of her children. In fact the petition may have been, at least in part, addressed to Zaïre by Jolicoeur, a public declaration of his sentiments for her.[28]

Who was Zaïre? The petition provides a few details about her: she was forty years old, had rendered "great service" as a slave, and was of the "Ibo nation." She, like Jolicoeur, was African-born, and a survivor of the Middle Passage. Her name, though, was not a reference to her place of origin; although slave ships docking in Saint-Domingue were sometimes described as having departed from the mouth of the Zaïre river, on the coast of Central Africa, she came from West Africa.[29] It is far more likely that, like many enslaved people in Saint-Domingue, she received the name as a reference to Voltaire's play.[30]

Enslaved people often had multiple names: those given to them by masters (and written down in registers) and others used within their own community. Of course, behind this name could have stood another she used with other slaves, perhaps even with her master Jolicoeur. Unfortunately, it is probably impossible to establish what the slave in question actually considered to be her own name, or names, and what relationship she had to the name Zaïre. And it is equally difficult to envision how she thought about her sexuality and about its relationship (or lack thereof) to her capacity for freedom and citizenship. If Jolicoeur and Zaïre were indeed partners, and her escape from slavery was also a way for them to more legitimately establish their relationship (as it was for couples elsewhere in the French Caribbean during the same period), it is in fact possible that the petition was actually a collaborative effort between them. There is even the possibility that the name "Zaïre" was made up specifically for use in the petition, although if Jolicoeur had to present earlier documents proving his ownership of her this would have been difficult. If Jolicoeur truly quoted lines from *Zaïre* to Zaïre, did they have other conversations about the play? Had she joined him at one of its performances? Did she know of the composition of the petition, and perhaps even participate in it, directly or less directly through her presentation of herself and her aspirations to Jolicoeur?

The fact that Zaïre was described as an Ibo added another layer of reference to the petition, which would have echoed Voltaire's portrayal of his Zaïre. The "Ibo," in Saint-Domingue as elsewhere, were often singled out as being particularly inconsolable and prone to suicide. Moreau de Saint-Méry, for instance, wrote that masters needed to watch their Ibo slaves very carefully, as the idea of suicide was "seductive" to them "because they adopt the dogma of the transmigration of souls."[31] Jolicoeur's portrayal of the "Ibo" Zaïre as inconsolable would have resonated with these broader stereotypes and could have served to further expand the potential for tragedy highlighted by the reference to Voltaire. Through *Zaïre*, Jolicoeur evoked the potential for murder, and through the naming of Zaïre as "Ibo" he was also evoking the specter of suicide. But he suggested that rather than seeking death as a route home, Zaïre could instead follow another "transmigratory" passage, from slavery to freedom.

What is powerful about this fleeting fragment from the broader archive of revolutionary Saint-Domingue is that it both refuses the narrative arc of the tragedy it invokes and embraces the broader vision that Voltaire brought to its composition. Voltaire killed off his lovers, Zaïre and Orosmane, as a way of illustrating the cost of a religious intolerance fed by narratives of past battles and the ghosts of dead martyrs. Decades later, Jolicoeur used the play to argue that it was within the power of the local government to avoid and eliminate a tragedy in their midst by allowing Zaïre's "elevated sentiments" and "beautiful soul" to flourish in freedom. Both authors used a theatrical tragedy in seeking to deflect and undo a social and political one. Both also, of course, heavily circumscribed and channeled Zaïre's public role by focusing on her sexual virtue as its major symbol. And the fact that we seem to have no way to approach her own views on liberty and virtue remains its own kind of tragedy. Still, the petition, placed in its context, powerfully illuminates the complicated circulation of texts, discourses, ideas, dispositions, and sentiments in the Atlantic context.

Minette

Minette's story was first told in detail in Fouchard's *Le théâtre à Saint-Domingue* (1955). It is essentially the climax and conclusion of his book. Titled simply "Minette et Lise," Fouchard's chapter describes the rise of the two sisters to the highest echelons of celebrity in Saint-Domingue. Born into poverty to a formerly enslaved woman of color, the sisters were trained in singing by local white actress Madame Acquaire who, working with others at the Port-au-Prince theater, took the bold step of presenting Minette to the public. Minette was such a success that she went on to star in several different theatrical works, appearing on stages throughout the colony and celebrated everywhere for her remarkable talent. Her sister Lise also had a significant performance career in the colony. Fouchard's work inspired the Haitian novelist Marie Vieux-Chauvet to write a novel woven around Minette's life, *La Dance sur le volcan*, which provides a rich portrait of colonial Saint-Domingue on the brink of revolution.[32]

Fouchard located a fascinating trace of Minette's own aesthetic choices in the form of a newspaper announcement for one of her performances in 1783, which explained Minette's decision to perform in the French opera *L'Infante de Zamora*. The reason was that this work was "in good taste" and one that "fans of beauty will always see again with pleasure." The play, she added, marked a contrast with "those ephemeral productions that have bastardized or we might say degraded the lyric stage for some time, plays that are only local and which often only focus on daily life in private society." This was a disparaging reference to locally written plays, some in Creole, including Clément's popular drama *Jeannot et Thérèse*. Fouchard interprets Minette's rejection of the local plays as a sign of her cultural Francophilia, situating her in a tradition of elite Haitian rejection of the Creole language and other forms of Haitian culture. Between her and her sister Lise, who did perform in Creole language plays, Fouchard sees the history of Haitian literary and cultural debates condensed.[33]

Fouchard ends his chapter with the claim that Minette probably died during a terrible few days of killings and fire in Port-au-Prince in late 1791. But over the past decade, Camier—in collaboration with other scholars—has tracked down a number of fascinating additional traces of Minette, which suggest that her life extended well beyond 1791. The first bit of evidence about her longer life emerged when I came across an announcement in a November 1806 announcement in a New Orleans newspaper, *Moniteur de la Louisiane*. It was for a performance by an "ancienne artiste" named Minette Ferrand. The advertisement noted that a long illness had left her in difficult circumstances, especially given that she was taking care of a "large family," and announced that Minette would perform *Euphrosine ou la Tyran Corrigé*, a popular French romantic opera set in medieval Provence. This was not a play Minette had staged in Saint-Domingue, but the tactic was a familiar one, for she had organized similar evenings in Port-au-Prince, where actors often supplemented their meager salaries through benefit performances.

Not long thereafter, in January 1807, Minette Ferrand died in New Orleans. Camier has used the names from her death record to reconstruct her remarkable story and family history. These traces have emerged from a range of sources, including notarial records, consular records relating to refugees in Cuba, and records from New Orleans. Camier's work offers up a strikingly different portrait of both Minette's family background and her life than the one sketched out by Fouchard. He convincingly argues that Minette's mother and grandmother were both free. He establishes that she was born on 4 July 1767, and that when she was baptized a few weeks later her grandmother, Elizabeth Dougé, was there. Her father, Marin Ferrand, a French treasurer working with the colonial government, was not. Minette seems to have been raised in comfortable circumstances and even may have owned two slaves. Though the evidence is circumstantial, Camier concludes that she had a romantic relationship with François Saint-Martin, manager of the Port-au-Prince theater, and had her first child with him at the age of fifteen. She went on to have two more children after his death, two girls named Marie Jeanne and Louise Françoise. And she probably raised them to adulthood, though not in Saint-Domingue. Fragments from the archive suggest that Minette embarked on a journey into exile in the early 1800s— she was in Cuba in 1802, Camier has found—before making her way to New Orleans by 1806. Camier's research into Minette's life in the 1790s and 1800s is ongoing.[34]

In her powerful portrayal of Minette's life, Chauvet offers us an imagined glimpse of what it must have been like to perform on Saint-Domingue's stages as a woman of color. She raises the question of precisely who this theater was for, reminding us of its varied audiences and the different histories and perspectives they carried with them. A key passage in *Dance on the Volcano* reminds us, too, of the way in which theater resides at a crossroads of experience, narrative, embodiment, and politics.

It is Minette's first performance on stage, and as the violin strikes its first chord, Minette opens her mouth but no sound comes out. The orchestra stops and starts again, but still she is frozen, and cannot sing:

> At that very moment, her eyes stopped seeing the extravagant, too-bright theater and focused further into the distance, higher up, towards the twenty-one boxes of the second tier where the people of color were seated. Jammed together and piled on top of one another, they seemed attached to each other in an immense

solidarity that suddenly revealed itself to her. They were waiting, too. There was something so distressing in their eyes it made her want to scream. Immediately a series of images unfurled in her memory at a dizzying pace: images of backs riddled with lashes of the whip—one scarred over, the other still bleeding from fresh wounds. A long shudder traversed her body. She heard those lashes of the whip in that very moment, striking thousands of bloody backs with a loud, dull sound. Joseph's voice whispered in her ear: *You've got to tell yourself you're playing for high stakes now. Your voice is your weapon and you're going to use it.*

The violin went quiet for a second time. Then it hit the note a third time as the orchestra waited, craning its neck towards the stage like everyone else in the theatre.

Minette opened her mouth, and this time her voice rang out, crystal clear, warm, and so full that a long murmur of admiration ran through the audience.

Now that she was singing, she did not see anything else, she did not hear anything else, she was entirely possessed by the incredible sounds pouring out of her. Everything else had disappeared, the theater, the orchestra, and even the twenty-one boxes where her friends were watching her. Something in her that came from far, far away was directing her gestures, her poses.[35]

Notes

1. Bernard Camier and Laurent Dubois, "Voltaire et Zaïre, ou Le Théâtre Des Lumières Dans l'aire Atlantique Française," *Revue d'histoire Moderne et Contemporaine* 54, no. 4 (April 2007): 39–69; Laurent Dubois and Kaiama L. Glover, "Staging Revolution: Jean Fouchard, Marie Vieux-Chauvet, and Writing the Theater of 18th-Century Saint-Domingue," in *On History's Stage*, ed. Jeffrey M. Leichmann and Karine Benac (Oxford: Oxford University Studies in the Enlightenment, forthcoming).

2. Jean Fouchard, *The Haitian Maroons: Liberty or Death* (New York: E. W. Blyden Press, 1981); Jean Fouchard, *Le Théâtre à Saint-Domingue* (Port-au-Prince: Imprimerie Henri Deschamps, 1988); Jean Fouchard, *Plaisirs de Saint-Domingue* (Port-au-Prince: Imprimerie Henri Deschamps, 1988); Jean Fouchard, *Artistes et Répertoire Des Scènes de Saint-Domingue* (Port-au-Prince: Imprimerie Henri Deschamps, 1988); Julia Prest, "Theater in Saint-Domingue, 1764–1791: Plays, Ballets, Operas," https://www.theaterinsaintdomingue.org/.

3. Bernard Camier, "Musique Coloniale et Société à Saint-Domingue à La Fin Du XVIIIème Siècle" (Thèse de doctorat, Université des Antilles-Guyane, 2004);

Lauren Clay, *Stagestruck: The Business of Theater in Eighteenth-Century France and Its Colonies* (Ithaca: Cornell University Press, 2013); David M. Powers, *From Plantation to Paradise: Cultural Politics and Musical Theater in the French Slave Colonies 1764–1789* (East Lansing: Michigan State University Press, 2014).

4. M. L. E. Moreau de Saint-Méry, *Description topographique, physique, civile, politique et historique de la partie française de L'isle Saint Domingue*, 3 vols. (Paris: Société française d'histoire d'Outre-Mer, 2004).

5. Dominique Rogers and Stewart King, "Housekeepers, Merchants, Rentieres: Free Women of Color in the Port Cities of Colonial Saint-Domingue, 1750–1790," in *Women in Port: Gendering Communities, Economies, and Social Networks in Atlantic Port Cities, 1500–1800,* ed. Douglas Catterall and Jodi Campbell (Leiden: Brill, 2012), 362.

6. Fouchard, *Théâtre*, 167.

7. The history of the play was first described in Fouchard, *Théâtre*, 281, 297–98. But its content and language were unknown until the recent discovery by Camier of a complete version of the play in the Public Record Office at Kew, in a series of papers from French ships captured during the revolutionary period (HCA 30/381). This manuscript contains a 1783 revision of the play, while a shorter fragment of the play located by Yvonne Fabella in the Library Company of Philadelphia, Du Simitière Papers, Scraps No. 60, comes from an earlier version. For an annotated transcription of the play in the original Creole, see Bernard Camier and Marie-Christine Hazael-Massieux, "Jeannot et Thérèse un opéra-comique en créole au milieu du XVIIIème siècle," *Revue de la société haïtienne d'Histoire et de Géographie*, 215 (2003): 135–66. For a linguistic analysis of the play, see Marie-Christine Hazaël-Massieux, "A propos de Jeannot et Thérèse: une traduction du Devin du village en créole du XVIIIe siècle?" *Creolica*, http://www.creolica.net/A-propos-de-Jeannot-et-Therese-une.

8. I explore this cultural context in Haiti in *The Banjo: America's African Instrument* (Cambridge: Harvard University Press, 2016), 97–102, 123–38, 178–81.

9. "Le Pillage du Cap. Révolte de Saint-Domingue, 1793: Analyse de l'aquarelle par Monsieur Jacques de Cauna," manuscript, Rubenstein Special Collections Library, Duke University.

10. Pierre-Jean-Louis Bouquet, "Pillage du Cap Français en 1793," 1795, John Carter Brown Library (record number 09–147, call number Fr795 B727 Oversize.) Available online at https://jcb.lunaimaging.com/luna/servlet/s/6tkawp. Bouquet's engraving of the burning of the city is in a private collection, but is reproduced on the cover of Laurent Dubois and John Garrigus, *Slave Revolution in the Caribbean, 1789–1804: A History in Documents*, 2nd ed. (New York: Bedford Books, 2017).

11. Except in cases where I have translated directly from the French to emphasize the original formulations, I draw from the English translation of Voltaire, *Alzire*, in *Seven Plays by Voltaire* (New York: Howard Vertig, 1988); see Alvarez's speech on pp. 6–8. On the writing of the play see Jeanne Monty, "Le Travail de composition d'*Alzire*," *The French Review*, 35, no. 4 (1962): 383–89; for the French text and a detailed analysis of the play's sources and composition, see T. E. D. Braun, ed., *Alzire, ou les Américains*, in *Les Oeuvres complètes de Voltaire,* vol. 14 (Oxford: Voltaire Foundation, 1989), 1–210.

12. Howard Brofsky, "Rameau and the Indians: The Popularity of *Les Sauvages*," in Allan W. Atlas, ed., *Music in the Classic Period: Essays in Honor of Barry S. Brook* (New York: Pendragon Press, 1985), 43–46.

13. The incident, dated to the mid-eighteenth century, is described in a fragment in the Centre des Archives d'Outre-mer F3 141.

14. Braun, "Subject, substance, and structure in *Zaïre* and *Alzire*," *Studies in Voltaire and the Eighteenth Century* 87 (1972): 181–97, 188.

15. On the costumes in Paris, see Marvin Carlson, *Voltaire and the Theater of the Eighteenth Century* (Westport: Greenwood, 1998), 49; *Affiches Américaines*, Port-au-Prince, 2 August 1783.

16. Laurent Dubois, *Avengers of the New World: The Story of the Haitian Revolution* (Cambridge: Harvard University Press, 2004), 14–15, 299–301.

17. M. Charles-Malo, *Histoire d'Haïti* (Paris: Louis-Janet, 1825), 196.

18. Constantin Dumervé, *Histoire de la musique en Haiti* (Port-au-Prince: Imprimerie des Antilles, 1968), 33; on Christophe's coronation, see the Washington-published newspaper *Intelligent national*, 25 July 1811, in Centre des Archives d'Outre-mer F3 267 fol. 538 and fol. 540; on the theater in Le Cap, see Moreau de Saint-Méry's note from 19 October 1816, Centre des Archives d'Outre-mer F3 141 bis fol. 316.

19. See Dubois, *Avengers*, 299–301.

20. *"le vengeur de l'Etat"*; *"vengeurs"*; *"foule heroique"*; *"venger l'Amérique"* (Voltaire, *Alzire*, 136, 157, 151).

21. The petition was printed in *Moniteur Général de Saint-Domingue*, 3, no. 81 (5 February 1793), 322.

22. See Eva Jacobs, ed., *Zaïre,* in *Les Oeuvres complètes de Voltaire,* vol. 8 (Oxford: Voltaire Foundation, 1988), 273–528; Jean Goldzink, ed., in *Voltaire: Zaïre—Le Fanatisme—Nanine—Le Café* (Paris: Flammarion, 2004). On the importance of Voltaire in French theater, see Goldzink's introduction and Jean-Pierre Perchellet, "Voltaire, tragique en son temps," *Revue Voltaire* 3 (2003): 267–87; and Carlson, *Voltaire and the Theater*, 42, 53, 99. There has been surprisingly little detailed textual analysis of the play, given its interesting themes. I draw here on Clifton Cherpack, "Love and Alienation in Voltaire's *Zaïre*," *French Forum* 2, no. 1 (1977): 47–57; L. Brian Price, "Symbolic Temporal Prisons in Voltaire's *Zaïre*," *CLA Journal* 20, no. 1 (1976): 40–47; and Braun, "Subject, Substance, and Structure in *Zaïre* and *Alzire*."

23. Between 1764 and 1797, the years researched by Fouchard, plays by Voltaire were advertised eighty-four times in the colony's newspapers; *Zaïre* was among the most popular, advertised eight times starting in 1768. See Fouchard, *Artistes et répertoire*, 91–271; on the 1791 performance, see Fouchard, *Théâtre*, 152–54.

24. List of "Africains domestiques," St. Marc, October 1793, in Archives Nationales (AN) DXXV 30. My sincere thanks to Rebecca Scott, who found this document and generously shared this information with me.

25. Moreau de Saint-Méry describes the "Fonds" simply as one of the people from the interior of the "Côte des Esclaves"; *Description*, 1:50; Gabriel Debien noted how, in the late seventeenth century, in a description similar to those later often given of the Ibo, Father Labat wrote that the Fons were inclined to eat dirt in order

to kill themselves, and "saddened easily," but the only examples of slaves being listed as "Fon" come from French Guiana; see *Les Esclaves des Antilles françaises (XVIIè-XVIIIè siècles)* (Fort-de-France: Société d'Histoire de la Martinique, 2000 reprint [1974]), chap. 2 and 396–97.

26. Centre des Archives d'Outre-mer CAOM, DPPC, Etat Civil de St. Marc, 4 February 1775. Scholars continued to debate the question of how to interpret the meaning of such terms. For recent contributions to the debate, see Alexander X. Byrd, "Eboe, Country, Nation, and Gustavas Vassa's *Interesting Narrative*," *William and Mary Quarterly* 63, no. 1 (2006): 123–48; Gwendolyn Midlo Hall, *Slavery and African Ethnicities in the Americas: Restoring the Links* (Chapel Hill: University of North Carolina Press, 2005); and Douglas Chambers, *Murder at Montpelier: Igbo Africans in Virginia* (Jackson: University of Mississippi Press, 2005).

27. Voltaire claimed the line made "a great impact" in the French theaters and on Louis XV; see *Oeuvres complètes de Voltaire* 52 vols. (Paris: Garnier Frères, 1877–85), 2, 607. The quotation comes from a scene in which Orosmane is seeking to understand Zaïre's reason for wanting to delay their marriage. Although Jolicoeur's version of the line—"A quoi! Zaïre, vous pleurez"—does not equate precisely with how it appears in the early published versions of the play, from 1738 and 1742, he could well have heard the version he wrote in a performance.

28. My thanks to Madison Smartt Bell for suggesting this last possibility to me.

29. In March 1793, for instance, one of the last slave ships to arrive in the colony—ironically called *La Nouvelle Société*, or "The New Society"—was arriving from the "Zaïre river," according to a newspaper advertisement; see Dubois, *Avengers*, 151.

30. Voltaire got the name for his character from Racine's well-known play, *Bajazet*, which was set in Turkey and featured a character named Zaïre; see Goldzink, *Voltaire*, 51; naming slaves after classical or literary figures was a common practice in the French Caribbean, and there were slaves in Saint-Domingue with the names Orosmane and Nerestan, clearly references to *Zaïre*; see Jacques de Cauna, *Au temps des isles à sucre: Histoire d'une plantation de Saint-Domingue au XVIIIè siècle* (Paris: Kharthala, 2003), 92.

31. Moreau de Saint-Méry, *Description*, 1:51.

32. For a full treatment of Minette's remarkable life and the links between the work of Fouchard and Chauvet, see Dubois and Glover, "Staging Revolution."

33. Fouchard, *Théâtre*, 270, 284.

34. See Bernard Camier, "Minette (Élisabeth, Alexandrine, Louse Ferrand dite) / Artiste libre de couleur á Port-au-Prince à la fine du XVIIIe siècle," *Journal de la Société d'Histoire et de Géographie d'Haïti*, no. 259–62 (January-December 2016): 237–41. An English version of the article is available as "A 'Free Artist of Color' in Late Eighteenth-Century Saint-Domingue: The Life and Times of Minette," *International Journal of the Study of Music and Musical Performance* 1, no. 1 (2019): 1–26. For an earlier articulation of Camier's thesis about Minette's family origins, now confirmed with substantial additional research, see "Minette, artiste de couleur à Saint-Domingue," *Revue de la société haïtienne d'Histoire et de Géographie*, no. 205 (October-December 2000), 1–11. See also David Powers's presentation of Minette's story in *From Plantation to Paradise*, 93–104.

35. Marie Vieux-Chauvet, *Dance on the Volcano*, trans. Kaiama L. Glover (New York: Archipelago Books, 2016), 66–67.

CONSUMPTION AND REMEDIATION

Cluster: Consuming Foreign Music and Theater in Eighteenth-Century Britain

Introduction: Consuming Foreign Music and Theater in Eighteenth-Century Britain

ALISON DESIMONE AND AMY DUNAGIN

When foreign performers started arriving in London in the late seventeenth and early eighteenth centuries, their presence provoked fierce debates concerning national identity, gender, party politics, and the state of England's own dramatic and musical traditions.[1] Fleeing wars and unstable economies, Continental composers, singers, instrumentalists, and dancers hoped to find a city that would provide ample financial and artistic opportunities for performance.[2] Instead, they found that England's capital was, paradoxically, of two minds: audiences were eager to hear foreign superstars who could sing and play the virtuosic music they so craved, and yet there were critics—often motivated by political and religious loyalties—ready to scapegoat imported culture in order to bolster native English musical and theatrical traditions.[3] In *The Spectator*, Joseph Addison summarized this confusion:

> At present our notions of music are very uncertain that we do not know what it is we like; only, in general, we are transported with any thing that is not English: so it be of a foreign growth, let it be Italian, French, or High Dutch, it is the same thing. In short, our English music is quite rooted out, and nothing yet planted in its stead.[4]

Although Addison's remarks are tinged with hyperbole, this cluster of essays explores the truth behind his politically charged sentiment from the perspective of a broader reception history—one that engages with both public discourse and private experiences concerning foreign culture. By focusing on the idea of consumption in early eighteenth-century England, the three essays here test Addison's claim that Continental culture "rooted out" English music. Our authors find that consuming foreign music and theater allowed audiences to explore new genres, sounds, and styles; debate and refine their own musical tastes; and engage with an expanding European world even from the comforts of London's theaters or their own drawing rooms.

These essays examine the eighteenth-century English reception of foreign musical and theatrical works from multiple disciplinary perspectives, including musicology, cultural history, and the history of theater. In soliciting these essays, we asked our contributors to consider why English men and women embraced foreign culture even as they increasingly defined English national identity in opposition to the Continent. The question is intimately connected to arguments persuasively made by Linda Colley concerning how the British used other nations and peoples (especially Catholic France and Italy, as well as those encountered in the colonies) to provide foils as they struggled to create a new national identity in the wake of the Acts of Union (1706–7).[5] While Colley provides a starting point from an historical perspective, musicologists have also posed this question—most often with regard to the reception of Italian opera.[6] Others have approached this question by exploring the reception of specific foreign musicians who found success in England.[7] More recently, musicologists and historians have turned to methodologies that focus not on prominent genres or historical figures, but rather on the circulation and consumption of the music itself.[8] The essays in this cluster build upon this scholarship by investigating how the consumption and reception of foreign music and theater, both on the public stage and in domestic spaces, presented an opportunity for the renegotiation of British cultural identity.

Two themes run throughout these essays. First, they all discuss how the British often defined their identity in opposition to another foreign culture. In "Opera, War, and the Politics of Effeminacy under Queen Anne," Amy Dunagin explores the ways in which early criticism of Italian opera participated in a heated political dispute over Britain's involvement in the War of the Spanish Succession. As fears circulated that British society might be undergoing a cultural emasculation that could lead to military weakness, some Whig commentators used opera criticism for political ends by attributing Tories' opposition to the war to the effeminizing effects of Italian opera, while other Whigs defended the controversial genre. Erica Levenson identifies similar patterns of ambivalence toward French performers and performances in "From Royalty to Riots: Nation and Class in the Reception of French Musical Theater in London." She explores how the enthusiasm for French popular theater in the period between 1718 and 1735 both mirrored and deflected political anxieties about the fraught Anglo-French relationship. In "'African' Songs and Women's Abolitionism in the Home, 1787–1807," Julia Hamilton similarly examines how "African" songs, written and sung by white Britons, often women, required a complex performance of multiple racial and national identities, including an emergent British identity as a nation opposed to slavery.

These three essays are also linked by their innovative use of sources, the second theme that runs throughout this cluster. Each author takes as a starting point the idea of consumption as personal and discursive engagement.[9] Dunagin, Levenson, and Hamilton show how various sources can illuminate the ways in which audiences experienced foreign culture, both directly and through the eyes of others. Dunagin, for example, draws on political poems, tracts, prologues, and epilogues from 1701–13 in order to show how public discourse attempted to shape reactions to foreign music during wartime. Levenson analyzes French plays and tunes found in English sources ranging from grammar books to ballad operas in order to demonstrate how French comic theater and song provided a creative space in which English men and women redefined their own Britishness in relation to French culture. Finally, Hamilton examines eleven "African" songs that adopted the perspective of an African narrator addressing a white British, and often female, listener— the consumer of this music. Composed and performed in the context of the British abolitionist movement, these songs employed both text and music to express with varying degrees of intensity the shame of British slavery.

Notes

1. Many scholars have confronted and illuminated the various ways in which musico-theatrical traditions in early eighteenth-century London reflected anxieties surrounding foreign culture. For some examples, see Brean S. Hammond, "Joseph Addison's Opera *Rosamond*: Britishness in the Early Eighteenth Century," *ELH* 73, no. 3 (2006): 601–29; Lowell Lindgren, "Critiques of Opera in London, 1705–1719," in *Il melodrama italiano in Italia e in Germania nell'eta barocca*, ed. Alberto Colzani, Norbert Dubowy, Andrea Luppi, and Murizio Padoan (Como: AMIS, 1995), 145–65; Thomas McGeary, *The Politics of Opera in Handel's Britain* (Cambridge: Cambridge

University Press, 2013); and Paul Monod, "The Politics of Handel's Early London Operas, 1711–1718," *Journal of Interdisciplinary History* 36, no. 3 (2006): 445–72.

2.　James A. Winn has discussed how foreign musicians integrated into London's musical scene during Queen Anne's reign; see Winn, *Queen Anne: Patroness of the Arts* (Oxford: Oxford University Press, 2014). For London's population explosion at the turn of the eighteenth century, see E. A. Wrigley, "A Simple Model of London's Importance in Changing English Society and Economy 1650–1750," *Past & Present* 37 (1967): 44–70. On the arrival of foreigners more generally, see Daniel Statt, *Foreigners and Englishmen: The Controversy over Immigration and Population, 1660–1760* (Newark: University of Delaware Press, 1995). London was not the only city experiencing such demographic change at the time. On the heightened mobility of foreign musicians in Europe more generally, see, for example, Reinhard Strohm, ed., *The Eighteenth-Century Diaspora of Italian Music and Musicians* (Turnout: Brepols, 2001).

3.　See, for example, McGeary, *Politics of Opera*; Monod, "Politics of Handel's Early London Operas"; and Amy Dunagin, "Secularization, National Identity, and the Baroque: Italian Music in England, 1660–1711" (Ph.D. diss., Yale University, 2014). On the role of party politics in shaping early eighteenth-century narratives of English music history, see Dunagin, "Tory Defenses of English Music: Thomas Tudway and Roger North," *Eighteenth-Century Life* 40, no. 2 (2016): 36–65. For how female opera singers were drawn into this political dispute, see Alison DeSimone, "'Equally Charming, Equally Too Great': Female Rivalry, Politics, and Opera in Early Eighteenth-Century London," *Early Modern Women: An Interdisciplinary Journal* 12, no. 1 (2017): 73–101.

4.　Joseph Addison, *The Spectator* 18 (21 March 1711). In this issue, Addison critiques Italian opera of the early eighteenth century, specifically the pasticcio opera, which he derides as nonsensical, especially given its performance in a mixture of languages depending on the singers involved. His negative commentary also probably stems from the poor reception of his own opera, *Rosamond*, just a few years earlier. See Hammond, "Joseph Addison's Opera *Rosamond*," especially 601–5.

5.　Linda Colley, *Britons: Forging the Nation 1707–1837*, rev. ed. (New Haven: Yale University Press, 2014), 6.

6.　Beyond those sources already cited in note 1, see Matthew Gardner and Alison DeSimone, eds., *Music and the Benefit Performance in Eighteenth-Century Britain* (Cambridge: Cambridge University Press, 2019); Roger Fiske, *English Theatre Music in the Eighteenth Century* (Oxford: Oxford University Press, 1973); Robert D. Hume, "The Sponsorship of Opera in London, 1704–1720," *Modern Philology* 85, no. 4 (1988): 420–32; David Hunter, "Bragging on *Rinaldo*: Ten Ways Writers have Trumpeted Handel's Coming to Britain," in *Göttinger Händel-Beiträge*, vol. 9 (Kassel: Bärenreiter Verlag, 2001), 113–31; Hendrik Knif, *Gentlemen and Spectators: Studies in Journals, Opera and the Social Scene in Late Stuart London* (Helsinki: Finnish Historical Society, 1995); Kathryn Lowerre, *Music and Musicians on the London Stage, 1695–1705* (Burlington: Ashgate, 2009); and the essays in Susan Wollenberg and Simon McVeigh, eds., *Concert Life in Eighteenth-Century Britain* (Aldershot: Ashgate, 2004).

7. Much of the literature on foreign musicians in eighteenth-century Britain focuses on Handel. For two recent biographies, see Ellen T. Harris, *George Frideric Handel: A Life with Friends* (New York: W.W. Norton, 2014) and David Hunter, *The Lives of George Frideric Handel* (Woodbridge: Boydell & Brewer, 2015). Other scholars have focused especially on Italian singers who arrived in London in the early eighteenth century. See, for example, Suzanne Aspden, *The Rival Sirens: Performance and Identity on Handel's Operatic Stage* (Cambridge: Cambridge University Press, 2013), and C. Steven LaRue, *Handel and His Singers: The Creation of the Royal Academy Operas, 1720–1728* (Oxford: Clarendon Press, 1995).

8. The most recent study to discuss musical circulation in Britain is Linda Austern, Candace Bailey, and Amanda Eubanks Winkler, eds., *Beyond Boundaries: Rethinking Music Circulation in Early Modern England* (Bloomington: Indiana University Press, 2017). The last four chapters in the collection address music in eighteenth-century Britain.

9. The essays in this collection do not focus on the economic aspects of consumer culture in the eighteenth century. For a broad overview of consumer culture in eighteenth-century Britain, see Neil McKendrick, John Brewer, and John H. Plumb, eds., *The Birth of a Consumer Society: The Commercialization of Eighteenth-Century Britain* (Bloomington: Indiana University Press, 1982). On the impact of Britain's expanding consumer culture on the arts, see John Brewer, *The Pleasures of the Imagination: English Culture in the Eighteenth Century* (New York: Farrar Straus Giroux, 1997).

Opera, War, and the Politics of Effeminacy under Queen Anne

AMY DUNAGIN

When Italian opera first came to the English public stage in 1705, its reputation as a frivolous, luxurious, and potentially effeminizing entertainment preceded it.[1] Five years before its debut, the dramatist John Dennis preemptively sowed the ground with salt.[2] In the prologue to his play *Iphigenia* in 1700, he has the genius of England "rise to a warlike symphony" and relate the muse of Tragedy's exclamation: "Oh is my *Brittain* faln to that degree, / As for effeminate Arts t' abandon me? / I left the enslav'd *Italian* with disdain, / And servile *Gallia*, and dejected *Spain*: / Grew proud to be confin'd to *Brittain's* shore / Where godlike Liberty had fix'd before."[3] Fearing a growing public taste for "those arts … that soften'd foreign braves, / And sunk the Southern nations into slaves," Dennis attempted to shame audiences by asking how England's past kings might have reacted "to see a bearded more than female throng / Dissolved and dying by an eunuchs song."[4] In issuing this warning about the dangers of opera, Dennis capitalized on a longstanding set of beliefs about the genre's birthplace. The association of Italy with various sorts of what was considered sexual degeneracy, including lust, effeminacy, and sodomy, was by this time well established in English sources.[5] To take just one example, in the same year, 1700, Daniel Defoe, in his well-known poem *The True-Born Englishman,* identified Italy as a "torrid zone," "where blood ferments in rapes and sodomy" and "nature ever burns with hot desires, / Fanned with luxuriant air from subterranean fires."[6] It is no surprise, then, that the trope of Italian licentiousness informed the public's reception of Italy's premier musico-dramatic export.

From its first introduction in London theaters at the start of the eighteenth century, Italian opera provoked scathing responses from some English critics, who perceived a threat to their nation's masculinity.[7] Critics of the opera argued that the spectacle and sensuality of Italian opera and the ambiguously sexed, or de-sexed, bodies of some of its star performers, the castrati, could have an effeminizing effect on individual British men and, even more troublingly, on British culture.[8] Musicologists have noted that this gendering of Italian opera as feminine was completed in England in the late seventeenth and early eighteenth centuries—around the same time Italian opera was being introduced—and that it had to do not merely with the characteristics of opera itself, which had not been gendered in the same way in Italy, but also with opera's association with a place that the British were invested in viewing as feminine.[9] These critiques of Italian opera as dangerously sensual and potentially effeminizing would be deployed against the genre for decades—in fact, centuries—to come. While some contemporaneous Continental opera criticism linked opera with effeminacy, early eighteenth-century English critics emphasized opera's supposed effeminizing, enervating effects with a unique intensity and alarm. Why should these characterizations of Italian opera have been particularly pronounced in England?[10] This article argues that an important facet of the explanation for the gendering of Italian opera in England was early opera criticism's relationship to the fierce partisan debate over England's (after 1707, Britain's) involvement in the War of the Spanish Succession.[11]

Italian opera arrived in England at a particularly fraught time. In the first decade of the eighteenth century, Britons contended with an era of hyper-partisanship during which Whigs and Tories vied for power, and partisan invective flowed from the pens of the era's most celebrated literary figures. In this hot political climate, the War of the Spanish Succession was the litmus test issue that most galvanized the two parties. In 1700, Whigs and Tories alike lamented the deathbed decision of the childless Spanish King Charles II to bequeath his throne to his grandnephew Philip, Duke of Anjou, a grandson of Louis XIV. Both parties feared, not unreasonably, that this succession could tip the balance of power irrevocably in the French king's favor, and England consequently joined a large European coalition to check him. Tories were tepid and, as expenses ballooned, increasingly hostile to the costly and seemingly endless war. Tories, the deficit hawks of early eighteenth-century England, worried that the Whigs' cure for European power imbalance—huge, potentially crippling war debt—might prove worse than the disease.[12] Their fiscal concerns were not unfounded: over the course of the war, national debt more than doubled, from 14.1 million to 36.2 million pounds.[13] Many Tories were thus prepared to seek a peace that would accept the Bourbon candidate as King of Spain. Whigs, on the other hand, viewed the total separation of the French and Spanish crowns as the principal reason for war, rallying under the slogan, "No Peace without Spain." They were not to have their way, as a ministerial shake-up in summer of 1710 brought the Tory party into power, allowing them to pursue secret peace negotiations, which prompted a tremendous outcry from Whigs once the news leaked and led ultimately to the Treaty of Utrecht in 1713.

It was in this context, as military losses abroad and monetary losses at home weakened support for the war, that commentators on the Italian opera expressed concern that a creeping emasculation of British society might be weakening public spirit and endangering the war effort.[14] In its first, experimental years on the London stage, Italian opera proved to be a *cause célèbre* uniquely suited to bolstering such arguments. The first Italian operas in London coincided with important developments in the war. For instance, *Arsinoe*, the first London "opera after the Italian manner," as it was billed, appeared in 1705, during a worrying lull after the Battle of Blenheim; the popular *Camilla* ran in 1706, during a series of victories; and George Frideric Handel's first London opera, *Rinaldo*, went up in 1711, as the newly empowered Tories moved toward a conclusion to the war that many distressed Whigs viewed as tantamount to defeat.[15] In this climate, discussions about a Continental genre already associated with effeminacy informed and were informed by arguments about the war.

During these years, numerous Whig pamphlets, newspapers, and poems chided Tories for unmanliness, evidenced by their hesitancy to commit fully to the war, and, later, by their efforts to end it.[16] To take one example, in his poem describing the victory at Oudenarde in 1708, "Jack Frenchman's Defeat," William Congreve set up a contrast between the weakness and effeminacy of two grandsons of Louis XIV and the valor of the Hanoverian prince already destined for the British crown.[17] When faced with danger, Louis's "grandchildren twain, / For fear of being slain, / Galloped off with the popish pretender," James Francis Edward Stuart, the Catholic claimant to the British throne. Louis XIV supported the Stuart cause, and some Tories preferred a Stuart restoration to the proposed Hanoverian Succession. In contrast to the cowardly Bourbons and Stuart, "Young Hanover brave," who would one day rule in Britain as George II, has his horse shot from under him, but nevertheless "fought it on foot like a fury" and, "Being kin to Queen Anne, / Did as were she a man, she would do."[18] The poem reminded readers that the Protestant Hanoverian succession rested on the successful outcome of the war.

Given the high stakes, commentators on the war obsessed over any potential vulnerability. One in particular alarmed them: many ascribed defeat, or the threat of it, to effeminacy. An anonymous pamphlet from the first year of the war entitled *The Present Succession of Spain Consider'd* pointed to the "weakness" and "effeminacy" of the Spaniards as the very things that made them vulnerable to French domination, implicitly admonishing the British to avoid a similar path.[19] A later Whig pamphlet lamented at the end of the war: "We were the Terror of Europe ... is our courage fled beyond sea with the Duke of Marlborough? Are our Blenheims and Ramillies forgot? ... Shameful Effeminacy!"[20] In 1704, the Whig political economist James Whiston spelled out the Whig case for the war in *England's State-Distempers*. He insisted that the commercial benefits that could accrue from victory far outweighed the cost of continued war and begged his readers to "embrace the offer'd occasion" to enrich the nation, which the "corrupt practices, luxury, and effeminacy" of some, namely the Tories, "endeavor to ... debauch."[21] The Whig writer and poet William Coward in his *Licentia poetica discuss'd* (1709) warned against "that sort of public constitution, which might in the shortest time corrupt the morals of a whole people, make them effeminate, and ... which might probably bring them to a condition of beggary and slavery at home, could they escape foreign danger." Once luxury had been introduced, Coward suggested, "the rich and luxurious will soon become effeminate," and feel themselves "free from any obligations of serving in the war."[22] Often, arguments like these invoked the widespread belief that the Roman Empire had collapsed due to the Romans' embrace of "Asiatic" luxury, weakening their public spirit; the comparison with Rome as a cautionary tale was a favorite Whig tactic.[23]

This causal linkage of luxury, effeminacy, and national decline, packaged in an historical Roman precedent, had important implications for how theater criticism, especially that devoted to Italian opera, would participate in the broader debate over the war. It figured prominently in George Ridpath's *The Stage Condemn'd*, in which he assembled the testimony of thinkers ranging from St. Chrysostom to Tertullian, Livy to Cicero, offering variations on the theme that the theater promotes effeminacy and same-sex desire among men. For instance, Ridpath has St. Chrysostom caution that men returning "from the stage more dissolute, wanton and effeminate," will find "the sight of [their] wi[ves] ... less pleasing," however beautiful they might be.[24] Though first published in 1698, *The Stage Condemn'd* was reissued in a second edition in 1706, just as the Italian opera debate, featuring similar arguments, was taking off. Arthur Bedford, who allied himself with Whigs, followed a similar line in *The Great Abuse of Musick* (1711), decrying those "who through too much effeminacy give themselves continually over" to the "delights" of theatrical songs "inticing to lust."[25]

Against the backdrop of these Whiggish arguments, it becomes easier to understand the notable prevalence in early Italian opera criticism of references to the war itself, to the weakening of British military resolve, to the feminization of politicians and soldiers, and to the threat of foreign luxury—which all seemed to forebode imperial catastrophe in an eighteenth-century echo of ancient Rome. Consider, for instance, Lord Halifax's lines about the effect that the celebrated Italian soprano Margherita de L'Epine had upon the Tory Admiral of the Fleet, Sir George Rooke: "And since the tawny Tuscan rais'd her strain, / Rook furls his sails, and dozes on the main. / Treaties unfinish'd in the office sleep, / And Shovel yawns for orders on the deep."[26] Here Sir Cloudesley Shovell, an admiral under Rooke's command, waits in vain for orders from his commander, who has been seduced away from his war responsibilities by the luxurious strains of an Italian voice. Another example can be found in the epilogue to *The Cares of Love*, which was acted at Lincoln's Inn Fields in 1705 and which explicitly discusses *Arsinoe*, the first "opera after the Italian manner": "As if exotic follies are too few, / Arsinoe comes in to charm you too. / Prophetick bays too well your palate knew! / When Battles he to harmony confin'd, / And all the Rage of War to notes consign'd."[27] The message across these and similar texts is plain: opera is seducing men away from their duty in a time of war.

The Whig politician and author Arthur Maynwaring contributed a positive version of this argument in an epilogue to a spoken play, addressed to officers bound for Flanders in 1705. The speaker expresses his certainty that even though many "tender souls, with opera's affected," have come to despise spoken plays, "the Brave" will never be so easily swayed by "musick's charms": "But when the brave return, we hope to find / You constant here, & to our wishes kind: / Then sav'd by heroes that our state protect / We'll praise your virtues, & your battles act."[28] The tone of the full epilogue is one of false confidence; the speaker hopes, more than believes, that martial vigor will inoculate British men-at-arms against frivolous musical entertainments. Another strain of argument emphasized the folly of adopting—as the Romans did—the cultural habits of one's enemies. In his prologue to the 1707 play *The Cuckold in Conceit*, Maynwaring noted that the British had recently trounced the French in the Battle of Ramillies: "Yet as the Romans brought the customs home / Of foes subdued & nations overcome, / So we, instructed by their great example, / Copy the mounsieurs, though on them we trample."[29] Though these lines strike a triumphant tone, lurking in the background is an allusion to what may happen next if Britain continues to follow Rome's example.

The association of opera with effeminacy proved indelible, infusing British conceptions of opera among detractors and advocates alike.[30] In the early years of the eighteenth century, as critics quickly branded opera as effeminizing luxury, its patrons and proponents had to be creative to justify their passion for it. This was particularly challenging for Whig opera advocates, of whom there were many, who faced the tricky task of defending their appreciation for the genre while stressing their manly public spirit and unwavering commitment to the war. Perhaps the finest attempt at a Whiggish defense of opera comes from a prologue that was added to the popular opera *Camilla* for the 23 May 1706 performance, following a series of military victories in the Spanish Netherlands.[31] Here, the rebuke of effeminacy is cleverly inverted. It is femininity that inspires (rather than weakens) martial bravery: "Ladies, to you our Gratitude we pay / For the late triumphs of a glorious day / Urg'd by your charms our troops their foes subdue, / And well may conquer, when inspir'd by you. / France wou'd have men more obstinate in fight, / If her faint women shin'd with eyes so bright." Moreover, it is precisely an indulgence in pleasure that offers the best expression of patriotic passion: "In pleasure thus your hours you well employ, / 'Tis almost treason not to shew your joy / ... Each faithful subject shou'd his zeal express / In transports equal to our vast success."[32] Indulging in pleasurable entertainment, according to this line of reasoning, is patriotic, and the entertainment should be as extravagant as the military successes. The argument vindicates enjoyment of Italian opera, the most extravagant entertainment available to Londoners wishing to express their zeal for English victory.

Though clever, this Whig defense of Italian opera failed to gain a lasting purchase. Rather, it was arguments about the supposed effeminizing effects of Italian opera, deployed in support of Whiggish calls for an aggressive policy in the War of the Spanish Succession, that reverberated through eighteenth-century English opera criticism. That Whigs espoused such divergent responses to Italian opera suggests both the ambivalence with which the English reacted to Italian opera and the factionalism that characterized Queen Anne's reign.[33] Italian opera's reception in England was highly political without being straightforwardly partisan; the critical debates ran through as well as between parties. Opera's first promoters included members of both parties, among them many prominent Whigs. Records make clear that even as Whig rhetoric mostly denounced Italian opera in service of pro-war and anti-Tory arguments, Whig money supported it, and Whig grandees made up a significant portion of its audience.[34]

If, then, Whigs were among the prominent supporters of Italian opera, why would they push an argument linking opera attendance to effeminacy, a strategy that risked implicating at least as many Whigs as Tories, and probably more? Two observations help to explain Whigs' seemingly self-defeating behavior. First, for some critics, the central message condemning the opera was not so much intended for Tories, who had already succumbed to the enervating effects of foreign luxury and lost their appetite for war, but for fellow Whigs, who might yet be dissuaded from their participation in the Italian opera fad, if they could only be convinced of the ill effects opera could have on their manly public spirit. Second, it is possible that the disagreement between the Whigs who patronized Italian opera and the Whigs who feared it reflected a crack along the ideological fault line within the party that would later widen, after the Hanoverian Succession, into a division between the Patriot and Establishment factions. Musicological scholarship on the Handelian period has meticulously traced the relationship between Whig politics and the politics of opera in this later period, the 1720s and 1730s.[35] This analysis makes clear that although individual taste for opera did not correlate very well with political affiliation, printed anti-Italian opera criticism was heavily concentrated on one side: that of the Patriot Whigs, whose newspapers and satires lambasted Robert Walpole and his cronies for risking public spirit by promoting luxurious, effeminate, foreign Italian opera.[36]

In this later period, the Patriots, now uneasily allied with Tories in opposition to the Walpole government, deployed to great propagandistic effect the same early Whig criticisms of Italian opera discussed in this article in order to buttress some of the same tenets: aggressive military intervention on the Continent, condemnation of vice and luxury, and a patriotic preference for British culture over Continental alternatives. Thus the author of a piece in the *Craftsman*, a widely read Opposition newspaper, fretted in the context of the siege of Gibraltar of 1727 that "the soft *Italian* musick" might have a negative impact on "[our polite Warriors'] Courage abroad."[37] And the following year, Jonathan Swift reacted to John Gay's *The Beggar's Opera*, which famously satirized both Italian opera and the Walpole regime, by praising it for "[exposing] with great Justice, that unnatural Taste for *Italian* Musick among us." Britain had been "overrun," he lamented, "with *Italian-Effeminacy*, and *Italian* nonsense."[38] These two examples typify a profusion of criticism and satire of Italian opera from the Walpole era; Patriots and Tories published many such lampoons as part of their broader critique of the Walpole regime in Opposition newspapers such as *The Craftsman*, *Common Sense*, and the Tory *Fog's Weekly Journal*. These critiques have received considerable study in part because of their association with the canonical operas of Handel. But Opposition writers did not invent this set of critiques of Italian opera to suit their anti-Walpolian political ends. Their arguments were not new; the foundations of the English critique of Italian opera—as well as the English defense of it—were laid years before in the context of the War of the Spanish Succession.

This article has traced how early Italian opera criticism in England participated in and was shaped by partisan debate over the War of the Spanish Succession. Of all the early commentators who connected Italian opera with the threat of military defeat in that war, none was more passionate or prolific than John Dennis, the dramatist and critic with whom we began. His 1706 *Essay on the Operas after the Italian Manner* has long been a first port of call for those wishing to learn about Italian opera's reception in England. Dennis had been building the arguments of the *Essay* for several years, in the prologue to *Iphigenia* quoted above and in the prologue to his 1704 anti-French play *Liberty Asserted*, in which he admonished the audience to remember the suffering of those who were then fighting in the war: "[T]o discover scenes of mortal woe, / Survey the Rhine, the Danube, and the Po. / No fancy'd tragedies are acting there, / There the distracted native rends his hair, / And shrieks and wrings his hands in true despair."[39] While the audience sits safe and sound at Lincoln's Inn Fields theater, enjoying a "pleasing moan" and "gently [sighing] with sorrows not [their] own," Dennis seeks to frighten them out of their complacency with a vision of invasion, in which the "tragic scenes" about to be acted would "yield to horror and mortal fright," when "impious Mars" would "descend to visit pale Britannia's shore." Dennis then turns to those who would permit such a fate: emasculated Britons, to whom "Already treason whispers, come away." Finally, he offers up his prescription for avoiding this fate: his own play, which the audience is about to see. For Dennis, theater—traditional, spoken, manly English theater—is as potent as opera, as capable of affecting public spirit, but its effects are salutary whereas those of opera are malignant. In the last bit of his prologue, Dennis calls on all "patriots" to work to prevent defeat—a "tragedy indeed, / Whose sad spectators would not weep, but bleed"—by convincing their Tory "foes" that they are deluded to believe that France will adhere to the terms of treaties or be a good neighbor after a peace and that they and their children will share in France's defeat when it finally comes.[40]

Turning finally to Dennis's *An Essay on the Opera's after the Italian Manner*, which had such a significant impact on the terms of English Italian opera criticism and on the writing of its history, we see the arguments we have been tracing distilled into their most vehement form: in the concern over the "influence the soft and effeminate measures of the Italian Opera has upon the minds and manners of men"; in the exclamation that "at a time when we are contending with our enemies for our very being; we are awkwardly aping their luxuries and their vices, … as if by certain foreboding delusion we were preparing our selves for slavery, and endeavouring to make our selves agreeable to our new masters"; and in the fervent expression of hope that "while the English arms are everywhere victorious abroad, the

English arts may not be vanquish'd and oppress'd at home by the invasion of foreign luxury."[41]

The early response to Italian opera in England is notable for its intensity. This form of entertainment garnered not just amused scoffs, but also extreme, even vitriolic, reactions. I suggest that the vehemence of some of this early criticism makes more sense when we reinterpret its passion as inherently political. Italian opera arrived at a time when its perceived characteristics (foreignness, luxuriousness, effeminacy) ideally suited it for co-option into a broader debate about the war. Opera commentary provided a discursive space in which to air intense anxieties about cultural degeneration leading inexorably to weakening resolve and ultimately, if the Tories could not be stopped, to military defeat. If, then, Dennis was using a political threat in order to buttress an argument he wanted to make about opera, he was also using a critique of opera to make an argument about the war. In doing so, he and his fellow opera critics helped fuse intense wartime fears about effeminacy and cultural degeneration to the very definition of Italian opera in England.

Notes

1. For private precursors to the public performance of Italian opera, see, for example, Andrew R. Walkling, *Masque and Opera in England, 1656–1688* (New York: Routledge, 2017), esp. 209–18.

2. Dennis became one of Italian opera's most fervent critics; his *An Essay on the Opera's after the Italian Manner* (London: John Nutt, 1706) remains one of the most frequently cited critical responses to Italian opera in early eighteenth-century England.

3. John Dennis, *Iphigenia* (London: Richard Parker, 1700), prologue.

4. Dennis, *Iphigenia*, prologue. Here Dennis employs a metaphorical connotation of "death" that had been in use since the Renaissance to imply that the castrato's voice has the power to induce not only female but also male orgasm.

5. Jeremy Black notes that sodomy "was regarded in Britain as a foreign vice of Mediterranean origins" and that "homosexuality had long been particularly associated with Italy" and "was indeed sometimes called 'the Italian vice.'" Jeremy Black, *Italy and the Grand Tour* (New Haven: Yale University Press, 2003), 130.

6. Daniel Defoe, "True-Born Englishman," in *Anthology of Poems on Affairs of State: Augustan Satirical Verse, 1660–1714*, ed. George de Forest Lord (New Haven: Yale University Press, 1975), 626.

7. On Britain's identification with masculinity as a national trait, in contrast to an ostensibly feminine, Continental "other," see Linda Colley, *Britons: Forging the Nation,*

1707–1837, rev. ed. (New Haven: Yale University Press, 2014), and Michèle Cohen, *Fashioning Masculinity: National Identity and Language in the Eighteenth Century* (New York: Routledge, 1996).

8. Extensive scholarship on castrati has illuminated the significance of these celebrity figures to developing conceptions of gender, sex, and sexuality in the early modern period. See esp. Roger Freitas, "The Eroticism of Emasculation: Confronting the Baroque Body of the Castrato," *The Journal of Musicology* 20, no. 2 (April 2003): 196–249; Wendy Heller, "Varieties of Masculinity: Trajectories of the Castrato from the Seventeenth Century," *Journal for Eighteenth-Century Studies* 28, no. 3 (2005): 307–21; Thomas A. King, "The Castrato's Castration," *Studies in English Literature, 1500–1900* 46, no. 3 (July 2006): 563–83; and Martha Feldman, *The Castrato: Reflections on Natures and Kinds* (Oakland: University of California Press, 2015).

9. For a brief historical summary of the association of music with effeminacy in England, stretching into the nineteenth century, see Gillen D'Arcy Wood, *Romanticism and Music Culture in Britain, 1770–1840: Virtue and Virtuosity* (Cambridge: Cambridge University Press, 2010), 94–97. On connections between eighteenth-century Italian opera, effeminacy, and luxury, see Suzanne Aspden, "'An Infinity of Factions': Opera in Eighteenth-Century Britain and the Undoing of Society," *Cambridge Opera Journal* 9, no. 1 (1997): 1–19. Michael Burden discusses the links between discourses of effeminacy and luxury within English opera criticism in "Opera, Excess, and the Discourse of Luxury in Eighteenth-Century England," *XVII–XVIII: Revue de la Société d'études anglo-américaines des XVIIe et XVIIIe siècles* 71 (2014): 232–48.

10. Thomas McGeary, in a compelling explanation that harmonizes with my own, proposes that the English characterization of Italian opera as effeminizing was related to a roughly contemporaneous recognition of homosexuality as a distinct sexual orientation, as distinguished from seventeenth-century conceptions of sodomy and effeminacy, neither of which necessarily connoted exclusive sexual preference of men for other men. Thomas McGeary, "Gendering Opera: Italian Opera as the Feminine Other in Britain, 1700–1742," *Journal of Musicological Research* 14, no. 1 (1994): 17–34. McGeary's article draws on Thomas Laqueur's *Making Sex: Body and Gender from the Greeks to Freud* (Cambridge: Harvard University Press, 1990). On changing conceptions of masculinity, effeminacy, and sexuality in late seventeenth- and eighteenth-century England, see also Randolph Trumbach, "Sex, Gender, and Sexual Identity in Modern Culture: Male Sodomy and Female Prostitution in Enlightenment London," *Journal of the History of Sexuality* 2, no. 2 (1991): 186–203; Cohen, *Fashioning Masculinity*; Philip Carter, "Men about Town: Representations of Foppery and Masculinity in Early Eighteenth-Century Urban Society," in *Gender in Eighteenth-Century England: Roles, Representations and Responsibilities*, ed. Hannah Baker and Elaine Chalus (New York: Routledge, 1997), 31–57; Philip Carter, "An 'Effeminate' or 'Efficient' Nation? Masculinity and Eighteenth-Century Social Documentary," *Textual Practice* 11 (1997): 429–43; Tim Hitchcock and Michèle Cohen, eds., *English Masculinities: 1660–1800* (New York: Routledge, 1999); Philip Carter, *Men and the Emergence of Polite Society, Britain 1660–1800* (New York: Routledge, 2014); E. J. Clery, *The Feminization Debate in Eighteenth-Century England: Literature, Commerce and Luxury* (New York: Palgrave Macmillan, 2004); and Karen Harvey, "The History of Masculinity, circa 1650–1800," *Journal of British Studies* 44, no. 2 (2005): 296–311.

11.   Early eighteenth-century discourse linking Italian opera to effeminacy should also be understood in the context of a longstanding association of music with the feminine in early modern England. See Linda Phyllis Austern, "'Alluring the Auditorie to Effeminacie': Music and the Idea of the Feminine in Early Modern England," *Music & Letters* 74, no. 3 (1993): 343–54.

12.   On party-political debates over war policy in the War of the Spanish Succession, see Steve Pincus, "Addison's Empire: Whig Conceptions of Empire in the Early Eighteenth Century," *Parliamentary History* 31, no. 1 (2012): 99–117; and Geoffrey Holmes, *British Politics in the Age of Anne*, rev. ed. (London: Hambledon, 1987).

13.   John Brewer, *Sinews of Power: War, Money and the English State, 1688–1783* (Cambridge: Harvard University Press, 1988), 30.

14.   John Dennis offers an especially vigorous articulation of this argument in *An Essay upon Publick Spirit* (London: Bernard Lintott, 1711).

15.   It should be noted that the earliest of these "Italian" operas encompassed a wide range of forms: some were *pasticcios*; some, like *Arsinoe*, were written in an Italian style by English composers; and some were performed in English or a mixture of English and Italian to accommodate both English and Italian singers. For the fluidity of musico-dramatic musical entertainments in the first decade of the eighteenth century, see Curtis Price, "The Critical Decade for English Music Drama, 1700–1710," *Harvard Library Bulletin* 26 (1978): 38–76; and Robert Hume, "Opera in London, 1695–1706," in *British Theatre and the Other Arts, 1660–1800*, ed. Shirley Strum Kenny (Washington: Folger Shakespeare Library, 1984), 67–91. See also Amy Dunagin, "Secularization, National Identity, and the Baroque: Italian Music in England, 1660–1711" (PhD diss., Yale University, 2014), 181–237.

16.   As Rachel Weil has shown, rhetoric equating isolationism with effeminacy had also featured in debates over the Nine Years' War. Rachel Weil, *Political Passions: Gender, the Family and Political Argument in England, 1680–1714* (Manchester: Manchester University Press, 1999), 110.

17.   To ensure a Protestant succession after the death of Queen Anne, who had no surviving children, Parliament passed the Act of Settlement in 1701, which barred any Roman Catholic from the throne and fixed the succession on the Protestant Sophia of Hanover and her heirs. Because Sophia died shortly before Anne in 1714, her son George acceded as King George I. His son is the "young Hanover" mentioned in the poem.

18.   William Congreve, "Jack Frenchman's Defeat," in de Forest Lord, *Anthology of Poems on Affairs of State*, 703–704.

19.   *The Present Succession of Spain Consider'd* (London: A. Baldwin, 1701), 12.

20.   *Treason Unmask'd: or, the Queen's Title, the Revolution, and the Hanover Succession* (London: n.p., 1713), 277.

21.   James Whiston, *England's State-Distempers* (London: John Nutt, 1704), 17.

22.   William Coward, *Licentia Poetica Discuss'd* (London: William Carter, 1709), 102.

23.   Numerous English commentators drew parallels between Britain and the Roman empire, with particular emphasis on learning from Rome's example by avoiding the pitfalls of powerful, expanding empires that were perceived to have led to Rome's decline. Chief among these was consumption of "Asiatic luxury." On the Roman analogy as it was applied to discussions of imperial decline in Britain, see Krishan Kumar, "Greece and

Rome in the British Empire: Contrasting Role Models," *Journal of British Studies* 51, no. 1 (2012): 76–101. On the Roman analogy in opera criticism and satire, see Burden, "Opera, Excess, and the Discourse of Luxury," 243–45.

24.   George Ridpath, *The Stage Condemn'd*, 2ⁿᵈ ed. (London: B. Bragg, 1706), 56.

25.   Arthur Bedford, *The Great Abuse of Musick* (London: John Wyatt, 1711), 48, 47.

26.   Charles Montagu, 1ˢᵗ Earl of Halifax, "On Orpheus and Signora Margarita," 1703, British Library, Add. MS 40060, f. 30r. Printed in Sir John Hawkins, *A General History of the Science and Practice of Musick*, vol. 5 (London: T. Payne and Son, 1776), 154–55. On l'Epine's identification with the Tory party, see Olive Baldwin and Thelma Wilson, "The Harmonious Unfortunate: New Light on Catherine Tofts," *Cambridge Opera Journal* 22, no. 2 (2010): 217–34; and Alison DeSimone, "'Equally Charming, Equally Too Great': Female Rivalry, Politics, and Opera in Early Eighteenth-Century London," *Early Modern Women: An Interdisciplinary Journal* 12, no. 1 (2017): 73–101.

27.   *The Cares of Love* (London: W. Davis, 1705), epilogue.

28.   Arthur Maynwaring, "Epilogue, Address'd to the officers bound for Flanders," 1705, British Library, Add. MS 61462, f. 1r.

29.   Arthur Maynwaring, prologue to *The Cuckold in Conceit*, 1707, British Library, Add. MS 61462, f. 5r.

30.   English audiences' association of Italian opera with effeminacy was surely also informed by Italian and French critiques of opera along these lines, some of which would have been familiar to elite English operagoers. Wendy Heller, for example, notes that "associations between singing and effeminacy" had become "a crucial issue for critics of opera in the early 18ᵗʰ century," in "Reforming Achilles: Gender, 'opera seria' and the Rhetoric of the Enlightened Hero," *Early Music* 26, no. 4 (1998): 567. See also Georgia Cowart, *The Origins of Modern Musical Criticism: Quarrels over French and Italian Music, 1600–1750* (Ann Arbor: UMI Research Press, 1981); Charles Dill, *Monstrous Opera: Rameau and the Tragic Tradition* (Princeton: Princeton University Press, 1998); and Downing A. Thomas, *Aesthetics of Opera in the Ancien Régime, 1647–1785* (Cambridge: Cambridge University Press, 2002).

31.   This is not the prologue printed in the libretto; it was written after the libretto's publication in response to new victories.

32.   Prologue to *Camilla*, 23 May 1706, BL Add. MS 61360, f. 6r.

33.   On factional divides within the Whig party during the War of the Spanish Succession, see Holmes, *British Politics*, 217–46.

34.   Paul Monod has suggested that the early debate over Italian opera was largely internal to the Whig party, and subscribers' lists indicate that opera patronage was bipartisan but more pronounced among Whigs than Tories. Paul Monod, "The Politics of Handel's Early London Operas, 1711–1718," *Journal of Interdisciplinary History* 36, no. 3 (2006): 448. A copy of the subscribers' agreement (Portland MS. PW2.571 at Nottingham University Library) for the Haymarket Theatre, built for the performance of operas, contains the names of twenty-nine subscribers. Judith Milhous describes its contents in "New Light on Vanbrugh's Haymarket Theatre Project," *Theatre Survey* 17 (1976): 150–59. On the financial aspects of Italian opera in early eighteenth-century England, see Curtis A. Price, "The Critical Decade for English Music Drama"; and Robert D. Hume, "The Sponsorship of Opera in London, 1704–1720," *Modern Philology* 85,

no. 4 (1988): 420–32. On the makeup of its audience, see David Hunter, "Patronizing Handel, Inventing Audiences: The Intersections of Class, Money, Music and History," *Early Music* 28, no. 1 (2000): 33–49.

35.   On the Whig Schism that inaugurated the ideological divide between Patriot and Establishment factions, see W. A. Speck, "The Whig Schism Under George I," *Huntington Library Quarterly* 40, no. 2 (1977): 171–79; and Amy Watson, "Patriot Empire: The Rise of Party Politics in the British Atlantic, 1716–1748" (PhD diss., Yale University, 2018), 29–41. On Whig factionalism in this period, see Nicholas Rogers, *Whigs and Cities: Popular Politics in the Age of Walpole and Pitt* (Oxford: Oxford University Press, 1989). On the cultural dimensions of the Patriot movement, see Christine Gerrard, *The Patriot Opposition to Walpole: Politics, Poetry, and National Myth, 1725–1742* (Oxford: Clarendon Press, 1994).

36.   Thomas McGeary observes that "throughout opposition polemic, Italian opera is singled out as symptom and agent of the corruption of morals and taste spawned by Walpole's ministry." Thomas McGeary, *The Politics of Opera in Handel's Britain* (Cambridge: Cambridge University Press, 2013), 97. Such arguments linking the government to corruption and luxury featured prominently in Opposition attacks leveled at the Walpolean regime by both Patriot Whigs and Tories. See also Gerrard, *Patriot Opposition*. On Opposition newspapers targeting the Walpole regime, see Isaac Kramnick, *Bolingbroke and His Circle: The Politics of Nostalgia in the Age of Walpole* (Ithaca: Cornell University Press, 1968), 17–38.

37.   *Craftsman*, no. 28 (10–13 March 1727). The author was Viscount Bolingbroke; for analysis of this letter see McGeary, *Politics of Opera*, 107.

38.   [Jonathan Swift], *The Intelligencer*, no. 3 (1728).

39.   John Dennis, *Liberty Asserted* (London: George Strahan, 1704), prologue.

40.   Dennis, *Liberty Asserted*, prologue.

41.   Dennis, *Essay upon the Opera's*, preface, 1, 2.

From Royalty to Riots: Nation and Class in the Reception of French Musical Theater in London

ERICA LEVENSON

Of the many foreigners to thrive on the early eighteenth-century London stage, George Frideric Handel has most consistently garnered the attention of scholars.[1] Yet alongside Handel's now canonic *opere serie*, more ephemeral, light-hearted entertainments flourished in the margins of high culture. When French acting troupes from Paris arrived in London in 1718, they quickly became showstoppers. Their repertoire had been shaped predominantly in Paris's fairground theaters, but also in the city's official theatrical institutions—the Comédie-Italienne and the Comédie-Française. Their performances blended music with dance and acrobatics with spoken comedy and often revolved around the stock characters from *commedia dell'arte*. Over the next two decades, French acting troupes, consisting of up to seventy members, performed nearly two hundred distinct musical comedies in London.[2] While French dancers and *commedia dell'arte* actors had been employed on London stages for afterpieces in decades prior, the troupes that performed between 1718 and 1738 became more than add-ons to the main theatrical attraction and could command the stage for an entire evening.[3] Offering an average of four different programs of theatrical entertainments per week, theirs was a fast-changing, ephemeral repertoire that was performed entirely in French. The troupes did not regularly perform

141

at the London equivalent of the Paris fair theaters, but rather at the official theaters used for serious dramas and operas, including Lincoln's Inn Fields and the King's Theatre. As a result, the royal family and London's aristocratic elite were often in attendance at their performances.

Given Britain's ongoing tense political relationship with France throughout the eighteenth century, one might assume that Londoners' predominant attitude towards the French performers was one of antagonism, especially since Britain and France had recently emerged from a twenty-five-year period of war.[4] However, the troupes' reception in London was not so clear-cut. It is true that they were condemned, belittled, and often parodied by many members of the "middling sort," a wide-ranging group that included "yeomen, financially independent trades, and knowledge-based professions."[5] However, the French performers found great appeal among London's elite and even gained patronage from the British royalty. Their twenty years of successful trips to London were in large part due to this royal support.

This article examines the reactions to the French troupes within the context of the rapid social changes of early eighteenth-century England. Chief among these transformations was a growing concern with social hierarchy, which developed during the 1720s and 30s in response to an increasingly unified ruling elite and the growth of the middling orders.[6] These changes eventually led to a heightened awareness of "social class" as a principle for describing the hierarchical nature of British society.[7] Although England had long been divided along lines of rank and aristocratic privilege, many eighteenth-century commentators began to see "class" as something that could be gained or lost; it thus could be performed, emulated, or even bought, resulting in new anxieties surrounding status.[8]

In response to these changing social norms, French musical comedies were interpreted as both high- and low-style entertainment once they were imported to England, depending largely on who was watching. For elites, attendance at the French plays could signal prestige and demonstrate their nuanced grasp of foreign culture. But among the middling orders the craze for French theater was indicative of widespread trends for consuming foreign luxuries that they believed would destabilize native English culture. Thanks to this divergent reception across social strata, the French performances became divorced from their earlier position at the lower end of the hierarchy of Parisian theatrical institutions.[9] Through this process of reinterpretation, the French performances helped to enact a mutable sense of class identity in ways that both negated and reinforced ideas of what France could represent in the transnational imagination.

The Royal Treatment

The widespread success of the French performers in the years 1718–38 depended, at least in part, on the support of the royalty and aristocracy. Although surviving first-hand accounts of the French plays from the perspective of the British royalty are few, evidence found in theatrical advertisements reveals that the nobility regularly attended, and even requested (or "commanded") the French performances, prolonging the London careers of the French troupes for multiple seasons.[10] Support began with the King himself, George I (1660–1727), who frequently attended the French plays and provided monetary gifts. At the first French play he attended on 26 November 1718 at Lincoln's Inn Fields, the King presented the troupe with 100 guineas for their performance of *Le Maître étourdi* and the afterpiece *Le Tombeau de maître André*.[11] He continued to request performances by the French troupes, with at least six French plays "by his Majesty's command" in their first London season alone.[12]

George I was not the first monarch with a penchant for French tastes; Charles II (1630–85) had employed French actors, composers, and musicians at his court during the Restoration. But while Charles II had brought French performers across the Channel in order to emulate the court of Louis XIV, the French troupes that arrived in London in 1718 became part of a competitive entertainment industry.[13] They arrived after a long period of war between England and France, when the flow of performing arts and cultural goods from across the Channel increased tenfold. For many among this new generation of London theatergoers, France represented the height of fashion, culture, and luxury; those who had the means of participating in French culture through travel, literature, language learning, or attending French plays could perform their social identity as part of a cosmopolitan elite.[14] The French troupes thus came to London at an opportune moment in the early eighteenth century, at a time when the consumption of French culture was viewed by some as a means of elevating one's social status.

Following their initial season at Lincoln's Inn Fields, the French performers were immediately employed at one of London's most illustrious theaters—the King's Theatre. They produced numerous plays there from 12 February to 19 March 1719 and, the following year, from 5 March to 21 June 1720.[15] In the 1719–20 season, the French actors shared the King's Theatre with Italian singers who had been hired for the Royal Academy of Music's subscription series of operas, many of them by Handel. Although scholars have often viewed this season as the foundation of Handel's fame in London and the showcasing of celebrity opera singers from Italy, it is less frequently noted that the same season also featured farcical French plays. In fact, raunchy musical comedies and high-style tragic operas were produced in alternation on the same stage, both of them appreciated by the same local audiences.[16]

Although tickets to the French plays cost half as much as a Handel opera, the French performers still attracted an elite demographic of theatergoers.[17] For example, the newspapers reported that "the King, the three young princesses, and a great number of nobility and gentry" attended the French company's debut at the King's Theatre.[18] With the regular attendance of the King at the French performances, the size of the audience would have also been quite robust; to catch a glimpse of the royal family was as exciting as the main theatrical attraction and helped perpetuate the feeling of social exclusivity at the theater.[19] On one occasion during the 1719–20 season, the French performers were in such high demand that they caused the delay of *Radamisto*, Handel's first opera for the Royal Academy of Music.[20] What premiered instead, "at the particular desire of several ladies of quality," was *La Fille capitaine*, by the French troupe, even though it had supposedly finished its season.[21] Such incidents reveal that the French troupe's popularity among this social group rivaled that of Italian operas. So great was the French performers' renown among the elites that for their third London season (1720–21), the nobility even financed a new theater—the Little Haymarket Theatre—expressly for their performances.[22]

Natural and Unnatural Taste

Beyond royal and aristocratic circles, the reception of French theater in London was less enthusiastic. The theaters were certainly open to members of the middling orders with sufficient disposable income to purchase a ticket. But critics profusely condemned the French plays in London's newspapers, spreading their antagonistic opinions to a wide readership.[23] In their writings, the critics frequently mocked the French performers' appearances and accents, criticized their plays for being too frivolous, and blamed them for stealing employment from well-deserving English actors.

Many commentators described French theater as the opposite of English theater, portraying English theater in terms of nature, sense, wit, and taste, while French theater was deemed unnatural, dim-witted, lewd, sensory, and ordinary. In some cases, this language was little more than prejudice, applied without concern for the actual performance. Such is the case in an anonymous letter to the editor of *The Weekly Journal; or, Saturday's Post* from 5 October 1717, a year before the French troupes actually arrived in London. Perhaps the author had seen the troupes perform in their native Paris, but more likely he was imagining what they would be like based on the French dancing and tumbling that could be seen at Lincoln's Inn Fields starting in 1714.[24] The author opens his letter by exclaiming "but now our nation is famous throughout the world for wit and sense, as well as for polite and solid learning; what will be said of us, if we prefer the French plays and actors to our own?" His pompous boasting continues: "Rome nor Athens never could boast a sett of actors so just to Nature, as at present adorn our English Theatres."[25]

In the next issue of *The Weekly Journal*, the same critic completes the other side of the dichotomy by painting French theater as unnatural. His critique takes the form of a mock "epilogue" wherein an imaginary French actor speaks in French-accented English:

> Sublime and swift Invention ve dispise,
> Dat is as coarse vid'us as to be vise ...
>
> Ve're all for sprightly Action and Grimace,
> And talk by shruggy Snear, Gesture of de Hand,
> Vat you, nor ve ourselves do understand ...
>
> Our Dancing too, such Vigour shews and Heat,
> Dat all believe our Brains lie in our Veet;
> Dis always de French Ladies does Command,
> Vor dis is all indeed they understand ...
>
> Our Singing likewise has most charming Note,
> It does so vinely rattle in de Troat ...
>
> Ve hope ye now be all convinc'd from hence,
> Ve're vers'd in ev'ry ting, but Vit and Sense."[26]

The critic's xenophobic commentary may have had a more locally aimed political message, however. Since *The Weekly Journal* was also one of the most popular opposition newspapers to King George I and his ministry, even a seemingly minor jab at the King's theatrical taste could have been a means of critiquing the King himself.[27] Regardless of whether the critic aimed at the King or the French, his portrayal of foreign theater as unnatural is here used symbolically to construct the image of a natural England untainted by foreign influence.

Nor did this type of criticism disappear after the French troupes arrived in London. Authors writing in *The Grub-Street Journal*, a publication that satirized the hack journalism of Grub Street, feared that the success of the French troupes pointed toward an erasure of English culture by foreign imports. One critic commented on the aspects of their performance of Molière's *L'Avare* (and the afterpiece *La Réunion des amours*) that he found unnatural, beginning with the appearance of the French actors: "What their natural faces were, I cannot tell: for they were so daubed with paint, that they seemed to act [in] masques." In addition to their gaudy makeup, the critic was equally struck by their incongruous costumes when the lover (who is supposed to be disguised as a servant) puts on a disguise more aristocratic than his master:

> I expected therefore to see this disguised lover make his appearance in a very shabby livery, or at least a very mean habit. Instead of which to my great surprize, he comes upon the stage with his hair finely curled, and powdered, a black bag, and solitair, a sword, red velvet coat, a brocaded waste-coat trimmed with gold fringe, &c. in short, so compleat a beau, that one would imagine he had thrown off the disguise of a domestic, and appeared in his proper person of a gentleman of family and fortune.[28]

Comedies about mistaken identities were rampant in England at the time, exploiting anxieties about the mutability of social class for humorous effect.[29] Here, however, the humor breaks down because of the differences between English and French perceptions of fashion: the ornate formality of French fashions made even those of the lower classes appear of higher class than their English equivalents.[30]

In addition, the declamatory acting style of the French performers translated poorly to English sensibilities:

> As this first scene is a conversation betwixt two young lovers, who had just given each other a promise of marriage; one would expect to hear and see the warmest and tenderest expressions of their mutual satisfaction, in their words and actions. Instead of which, we saw two persons standing the greatest part of this scene at a distance; looking now and then at one another, in as cold a manner as if they had been married seven years; and repeating alternately, not to each other, but to the spectators, the poet's fine speeches, in two different tones perpetually recurring, with very little action, and that very improper, and altogether unaffecting.[31]

The critic is here describing the declamatory style of acting from seventeenth-century France, which derived from ancient practices of oratory that required the actor to face the audience more than the other performers on stage.[32] He finds this style so unnatural that it appears a "comical sight," and he continually emphasizes the "impropriety and improbability" of the French actors' physical manifestations of emotions, such as love.[33]

The most unnatural element for many critics was the performance of plays entirely in French. This language barrier would not have been an obstacle for the royal family and most of the nobility, who spoke the *lingua franca* of the time; however, the general public possessed widely varying levels of French fluency.[34] Another critic in *The Grub-Street Journal* parodies the conglomeration of foreign languages spoken on London stages by introducing a five-step plan to create a mock entertainment titled, *The History of the Fall of the Tower of Babel.* The third step of this plan ridicules the use of inaccessible foreign languages in the theater: "3rdly, I shall perform in High Dutch, and this for these reasons: 1ˢᵗ, my actors speak no other; 2ndly, as the learned Goripius Becanus informs us, this was the original language, and therefore probably that which the builders of Babel spoke; and lastly, it will be in no danger of being understood by any of my audience."[35] The author's parody highlights what some feared and others thought a distinct benefit of foreign performances in London: varying levels of comprehension of foreign languages could serve to create a hierarchy among the social classes brought together to watch the performances. For many critics, French—long connected to social prestige—felt exclusionary, even though the French plays were as reliant on musical entertainment and visual spectacle as they were on verbal wit, and so could have been enjoyed by non-French speakers as well.

High and Low Taste

Other critics couched their concerns in the vague yet powerful language of "taste." Although taste had emerged as a topic of aesthetic theory in seventeenth-century France as part of the debate between the ancients and the moderns, in eighteenth-century Britain, it became a means of critiquing luxury in an increasingly commercial society.[36] In this context, one who had good taste avoided an overconsumption of luxury goods, which were seen as effeminate, elitist, and foreign (particularly French). This rhetoric was especially useful for critics, many from the middling orders, to critique the consumption habits of the elite and even those of their own ranks who aspired to enter the upper echelons of society.

In an age of increasing patriotism among the British middling orders, the rhetoric of taste helped to paint elites as un-British and overly obsessed with foreign goods.[37] As a critic wrote in *The Grub-Street Journal,*

> For sure 'tis impossible, that any *English-man* who has been transported with the passionately-expressive images of Shakespeare, or the melting softness of Otway, or has been delighted with the fine humour of Ben Johnson, the elegant thoughts and diction of Mr. Dryden, or the genteel wit of Mr. Congreve, could ever give immediate sanction to the low conceits

and groveling invention of Farce, either *French* or *English*; or to
the monkey tricks or grotesque postures of a Merry-Andrew, tho'
disguised under the name of *Monsieur* Francisque, or *Monsieur*
Lun senior or junior.[38]

This author here juxtaposes the low style of the French comedies with the
high style of famous British dramatists, perhaps hoping to undermine the
prestige that French culture enjoyed within elite circles. The unstated—and
likely unrealized—irony in this passage is that these British authors, among
many others, were avid borrowers of French theater.[39]

Similar criticism also appears in private conversations, such as a letter
written by the clergyman Thomas Rundle to a "Mrs. Sandys" on 24 March
1720. Having recently attended a French play in London, he relays his
opinions on what he witnessed: "Our playhouse is put under the greatest
discouragement that can possibly be, to encourage the facetious lewdness
of a company of *French* strolling mountebanks, who are in high reputation
at the theatre in the *Haymarket*, among all people who are above being
entertained by nature and art, or in other words, old Shakespeare at Drury-
lane."[40] In this sarcastic remark, Rundle casts the French entertainers, or
"mountebanks," as unduly popular, appealing to those without taste for
high art. That he compares Shakespeare to high art is unsurprising, since
the bard had already been canonized over the previous century.[41] Yet
Rundle also evokes the natural, which as we saw above, was code for art
that exemplified Britishness. Such commentary reveals how the rhetoric of
taste often amplified the rhetoric of naturalness, a combination that sought
to normalize and elevate British over French culture.

∽

The reception of French musical comedies in London across different
social strata reveals the complex realities into which French culture actually
arrived. When viewed through the lens of popular theatrical culture, this
world was more complicated than either accounts of Anglo-French political
antagonism or accounts of France's enlightening, civilizing influence have
acknowledged.[42] On the one hand, France did become wrapped up in the
image of an elite, cosmopolitan sensibility in London; but, on the other,
there were also many who railed against its claims to a civilizing progress.

In the end, however, it was the critics of the French performers who
prevailed. In 1738, the French performers attempted a new season at the
Little Haymarket Theatre, only to be "cat-called" off the stage.[43] The riot was
partially instigated because royal patronage supporting the French performers
allowed them to dodge the new rules introduced by the Licensing Act of

1737, which required all play scripts to be reviewed, prior to performance, by a government censor.[44] English playwrights and actors became enraged that the French could perform without being subject to the same regulations as the English. Incensed by the blatant privileging of the foreign over the domestic by the British government, London audiences rioted at the playhouse on the evening of the French troupe's first performance on 9 October 1738.

These riots soon came to be seen as a turning point in the history of French and English theatrical exchange. Twenty years after the fact, the theater impresario Benjamin Victor claimed he had witnessed the riot in 1738:

> Then [the French Actors] began the Serenade; not only Catcalls, but all the various portable Instruments, that could make a disagreeable Noise, were brought up on this Occasion, which were continually tuning in all Parts of the House; and as an Attempt to speaking was ridiculous, the Actors retired, and they opened with a grand Dance of twelve Men and twelve Women; but even that was prepared for, and they were directly saluted with a Bushel or two of Peas, which made their Capering very unsafe. After this they attempted to open the Comedy; but had the Actor the Voice of Thunder, it would have been lost in the confused Sounds from a thousand various instruments.[45]

The riots effectively halted the French troupe's performances at the Little Haymarket Theatre that season, and the War of the Austrian Succession (1740–48) soon precluded the possibility of further returns for the next decade. After the war, in 1749, another troupe of French performers, led by the director of the Opéra Comique in Paris, Jean Louis Monnet, attempted to perform in London. That season, too, was aborted by violent riots.[46] The London theaters had once been spaces where French and English plays alike had elicited laughter. But by mid-century, they became a battlefield where ideas at the intersection of class, taste, and national identity were fought through both verbal and physical violence.

Notes

I wish to thank Rebecca Harris-Warrick and J. Mackenzie Pierce for their detailed readings of this article at various stages. Special thanks are also due to Alison DeSimone and Amy Dunagin for organizing this cluster.

1. For a recent example, see Colin Timms and Bruce Wood, eds. *Music in the London Theatre from Purcell to Handel* (Cambridge: Cambridge University Press, 2017).

2. For a full listing of these performances, see Erica Levenson, "Traveling Tunes: French Comic Theater and Opera in London, 1714–1745" (Ph.D. diss., Cornell University, 2017), 175–239. See also *The London Stage, 1660–1800: A Calendar of Plays, Entertainments & Afterpieces,* vols. 2–3 (Carbondale: Southern Illinois University Press, 1960).

3. On French theatrical imports before 1718, see Jeremy Barlow and Berta Joncus, eds. *The Stage's Glory: John Rich, 1692–1761* (Newark: University of Delaware Press, 2011); Antoni Nicholas Zalewski Sadlak, "Harlequin Comes to England: The Early Evidence of the Commedia dell'arte in England and the Formulation of English Harlequinades and Pantomimes" (Ph.D. diss., Tufts University, 1999).

4. Linda Colley focuses predominantly on the antagonistic responses to French culture that created British national identity in *Britons: Forging the Nation, 1707–1837* (New Haven: Yale University Press, 1992).

5. On the definition of "middling sort," see H. R. French, "The Search for the 'Middle Sort of People' in England, 1600–1800," *Historical Journal* 43 (2000): 277–93.

6. Frank O'Gorman, *The Long Eighteenth Century: British Political and Social History, 1688–1832* (London: Bloomsbury, 2016), 107–20.

7. While "social class" is often considered anachronistic to early eighteenth-century Britain, I use it here to indicate a shift to a more fluid understanding of social identity, one that moved away from the idea of an inherited status that was fixed from birth.

8. P. J. Corfield, "Class by Name and Number in Eighteenth-Century Britain," *History* 72 (1987): 38–61; Lawrence Klein, "Politeness for Plebes: Consumption and Social Identity in Early Eighteenth-century England," *The Consumption of Culture, 1600–1800: Image, Object, Text* (New York: Routledge, 1995), 362–82.

9. This hierarchy in Paris was also becoming more fluid in the early eighteenth century, and social classes often mixed at the fair theaters. See Jeffrey Ravel, *The Contested Parterre: Public Theater and French Political Culture, 1680–1791* (Ithaca: Cornell University Press, 1999), 100–101; Georgia Cowart, *Watteau, Music, and Theater*, ed. Katharine Baetjer (New Haven: Yale University Press, 2009), 14.

10. Instead of the initially planned single season, the French performers returned for seven full seasons in London: 1718–19, 1719–20, 1720–21, 1721–22, 1724–25, 1725–26, and 1734–35. They usually arrived in London during the fall and departed in the spring.

11. *Original Weekly Journal*, 29 November 1718.

12. *The London Stage*, part 2, vol. 2, 513–32. It is probable that he commanded even more than six, just as he was thought to have commanded many more performances of Italian opera than were documented in *The London Stage*. See Donald Burrows and Robert Hume, "George I, the Haymarket Opera Company, and Handel's *Water Music*," *Early Music* 19 (1991): 324.

13. Andrew Walkling, *Masque and Opera in England, 1656–1688* (New York: Routledge, 2017), 264–90. On Charles II's failed emulation of Louis XIV, see Rebecca Herissone, "Playford, Purcell, and the Functions of Music Publishing in Restoration England," *Journal of the American Musicological Society* 63 (2010): 243–89.

14. Jeremy Black, *A Subject for Taste: Culture in Eighteenth-Century England* (New York: Palgrave Macmillan, 2005), 211–15.

15. Levenson, "Traveling Tunes," 180–90.

16. *The London Stage*, part 2, vol. 2, 575–87.

17. At the King's Theatre, the French plays cost 5 shillings for pit and boxes, 7s 6d for stage boxes, and 2s for the gallery. These tickets could also be bought by subscription. The only difference in the price to attend the French plays at Lincoln's Inn Fields the previous season was 3s (instead of 5s) for the pit and boxes. See *The London Stage*, part 2, vol. 2, 513, 527.

18. *The London Stage*, part 2, vol. 2, 527.

19. Judith Milhous and Robert Hume, "Heidegger and the Management of the Haymarket Opera, 1713–1717," *Early Music* 27 (1999): 80.

20. J. Merrill Knapp, "Handel, the Royal Academy of Music, and its First Opera Season in London (1720)," *The Musical Quarterly* 45 (1959): 154.

21. *The London Stage*, part 2, vol. 2, 578.

22. William Burling, *Summer Theatre in London, 1661–1820, and the Rise of the Haymarket Theatre* (Madison: Fairleigh Dickinson University Press, 2000), 79. The French troupes had exclusive use of this theater for the following two seasons and continued to perform there for the remainder of their London visits.

23. Periodicals, including *The Grub-Street Journal*, *The Weekly Journal, or Saturday's Post*, and *The Prompter*, provide the main source of surviving first-hand accounts of French performers and plays in London from the years 1718 to 1738.

24. Moira Goff, "John Rich, French Dancing, and English Pantomimes," *The Stage's Glory*, 85–98.

25. *The Weekly Journal; or, Saturday's Post*, 5 October 1717, issue 43.

26. The full epilogue is printed in *The Weekly Journal; or, Saturday's Post*, 12 October 1717, issue 44. A mock prologue is included in the previous issue (5 October 1717).

27. "The Weekly Journal or Saturday's Post," *17th-18th century Burney Newspapers Collection*.

28. Patriophilus, *The Grub-Street Journal*, 7 November 1734, issue 254.

29. Black, *A Subject for Taste*, 112–13.

30. Madeleine Delpierre, *Dress in France in the Eighteenth Century*, trans. Caroline Beamish (New Haven: Yale University Press, 1997), 58–60, 105.

31. Patriophilus, *Grub-Street Journal*.

32. On seventeenth-century French acting styles, see Sabine Chaouche, *L'Art du comédien: déclamation et jeu scénique en France à l'âge classique (1629–1680)* (Paris: Honoré Champion, 2001).

33. A more "naturalistic" acting style is usually attributed to the innovations of David Garrick, beginning in the 1740s. This reviewer's comment suggests that such a naturalistic acting style prevailed in London even before Garrick's rise to fame.

34. On the spectrum of foreign language competencies at this time, see John Gallagher, *Learning Languages in Early Modern England* (Oxford: Oxford University Press, 2019). On French as the *lingua franca*, see Marc Fumaroli, *When the World Spoke French*, trans. Richard Howard (New York: New York Review of Books, 2011).

35. Arlequin Chef d'oeuvre, *The Grub-Street Journal*, 20 February 1735, issue 269.

36. Georgia Cowart, *The Origins of Modern Musical Criticism: French and Italian Music, 1600–1750* (Ann Arbor: UMI Research Press, 1981), 35–39, 67; John Styles and Amanda Vickery, eds., *Gender, Taste, and Material Culture in Britain and North America, 1700–1830* (New Haven: Yale University Press, 2006), 14–16.

37. Christine Gerrard, *The Patriot Opposition to Walpole: Politics, Poetry, and National Myth, 1725–1742* (Oxford: Clarendon Press, 1994). There are parallels here with the debates that took place in France, especially in the musical criticism of Le Cerf and Raguenet. See Cowart, *The Origins of Modern Musical Criticism*, 67–85.

38. *The Grub-Street Journal*, 13 March 1735. Francisque Moylin was the leader of the French troupe that came to London in 1718 and again in 1735; *Monsieur Lun* refers to John Rich, manager of Lincoln's Inn Fields, who went by that stage name. Both actors played the role of Harlequin.

39. Thomas Otway, for one, adapted *Titus and Berenice* from Racine's *Bérénice* and *the Cheats of Scapin* from Molière's *Fourberies de Scapin*.

40. *Letters of the late Thomas Rundle, L.L.D., Lord Bishop of Derry in Ireland, to Mrs. Barbara Sandys*, with introduction by James Dallaway, 2 vols. (Gloucester: R. Raikes, 1789), 1:18–20.

41. Emma Depledge, *Shakespeare's Rise to Cultural Prominence: Politics, Print, and Alteration, 1642–1700* (Cambridge: Cambridge University Press, 2018); Michael Dobson, *The Making of the National Poet: Shakespeare, Adaptation, and Authorship, 1660–1769* (Oxford: Clarendon Press, 1992).

42. For recent challenges to the narrative of France's civilizing influence, see Rahul Markovits, *Civiliser l'Europe: politiques du théâtre français au XVIIIe siècle* (Paris: Fayard, 2014).

43. Most of the scholarship on the French theatrical presence in London revolves around this single incident. See, for example, Thomas Lockwood, "Cross-Channel Dramatics in the Little Haymarket Theatre Riot of 1738," *Studies in Eighteenth-Century Culture* 25 (1996): 63–74.

44. Cheryl Wanko, *Roles of Authority: Thespian Biography and Celebrity in Eighteenth-Century Britain* (Lubbock: Texas Tech University Press, 2003), 215.

45. Benjamin Victor, *History of the Theatres of London and Dublin* (London: Printed for T. Davies, 1761), 57–58.

46. *The Daily Advertiser,* 16 November 1749.

"African" Songs and Women's Abolitionism in the Home, 1787–1807

JULIA HAMILTON

During the first wave of antislavery activism in Britain—from about 1787 to 1807—the nation's musical marketplace saw a new trend for scores composed on the themes of West Indian slavery, the transatlantic slave trade, and African identity.[1] At least fifty of these scores were so-called "African" songs: that is, songs by white British composers and poets whose texts used first-person narration from the imagined point of view of an African.[2] These songs ranged in tone and subject matter from sentimental complaints about the slave trade to expressions of hospitality for white travelers in Africa to songs of cheerful slavery. Whether their texts advocated for the abolition, amelioration, or continuation of slavery, all of the songs promoted racialized thinking by producing and circulating stereotypes about Africans. Yet these problematic songs are important historical sources, particularly as they bring to light new musical performance contexts in which the debates over abolition played out.

Scholars have already begun to explore the relationship between music and popular abolitionism, studying the texts of antislavery ballads sung on the streets and so-called "Negro" songs performed on the stage.[3] Brycchan Carey's work on abolitionist ballads by William Cowper has pointed to another performance venue for "African" songs: the home.[4] Indeed, the format in which most "African" songs were published—short musical scores for voice with accompaniment by a keyboard instrument or harp—

was ideally suited for domestic consumption. Women in particular were encouraged to cultivate their keyboard, harp, and vocal skills, and their music collections were filled with such scores.[5] In fact, I have located personal copies of "African" songs and keyboard pieces on African themes that were originally owned by nineteen different British women. Eleven of these women owned at least one "African" song whose text contained explicitly antislavery rhetoric.[6] For instance, Lady Maria Beauclerk (ca. 1779–1822) transcribed into her manuscript copybook John Wall Callcott's "Forc'd from Home and all it's [sic] Pleasures" (ca. 1799), a new setting of Cowper's "The Negro's Complaint."[7] Lydia Hoare Acland (1786–1856) of Killerton House likewise owned two antislavery songs by William Carnaby: "The Negro Girl" (ca. 1801) and "Azid, or the Song of the Captive Negro" (ca. 1802)."[8] Mary Edmeades (1772–1840) of Owletts included Edward Miller's "The Negro Boy, Who was Sold by an African Prince, for a Metal Watch" (1792) and William Reeve's "The Desponding Negro" (ca. 1793) in a single binder's volume, which was later used by her two daughters.[9]

The existence of these scores in women's music collections is especially significant because we already know that British women actively supported abolition by writing antislavery literature, abstaining from slave-produced sugar, and wearing antislavery medallions.[10] The scores, therefore, introduce to scholarship a previously unknown group of women who opposed the slave trade and recast domestic music-making as a potentially abolitionist activity. With that said, the specifics of women's day-to-day musical practices are notoriously difficult to uncover. Amateur musicians rarely left written evidence of the music that they played on any given day, let alone descriptions of how the political message in a song's text affected their worldview. How then might we understand a musical score as evidence of antislavery activism?

This article thinks through what it might have meant for a contemporary British woman who opposed the slave trade to use the score of one abolitionist "African" song, William Howard's "The Negro's Lamentation" (1800), in her home.[11] I outline some of the musical activities that are likely to have been involved in the domestic consumption of this score: studying the meaning and sentiment of the song's text, singing the words of the first stanza to the tune, working to find suitable text-settings for later stanzas, and accompanying oneself while singing. Each of these activities, I argue, would have entailed spending time working through the lyrics. And since the song's text forces the reader to reflect on her complicity in Britain's involvement in slavery, practicing and performing this song in the home meant engaging with and perhaps even internalizing an antislavery argument.

In my attempt to imaginatively reconstruct this particular situation, I use singing treatises published in the period as evidence of advice that would have been available to female amateurs at the time—acknowledging, of course, that this advice would have been supplemented or perhaps contradicted by in-person music lessons. Inspired by the performance-based music analyses of Elisabeth Le Guin, Nicholas Cook, and Elizabeth Morgan, I also rely on my own experiences in working with the score for "The Negro's Lamentation."[12] I make a similar argument to the one Morgan makes in her article on "battle pieces" composed during the American Civil War: just as American women learned about important battles by playing piano music, British women learned about key anti-slave trade arguments by practicing "African" songs. Certainly, my own experiences singing and playing this song as a white American woman in 2021 differ greatly from those of a white British woman in 1800.[13] My discomfort with the song's text comes from its title, its appropriation of the voice of an enslaved African, and its positioning of the narrator as pitiable and in need of the reader's sympathy. Presumably, a woman in this period would have been most uncomfortable with the song's accusation that all Britons were complicit in the slave trade. Nevertheless, my experience playing the music was central to my understanding of the score as an object of domestic consumption.

Before turning to the score, it will be useful to provide some context for the abolitionist argument made by the song's text. A number of scholars have shown that abolitionists cast Britain's involvement in the slave trade as a "national sin," complicating the British public's belief that they were citizens of a nation that upheld Protestant Christian moral values and possessed a supposedly unique affinity for liberty.[14] Two examples from private writings illustrate the effect that this rhetoric had on the lives of contemporary Britons. The first comes from the diary of Hannah Lightbody (later Hannah Greg, 1766–1828), a Unitarian resident of Liverpool who maintained close relationships with proslavery and antislavery advocates alike. Lightbody's diary records a sermon the Reverend John Yates preached against the slave trade in Liverpool on 28 January 1788, in which he emphasized the discrepancy between his parishioners' status as the nation's most prolific slave-traders and their profession of Christianity: "What opinion were the poor victims of our Avarice to form of that Religion whose votaries practiced such inhumanity?—how would they abhor a system which they would suppose from the conduct of its professors gave a sanction to Cruelty. ... he was unhappy to say that 2/3rds of the Slave trade carried on by Britons was by his Townsmen."[15] Lightbody notes that following his explicitly anti-slave trade sermon in the morning, Yates preached on "the duty of Self Examination" that same afternoon.[16] She seems to have taken Yates's words to heart, for her diary mentions several discussions about the slave trade that she had with abolitionist friends in the months following the sermon. For example, two nights after she heard the sermon, she "lay awake endeavouring to recollect the Negro's Complaint," an antislavery poem written by her abolitionist friends James Currie and William Roscoe.[17] Of course, Lightbody's connections to slavery through her brother-in-law and family friends necessarily made self-examination on the topic of slavery personal.[18] But even for Britons with no personal connections to slavery, the nation's contradictory promotion of both liberty and slavery, honor and cruelty, prompted feelings of collective guilt. Regarding Britain's slow response to evidence of the slave trade's inhumane practices, the poet William Cowper wrote: "It had been less dishonourable for England never to have stirred in it, than after having done so, to fall asleep again. Till now, we were chargeable perhaps only with Inattention, but hereafter, if the poor creatures be not effectually redressed, and all buying and selling of them prohibited for ever, we cannot be wrong'd by the most opprobrious appellations. Call us, who will, deliberately cruel and Tyrants upon principle, we are guilty and must acknowledge it."[19] Though he had no immediate connections to the British slave trade, Cowper took the issue personally, including himself among the guilty by virtue of his nationality.

With this context in mind, let us turn to the score of William Howard's "The Negro's Lamentation" (see fig. 1). The song was printed in 1800 as a two-page score in an upright format, with the parts for voice and accompaniment printed on two staves. As was typical for strophic songs, in which each stanza of text was sung to the same tune, only the first stanza is notated musically. The rest of the stanzas are printed without music at the end of the score. At the bottom of the second page, the melody is printed for German Flute. The copy I consulted at Yale University's Beinecke Rare Book and Manuscript Library contains no indications of its original owner. Still, its musical and textual contents, coupled with its piano-vocal format, place it firmly within the female-dominated context of domestic music-making.[20]

Singing treatises provided differing advice on how exactly one should approach practicing a song like this for the first time, but as Robert Toft has convincingly shown, most treatises instructed singers to begin by studying and "recit[ing] their texts as spoken dramatic readings."[21] For example, in 1771, Anselm Bayly suggested that singers should "first study the sentiment of recitatives and airs, how to speak the words, and you will seldom fail in singing the notes."[22] In his *Introduction to the Art of Sol-Fa-Ing and Singing* (ca. 1807), Jean Jousse gave clearer directions for learning "how to speak the words," telling singers to "read several times over the words of the Piece which you are to sing, observe the punctuation where the emphasis

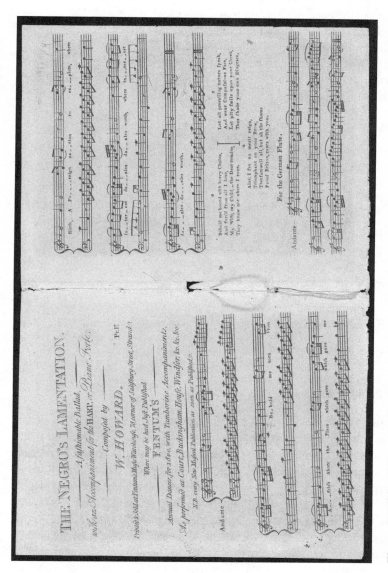

Figure 1. William Howard, "The Negro's Lamentation. A fashionable Ballad, with an Accompaniment for the Harp, or, Piano-Forte, Composed by W. Howard" (London: Fentum's Music Warehouse, 1800). Beinecke Rare Book and Manuscript Library, Yale University, JWJ-V4 H833 N32.

lies, ponder the sense, try to make your own the sentiments express'd by the Notes."[23] William Kitchiner spent much of his 1821 treatise discussing this question of "where the emphasis lies," expounding upon the necessity of studying both "accent" and "emphasis" in the poetic text.[24] By "accent" and "emphasis," he meant that singers should recognize the meter of the poem and identify important words in each line.

If a consumer of William Howard's "The Negro's Lamentation" received this standard advice to "study," "speak," "read over," observe," and "ponder" the words before singing, she would have begun her study of this song by reading the following words aloud:

> Behold me torn from Afric's shore
> The place which gave me birth,
> A foreign nation to explore
> Where interest dazzles worth.
>
> Behold me bound with heavy Chains,
> And forc'd from all I love,
> My wife, my child, _ the Dear remains,
> They know not where I rove.
>
> Let all prevailing nature speak,
> And wear Compassions Face,
> Let pity smile upon your Cheek,
> Thus shade your own Disgrace.
>
> Alas! I see no merit reign,
> Triumphant on your Brow,
> Then farewell all, but ah the shame
> Proud Briton, rests with you.

On this first reading, she might have observed the formal qualities of the poem, reading for accent, emphasis, and punctuation. Reading aloud, she would have heard the poem's use of common meter—that is, the alternation between eight-syllable lines in iambic tetrameter and six-syllable lines in iambic trimeter. Knowing this, she would have needed to consider which words ought to be emphasized in each line. For example, when speaking aloud the third line of the first stanza ("A foreign nation to explore"), she would have ideally emphasized the words "foreign," "nation," and "explore," rather than the word "to," despite the fact that the word "to" is technically a stressed syllable in this line of iambic tetrameter. In terms of punctuation, carefully attending to exceptions to the fairly regular use of commas and periods at the end of the lines could have helped her to understand the text's emphasis and sentiment as well. For instance, the exclamation point after "Alas!" in the first line of the fourth stanza ("Alas! I see no merit reign,") might have led her to emphasize this word when reciting the text. Additionally, she might have read the underscore in the third line of the second stanza ("My wife, my child, _ the Dear remains,") as a choked-up pause or sentimental sigh. As literary scholars have long pointed out, authors of sentimental literature creatively used punctuation marks such as dashes to convey emotionally charged sighs, gasps, and pauses that could not be described in words.[25]

Reading the text "several times over," this female consumer of "The Negro's Lamentation" would have had plenty of time to further "ponder the sense" and "study the sentiment" of its text.[26] In its use of first-person narration, the poem creates the same "oscillation between identification with the speaking 'I' of the slave and identification with the addressed white Briton" that Lynn Festa observes in William Cowper's more famous antislavery poem, "The Negro's Complaint."[27] The poem places the reader in an imaginary exchange of gazes between herself and the enslaved African narrator of the poem. In the first two stanzas, the narrator tells the reader to "behold" him, directing her to note that he has been "torn from Afric's shore" and that he is "bound in heavy chains." While the reader learns details about the cruel treatment the narrator has received at the hands of his enslavers—his forced separation from his homeland and family and the shackles he is made to wear on his body—the narrator does not directly name the sentiment he feels. The reader must therefore study the narrator's sentiment, pondering the use of the word "lamentation" in the song's title and attending to expressive punctuation marks.

If the first two stanzas leave the reader to piece together the sentiments of the narrator, the third and fourth stanzas make it very clear how the reader is supposed to feel. Here, the narrator returns the gaze of the reader. In the third stanza, he expresses his expectation that there will be visible proof of the reader's sentimental reaction on her face in the form of a blush on her cheek: "Let pity smile upon your Cheek / Thus shade your own Disgrace." In the final stanza, the narrator accuses the reader of not reacting with compassion, claiming that "your Brow" displays "no merit." The line "Then farewell all" at the end of the poem hints at the narrator's possible suicide—a common trope in antislavery poetry of the time. Nevertheless, the narrator's tone at the end of the poem has altered from the lamentation of the opening stanzas to a bold, perhaps indignant critique of the reader: "but ah the shame / Proud Briton, rests with you." If the reader's impulse is to distance herself from the poem's addressee, protesting that she did in fact blush or furrow her brow, these final lines force her to rethink her innocence. Drawing on the abolitionist portrayal of the slave trade as a national sin, the narrator calls the reader a "proud Briton" to remind her that by virtue of being British, she is guilty. So far, by reciting the poem several times, the singer would have contemplated the emotional and physical impact the slave trade made upon enslaved Africans, considered her own capacity to feel pity for the enslaved, and subjected her own British identity to potential critique. But singing a song, of course, did not stop with speaking the text. The next step in the domestic consumption of this score was to sing the melody.

Authors of singing treatises differed in their level of specificity about how a singer ought to approach a melody. On one end of the spectrum, Gesualdo Lanza advocated for a multi-step process that included speaking the names of the solfege syllables in rhythm, singing the melody using solfege syllables, and singing the poetic text to the melody.[28] Most, however, seemed to imply that a singer could use the song's text on her first attempt at singing the melody, as long as she had studied the text first. No matter how she initially approached learning the melody, she would have found herself singing a simple melody replete with sighing appoggiatura figures over an arpeggiated accompaniment (see fig. 2).[29] As one contemporary reviewer of "The Negro's Lamentation" put it, "the melody, though it exhibits no remarkable trait of novelty, is pleasingly expressive, and the *arpeggio* bass murmurs through the strain with an appropriate and interesting effect."[30]

Figure 2. Howard, "The Negro's Lamentation" (1800), measures 9–16.

The song's style would have been especially familiar to British operagoers, who frequently heard sentimental heroines sing similarly slow, tuneful arias in major keys that featured sighing appoggiaturas and uncomplicated accompaniments. In 1797, 1798, and 1800, for example, London audiences heard the sentimental heroine of Giovanni Paisiello's *Nina, o sia La pazza per amore* (1789) sing "Il mio ben quando verrà," an aria that features these same musical traits (see fig. 3).[31] In other words, Howard's setting of "The Negro's Lamentation" placed the plight of the enslaved African in the musical language of the virtuous heroine in distress. For a female amateur musician, this shared musical style may have helped her to connect her own experiences to the narrator's, or, as Jean Jousse put it, to "make [her] own the sentiments express'd by the Notes."[32] Making the leap between gendered oppression and race-based chattel slavery would likely have seemed natural to white British women in the period, many of whom metaphorically described their own "slavery" in their published abolitionist writings.[33]

Figure 3. Giovanni Paisiello, "Il mio ben quando verrà" from *Nina, o sia La pazza per amore* (1789), measures 9–16.

Having sung through the first stanza to this "pleasingly expressive" melody, the musician now needed to sing through the later stanzas of this strophic song to the same music. This was not as straightforward as it may seem; as William Kitchiner pointed out, "SECOND VERSES of Songs seldom fit the notes so well as those of the First Stanza."[34] Rhythms often needed to be changed in order to fit the number of words included in the lines of subsequent stanzas and to avoid stressing the incorrect syllables. Some composers and publishers acknowledged this by including notated rhythms and pitches in small type next to or above the words of later stanzas that fit awkwardly with the melody.[35] Others, including Howard, did not give any hints as to suitable text-settings of subsequent stanzas.

In my own experience singing the later stanzas of "The Negro's Lamentation," there were several lines that required me to pause and work out the best possible text-setting. For example, in the second line of the first stanza, Howard repeats the words "which gave" two times (see fig. 2, measures 13–16). When singing the corresponding line of the third stanza ("And wear Compassions [*sic*] Face"), I could not repeat the syllables that fell on the exact same part of the melody, as this would have meant repeating the first two syllables of the word "compassion." Instead, I chose between the two options presented in Figure 4.

Figure 4. Howard, "The Negro's Lamentation" (1800), stanza 3, line 2, measures 13–16. Options 1 and 2.

Throughout my trial-and-error phase, I found myself repeating crucial words in the poem, including ones that might have embarrassed a white Briton living in the time of slavery. This was the case in the final line of the fourth stanza. In the corresponding line of the first stanza, Howard expands the length of the word "interest" from the two syllables that would be used to speak the line in iambic trimeter ("Where in-terest daz-zles worth") to three equally stressed syllables ("in-ter-est") (see fig. 5).

Figure 5. Howard, "The Negro's Lamentation" (1800), stanza 1, line 4, measures 21–24.

This created a problem for me when setting the same music to the two-syllable word, "Briton," in the last line of the fourth stanza ("Proud Bri-ton rests with you"). When I went to practice this line, I found myself singing the words "Proud Briton" many times as I tried out possible settings. I first tried leaving out the pickup in an attempt to mimic the way Howard set each syllable of the word "in-ter-est" as a pair of slurred eighth notes (see fig. 6).

Proud Bri - ton_ rests____ with rests____ with you

Figure 6. Howard, "The Negro's Lamentation" (1800), stanza 4, line 4, measures 21–24. Option 1.

I then tried placing a four-note melisma on the second syllable of the word "Briton" (see fig. 7).

Proud Bri - ton_____ rests____ with rests____ with you,

Figure 7. Howard, "The Negro's Lamentation" (1800), stanza 4, line 4, measures 21–24. Option 2.

This altered the sense of the line's iambic trimeter, though, putting too great a stress on the second syllable of the word "Briton." Ultimately, I decided to place the melisma on the first syllable of that word (see fig. 8).

Proud Bri - ton_ rests____ with rests____ with you,

Figure 8. Howard, "The Negro's Lamentation" (1800), stanza 4, line 4, measures 21–24. Option 3.

My point here is not to exaggerate the difficulty of this piece, but to illuminate the ways that practicing a strophic abolitionist song might force an amateur to repeatedly sing words that would have forced her to confront her nation's (and therefore her own) tarnished reputation.

One final mode of consuming this song at home involved accompanying oneself at the keyboard or harp. Although authors of singing treatises typically focused on singing, rather than singing while playing, they did occasionally allude to the practice of accompanying oneself. Gesualdo Lanza directed singers to "avoid accompanying yourself, if you can get a competent person to do it," while Domenico Corri reminded singer-accompanists that "if you do accompany yourself, remember that the voice is principal."[36] In any case, the novels of Jane Austen provide plenty of examples of this practice; Emma Woodhouse and Jane Fairfax of *Emma* and Marianne Dashwood of *Sense and Sensibility* all sing songs while accompanying themselves at a keyboard instrument.[37] I do not play the harp, so I could not test out the experience of consuming the score as a singer-harpist, but I did practice singing this song while playing the piano. Although the musical material was not complicated, I discovered that the layout of the score—with its placement of the texts of stanzas two through four at the end of the second page—increased the difficulty of singing and playing the later stanzas with fluency. I found myself glancing back and forth between the musical notation provided for the first stanza and the non-notated texts found on the second page. This involved some partial memorization, both of the keyboard part and the words of the later stanzas. It made me wonder: if the score's layout required me to memorize at least part of the sentimental music and accusatory text, how might this experience have affected someone like Hannah Lightbody, who felt herself to be guilty of the national sin? Perhaps after reciting the song's text, singing it to music, working out text-settings for later stanzas, and accompanying herself at the keyboard, she would lie awake at night "endeavouring to recollect" Howard's song.[38] Possibly, too, consuming the song in this manner would inspire her to further abolitionist activity.

While scholars of the British antislavery movement have brought to light the names and activities of many women who opposed the slave trade in the years between 1787 and 1807, the presence of "African" songs in the music collections of female amateur musicians from this period suggests that a great many more women promoted abolition with their singing voices, keyboard instruments, and harps. Following the advice provided in contemporary treatises on singing instruction, female amateurs recited, sang, and memorized antislavery poetry, which was often written from the perspective of an enslaved African. In this way, they gained intimate knowledge of abolitionist arguments, such as the assertion that the slave trade was Britain's national sin. Future studies might consider other modes of consuming antislavery songs, such as performing in and listening to private concerts, copying out scores by hand, or binding printed scores into a volume of favorite songs. We might also consider what it meant for women to consume "African" songs that did *not* contain explicitly antislavery messages and interrogate the ways that "African" songs perpetuated conceptions of whiteness even as they attempted to depict blackness. In all of these cases, "African" songs suggest new avenues for uncovering and describing the ways that women engaged with the political movement that was gripping the nation in the late eighteenth century.

Notes

1. These years were marked by widespread debate over the slave trade: the Society for Effecting the Abolition of the Slave Trade was established in 1787 and the Act for the Abolition of the Slave Trade was passed in 1807.

2. While the repertory I examine had no agreed-upon name in the period, I adapt a phrase in contemporary usage, "African songs," to refer to the group as a whole. I place this group of songs in conversation with a larger corpus of British music relating to slavery and African identity, including music by Black British composers, in my forthcoming "Political Songs in Polite Society: Singing about Africans in the Time of the British Abolition Movement," (PhD diss., Columbia University, 2021).

3. See, for example, Ivan Ortiz, "Lyric Possession in the Abolition Ballad," *Eighteenth-Century Studies* 51, no. 2 (2018): 197–218; Felicity Nussbaum, "'Mungo Here, Mungo There': Charles Dibdin and Racial Performance," in *Charles Dibdin and Late Georgian Culture*, ed. Oskar Cox Jensen, David Kennerley, and Ian Newman (Oxford: Oxford University Press, 2018), 23–42; and Roxann Wheeler, "Sounding Black-*ish*: West Indian Pidgin in London Performance and Print," *Eighteenth-Century Studies* 51, no. 1 (2017): 63–87. There is also a growing body of literature on the use of the profits derived from slave labor to fund various aspects of musical culture in the period. See David Hunter, "The Beckfords in England and Italy: A case study in the musical uses of the profits of slavery," *Early Music* 46 (2018): 285–98; Glenda Goodman, "Bound Together: The Intimacies of Music-Book Collecting in the Early American Republic," *Journal of the Royal Musical Association* 145 (2020): 1–35.

4. Brycchan Carey, *British Abolitionism and the Rhetoric of Sensibility: Writing, Sentiment, and Slavery, 1760–1807* (Basingstoke: Palgrave Macmillan, 2005), 100–101.

5. For women's musical collecting habits, see Jeanice Brooks, "Musical Monuments for the Country House: Music, Collection, and Display at Tatton Park," *Music & Letters* 91, no. 4 (2010): 513–35.

6. I made the case for women as the primary consumers of antislavery "African" songs in my paper, "Politics at the Piano: Women's Musical Abolitionism in the Home, ca. 1787–1807" (presented at the American Musicological Society meeting, Boston, Massachusetts, 1 November 2019).

7. The University of Chicago Library, Special Collections Research Center, obl M1 f. S17 v. 28.

8. Killerton, National Trust, Vocal Music (M5) 1 14 B. See Leena Rana, "Music and Elite Identity in the English Country House, c.1790–1840" (PhD diss., University of Southampton, 2012), 70–85.

9. Owletts, National Trust, inventory numbers NT 3194779.3 and NT 3194779.9.

10. Elizabeth J. Clapp and July Roy Jeffrey, eds., *Women, Dissent, and Anti-Slavery in Britain and America, 1790–1865* (Oxford: Oxford University Press, 2011); Charlotte Sussman, "Women and the Politics of Sugar, 1792," *Representations* 48 (1994): 48–69; Clare Midgley, *Women against Slavery: The British Campaigns, 1780–1870* (London: Routledge, 1992).

11.   My analysis of this score is indebted to recent studies of scores as physical objects. See Glenda Goodman, *Cultivated by Hand: Amateur Musicians in the Early American Republic* (Oxford: Oxford University Press, 2020); Jeanice Brooks, "Making Music," in *Jane Austen: Writer in the World*, ed. Kathryn Sutherland (Oxford: Bodleian Library, 2017), 36–55; James Davies, "Julia's Gift: The Social Life of Scores, *c.* 1830," *Journal of the Royal Musical Association* 131, no. 2 (2006): 287–309.

12.   Elisabeth Le Guin, *Boccherini's Body: An Essay in Carnal Musicology* (Berkeley: University of California Press, 2006); Nicholas Cook, *Beyond the Score: Music as Performance* (Oxford: Oxford University Press, 2013); Elizabeth Morgan, "War on the Home Front: Battle Pieces for the Piano from the American Civil War," *Journal of the Society for American Music* 9 (2015): 381–408.

13.   All the female owners of "African" songs I have been able to identify were white; future studies might fruitfully consider what the consumption of such scores would have meant for Black British women in the same period.

14.   See Katie Donington, Ryan Hanley, and Jessica Moody, introduction to *Britain's History and Memory of Transatlantic Slavery: Local Nuances of a "National Sin,"* ed. Katie Donington, Ryan Hanley, and Jessica Moody (Liverpool: Liverpool University Press, 2016), 1–20; Srividhya Swaminathan, *Debating the Slave Trade: Rhetoric of British National Identity, 1759–1815* (Farnham: Ashgate, 2009); Linda Colley, *Britons: Forging the Nation, 1707–1837*, rev. ed. (New Haven: Yale University Press, 2009), 357–68.

15.   David Sekers, ed., "The Diary of Hannah Lightbody, 1786–90," *Enlightenment and Dissent* 24 (2008): 58.

16.   Sekers, "The Diary of Hannah Lightbody," 58.

17.   Sekers, "The Diary of Hannah Lightbody," 59.

18.   Hannah Lightbody was connected to both the slave trade and plantation slavery. Her sister was married to Thomas Hodgson, who acted as an investor in slave trading voyages, an agent for a slave trader, and, at one point, an owner of a slave trading fort in his own right (see Sekers, "The Diary of Hannah Lightbody," 13–14). In addition, the year after she heard Yates's sermon, Lightbody married Samuel Greg, who was an heir to his uncle's slave plantation (see David Sekers, *A Lady of Cotton: Hannah Greg, Mistress of Quarry Bank Mill* [Stroud: The History Press, in association with the National Trust, 2013], 73). Sekers mentions a number of other people in Lightbody's circle who were connected in some way to the slave trade and/or slavery, but does not specify what the connections were (see Sekers, "The Diary of Hannah Lightbody," 14).

19.   Letter from Cowper to Lady Hesketh, 31 March 1788, in James King and Charles Ryskamp, eds., *The Letters and Prose Writings of William Cowper*, Vol. 3, Letters 1787–1791 (Oxford: Clarendon Press, 1982), 140.

20.   The foundational work on gender and domestic music making is Richard Leppert, *Music and Image: Domesticity, Ideology, and Socio-Cultural Formation in Eighteenth-Century England* (Cambridge: Cambridge University Press, 1988). However, more recent scholarship has challenged and nuanced various aspects of Leppert's work, especially his argument that domestic music-making effectively contained and oppressed women. See Elizabeth Morgan, "Pertinacious Industry: The Keyboard Etude and the Female Amateur in England, 1804–20," in *Crafting the Woman Professional in the Long Nineteenth*

Century: Artistry and Industry in Britain, ed. Kyriaki Hadjiafxendi and Patricia Zakresk (Farnham: Ashgate, 2013), 69–87; and Leslie Ritchie, *Women Writing Music in Late Eighteenth-Century England: Social Harmony in Literature and Performance* (Aldershot: Ashgate, 2008).

21. Robert Toft, *Heart to Heart: Expressive Singing in England, 1780–1830* (Oxford: Oxford University Press, 2000), 16.

22. Anselm Bayly, *A Practical Treatise on Singing and Playing with Just Expression and Real Elegance* (London: J. Ridley, 1771), 62.

23. Jean Jousse, *Introduction to the Art of Sol-fa-Ing and Singing* (London: Goulding & Co., [1807]), xi.

24. William Kitchiner, *Observations on Vocal Music* (London: Hurst, Robinson, and Co., 1821), 29–30.

25. Janet Todd, *Sensibility: An Introduction* (New York: Methuen, 1986), 5–6.

26. Jousse, *Introduction to the Art of Sol-fa-ing*, xi; Bayly, *Practical Treatise*, 62.

27. Lynn Festa, *Sentimental Figures of Empire in Eighteenth-Century Britain and France* (Baltimore: Johns Hopkins University Press, 2006), 164. On the dehumanizing implications of abolitionist empathy, see also Saidiya V. Hartman, *Scenes of Subjection: Terror, Slavery, and Self-Making in Nineteenth-Century America* (New York: Oxford University Press, 1997), 17-48.

28. Gesualdo Lanza, *Elements of Singing in the Italian & English Styles*, vol. 3 (London: Chappell, 1813), 43.

29. Treatises from this period use the word "appoggiatura" to indicate any non-chord tones notated with smaller type, regardless of whether they were approached or left by leap or step. That is, pitches we might mark as suspensions or retardations today were labeled as "appoggiatura" at the time. I follow contemporary usage here to describe the appoggiaturas in measures twelve and sixteen.

30. "'The Negro's Lamentation,' a Ballad, with an Accompaniment for the Harp, or Piano-Forte. Composed by W. Howard. 1s. Fentum," *The Monthly Magazine; or, British Register* 9 (June 1800): 480. The review was possibly by Thomas Busby, who is known to have contributed music reviews to *The Monthly Magazine*. See Carrol Grabo, "The Practical Aesthetics of Thomas Busby's Music Reviews," *The Journal of Aesthetics and Art Criticism* 25, no. 1 (1966): 37–45.

31. My transcription in Figure 3 is adapted from Example 6.6 in Stefano Castelvecchi, *Sentimental Opera: Questions of Genre in the Age of Bourgeois Drama* (Cambridge: Cambridge University Press, 2013), 176. See also Frederick C. Petty, *Italian Opera in London, 1760–1800* (Ann Arbor: UMI Research Press, 1972), 311–30. For a contemporary London score, see Giovanni Paisiello, "Il mio ben. A favorite song, sung by Madm. Banti" (London: Longman and Broderip, ca. 1795).

32. Jousse, *Introduction to the Art of Sol-fa-Ing,* xi.

33. The tradition of connecting white women's experiences to Black slavery was long-lasting and pernicious. See Moira Ferguson, *Subject to Others: British Women Writers and Colonial Slavery, 1670–1834* (New York: Routledge, 1992), 176; Clare Midgley, "Anti-slavery and the roots of 'imperial feminism,'" in *Gender and Imperialism*, ed. Clare Midgley (Manchester: Manchester University Press, 1998), 161–79.

34. Kitchiner, *Observations on Vocal Music*, 66.

35. See, for example, the second stanza of Edward Miller, "The Negro Boy, who was sold by an African Prince for a Metal Watch, A Favorite Song Sung by Mr. Burrows, at the Public Concerts, Composed by Dr. Miller" (London: J. Dale, 1792).

36. Lanza, *Elements of Singing*, 170; Domenico Corri, *The Singers Preceptor or Corri's Treatise on Vocal Music* (London: Chappell, 1810), 72.

37. Jane Austen, *The Novels of Jane Austen, Vol. 4: Emma*, 3rd rev. ed. R. W. Chapman (Oxford: Oxford University Press, 2015), 227; Jane Austen, *The Novels of Jane Austen, Vol. 1: Sense and Sensibility,* 3rd rev. ed., ed. R. W. Chapman (Oxford: Oxford University Press, 2015), 35, 83.

38. Sekers, "The Diary of Hannah Lightbody," 59.

CONSUMPTION AND REMEDIATION

Cluster: Remediating Eighteenth-Century Texts

Manuscript Notations and Cultural Memory

MICHAEL EDSON

Historians using manuscript notes to reconstruct reading practices from the past have traditionally focused on single annotators with marginalia in many volumes. Think of William Sherman's work on John Dee, Lisa Jardine and Anthony Grafton's on Gabriel Harvey, or Heather Jackson's on Samuel Taylor Coleridge.[1] Such studies have advanced substantially our understandings of reading, and we would not wish them away. But they point to dissonant trends. Where literary studies continues to shun single authors (at least as the subjects for new monographs) and to question the privileging of an author's biography as the key to interpretation, studies of single annotators still dominate histories of reading. Known marginaliaists, often wealthy and male, disproportionately define the field. And while undertakings such as Book Traces (University of Virginia) and The Reading Experience Database (The Open University) have enlarged awareness of marginalia by readers about whom often little is known, both projects are, at least currently, too miscellaneous to permit comparisons across many annotated copies—comparisons promising broad insights into collective reading practices at certain times.[2]

In response to these patterns in print and digital scholarship, I would like to propose another method of doing the history of reading: comparing manuscript notations across many, if not all, surviving copies of single titles. This labor-intensive, comparative analysis has been done occasionally in the past, but largely, again, in terms of the intentions and biographies of authors and identifiable annotators.[3] By contrast, I will show what possibilities emerge through the study of marginal notes by large numbers of readers without traceable lives or intentions. To illustrate, I will analyze the handwritten notations by the mainly anonymous readers of the roughly ninety extant copies of Lady Anne Hamilton's 1807 satire, *The Epics of the Ton; Or, The Glories of the Great World: A Poem*. Leaving behind a larger-than-usual number of annotated copies, *Epics of the Ton* is a perfect subject for a comparative analysis of marginalia. Part of a larger project, the analysis to follow will raise questions that our current methods and priorities are unable to answer. My suggestions here model one possible approach beyond the single-annotator study, revealing manuscript notation to be a potentially rich source for studying cultural memory, which is to say, for studying what was foremost in the minds of readers at certain times and how it got there. This approach also requires that we see satire like Hamilton's as a kind of literacy game, with the goal being above all to assign names to the satiric targets. Unable to offer individualizing accounts for the names left by the many unknown readers of *Epics of the Ton*, scholars must seek out larger, social explanations for patterns in notation, including partisan identities and competing information sources.

Published anonymously, Hamilton's *Epics of the Ton* decries gambling and illicit sex in London high society. In part a defense of Caroline, Princess of Wales, for whom Hamilton (1766–1846) was for a time a lady in waiting, and in part a gossipy satire on philandering Regency elites, *Epics of the Ton* exploits the media-driven clamor for celebrity scandal in eighteenth- and early nineteenth-century England.[4] The division into two gendered sections, titled the Male Book and the Female Book, makes *Epics of the Ton* unique among satires. The work ridicules seventeen men and twenty-five women, mainly aristocrat-politicians and society hostesses, who are identified in the Table of Contents and the section headers only by initials: D— of B—, V— C—, etc. (fig. 1).[5] Additional blanks throughout the poem and its footnotes invite readers to put names to the textual clues, in effect doing the work Hamilton begs of her muse: "From next year's Lethe, and oblivion drear, / Come save the deeds" of the London beau monde.[6] Reacting to the poem's "lust [for] personal defamation," the poet Anna Seward wrote that she wished *Epics of the Ton* would suffer a "total famine of readers."[7] Yet feast, not famine, better describes the poem's brief, intense popularity, as it saw three editions, all in 1807, and perhaps would have enjoyed more had it not cost an expensive 7s. 6d. Excerpts were reprinted in papers as far

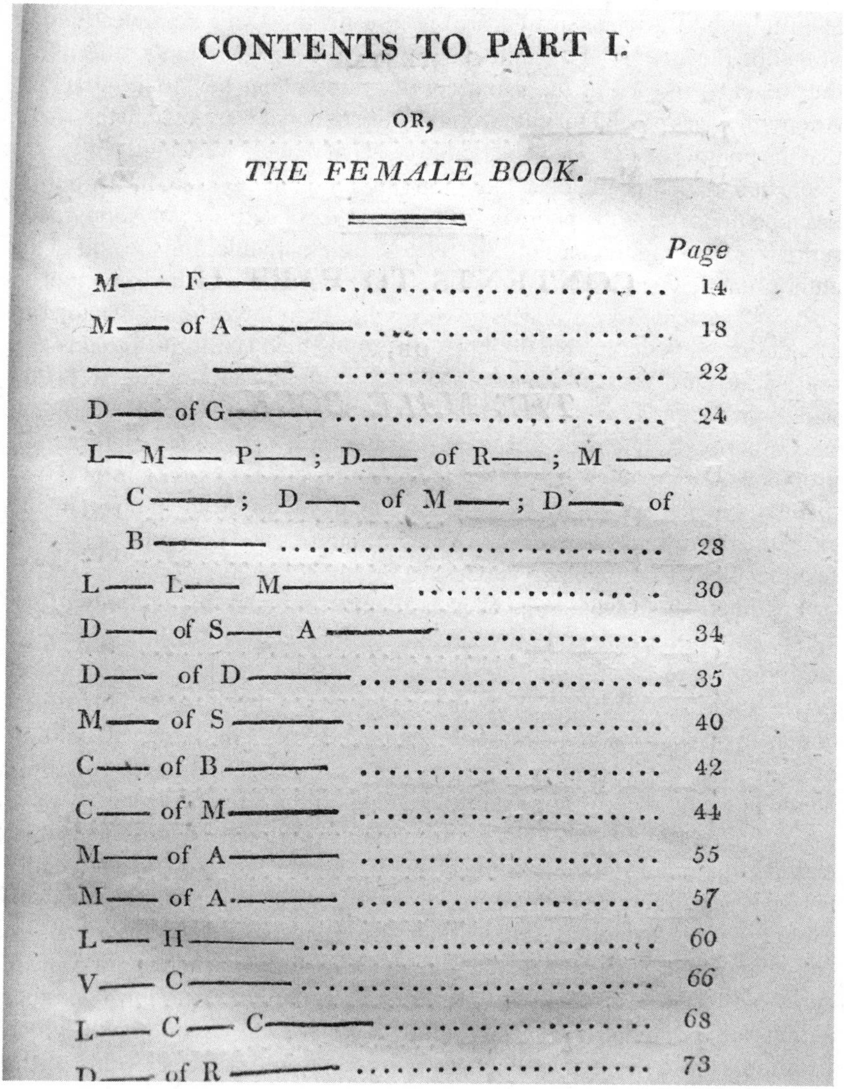

CONTENTS TO PART I.

OR,

THE FEMALE BOOK.

═══════

Figure 1. Table of Contents to *The Epics of the Ton*, 3rd ed. (1807). Author's copy.

away as Bombay (Mumbai). In later years, the title persisted as a popular byword for ugly gossip.[8]

Hamilton—a Scot, the daughter of Archibald Hamilton, 9th Duke of Hamilton, and a partisan of Caroline during the Delicate Investigation of 1806, the official Parliamentary inquiry into Caroline's fidelity to the Regent—moved in the same courtly circles that her poem attacked. Anonymity was crucial for elite women satirists, and it was not until the 1880s that the poem was attributed to Hamilton.[9] That readers were apparently less interested in identifying the anonymous author than they were in attributing the scurrilous deeds the poem describes should not surprise us. Anonymous satire was so commonplace in 1807 as to be unremarkable, and the pull of the author function was weaker than usual in *Epics of the Ton*, which announced itself as a patchwork of public gossip rather than the original disclosures of a unique personality. No doubt anonymity helped Hamilton avoid social reprisal, even if most of the poem's tawdry tidbits had already circulated widely in the press. That Hamilton attacks her own is also not surprising. As Catherine Keane observes, "satiric attack is a vehicle for marking out groups that are dangerously close to the satirist."[10] Perhaps Hamilton was disturbed by her proximity to the gambling and adultery she mocks. In any case, the poem's criticism of the sexual infractions and domestic neglect of fashionable London women appears to be sincere enough.[11]

For historians of reading, what is of most interest about *Epics of the Ton* is how early readers responded to the gutted names. Of the eighty-nine surviving copies of *Epics of the Ton* that I have located at institutional and house libraries worldwide, at least forty-five show traces of readers filling blanks in one or both of the Male and Female Books. I have seen all but four of these forty-five copies. Attempted identifications, sometimes by multiple hands in a single copy, appear in the blanks in the Table of Contents or in the margins. Eight copies have full manuscript keys, and it is likely that penciled-in names in some copies have been erased and could potentially be recovered through multispectral imaging.[12] This flood of notations—in roughly half of extant copies—is both rare and typical. Dashed-out names were part of the satirist's arsenal going back to the late seventeenth century and would have been familiar to Hamilton's contemporaries through other recent satires, such as Charles Pigott's *The Jockey Club* (1792), which featured even more blanks than *Epics of the Ton*. And, as veterans of the archive know well, copies of satires, from Restoration squibs to Romantic declamations, often have names written into the blanks by readers.[13] But Hamilton (or her publishers, C. and R. Baldwin) seemed unusually eager to invite reader involvement. Not only did the advertisements for *Epics of the Ton* feature blanked-out names, but Hamilton also omitted all but initial letters where Pigott had omitted vowels alone.[14] Heightening curiosity and increasing the range of names assigned seemed more the goal than avoiding libel charges. As Andrew Benjamin Bricker has shown, blanks and initials rarely spared earlier satirists from legal proceedings, though they did lend a marketable air of mystery to satire.[15] Whatever the reason, Hamilton's blanks generated an outpouring of response from readers. The high number of marked copies of the same title offers a rare opportunity to compare notations by many readers and to generalize about their reading practices.

One is struck by the unevenness of notations in marked copies. Hannah Grieg, one of the few scholars to give *Epics of the Ton* a passing mention, declares that Hamilton's contemporaries needed "little effort to establish [who] these were attacks on."[16] One reviewer in 1808 was much less confident, admitting, "We are not sure we are *tonnish* enough to guess at all the subjects … from their mere initials."[17] The reviewer gets it right. In the forty-one reader-annotated copies of the Female Book I have inspected, some names were more frequently identified than others. In roughly 98 percent of these copies M— F—, D— of G—, D— of S— A—, and D— of D— were filled in. The names given are also highly consistent: M— F— as Maria Fitzherbert, one of the Prince Regent's mistresses; D— of G— as the Duchess of Gordon; D— of S— A— as the Duchess of St. Albans; and D— of D— as the Duchess of Devonshire. Based on the frequency and consistency of identification, thirteen of the female targets were easily recognized, either because of contextual knowledge or textual details. The other twelve appear to have challenged readers, as these often received no or conflicting identifications. Least filled were C— of M—, L— C—, and L— P—, the last identified in only 33 percent of copies. L— P— is most often identified as Lady Petre, though some copies also volunteer Payne, Percy, Perth, Pomfret, and Portsmouth. Roughly equal numbers of copies identify another portrait, C— of B—, as the Countess of Bath and as the Countess of Buckinghamshire. As such variations suggest, scholars today often overrate reader knowledge. Unlike literary allusions, which become more intelligible to readers higher on the social ladder with greater access to education and books, knowledge of celebrity scandal depends on the newspapers one reads and the social circles one frequents. The assumption that an author's contemporaries had no trouble filling the blanks, or that blanks and initials signal widespread knowledge among first or early readers about the names such marks obscure or replace, is belied by the uneven identification of celebrities in copies of *Epics of the Ton*. Some deeds and names needed saving from "Lethe, and oblivion drear" more than others.

Readers felt more confident about the male portraits. Eighty-two percent of all blanks in annotated copies of the Male Book are filled, compared to seventy-one in copies of the Female Book. In fifteen copies every male blank is filled, something achieved in the case of the female blanks in just one copy.[18] Granted, more surviving copies overall contain notations to the Female Book than the Male Book: forty-one to thirty-six. Maybe this discrepancy indicates that the guessing game in the Female Book was more fun, or that by the time they reached the Male Book in the latter half of the volume readers had tired of the gimmick. Either way, unfilled blanks do not always imply difficulty or failure. Readers doze; pens break. The female portraits L— P— and L— C— may have been too difficult, but some readers may have just skipped them. At a time when writing was more labor intensive than it is today, readers needed an incentive to fill blanks, and perhaps not all of Hamilton's portraits equally succeeded at overcoming the inertia. Some targets, perhaps, were too obvious for readers to bother annotating. That so many blanks in copies of *Epics of the Ton* were in fact filled confirms Peter Stallybrass's sense of the affinity between print and manuscript and of print's functioning often as "an incitement to writing by hand."[19] In Hamilton's case the stimulus was rather different than that involved in the indulgences and tax forms that Stallybrass discusses. Part of a larger, print-based economy of celebrity and affect, Hamilton's poem promised readers intimacy with the celebrities whose deeds the poem described. Putting names to targets offered readers the further gratification of feeling "in the know," together with the sense of empowerment that comes with thinking that one has information that others do not.[20]

Instead of simply counting unfilled blanks as evidence of difficulty or failure, we might better infer difficulty from blanks showing a low identification rate *and* a high variation in the names given when identification is attempted. By this measure, the most difficult portraits in the Female Book were C— of M—, D— of R—, L— P—, and C— of B—, which received four, five, six, and eight different names while being identified in just 50, 68, 34, and 59 percent of the extant copies. In the Male Book, E— of C— proved the most challenging; left blank in eleven cases, it received six different appellations in the twenty-five cases in which it was annotated: Earl of Chatham, Carlisle, Cardigan, Carnarvon, Castlereagh, and Covington (or possibly Carrington, since the name in the blank is nearly illegible). Confidence seems to have improved over time, as the number of unfilled blanks decreases in annotated copies of the third edition. But this trend could be an accident of which copies of the third edition happen to survive.

I have so far stressed confidence, not accuracy. With attention and context, we might be able to reduce every one of Hamilton's satiric portraits to a single, most likely target. Declining in most cases to offer multiple identifications or to interpret the portraits as composites, early annotators seem also to have thought a single target was intended or was at least more interesting than listing several possibilities. But such identificatory work has already been done: in 1881 the Edinburgh Aungervyle Society printed "A Key to 'Epics of the Ton,'" an odd antiquarian exercise with no justifications for the names it supplies.[21] Accordingly, I propose that we stop worrying whether readers assigned the right names to the blanks, or even who the intended targets were. For one thing, Hamilton's use of first letters encourages varied identifications. This is not to claim that recovering the intended targets is impossible, rather, that attempting to do so ignores the likelihood that the poem's main appeal in 1807 was guessing at the victims and not parsing, scholar-like, the themes manifested once all the victims' identities had been decided through contextual research. For another, by focusing only on the probable or accurate identities of Hamilton's victims we overlook the other story that manuscript notations have to tell. Too focused on right answers, scholars fail to ask why readers get things wrong, or at least why they identify blanks so differently.

What the notations in *Epics of the Ton* reveal is satire as a kind of interactive play: a game of speculation and uncertainty in which the self-declared winners supplied names for as many of the blanks as possible, even names that to later observers seem unlikely or incorrect. Annotators presumably worked independently, but it seems possible that some knew one another and talked about the poem. It also seems likely that considerable social interaction stands behind even the identifications in a single hand. We can easily imagine three or four readers together, one filling blanks while over her shoulder the others debate the identifications offered by friends or relations in letters and recent conversation. As part of this social gameplay, this collective puzzle-solving, *Epics of the Ton* didn't invite *reading* in the way scholars usually understand it. The users of *Epics of the Ton* processed the text discontinuously, rather than continuously, more often hunting around for occasions to show off their knowledge of celebrity gossip than allowing textual details to dictate the identification. Assigning some, indeed, any name, no matter how imposed or far-fetched it seems to us today, earned users social capital in this friendly battle of wits. Such interaction would not have been guided by accuracy or some concept of authorial intention. In fact, affixing the wrong name to a blank knowingly, or even refusing an offensive individual the courtesy of an identification, could heighten the pleasure of the game. Blanks may be left blank for reasons other than obscurity.

Epics of the Ton teaches the rules of this satire game, although *rules* is perhaps too dignified a term. Hamilton's readers were playful, fickle, partisan. The annotator of the Newberry Library copy identified L— C— in the Female Book as "Lord Canning," presumably making a joke about the lack of leadership or manliness displayed by George Canning, then Foreign Secretary and, later, Prime Minister.[22] Annotators of D— of R— in the Female Book were often indecisive, as the first identification of Rutland in the Columbia University copy is scratched out with Roxburghe given in the margin.[23] The initial identification of Rutland in the University of Wyoming copy is also cancelled with no alternative hazarded.[24] So challenging was D— of R— that one of the British Library copies of *Epics of the Ton*, in a rare case, offers two names, "Rutland" and "Roxburgh," above the blank.[25] The blanks were also used at times to vent political opinions. In the Clark Library copy, the initials L— G— (most often identified as Lord Grenville) are struck out and replaced with "C[harles] Fox," the former Whig Prime Minister. The Clark annotator seems to have had a partisan animus against Fox.[26] As this instance suggests, initials were no curb on annotators who wished to appropriate or personalize the blanks. Confirmation bias and partisan zealotry are not unique to our own fake news era.

Notations in many cases show readers engaging only fleetingly with Hamilton's text. They sought what Andrew Elfenbein calls "the gist" without worrying overmuch if the names assigned fit all the details of the portrait.[27] For example, one of the female portraits, C— of B—, mentions a "Laura" (*ET*, bk. 1, line 374), presumably Laura Pulteney, Countess of Bath, but neither Bath nor Albinia Hobart, Countess of Buckinghamshire, the two nobles most often assigned to this blank, spent significant time in Scotland, as the portrait claims. Some readers took the clue ("Laura"), fit a name to the initials, and ignored the rest. Others, privileging the mention of Scotland, ignored the disconfirming name and identified the target as a Scottish noble, either the Countess of Breadalbane or the Countess of Bute. Ultimately, "Laura" appears more a stock name than a real clue, as Laura could be one of a number of romance-type names—including Belinda, Dorinda, and Strephon—that Hamilton uses in other portraits. But early readers of *Epics of the Ton* were misled by far less than this. It seems surprising now that any reader could identify M— of A— as other than Lady Craven, the Marchioness of Anspach, with the rhyme in one of the couplets in her portrait giving away the answer: "To Jove's imperial bird convert the raven, / And Lady Mary make of Lady —" (*ET*, bk. 1, lines 137–38). The same strategy appears in the portrait for another M— of A— later, presumably the Marchioness of Abercorn: "She, that once held her name, the theme of scorn, / Does the thought move the sprightly — ?" (bk. 1, lines 570–71). But in three copies the first M— of A— went unidentified, and in a whopping fifteen copies the later M— of A— was left blank or identified as a different figure. Hamilton's readers were not at all "close readers" in the standard scholarly sense.

If we accept Leah Price's view that a blank margin can often indicate absorbed reading, then the filled margins and blanks in copies of *Epics of the Ton* may indicate readers distracted by petty concerns and chauvinisms.[28] Of course, as the number of names of women with Scottish (Breadalbane, Bute, Gordon, Roxburghe) and Irish (Abercorn, Cloncurry, Moira) ties by either birth or title assigned to the blanks imply, we cannot underrate political and regional rivalries in shaping how Hamilton drew her portraits and how readers identified them. Jane, Duchess of Gordon (most often identified as D— of G—) was a Tory socialite; Georgiana Cavendish, Duchess of Devonshire (most often identified as D— of D—), was, of course, a famous Whig hostess and notorious gambler. As Mark Towsey reminds us, readers "create[d] meanings ... informed by their professional interests, political loyalties, existing commitments, worries and deeply-held beliefs."[29] Hamilton's use of initials did not allow just anyone to be inserted into the blanks, but most of the portraits were probably vague enough to accommodate whatever beliefs or biases readers happened to bring to the poem. Readers may have turned a satire on peeresses of all places and politics into an attack on women predominately of one region or political party. One wonders if two of the more questionable identifications to be found in copies of the Female Book, of M— of S— as Marchioness Sligo and of V— C— as Viscountess Cremorne, both of Ireland, reflected readers all too eager to pin the worst of anything on the Irish.[30]

How representative the extant copies are of interactions that did not leave traces in the form of notations cannot be known. How representative these copies are of wider reading is also debatable. Wealthy, educated readers are likely overrepresented in annotated copies of a pricey social satire like *Epics of the Ton*. But these readers are not the experts that often show up in studies of reading—the John Dees, the Coleridges, perhaps the Anna Larpents.[31] An educated reader is not necessarily a diligent reader or "in the know." *Epics of the Ton* does not require literary expertise, and, as my analysis suggests, readers approached the poem more as a gossipy game to be played with abandon than as an artwork to be studied with care. There is no reason to think that the love of unmasking appealed to in *Epics of the Ton* was limited to the social rank most represented in the surviving marked copies. Popular, cheap formats of other works—broadsides, ballads, pamphlets—contain blanks and innuendo as well, even if their narrow margins dissuaded readers from recording their identifications for posterity.

Marginalia in copies of *Epics of the Ton* challenge a common methodical assumption: that in the absence of wider evidence, annotation by a single known annotator, especially one with ties to the work's author, can be taken as authoritative, if not necessarily representative of how most audiences of the time read. Among her correspondents with literary associations, Hamilton counted Sir Walter Scott, who left behind one of the few copies of *Epics of the Ton* annotated by someone identifiable, and indeed famous.[32] There is no evidence that Scott possessed inside information about Hamilton's targets or knew that Hamilton was the author. Like the nameless annotators we have been examining, Scott left some blanks empty (L— L— M—, L— P—, and L— C—). He filled his blanks with the same names as many of the other, unidentified annotators of *Epics of the Ton*. But Scott's notations are not always representative of the general response. Where Scott leaves L— L— M— blank, 73 percent of the copies make an identification, all agreeing on Lady Louisa Manners, whose Scottish origins and famous portrait by Sir Joshua Reynolds would have, one might guess, made her familiar to Scott as well. Or perhaps Scott recognized Hamilton's sketch as Manners and yet, out of politeness or sympathy or gallantry, declined to affix her name. In any case, for Scott, as for the many unidentified readers of *Epics of the Ton* for whom we lack contextual information, we have to look elsewhere to explain the patterns in blanks filled and names given.

Where might we look? I would argue that we should look to social memory. That is, beyond recovering reading practices, manuscript notes and identifications across many copies of a single title can gauge the staying power of anecdotes in the public mind. For example, if C— of D— is Elizabeth (née Farren), Countess of Derby, as most annotators of *Epics of the Ton* agreed, then they had to have recalled, in 1807, the Earl of Derby's courtship of the actress Farren in the 1780s and their marrying soon after his estranged first wife died in 1797. In giving or not giving a name for C— of D—, annotators hint at what information was current in 1807 (and what was no longer so). Likewise, it is surprising that more readers of *Epics of the Ton* did not decline, with Walter Scott, to identify L— L— M—, given that readers who volunteered Lady Manners presumably had to recall her husband's death in 1792, fifteen years prior. To be sure, the initials L— L— M— did not permit many other names to be assigned, but the question remains: why was Manners sufficiently present in communal memory that she was the preferred identification in over two-thirds of the surviving copies? The same could be asked of the printed identifications offered by the Aungervyle Society key: how was *Epics of the Ton* and the social world it represents recalled in the late 1800s? To what extent do the key's contents reveal how the scandalous celebrities of the Regency were remembered in 1881, rather than who the likely or intended targets were in 1807?

Manuscript annotations may record memory over time as well as first or early responses. Dating the notations to *Epics of the Ton* is hard: even when marks of provenance are present, the title-pages of copies crowd with multiple, undated signatures in hands often different than those of the notations. The notations are in "contemporary hands," but, in the absence of other evidence, script from 1807, 1827, or 1847 can look nearly identical. At first it seems unlikely that a gossipy poem would carry interest twenty years on. Then again, if Charles Lamb could report in 1822 relishing a number of the gossipy *Town and Country Magazine*, defunct since 1796, then there is no telling how late *Epics of the Ton* had appeal.[33] That many copies contain notes in two hands, one in ink, another in ink or pencil over the first, indicates that later readers updated earlier identifications. How much later? The few dated or dateable annotations range widely: one Huntington copy of *Epics of the Ton* was annotated no earlier than 1814, as E— L— is identified as the "late" Edward Lascelles, who had died that year.[34] The V&A copy, once owned by Alexander Dyce, has notations dated 1859.[35] If some copies were marked by Victorians, then their marginalia reflect what names stuck over time or gained renewed currency decades later. In this case the utility of such notations for recovering public memory would expand. They help us recover the dynamics of memory in, say, 1837 as much as in 1807.

Reinforcing the idea that some readers were guessing at the names years after the fact, manuscript notations sometimes show apparent misremembering. In one copy V— C— in the Female Book (typically identified as Viscountess Castlereagh) is identified as "Castleborough."[36] First names could be challenging: L— C— C— (typically identified as Lady Charlotte Campbell) is identified once as "Lady Caroline Campbell."[37] Both kinds of error seem less likely to have occurred in 1807 than at some later time, when the names were no longer fresh in readers' minds. Titles also presented problems. Grieg tells the story of a James Hobart, who, claiming to be the non-existent Duke of Ormond, in 1791 scammed a banker out of £200, the banker confusing the imaginary Duke with the real-life Earl of Ormonde.[38] Readers of *Epics of the Ton* could be similarly muddled, with one annotator of the Male Book inventing an "Earl of Castlereagh" for E— of C— (Robert Stewart was at different times Marquess, Viscount, and Lord Castlereagh, but only ever Earl of Londonderry).[39] And even with the correct title, readers both early and late may have been baffled by the way noble titles were attached to multiple persons over time. After identifying M— of A— as the Marchioness of Abercorn, one still had to decide: was this Catherine Copley, who died in 1791; Lady Cecil Hamilton, who was divorced in 1799; or Lady Anne Jane Gore, who wed the Marquess in 1800? If readers managed to identify D— of R— as the Duchess of Roxburghe, then they met with a similar conundrum: was this Mary Innes-Ker, who died in 1807, the year *Epics of the Ton* appeared; or was this Harriet Innes-Ker, the Duke's second wife, whom he married the same year?

How readers settled these questions probably involved many factors, including personal and political taste as much as textual evidence. Why they remembered and forgot what they did is also an intriguing question. Memorability often has less to do with accuracy or authenticity than we might want to believe. As Ann Rigney observes, "certain things are remembered not because they are actually true … but because they are somehow meaningful in the present. In other words, 'authenticity' may not always be relevant to memorial dynamics."[40] The way false and exaggerated rumor shapes remembrance becomes clear in the case of one of the four most often identified portraits in the Female Book, D— of D—, who was seen to be the Duchess of Devonshire. In this portrait, Hamilton explicitly describes the target as "urged by faction midst the rabble tribe, / [to] kiss a greasy butcher with a bribe" (*ET*, bk. 1, lines 342–43). These two lines seem to refer clearly to Thomas Rowlandson's 1784 graphic satire, *The Devonshire, or Most Approved Method of Securing Votes*, which depicted the Duchess embracing a butcher while canvassing for Fox during the 1784 Westminster election.[41] Whether Georgiana ever fondled a butcher, which seems doubtful, the high number of copies identifying D— of D— as the Duchess of Devonshire indicate that this scandalous anecdote remained connected to her in public memory more than twenty years after Rowlandson's print. Devonshire had died in 1806, right before *Epics of the Ton* was published, so old rumors may have gained renewed circulation, which could have assisted readers in identifying the portrait.

Another factor in memorability was available information, what news readers had recently and frequently heard. Consider the higher rate of filled blanks in the Male Book. Maybe the male portraits are more precise than the female ones, leading to more frequent and more consistent identifications. But annotators likely also had a larger pool of names with which to fill the male blanks. Male ministry officials were more familiar to the public from Parliamentary Reports and the newspapers than most women, making readers better able to supply some name, correct or otherwise. Trends in the Female Book also show how marginalia can illuminate the dynamics of cultural remembering. Since *Epics of the Ton* mentions several scandalmongering periodicals, let us consider one of these, *The Morning Post*, which in 1807 had regular columns devoted to the bon ton, including its women. If we take the names most given for the poem's most identified blanks (M— F—, D— of G—, D— of S— A—, D— of D—; see above for their full names) *and* the names most given for the least identified ones (C— of M—, L— C—, and L— P—, which, when identified, are most commonly Countess Moira, Lady Cloncurry, and Lady Petre) and run them through *The Morning Post* on Gale's British Library Newspaper database, we get some suggestive results. As the chart in Figure 2 indicates, the most regularly identified names were

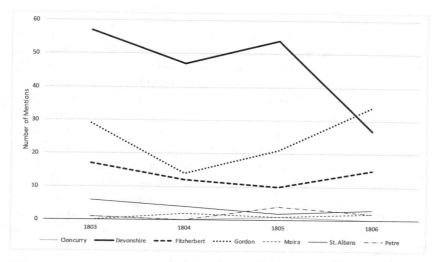

Figure 2. Mentions of Names in *The Morning Post*, 1803–1806.

the names readers encountered most often in the press during the preceding years. Maybe the names fit the portraits, too, but availability seems to have been central. The exception is St. Albans, who was not widely mentioned in *The Morning Post*. Perhaps coverage of St. Albans appeared in another newspaper. Or perhaps the longer name (as with Lady Louisa Manners) reduced the number of possibilities and so made the blank easier to decode.

Another illustration of the promise of marginalia for studies of cultural memory emerges with the notations to L— C— in the Female Book. None of the surviving annotated first editions (ten copies) identify L— C— as Lady Cloncurry (Elizabeth Georgiana Morgan), but the second and third editions (thirty-one copies total) do in 52 percent of cases. If we assume that most of these copies were annotated soon after publication, what happened in early 1807, after the first edition, to explain this increase in identification? In February news broke of the criminal conversation (adultery) suit brought against Sir John Piers for his liaison with Lady Cloncurry.[42] Thus, when the two later editions appeared, readers were more familiar with her name. Maybe Hamilton's portrait fit Cloncurry's details; maybe the portrait was meant for Cloncurry. But what mattered was readers having her name at their disposal. Patterns in filled blanks reveal not only what names and stories persisted over time, then, but also record what news and gossip were trending at particular moments.

Marginalia in copies of Hamilton's *Epics of the Ton* offer valuable evidence of collective reading and memory, including how eighteenth-century fashionable society was regarded after 1800. The names assigned to blanks in *Epics of the Ton* and similar fill-in-the-blank satires with manuscript notations surviving in many copies promise to help us reconstruct information flows, recover otherwise unrecorded gossip, and understand which names and stories stuck in the public mind and which others slipped quickly from memory. This essay has suggested, in a preliminary and speculative manner, what this method might look like. To realize the possibilities of this method, however, we need to adopt expansive, collective approaches to the study of marginalia and rethink generalizing from single, recognizable annotators. We also need to set aside the related preoccupation with judging the accuracy of marginalia and instead recognize the game-like quality of manuscript notation and focus on what the patterns in these notations reveal about cultural memory as it was shaped by partisanship and the availability of information. In terms of politics or literary quality, *Epics of the Ton* may be, as an early reader scrawled in one copy, "not worth a damn."[43] But in modeling new angles on the history of reading, *Epics of the Ton* and similar satires are surely worth more scholarly attention.

Notes

For advice on drafts of this essay, I want to thank the Wyoming Institute for Humanities Research (WIHR) Writing Group. I also thank WIHR for funding to support this research.

1. William H. Sherman, *John Dee: The Politics of Reading and Writing in the English Renaissance* (Amherst: University of Massachusetts Press, 1995); Lisa Jardine and Anthony Grafton, "'Studied for Action': How Gabriel Harvey Read His Livy," *Past & Present* 129 (1990): 30–78; H. J. Jackson, *Romantic Readers: The Evidence of Marginalia* (New Haven: Yale University Press, 2005).

2. See Book Traces, https://booktraces-public.lib.virginia.edu, and The Reading Experience Database, http://www.open.ac.uk/Arts/RED/index.html.

3. For this approach, see Alan Roper, "Who's Who in *Absalom and Achitophel*," *Huntington Library Quarterly* 63 (2000): 98–138; and Stephen Karian, "Reading the Material Text of Swift's *Verses on the Death*," *SEL* 41 (2001): 515–44.

4. For celebrity culture in this era, see Anna Clark, *Scandal: The Sexual Politics of the British Constitution* (Oxford: Oxford University Press, 2004); Marilyn Morris, *Sex, Money, and Personal Character in Eighteenth-Century British Politics* (New Haven: Yale University Press, 2014); and the essays in *Romanticism and Celebrity Culture, 1750–1850*, ed. Tom Mole (Cambridge: Cambridge University Press, 2009).

5. The first edition contains fifteen male portraits. In the 2nd edition, the Male Book adds two portraits (E— L—, commonly identified as Edward Lascelles, and T— S—, commonly identified as Thomas Sheridan).

6. [Lady Anne Hamilton], *The Epics of the Ton; or, The Glories of the Great World: A Poem, In Two Books, with Notes and Illustrations* (London: Printed by and for C. and R. Baldwin, 1807), bk. 1, lines 27–28, henceforth cited parenthetically in the text as *ET*.

7. Anna Seward to Walter Scott, 5 November 1807, *Letters of Anna Seward: Written between the Years 1784 and 1807*, ed. Archibald Constable, 6 vols. (Edinburgh: Printed by George Ramsay for Archibald Constable, 1811), 6:388.

8. See *The Bombay Courier* 805 (13 February 1808) and 807 (27 February 1808). For the title as shorthand for nasty gossip, see Sarah Green, *Romance Readers and Romance Writers: A Satirical Novel*, 3 vols. (London: T. Hookham, Junior, and E. T. Hookham, 1810), 2:209–10.

9. The attribution is made by Samuel Halkett and John Laing, *A Dictionary of the Anonymous and Pseudonymous Literature of Great Britain*, 4 vols. (Edinburgh: William Paterson, 1882–88), 1:777. Halkett and Laing are often unreliable, but in the absence of contrary evidence, I have accepted the attribution.

10. Catherine Keane, *Figuring Genre in Roman Satire* (Oxford: Oxford University Press, 2006), 90.

11. For Hamilton's politics of domesticity, see Adeline Johns-Putra, "Satirising the Courtly Woman and Defending the Domestic Woman: Mock Epics and Women Poets in the Romantic Age," *Romanticism on the Net* 15 (1999), *https://www.erudit.org/en/journals/ron/1999-n15-ron427/005863ar/*.

12. Although some copies evidence two annotators, I have not tried to distinguish them. Illegible identifications are included in my reported tallies of the total number of identifications for each blank.

13. See, for example, the British Library's copy of *The Jockey Club, or a Sketch of the Manners of the Age. Part the First*, 6th ed. (London: Printed for H. D. Symonds, 1792), shelf mark 785.e.14.

14. See, for example, the advertisement for *Epics of the Ton* in *The London Star*, 30 May 1808.

15. Andrew Benjamin Bricker, "Libel and Satire: The Problem with Naming," *ELH* 81 (2014): 889–921.

16. Hannah Greig, *The Beau Monde: Fashionable Society in Georgian London* (Oxford: Oxford University Press, 2013), 253.

17. *British Critic* 31 (February 1808): 197–98, 198.

18. Huntington Library, call number 436710.

19. Peter Stallybrass, "Printing and the Manuscript Revolution," in *Explorations in Communication and History*, ed. Barbie Zelizer (London: Routledge, 2008), 111–118, 117.

20. For more on the "hermeneutic of intimacy" and the reading of poetry for celebrity disclosure, see Tom Mole, *Byron's Romantic Celebrity: Industrial Culture and the Hermeneutic of Intimacy* (Basingstoke: Palgrave, 2007).

21. J. Davies Barnett, "A Key to 'Epics of the Ton,'" in *Aungervyle Society Reprints* (Edinburgh: Aungervyle Society, 1881–82), 33–36.

22. Newberry Library, call number Y185.H179.

23. Columbia University Rare Book and Manuscript Library, call number PR4739.H15 E6 1807g.

24. Toppan Rare Books Library, University of Wyoming, call number PR4739.H15 E65 1807.

25. British Library, shelf mark 1162.I.25.

26. Clark Library, UCLA, call number PR4739.H15 E6 1807a*.

27. See Andrew Elfenbein, *The Gist of Reading* (Stanford: Stanford University Press, 2018).

28. Leah Price, "Reading: The State of the Discipline," *Book History* 7 (2004): 303–20, esp. 312–13.

29. Mark R. M. Towsey, *Reading the Scottish Enlightenment: Books and their Readers in Provincial Scotland, 1750–1820* (Leiden: Brill, 2010), 231.

30. For Sligo, see Bodleian Library, University of Oxford, shelf mark 280 e.3621; for Cremorne, see British Library, shelf mark 11642.c.49.

31. John Brewer, "Reconstructing the Reader: Prescriptions, Texts, and Strategies in Anna Larpent's Reading," in *The Practice and Representation of Reading in England*, ed. James Raven, Helen Small, and Naomi Tadmor (Cambridge: Cambridge University Press, 1996), 226–45.

32. Advocates Library, National Library of Scotland, Abbotsford Collection, no shelf mark.

33. Charles Lamb, "Detached Thoughts on Books and Reading," *London Magazine* 6 (July 1822): 33–36, esp. 35.

34. Huntington Library, call number 436710.

35. Victoria & Albert Museum, shelf mark Dyce M 8vo 3473.

36. Noel Library, Louisiana State University–Shreveport, call number PR4739.H15 E65 1807 copy 2.

37. Johns Hopkins University Library, call number PO4739.H4 E4 1807 c. 1.

38. Greig, *The Beau Monde*, 226.

39. Wake Forest University Library, call number PR4739.H15 E6.

40. Ann Rigney, "Portable Monuments: Literature, Cultural Memory, and the Case of Jeanie Deans," *Poetics Today* 25 (2004): 361–96, 381.

41. For the doubtfulness of this anecdote, see Amelia Rauser, "The Butcher-Kissing Duchess of Devonshire: Between Caricature and Allegory in 1784," *Eighteenth-Century Studies* 36 (2002): 23–46.

42. See "Sir John Piers and Lady Cloncurry," *The Morning Post* (25 Feb 1807).

43. National Library of Israel, shelf mark S2010 C26860.

Henry Fielding's Theatrical Reminiscences: Another Look at Sophia Western as Jenny Cameron

ANACLARA CASTRO-SANTANA

In an alphabetical companion to Henry Fielding, written by a foremost Fielding scholar, Sophia Western is described as "the beautiful and virtuous daughter of Squire Western, Allworthy's neighbor. She is in love with Tom as he is with her. ... HF hints that she is the idealized figure of his beloved first wife Charlotte Cradock Fielding."[1] This explanation accords Sophia a marginal role in the text as "the daughter of," the beloved of, and the fictionalization of a real-life "wife of," while it also wrests complication away from the character by considering her merely "beautiful and virtuous." Admittedly, it is an appraisal written nearly twenty years ago; moreover, the entry limits itself to the bare bones of this and other characters, works, and topics. Nonetheless, the entry exemplifies most of what is still said of the heroine of *The History of Tom Jones, A Foundling* (1749) in non-specialized criticism.[2] This notion, in turn, tends to seep into classroom discussions, entrenching the enduring cliché that Fielding is a male chauvinist, oblivious to and uninterested in the multidimensionality of women's personalities—in the apt words of Robert D. Hume: "a 'manly' writer touting frat-boy verities and cheery about sowing wild oats."[3]

The recognition of the complexity of Fielding's approach to gender issues has been nourishing eighteenth-century scholarship for the past three decades.[4] It is now frequently acknowledged that the writer's attitude towards gender inequality is at least ambivalent, if not openly averse. Around the time of publication of the companion cited above, for instance, Earla A. Wilputte argued persuasively that Fielding "calls attention to the plight of eighteenth-century women to whom his culture denied an education, a political voice, any tangible social significance, and even identity once she was married."[5] In a more recent study, Simon Dickie notes Fielding's bending of the sexual double standard in his positive depiction of desiring women.[6] There is still work to do in that respect, however. That Sophia is a central and complex figure, far more than kin to the male characters of the novel and a surrogate wife for the writer, cannot be stressed enough. Neither can the fact that her characterization goes beyond a straightforward portrayal of virtuous femininity grounded in modesty and outward beauty. After all, it is Sophia's resolute abandonment of the paternal household that moves the narrative forward and towards its romantic conclusion from the second third of the book onwards.

Sophia's rebelliousness is a point of particular interest that crops up in discussions of another question that continues to perplex critics: Fielding's engagement with the Jacobite Rebellion of 1745. The fact that Fielding's political pamphlets and periodicals took a vociferous stance against the Jacobites is often taken as unmistakable proof of his anti-Jacobitism, which, the argument goes, finds its fictional expression in *Tom Jones*.[7] Yet, as some critics have also shown, Fielding's treatment of Jacobitism in his masterpiece is complicated to the point that it seems contradictory.[8] Particularly mystifying is Sophia's simultaneous endorsement by the narrative as a fitting companion (and moral compass) for a hero who would seem to stand for Hanoverian principles—but who is also endowed with the youthful impetuousness and charm of Charles Edward Stuart—and her association, albeit fleeting and mistaken, with Jenny Cameron, the Young Pretender's reputed mistress.

A key piece in this critical jigsaw puzzle of the relationship between Sophia and Jenny Cameron has not yet been successfully placed, however. By this I mean the appearance of the Jacobite heroine in a pantomime staged in London around the time when Fielding was hard at work on the novel. Given the author's crucial, though frequently neglected, investment in the theatrical world, which continued long after he had ceased to be a practicing dramatist, taking a close look at this piece—and paying particular attention to the actress who performed as Cameron—sheds new light on the old problem of the representation of the Stuart rebellion in *Tom Jones*. It emphasizes the centrality and complexity of female characters in Fielding's works, and it reminds modern readers that the pioneer novelist was at heart a man of the theater.[9] This is what I set out to do in the pages that follow.

Jenny Cameron Calls on the London Stage

On the evening of Monday, 3 March 1746, a new musical pantomime was staged at Drury Lane starring the celebrated actress and singer Catherine (better known as Kitty) Clive. Its title: *Harlequin Incendiary; or Colombine Cameron*. Its subject: the latest, and, as it turned out, the last Jacobite rebellion, which began in the summer of 1745 and was finally quelled in a sanguinary battle on 16 April 1746 at Culloden Moor. The libretto for this piece, hereafter abbreviated as *Colombine Cameron*, was published soon after the premiere, in April of the same year.[10] To modern readers versed in eighteenth-century Jacobitism, the title of the pantomime seems to announce yet another satirical portrayal of Jenny (also known as Jean, Jeanie, or Jane) Cameron, the putative—and much-abused—mistress of Charles Edward Stuart, who became one of the stellar characters of the '45 in the chronicles written by observers from both sides of the conflict. Extolled in Scottish ballads and besmeared first by sensationalist English newspapers and later by spurious biographies, Cameron acquired a celebrity status that endured long after the revolt.[11]

The most inventive, cruel, and best known of the stories about this Jacobite heroine, however, had not yet been published by the time *Colombine Cameron* premiered on the stage. The anonymous *Brief Account of the Life and Family of Miss Jenny Cameron* (1746), for instance, which propagated the most notorious rumors about her supposed immorality, did not appear in print until August of that year.[12] The other extensive volume dedicated to Cameron's life and exploits, Archibald Arbuthnot's *Memoirs of the Remarkable Life and Surprizing Adventures of Jenny Cameron*, ends with a report of her release on bail from Edinburgh Castle in November of 1746, which indicates that the book was written several months after the staging of the pantomime and the printing of its libretto. What London audiences knew about the Pretender's supposed mistress in the first months of 1746 came mainly from short press reports in which she appeared as Prince Charles's ministering companion, with whom he shared a coach—and presumably a bed.[13]

It is plausible to assert, then, that *Colombine Cameron* was the first substantial work in which the Jacobite rebel featured as the central figure, fueling, perhaps, a keener interest in Cameron as a character. Combined with what to loyalist Londoners was a period of intensified anxiety about the outcome of the revolt, the lavish scenery of the playhouse, and the musical arrangements of Thomas Arne—the favorite English composer of the moment—the first performances of this piece would have enhanced its memorability among the original audiences. That pantomimes did not frequently address political topics makes this an unusual one, further strengthening its appeal.[14] Moreover, given Clive's celebrity status, her embodiment of Cameron created a fundamental link between the two, connecting the actress and the character in the minds of the audience to the point that the fiction could seep into the performer and vice versa.

Despite being the first, *Colombine Cameron* is not the most emblematic fictional representation of the Jacobite rebel. The Colombine played by Clive is very much the standard version of the character as it appeared in other pantomimes of the period: a beautiful and vain female trickster involved in a series of love skirmishes with Harlequin and a host of inane would-be lovers. The libretto provides its readers with two explicit reminders of who the character is supposed to represent. First, readers are informed by a stage direction that Harlequin arrives in Edinburgh carrying a letter "directed to *Jenny Cameron*," and later that "the Pretender and his Party meet Colombine, who, with all the Affection of Jenny Cameron embraces and receives him."[15] It is impossible to ascertain what spectators saw, but we know that the scenery and decorations were new and that the performance featured "Scenes in Scotland."[16] We can also speculate that Harlequin showed the letter bearing Cameron's name to the audience and that the actress playing Colombine could have worn something to remind viewers of the person to whom her character alluded. To avoid imputations of sedition or treason, though, any visual display would have had to be discrete and explicitly satirical.[17] Being a pantomime, *Colombine Cameron* does not offer a naturalistic portrait of the Young Pretender's supposed mistress. Rather than weakening the link between Clive and Cameron, however, this lack of particularization cemented the correlation, for it rendered the Jacobite heroine a blank slate of sorts, to be filled in with the attributes of a Colombine, and, as I shall explain in greater detail further on, with those of the imagined persona of the actress who played the part.

In fusing topicality with the appeal to the senses that was characteristic of pantomimes, *Colombine Cameron* offered its original spectators an audiovisual treat that simultaneously tapped the nervous excitement of the bellicose atmosphere and took the gravity of the situation off the viewers' minds. Given that pantomimes were ostensibly frivolous entertainments, the prominence accorded to Cameron in the title and the content of the piece could be attributed to mere expediency or a marketing strategy. The potential for instruction inherent in even a fleeting portrayal of a female companion of the much-admired and equally as dreaded Young Pretender should not be underestimated, however. The sole mention of Cameron's name invoked key points of contention at the heart of the Jacobite scare of the 1740s: gender roles and boundaries, the proper forms of authority in the public and domestic spheres, and changing notions of heroism.[18]

Also, in a paradox that characterizes the genre of pantomime itself, the trivialization of a serious subject had the effect of foregrounding it, which rendered this form of entertainment an apposite medium for exploring controversial issues. As John O'Brien observes, in mustering up the protagonists of the Jacobite Rebellion to become characters in a lesser form of theatrical entertainment presented in a royally sanctioned venue, *Colombine Cameron* stands out as "a resource for staging political satire from within the London establishment, a vehicle that enabled ridicule of the crisis that was possible no other way."[19] Writing the '45 into a pantomime advanced the notion that the rebels—Cameron in particular—were little more than dramatic types, something that indulged an eighteenth-century fascination with the blurriness between the fictional and the factual. Moreover, Clive was an actress who made a particular effort to disassociate her private reputation from the roles that she played on stage, which added another layer of complexity to the reception of her Cameron. All these begetters of ambiguity and multiplicity of meaning that infused *Colombine Cameron* come to bear in the famous mistake of identities that occurs at the beginning of the Upton episode in *Tom Jones*, to which I shall now turn.

Sophia's Spirited Propriety

As those who have read *Tom Jones* probably remember, Fielding's novel takes place between November and December of 1745, in the heyday of the Jacobite scare from the point of view of loyalist Londoners. In Book XI, Sophia and her maid Honour arrive late at night at an inn in Upton on their way from Somerset to London. There, they are mistaken by the landlord and his wife for "some of the Rebel Ladies, who, they say, travel with the young Chevalier."[20] Upon the reception of, as it turns out, false news that the Jacobite forces were just "a Day's March towards London," the landlord becomes convinced that Sophia is "no other than Madam Jenny Cameron herself" (*TJ* 578). Thinking this to be true, and delighted with Sophia's good manners and amiability, the landlady of the inn "became in a Moment a staunch *Jacobite*, and wished heartily well to the young Pretender's Cause" (580). Two chapters later, readers are informed how "the Mistake of the Landlord throws Sophia into a dreadful consternation" (591), as she fears her identity is known (which it is not) and that her father might be alerted of her elopement and on the way to fetch her (which he is). All of this takes place in about an hour of diegetic time and a couple dozen pages. The speed with which inferences are drawn, opinions formed, and allegiances pledged recreates, in a nearly farcical format, the atmosphere of the '45. The dramatic irony, characteristic of Fielding, endows readers with a sense of hauteur, encouraging them to agree with his critique of the excesses of thought and action brought about by the Jacobite crisis. At the same time, the passage draws attention to how personal charisma could tip the scales in favor of a cause or a set of beliefs, regardless of their worth—similar to what social commentators feared about theatergoers coming to admire immoral characters played by talented performers.

It is a critical consensus that the '45 informs the background of Fielding's novel in a way that allows him to work out in comic form the atmosphere of uncertainty that plagued British subjects, irrespective of their monarchical loyalties, in the convulsive years before and after the rebellion. Most critics argue that *Tom Jones* confirms the anti-Jacobite stance that Fielding displays in "A Dialogue between the Devil, the Pope, and the Pretender" (1745), *A Serious Address to the People of Great Britain* (1745), and *A Compleat and Authentick History of the Rise, Progress, and Extinction of the Late Rebellion* (1747), as well as in his periodicals *The True Patriot* (1745–46) and *The Jacobite's Journal* (1747–48). In the words of J. A. Downie, "Fielding in *Tom Jones* is unequivocal in his support for the Hanoverian Succession, and as damning in his indictment of the absurd and 'exploded' doctrine of indefeasible hereditary right as he is in any of his political pamphlets or the *Jacobite's Journal*."[21]

A few critics, however, see some ambivalence towards Jacobitism in *Tom Jones,* or at least a recognition of how attractive the main actors of the '45 and the kinds of narratives that they constructed were. To Peter Carlton, for instance, Fielding's attitude toward Jacobitism in *Tom Jones* is "mixed," a state that becomes most evident in the characterization of Sophia, a heroine who represents "a union of politically significant opposites: Whig heroine on the one hand, 'Jenny Cameron' and her Jacobite father's daughter on the other."[22] Similarly, John Allen Stevenson argues that in the middle section of *Tom Jones,* there is an intriguing "parallel between Fielding's hero, Tom Jones, and the central figure in the rebellion (and future novel reader), Charles Edward Stuart." This, according to Stevenson, stems from Fielding's realization "that the Stuarts' stories were better than the tales Hanoverians told."[23] The resemblances between Tom and the legendary figure of "Bonnie Prince Charlie" do not in themselves betray a secret affinity for Jacobitism on the side of Fielding. Nonetheless, they signal the author's understanding of the complexity and nuance in all political causes, as well as the ways in which sympathy could be elicited by a well-crafted narrative. Something similar, I believe, is at stake with the implied parallel between Sophia and Jenny Cameron.

Critics have only sporadically considered the Jenny Cameron episode in their assessments of the Jacobite question in Fielding's novel. However, instances can be found in Carlton's work and in that of Jill Campbell, who additionally finds Sophia to be characterized in a way that combines Whig and Jacobite models of femininity, the one domestic and the other unruly.[24] To these scholars, the merging of contradictory traits in a single character attests to Fielding's ambiguity regarding the Jacobite cause, to his uncertainty about the woman question, and to his endorsement of the ideology of the companionate marriage, which, in turn, depended on the implementation of new models of domestic masculinity and femininity. According to Campbell, who builds on Carlton's assessment of Sophia, "Fielding shows a particular interest in creating scenes of sustained conflict between these opposed traits [Whig Liberty and Jacobite Vitalism], rather than cleanly reconciling them in a character who can embody 'the best aspects of both.'"[25] Following this last argument, then, the primary purpose of Fielding's hybrid characterization of his heroine as one who moves between Whiggism and Jacobitism would be to emphasize the difference between Jacobite and Whig stereotypes, as well as to show the difficulties of reaching a middle ground, leaving the matter open to the judgment—good or bad—of his readers. By the same token, the introduction of the Cameron confusion would function as an attempt to showcase the conflict between ideologies that were frequently expressed through political faction. More recently, in a short piece intended as an aid for the teaching of *Tom Jones,* Eric Leuschner makes a convincing case that Sophia's "surreptitious smile" when learning about the landlord's mistake, "evokes sympathy for Jenny Cameron" and prompts readers to remember the attractiveness of the Stuarts in the 1740s, which is to be read alongside the conventionally positive attributes of Sophia as a paragon.[26]

To my mind, the misunderstanding does not imply Jacobite support on the part of Fielding, but it does complicate our assessment of Sophia in welcome ways. For instance, it makes readers acutely aware that the errant behavior of this otherwise blameless heroine is all too similar to that of the women who supported and marched alongside Prince Charles. This does not entirely negate a recent proposed allegorical reading of Sophia as Mary II, but it does foreground the extent to which Jacobite figures possessed qualities that endeared them to the public, that conventional Whig figures lacked.[27] In fact, it signals the absence of legendary female characters on the loyalist side, which Fielding proceeds to supply in the character of Sophia. At the same time, given that the narrator—who is ever prone to convey his viewpoints about the probity, or lack thereof, of his characters—makes no negative comment regarding Sophia here, the passage can be read as tempering the criticisms made of the female rebels, who, like the heroine of *Tom Jones,* may have had personal justifications for their conduct. In fact, for all the animosity that Fielding displays toward the Jacobites in his pamphlets and periodicals, the two mentions of Jenny Cameron that appear in his *Jacobite's Journal* are not hostile at all. In one, his ironic persona John Trott-plaid simply claims that the woman in the frontispiece to the *Journal* is not meant to represent "the famous *Jenny Cameron.*"[28] In the other, Trott-plaid argues that if, as the Whigs claim, women on their side were the most beautiful, it should be acknowledged that "all the Women of Spirit are on ours," none more so than "the famous Jenny Cameron, and many others who marched forth with the Men."[29] The ironic diction with which Fielding endows Trott-Plaid tempts readers to interpret all his statements as judgments contrary to those of the writer. However, as is the case with some remarks elsewhere in the *Journal*, the commendation of the "spirit" of Jacobite women is probably an exception, for this is an attribute of Sophia commended in earnest throughout *Tom Jones.*[30] The unequivocal objects of criticism in the episode of the Sophia/Cameron juxtaposition are the smug stupidity of the innkeeper, the naïveté of his wife and, later on, the overblown sense of aggravation that causes Honour to "claw the Rascal" and leave "the Marks of my Nails in his Impudent Face" upon learning that the landlord believes her mistress to be (in the words of Honour) "that nasty, stinking W—re, (*Jenny Cameron* they call her) that runs about the Country with the Pretender" (*TJ* 603).

The comic identification of Sophia with a Jacobite insurgent, along with her vivacity and daring, presents the possibility that she is, in Carlton's apt words, "her Jacobite father's daughter."[31] It activates, in case it had been overlooked, the dormant potential for transgression in the heroine's actions so far. For instance, although Sophia does not don male garb (like the Cameron of the scandalous accounts), she does carry with her a conventionally masculine artifact, loaded with phallic symbolism. In Book VII, as Honour and Sophia plan their escape, the latter reassures the former's misgivings about the dangers of the road with the promise: "I will defend you; for I will take a Pistol with me" (*TJ* 351). If readers had missed this slight breach of strict eighteenth-century decorum, the Cameron mix-up that takes place some books later acts as a retrospective warning. In yoking together Sophia's and Cameron's names—even if only in a case of mistaken identity—the novel foregrounds its heroine's contumacy.

This, however, is trumped by the fact that several other aspects of Sophia's characterization seem to locate her on the side of post-Revolutionary Whiggism, as well as to endorse what Ian Watt long ago dubbed the "new feminine code"—or "the decarnalisation of the public feminine role"— recommended by fiction writers and social commentators from mid-century onwards, which dictated that ideal women were to be domestic, maternal, and sexually passive.[32] Take, for example, the episode of the pistol referenced above. In contrast to Cameron, who in spurious biographies, such as the *Brief Account of the Life and Family of Miss Jenny Cameron,* was said to transgress gender norms of dress and comportment out of curiosity and for her own amusement, Sophia's temporary masculinization in carrying a firearm is far from flamboyant.[33] The narrative makes clear that Sophia would only use the weapon to defend herself and (her) Honour.

Sophia's latent unruliness is usually tempered by her judiciousness and her sense of decorum. She embodies the golden mean that the misogynistic writer of the *Memoirs of the Remarkable Life and Surprizing Adventures of Jenny Cameron* regards as an impossibility for women, who are "generally observed to act in Extremes; and whatever Capacity or Station of Life a Woman appears in, you will find her notoriously bad, or wondrously good." "Seldom," he continues, "do we see a Female behave with Moderation in any Thing; she knows no Medium, but is hurried on from one Extreme to another, by that Passion which is most prevalent in her."[34] In her compromise between the attractive femininity of "rebel ladies" such as Cameron and the acceptable conduct of the "new feminine code," Sophia exemplifies what might be termed spirited propriety. She is decidedly not just the "virtuous and beautiful daughter of Squire Western" that Martin Battestin sets her up to be.[35] Paragon of the story notwithstanding, Sophia is an instance of Fielding's rejection of a conventional eighteenth-century notion, (in)famously voiced by Alexander Pope, purporting to quote Martha Blount, that "most women had no characters at all."[36] The whole passage implies that there is more than one side to Sophia, something that can well be applied to political matters—which is why people should make sure to ponder matters carefully.

Acting the Part of a Rebel

By having a modest heroine like Sophia become an insurgent in the eyes of an undiscerning onlooker, Fielding tapped into the notion that it was possible for someone to display ostensibly contradictory personalities. More precisely, Fielding suggests that character is performative: one can act the part of a rebel when necessary, as well as that of a modest, proper, unassuming woman when the situation so demands. This idea about the performativity of character was especially apparent to people working in the theater, as Fielding had for the first decade of his literary career when he wrote over twenty-five plays and became the manager of a boisterous theatrical troupe until the Licensing Act of 1737 effectively put him out of business and prompted him to explore other vehicles for creativity and cultural influence.[37] It was during those formative years that Fielding met and established a fruitful professional relationship with Kitty Clive, who would take on the role of Cameron around the time when he was writing *Tom Jones*.[38]

As I tried to suggest earlier, Clive's original performance as Colombine Cameron added to the audience's imagining of the historical Cameron by establishing an implicit link between the two, endearing the admirers of the actress to the unruly woman that she played onstage. By the 1740s, Clive was a particularly beloved performer, as well as a socially respected figure. As a singer, she was said to be "without a Superior, if we except the foremost Voices in the Italian Operas."[39] Not only was she part of the cast of the first London performance of Handel's *Messiah* in 1743, she was also the composer's favorite soprano, for whom he wrote several songs and oratorio roles throughout the 1740s.[40] As a comic actress, Clive earned the admiration of even those who were her rivals in courting the esteem of the theater-going public. Samuel Foote, for instance, famously declared her to be "the best Actress in her Walk that I, or perhaps any Man living, has seen."[41] Fielding made a similar remark a few months before the publication of *Tom Jones*, praising "Mrs Clive (who in Comedy is certainly the best Actress the World ever produced)."[42] The caveats inserted by Foote and Fielding about the type of acting in which Clive excelled must be noted, for they foreshadow the polemic that plagued the reception of her tragic parts, which in turn provides an instance of the frailty of actresses' (and women's) standing at the time.

Clive's most famous roles were of rebellious women across the social spectrum, from pert servants to disobedient heiresses. These included coveted parts in well-established comedies of the repertory, such as Phillis in Richard Steele's *The Conscious Lovers* (1722), Miranda in Susannah Centlivre's *The Busie Body* (1709), Phillida in Colley Cibber's *Damon and Phillida* (1729), Nell in Charles Coffey's *The Devil to Pay* (1731), and Polly in *The Beggar's Opera* (1728), as well as characters created for her, like Maria in James Miller's *The Man of Taste* (1735) and Miss Kitty (a dramatization of Clive herself) in Miller's *The Coffee House* (1737).[43] She was also the leading actress and singer in several of Fielding's comedies and ballad operas, including Chloe in *The Lottery* (1732), Kissindra in *The Covent-Garden Tragedy* (1732), Lappet in *The Miser* (1732), Dorcas in *The Mock-Doctor* (1732), Deborah in the play of the same title (1733), Lettice in *The Intriguing Chambermaid* (1734), and Lucy in *An Old Man Taught Wisdom; or the Virgin Unmask'd* (1735) and its sequel, *Miss Lucy in Town* (1742). All of these parts were conceived as vehicles for Clive.[44] Many of these roles exploited the comic potential of having a naïve country girl become acquainted with the sophistication (and vices) of the metropolis, similar to what happens to Sophia in the third section of *Tom Jones*. Most of the plays that launched Clive to fame were still part of the repertory at the time of *Colombine Cameron*'s premiere. Indeed, the third performance of this pantomime followed a staging of Fielding's *Miser*, in which Clive took on her customary role as Lappet.[45] Clive was likewise famous for delivering epilogues written for her, the content of which frequently revolved around the place of women on the stage and in society at large.[46] All of this helped create a stage persona of an outspoken, willful, and witty woman.

Unlike other renowned actresses who came before her, however, Clive managed to maintain a reputation of a morally blameless private life. She generally eschewed scandal, particularly of the sexual kind. She had no children out of wedlock, and although she separated from her husband soon after their marriage, she did not indulge in extramarital affairs—or, if she did, she was discreet enough that they were never publicly known.[47] Later in life, Clive sought to promote the idea that she was a homely "good country gentlewoman," an identity that was at odds with the roles that launched her to fame.[48] Fielding was one of the main promoters of Clive's private probity, as evidenced in the much-quoted "Epistle to Mrs Clive" appended to *The Intriguing Chambermaid,* in which he praised her for "acting in real Life the Part of the best Wife, the best Daughter, the best Sister, and the best Friend." Domestic virtue did not preclude displays of bravery, for later in the same document Fielding commended the way that Clive exerted herself to defend her convictions in the actors' rebellion of 1733, and he claimed that this single feat "would have given [her] the Reputation of the greatest Heroine of the Age," had the dispute concerned members of the social elite.[49]

The strident contrast between Clive's private life and the roles that she played onstage exemplifies a conflict that Lisa Freeman sees as characteristic of the eighteenth century, a period in which audiences demanded increasing access to the personal lives of celebrities, especially those in the theatrical world. According to Freeman, "the fictional persona created by a playwright often had to compete with the persona or public reputation of the actor or actress taking that part. In this very basic sense, the 'character' presented to an audience was neither singular nor unitary, but rather manifold and incongruous."[50] Given that Clive was a woman, the crafting of her dual persona was also at the heart of an ongoing problematization of the notions of virtue and reputation for women who participated in the public sphere, namely authors and actresses. Acting as a profession, and, more specifically, being a famous actress, epitomized the idea of the performativity of character and was central to a reconsideration of what it meant to be a public woman. As Felicity Nussbaum explains, "the audience's imagined intimacy with the theatrical and social being of the celebrated actress flourished throughout the century," and this "brought a newfound recognition that women's personalities exposed in public could be translated into profit, but could also redefine feminine virtue."[51] Because women were increasingly present in the public sphere, the taste for gossip about their private lives grew, making actresses easy targets of misogynistic satire. At the same time, the celebrity status that actresses acquired allowed them to "carve out a coherent personhood while projecting an accessible, layered interiority that traversed the boundaries between dramatic character and private self, between public display and personal revelation."[52] This phenomenon can be observed clearly in Clive, who, according to Nussbaum, succeeded in "heighten[ing] her marketability by aligning decorous womanhood with theatrical femininity at the very time when the larger culture was struggling with the incongruous linkage of these terms."[53] A Colombine Cameron conceived for and played by Clive carried with her all the personality traits of the actress's imagined identity.

According to Clive's biographer Berta Joncus, the soprano actress had three recognizable personas at the height of her career: "the sentimental heroine/titillating shepherdess of her early ballad operas (1728–33); the 'smart chambermaid' whose onstage willfulness was offset by her virtuous offstage conduct (1733–37); and the doyenne of the English musical and comedy stage who exemplified British values and cultural pre-eminence (1737–45)."[54] In Clive's role as Colombine Cameron, the first and last of these identities fuse. Not only is she a beautiful rustic maiden endlessly pestered by suitors, but by the end of the pantomime, rather than taking on her putative role as Prince Charles's ally, she becomes instrumental in his defeat, thus emerging as a patriotic figure for her London audiences. This fusion was enhanced by her performance of songs composed by Arne, the same artist who set to music James Thomson's "Rule Britannia." Harlequin likewise toys with the expectations raised by the full title of the pantomime (his being "Incendiary") as he outmaneuvers the Pope and the Devil, who in the initial scenes of the piece conjure him up as an envoy to help betray Protestant England to Rome and then send it to Hell. Near the end of the pantomime, Harlequin and Colombine convince the latter's Scottish admirers to join with the Pretender's forces, which they do. Harlequin then transforms "an English Palace" into which the Pretender and his army "rush in, Sword in Hand ... into a Prison" (23), which brings about the end of the rebellion. Thus, the ostensible miscreant is revealed as unexpectedly loyal—something that is also true of the hero of *Tom Jones*. Like Colombine and Clive, Sophia sports personality types that are ultimately joined in a patriotic gesture: the tantalizing country girl (besieged by unworthy suitors and whose muff is made much ado about by the narrative) and the domestic heroine embodying British values.[55]

Given that, as discussed earlier, *Colombine Cameron* was probably the first substantial work in which Prince Charles's reputed mistress featured as a protagonist, the character of Cameron was infused with the qualities attributed to Clive and the roles that made her famous (including her other performances as Colombine). This merging of Clive's stage persona with Cameron's legend encouraged the identification of portraits of the actress as likenesses of the Jacobite heroine by Stuart sympathizers, a conflation that continues to this day.[56] At the same time, the actress's decorous offstage life offered what in the eyes of eighteenth-century commentators were the best aspects of Sophia as a model of femininity. The contradictory qualities that were subsumed within Clive's personality can thus be regarded as a crucial link between Cameron and Sophia. The juxtaposition of Sophia (a fictional creation) and Cameron (a historical character, fictionally constructed) mirrors Clive's full character, with the real and fictional sides blended. Like that of the real Cameron, Clive's family heritage was not unambiguously English, for she was Irish on her father's side. Like the fictional Sophia, Clive was the daughter of a Jacobite, whose support for James II during the Glorious Revolution cost him his estate and social standing.[57] Similar to Clive, Sophia "was a perfect mistress of music, and would never willingly have played any but Handel's songs," but she also "learnt [popular] tunes to oblige" (*TJ* 169) her less sophisticated audiences (Squire Western in the case of the fictional heroine; enthusiasts of ballad opera in the case of the actress).[58] Like Cameron, Clive was an attractive and independent woman. Like Sophia, she was mindful of her reputation.

That the dynamics of on- and off-stage personalities—and their nearly automatic merging in the eyes of the audience—are relevant to *Tom Jones* is evident from the moment that Sophia is introduced. Upon the first mention of the heroine's name and a hint of her character at the end of Book III, the narrator pauses the narrative to begin anew, so as to grant the subject its due importance. The inaugural chapter of Book IV, which prefaces the proper introduction of Sophia, is a telling disquisition on characterization, in which the narrator relates an ostensibly trivial anecdote about the drinking habits of Barton Booth, the leading male actor of the preceding generation. With calculated nonchalance, the narrator refers to the actor as "King Pyrrhus," after the role for which he was most famous, as if stage performance seeped through, or indeed replaced, offstage personality. Having acted the part of Pyrrhus in the original production of Ambrose Philips's *The Distrest Mother* (1712), Booth becomes and is thereafter identified with the quasi-historical figure of Pyrrhus, as represented in a popular play. In the context of the arguments explored here, this detail is strongly suggestive, for it illustrates how eighteenth-century audiences were attuned to the curious fusion of a historical figure, a theatrical character, and the performer of the role, which occurs as a result of repeated playacting.[59]

This, I believe, is what is at stake with the insertion of Cameron as a comic model for Sophia. Rather than functioning as an endorsement of Jacobitism or as a criticism of Sophia, the invocation of the Jacobite rebel demonstrates the multidimensionality of character, as well as the difficulties of attempting a definite assessment of personhood. The Jacobite rebel is invoked as not only an historical figure or as the scandalous amazon of spurious biographies but also as *Clive* Cameron: a three-way conflation of Cameron (the political personage who was made into a pantomime character), the stage persona of the star actress Mrs. Clive, and the carefully constructed private character of Fielding's friend Catherine. All of these personae become one in performance. All three layers are present at once in Sophia, but not everyone can read them—only those whom Fielding calls his "sagacious readers."[60]

Reading Sophia

Colombine Cameron has several attributes that would appeal to the otherwise pantomime-averse Fielding. In fact, there are specific echoes between this pantomime and an earlier political text by Fielding. *Colombine Cameron* opens with the three characters of Fielding's "Dialogue between the Devil, the Pope, and the Pretender" (published a few months earlier), plotting against Britain. As in Fielding's pamphlet, in the pantomime their plans are thwarted on account of betrayals among the conspirators.[61] Although, as O'Brien points out, "there is probably no such thing as a fully representative eighteenth-century pantomime," *Colombine Cameron* (described on its title page as a "musical pantomime") does sport a few peculiarities that separate it from other pantomimes of the period and that move it closer to the ballad operas that were so popular after John Gay's *Beggar's Opera,* and of which Fielding wrote various specimens in the 1730s.[62] Despite its abundance of songs, *Colombine Cameron* contains more spoken lines than other pantomimes of the first half of the century and so less "dumb show"— unscripted episodes involving dancing and slapstick action.[63] Additionally, unlike most pantomimes of the period, there was no separation between the "serious" and "comic" parts of *Colombine Cameron*. Perhaps its greatest departure from convention, though, lies in the self-ironizing remarks about pantomime that are found in the libretto. For instance, readers are informed that Colombine is afraid of Harlequin at first, but "this is short, lest we should run out of Nature by making a Colombine not soon familiar with a Harlequin" (*CC* 12). Similarly, a magic trick is described as the "first feat of Harlequin that ever had any Moral to it" (14). These aspects betray a certain hostility of the work towards its own genre, a sense of self-mockery that recalls the afterpieces that Fielding staged during his tenure as manager of the Little Theatre at the Haymarket in the mid-1730s.[64]

Much of this might have been lost on audiences who did not have access to the printed version. The more so if, as was often the case with pantomime, they were distracted by the spectacle of the show (the scenery, the music, the singing and dancing) or rowdy fellow playgoers and did not pause to consider the broader implications of what they saw. This kind of onlooker might fuse, without further reflection, the stage persona and the fictionally constructed private personhood of Clive with the figure of Cameron. To a writer deeply invested in the power of the written word, as Fielding was, such spectators were dangerously liable to be mistaken in their views, as occurs with the foolish innkeeper in *Tom Jones*. The dynamics of the stage involve an implicit probing of the notions of deception and enactment—and of proper and improper interpretation. The novel, by contrast, allows for an explicit examination of these concepts. It is not surprising, then, that, having found in prose fiction an alternative outlet for exerting cultural influence, Fielding would want to explore these problems in earnest in the characterization of the heroine of his most carefully constructed novel.

Moreover, the novel as a form proved an effective mode of writing to counter the spectacle associated with the Stuarts. As Elaine McGirr convincingly demonstrates, from around the time of the Glorious Revolution up to the final Jacobite Rebellion, heroism was "closely associated with court culture," and so "the heroic was connected to the threat of Jacobitism." As far back as the reign of Queen Anne, commentators such as Richard Steele and Joseph Addison envisioned a new kind of hero who could be both polite and virtuous, thus replacing the model of the carefree cavalier endorsed by Restoration comedy. This, however, McGirr adds, "was not fully realized until the mid-eighteenth century and then only in a new genre, the domestic novel," with the protagonists of Fielding's *Tom Jones* and Samuel Richardson's *Sir Charles Grandison* as key exemplars.[65] Tom's gradual abandonment of pseudo-cavalier attitudes in favor of a domestic(ated) ethos is thus indicative of Fielding's attempt to replace the martial heroism associated with the Stuarts with the marital respectability that the Hanoverian regime sought to endorse. Even the way the protagonist's licentiousness is explained away as a product of his youth, his passionate constitution, and his deference to the opposite sex can be seen as responding to this notion. The domestic fiction of writers like Fielding fostered new types of relationships between readers and characters, which generated a sense of rapport. In McGirr's apt words, "the mid-century novel promoted sympathy—feeling with—to counter the heroic's awe—wonder at."[66] Tom is not offered as a paragon to be admired, or even feared—as conventional Restoration rakes such as Dorimant from George Etherege's *The Man of Mode* (1676) were— but as a representative of a slightly flawed but essentially good-natured, and thoroughly perfectible, human nature. Readers are entreated continuously to understand Tom's inner motivations. Something similar could be argued of Sophia, the female counterpart to this new type of hero.

As we saw, the character of Colombine Cameron, as performed by Clive, carried with it the many layers associated with the public persona of the actress and her most famous roles, which, together with Colombine's ultimate betrayal of the Pretender, worked to endear the figure to loyalist audiences. This could backfire on the Hanoverian position endorsed by the pantomime, for it could augment the sense of charisma and awe associated with the Stuarts and their supporters—similar to what happens to the innkeeper's wife in *Tom Jones* who is charmed by Sophia and, taking her for Cameron, becomes "in a Moment a staunch *Jacobite*" (*TJ* 580). Like the horse who is inexplicably charmed by Sophia's voice to the point that it refuses to obey his rider, theatrical audiences could fall for Clive's vocal virtuosity and forget that she was neither the real Jenny Cameron, nor an advocate for the Jacobite cause. Revisiting the argument in a different genre, that of prose fiction, allowed Fielding more control in guiding the audience's interpretation of the heroine. As Deidre Lynch points out, the novel was "founded in the promise that it was this type of writing that tendered the deepest, truest knowledge of character," while, at the same time, the novel fed from well-established characters in other media.[67] In order to elicit sympathy, Fielding's portrayal of Sophia strove to go beyond the admiration, the (virulent or benevolent) mockery, and the comic enjoyment associated with both Jenny Cameron and Kitty Clive. This "quality of being affected by the affection of another," as Samuel Johnson put it, was a concept rapidly gaining in social and philosophical esteem around mid-century.[68] As a character of pantomime, ballad, malicious biography, or news report, Cameron could be disparaged or applauded, but not fully understood. By contrast, Sophia is designed to be comprehended in all her intricacy through careful reading.

However, reading closely—and correctly—is not an easy task; it demands perceptive readers, or so Fielding argues both explicitly and implicitly in *Tom Jones*. Thus, another crucial matter to which the conflation of Sophia with her Jacobite avatar draws attention is that of misinterpretation or incorrect reading. Throughout the story, all sorts of characters misjudge Sophia and misconstrue her reactions. As we have seen, nosy innkeepers mistake her for a Jacobite insurgent. Her foolish father never knows what to make of her. Her learned and otherwise perspicacious aunt believes her to be infatuated with Blifil (whom she loathes). Allworthy (who despite being a well-meaning magistrate is the poorest judge of character in the whole novel) misinterprets her politeness as a proof of her regard for the intellectual subordination of women to men.[69] Even Tom, who is the character most closely connected to her, is slow to recognize her signs of love for him.

These errors of judgment, which not only affect Sophia, but also are ubiquitous throughout the text, stem from a combination of a lack of discernment on the part of characters and either a careless or a purposefully misleading arrangement of facts in the narrative.[70] Just before the Cameron confusion, for example, the acumen of the innkeeper is called into question in the following terms:

> This Landlord had the Character, among all his Neighbours, of being a very sagacious Fellow. He was thought to see farther and deeper into Things than any Man in the Parish. ... In his Deportment he was solemn, if not sullen; and when he spoke, which was seldom, he always delivered himself in a slow Voice; ... nay he commonly gave [his hearers] a Hint, that he knew much more than he thought proper to disclose. (*TJ* 576)

Readers of this passage are invited to mock the affectation of the innkeeper as much as the credulity of the parishioners who take his calculated mannerisms as evidence of shrewdness. By the time this obtuse and arrogant man takes Sophia for a rebel, readers are meant not only to scoff at his foolishness but also to reflect on the factors implicated in making inaccurate judgments more generally. Rumormongering has other nefarious consequences in *Tom Jones*—as, for instance, when the Jacobite Partridge tittle-tattles about Sophia's supposed infatuation with Tom. Sophia lays the blame on her beloved, and, living up to Clive's reputation of being as big-hearted as short-tempered, her outrage is categorical. "He is not only a Villain," she declares, "but a low despicable Wretch. I can forgive all rather than his exposing my Name in so barbarous a Manner. That renders him the Object of my Contempt" (545). As part of the Upton episode, in which Sophia is mistaken for a Jacobite rebel, this passage harks back to the way that newspapers, many of them pro-Jacobite, divulged unverifiable information about the supposed affair between Cameron and Prince Charles in an attempt to bolster their sales. These publications were adept at constructing characters that readers would either dread or admire without further reflection. Gossipers like Partridge, and all those willing to consume the information he divulges, exemplify the taste for the old heroic mode that, as McGirr shows, was decisively on its way out after the '45. Like the enthusiasts of pantomime, Partridge and the innkeepers are shown to be dazzled by spectacle and reputed deeds.

The Sophia/Cameron confusion, then, also implies a criticism about popular forms of entertainment and the endorsement of an alternative mode in Fielding's own "history." The latter, Fielding suggested in the theoretical disquisitions scattered throughout *Joseph Andrews* (1742) and *Tom Jones*, could only be written by talented writers (like himself) and accessed in all its multidimensionality by the "sagacious readers" that he idealized. Fielding's illustrations of unwitting delusion go beyond topicality to make a larger point about human nature—a favorite device in Fielding's writings. Ironically, the complexity of the characterization of Sophia might be lost on readers who, like the good-natured but short-sighted Allworthy, are too keen to accept beauty and modesty as the desirable and univocal attributes of a female paragon. The theater and its characters did not leave Fielding as he turned to writing novels. Among the many lessons that the stage taught him was an awareness of the competence of women and the significance of their public roles. In the many-faceted virtuousness of Sophia, Fielding brought to fiction Clive's project of a protean character that was alluring in its rebelliousness but ultimately commended for its propriety. Unlike the vehicles that Fielding and others created for Clive on the stage, however, the multidimensionality of Sophia's character was not to depend on what the personhood of the actress brought to the part, which is likely to be forgotten once the performer (and the witnesses to her art) are no more. As my analysis hopes to have shown, Fielding carried the theater into his novels in ways that might not be evident to readers nowadays. With Sophia, who is a more complex character than critics usually acknowledge, even seemingly trivial mistakes are endowed with unexpected significance. Paying close attention to these inter- and extra-textual dynamics sheds light on the intricate and fascinating relationship that existed between drama and prose fiction, as well as between national politics and gender roles. This, in turn, may remind us as critics to never stop probing into the (covert) complexity of their characters.

Notes

1. Martin C. Battestin, *A Henry Fielding Companion* (Westport: Greenwood Press, 2000), 282.

2. In the online version of the *Encyclopaedia Britannica*, for instance, Sophia is presented as a "fictional character, the beloved and, eventually, the wife of Tom Jones, hero of Henry Fielding's picaresque novel *Tom Jones* (1749)" *https://www.*

britannica.com/topic/Sophia-Western. Sparknotes, a site frequented (confessedly or not) by English undergraduates, tells its readers that Sophia is "an allegorical figure, meant to represent the feminine ideal and therefore kept as anonymous as possible. ... Although Sophia's decision to run away from her violent father Squire Western signals her courage and bravery ... she actually does very little in the novel. As a woman and obedient daughter, Sophia must allow herself to be acted upon, and even though she falls in love with Tom Jones before he falls in love with her, she cannot, in all decency, say anything" *https://www.sparknotes.com/lit/tomjones/ character/sophia-western/.* Browsers of Shmoop learn that Sophia is "Tom's love interest, ... also beautiful, graceful, and talented in her own right. ... the main core of her characterization is that she is in love with Tom" *https://www.shmoop.com/ tom-jones-book/sophia-western.html.*

3.   Robert D. Hume, "Henry Fielding at 300: Elusive, Confusing, Misappropriated, or (Perhaps) Obvious?" *Modern Philology* 108, no. 2 (2010): 249.

4.   The pioneering studies in this respect are Angela Smallwood, *Fielding and the Woman Question: The Novels of Henry Fielding and Feminist Debate, 1700–1750* (New York: Harvester Wheatsheaf, 1989); and Jill Campbell, *Natural Masques: Gender and Identity in Fielding's Plays and Novels* (Stanford: Stanford University Press, 1995).

5.   Earla A. Wilputte, "Women Buried: Henry Fielding and Feminine Absence," *Modern Language Review* 95, no. 2 (2000): 324.

6.   Simon Dickie, "*Amelia*, Sex, and Fielding's Woman Question," in *Henry Fielding (1707–1754) Novelist, Playwright, Journalist, Magistrate: A Double Anniversary Tribute,* ed. Claude Rawson (Newark: University of Delaware Press, 2008), 115–42, esp. 120. In another article in the same collection of essays, Guyonne Leduc considers the extent to which Fielding might be considered a pre-feminist, finding that "his attitude towards women's role is double. As a conservative, he would perpetuate their function as wives and mothers, limiting their ambitions to domestic life. More open-mindedly, he approves of intellectual, or rather moral, emancipation"; "Was Fielding a Prefeminist," in *Henry Fielding (1707–1754),* 271–92, 284.

7.   See, for instance, Anthony Kearney, "Tom Jones and the Forty-Five," *Ariel* 4 (1973): 68–78; Thomas Cleary, "Jacobitism in Tom Jones," *Philological Quarterly* 52 (1973): 239–51; Lawrence Lipking, "The Jacobite Plot," *ELH* 64, no. 4 (1997): 843–55; J. A. Downie, *A Political Biography of Henry Fielding* (London: Pickering and Chatto, 2009), 173–84; and, more recently, Kelly Fleming, "The Politics of Sophia Western's Muff," *Eighteenth-Century Fiction* 31, no. 4 (2019): 659–84.

8.   See Ronald Paulson, "The '45 and Bonnie Prince Charlie," *Popular and Polite Art in the Age of Hogarth and Fielding* (Notre Dame: University of Notre Dame Press, 1979), 190–207, an argument he repeats in *The Life of Henry Fielding, a Critical Biography* (Oxford: Blackwell), 204; Peter Carlton, "The Mitigated Truth: Tom Jones's Double Heroism," *Studies in the Novel* 19, no. 4 (1987): 397–409, as well as Carlton's "*Tom Jones* and the '45 Once Again," *Studies in the Novel* 20, no. 4 (1988): 361–73; Campbell, *Natural Masques,* 166–75; John Allen Stevenson, *The Real History of Tom Jones* (New York: Palgrave Macmillan, 2005), 17–47.

9. My argument is thus positioned at the crossroads of two of what Hume labels the "problem areas" of Fielding studies (i.e., gender issues and partisan politics), as well as one that he identifies as a neglected but promising direction for further inquiry: the intersections between Fielding's drama and his fiction. Hume, "Henry Fielding at 300," 243.

10. See the list of "Books and Pamphlets published" for April 1746 in *The Gentleman's Magazine* 16 (1746): 224, item 33. Although the customary shortening of the title of this pantomime is *Harlequin Incendiary*, for this essay, I select the subtitle (a practice not uncommon with other plays of the period) to emphasize the character on which my critical inquiry focuses.

11. The best instance of a positive popular depiction is the ballad "Bonnie Jeanie Cameron," which recounts the story of how, overcome with illness, "Rare, O rare, bonnie Jeanie Cameron!" calls for the aid of Charlie, who comes to her rescue. In turn, she informs him "who were his friends and who were his foes." Emile Berger and George Eyre-Todd, eds., *Ancient Scots Ballads: With the Traditional Airs to Which They Were Wont to Be Sung* (London: Bayley & Ferguson, 1894), 7–12. Satiric portrayals can be found in *Ascanius: Or the Young Adventurer; a True History. ... and Interspersed with Remarks on the Characters of the Principal Persons Who Appear'd in the Interest of Ascanius; Particularly the Celebrated Miss Cameron* (London: T. Johnson, 1746), 284–86; *Brief Account of the Life and Family of Miss Jenny Cameron* (London: T. Garner, 1746); Archibald Arbuthnot, *Memoirs of the Remarkable Life and Surprizing Adventures of Jenny Cameron* (London: R. Walker, 1746); Walter Turnbull, *Some Verses Composed upon the Insurrections of the Jacobites in the Kingdoms of Great-Britain and Ireland from Their First Rise to the Present Time* (Newcastle Upon Tyne: for the author, 1746); *The Fool: Being a Collection of Essays and Epistles: Moral, Political, Humorous and Entertaining.* Vol. 2 (London: Nutt, Cooke and Kingman, 1748), 346–53; and John Teacle, *An Excellent New Song on the Battle of Culloden* (Edinburgh: n.p., 1776).

12. See the advertisement in the *London Evening Post* 26 August 1746 announcing its forthcoming publication.

13. The first publication to divulge information that sullied the moral standing of Cameron (suggesting not only that she was Prince Charles's mistress but also that she had grown intimate with him upon their very first acquaintance) was the Tory pro-Jacobite paper *The London Evening Post* (in the issue for 14–17 December 1745). In all probability, the editors (at the time Richard Nutt and John Meres) were trying to awaken their readers' passions by inflating Prince Charles's reputed charisma and by calling attention to the vivacity and the human side of the rebels.

14. As John O'Brien shows, it was unusual for pantomimes to engage in direct political commentary of any kind, which is not to say that they were apolitical. They participated in politics in more complicated ways, having to do with the prominence of the genre itself in the public sphere and their symbolic suggestion that, if all the world was a stage, the ways of the government resembled the absurdity, inanity, and mercantilism supposedly appertaining to pantomime. *Harlequin Britain: Pantomime and Entertainment, 1690–1760* (Baltimore: Johns Hopkins University Press, 2004), esp. chapters 4 and 6.

15. *Harlequin Incendiary; or Colombine Cameron* (London: M. Cooper, 1746), 10, 19, henceforth cited parenthetically in the text as *CC*.

16. Arthur H. Scouten, *The London Stage, 1660–1800; A Calendar of Plays, Entertainments & Afterpieces, Together with Casts, Box-receipts and Contemporary Comment*, 5 vols. (Carbondale: Southern Illinois University Press), 3.2:1222.

17. Standard signifiers of Jacobitism include plaid fabric, white roses (or white dress in general), oak trees, and Cavalier King Charles Spaniels. See Murray Pittock, *Material Culture and Sedition, 1688–1760: Treacherous Objects, Secret Places* (Basingstoke: Palgrave McMillan, 2013), 54–83. For discussion of a print identified as Kitty Clive performing as Cameron in which such symbols may be identified, see note 56. A similar principle can explain why Cameron's name is not present in the spoken parts of the piece, which was mainly composed of songs. The songs of ballad operas and other musical entertainments tended to be repeated after the performance, some even turning into unofficial anthems, or war cries, as was the case with James Thomson's "Rule Britannia," set to music by Arne in *Alfred* (1740), and Fielding's own "The Roast Beef of Old England," created for *The Author's Farce* (1731).

18. On the relationship between Jenny Cameron and the ideological debates around the '45 see Campbell, *Natural Masques*, 154–57.

19. John O'Brien, "Pantomimic Politics," in Julia Swindells and David Francis Taylor, eds., *The Oxford Handbook of Georgian Theatre 1737–1832* (Oxford: Oxford University Press, 2014), 402. O'Brien also notes a relation between this piece and Fielding's novel having to do with the way that both were "occasioned … by the '45," which provided their plots with "a national framework" (399) that was then left aside for a significant portion of the work itself. He also points out the "structural similarities [of *Tom Jones*] to the *commedia dell'arte* sections of Georgian pantomime (hero, heroine, blocking figure)" (400). He does not, however, dwell on the possible implications of these resemblances.

20. Henry Fielding, *The History of Tom Jones, A Foundling*, ed. Fredson Bowers and Martin C. Battestin (Hanover: Wesleyan University Press, 1975), 577, henceforth cited parenthetically in the text as *TJ*.

21. Downie, *Political Biography of Henry Fielding*, 184.

22. Carlton, "*Tom Jones* and the '45 Once Again," 361, 369.

23. Stevenson, *Real History of Tom Jones*, 20, 24.

24. Carlton, "*Tom Jones* and the '45 Once Again"; Campbell, *Natural Masques*, 166–75.

25. Campbell, *Natural Masques*, 173.

26. Eric Leuschner, "Sophia's Smile: Reading Jenny Cameron in the Margins of *Tom Jones*," in *Approaches to Teaching the Novels of Henry Fielding*, ed. Jennifer Preston Wilson and Elizabeth Kraft (New York: Modern Language Association of America, 2015), 145.

27. Kelly Fleming's political reading of Sophia's muff leads her to endorse an allegorical interpretation of Tom as a figure for William of Orange and to suggest that Sophia should therefore be seen as Mary II. Persuasive though her argument is, Fleming glosses over the Jenny Cameron confusion too quickly to my taste, arguing that "the innkeeper's mistake rather than stemming from Jacobitism, likely results

from most men of the period being predisposed to assume women travelling alone in gold-laced riding dresses were sex workers." Fleming, "The Politics of Sophia Western's Muff," esp. 678–79, note 77.

28. Henry Fielding, *The Jacobite's Journal* 2 (12 December 1747), in *The Jacobite's Journal and Related Writings,* ed. W. B. Coley (Oxford: Clarendon Press, 1974), 173.

29. Fielding, *Jacobite's Journal* 13 (27 February 1748), in *The Jacobite's Journal,* 98.

30. Sustained irony is difficult to achieve and easy to misinterpret. Fielding acknowledged as much in the *Jacobite's Journal* itself, observing that there was "no kind of Humour so liable to be mistaken" and none more "dangerous to the Writer" as irony (17 [6 March 1748], in Coley, *The Jacobite's Journal,* 211). For an illuminating discussion of Sophia's "Spirit" as a positive quality in *Tom Jones,* see Campbell, *Natural Masques,* 171–72.

31. Carlton, *"Tom Jones* and the '45 Again," 369.

32. Ian Watt, *The Rise of the Novel: Studies in Defoe, Richardson and Fielding.* 2nd American ed. (Berkeley: University of California Press, 2001), 163.

33. Cameron supposedly went out cross-dressed with two servants, picked up "Women of the Town," and otherwise "acted the Cavalier to a Miracle" (*Brief Account,* 24).

34. Arbuthnot, *Memoirs of the Remarkable Life,* 13–14.

35. Battestin, *A Henry Fielding Companion,* 282.

36. Alexander Pope, "Epistle to a Lady: Of the Characters of Women," in *Moral Essays, in Four Epistles* (Glasgow: R. Urie, 1754), 21, line 2.

37. Of the twenty-eight plays that Fielding wrote throughout his life, twenty-five were the product of his work between 1728 and 1737. For illuminating discussions of Fielding's theatrical career, see Peter Lewis, *Fielding's Burlesque Drama: Its Place in the Tradition* (Edinburgh: Edinburgh University Press, 1987); Robert D. Hume, *Henry Fielding and the London Theatre, 1728–1737* (Oxford: Clarendon Press, 1988); Albert Rivero, *The Plays of Henry Fielding: A Critical Study of His Dramatic Career* (Charlottesville: University Press of Virginia, 1989); and Henry Fielding, *Plays,* ed. Thomas Lockwood. 3 vols. (Oxford: Clarendon Press, 2004–11).

38. The period of composition for *Tom Jones* is a contested matter. Some believe that Fielding started writing the novel after the defeat of the Jacobite rebels, at some point in 1746. For this view, see Hugh Amory, "The History of 'The Adventures of a Foundling': Revising *Tom Jones," Harvard Library Bulletin* 27 (1979): 277–303. By contrast, Martin Battestin advances the hypothesis that Fielding began writing the novel well before the '45 but that he abandoned the project for some years and returned to it after the rebellion. See Battestin's "General Introduction" to *Tom Jones.* ed. Fredson Bowers and Martin Battestin, xxxv–xlii. In either case, it is safe to assume that Fielding was working on *Tom Jones* in the months surrounding the staging and publication of *Colombine Cameron.*

39. *The Comedian, or Philosophical Enquirer* 7 (October 1732), 40.

40. On the mutually beneficial relationship between Handel and Kitty Clive, see Berta Joncus, "Handel at Drury Lane: Ballad Opera and the Production of Kitty Clive," *Journal of the Royal Musical Association* 131, no. 2 (2006): 179–226.

41. Samuel Foote, *The Roman and English Comedy Consider'd and Compar'd, with Remarks on the Suspicious Husband* (London: T. Waller, 1747), 41.

42. Fielding, *The Jacobite Journal* (30 January 1748), in Coley, *The Jacobite's Journal*, 146–47.

43. Clive received the extremely sought-after part of Polly Peachum in 1732, and it bolstered her fame from then onwards. Her performance was praised in a short note in *The Daily Journal,* in which she was referred to as "the Darling of the Age". See K. A. Crouch, "Clive [née Raftor], Catherine [Kitty]," *Oxford Dictionary of National Biography* (Oxford: Oxford UP, 2014).

44. In her recent biography of Clive, Berta Joncus argues that the first roles that Fielding created for her were detrimental to her reputation in that they over-sexualized her image and made her subservient to the characters played by Theophilus Cibber. After the actors' revolt in 1733, Joncus claims, Fielding found it more convenient to stay in Drury Lane (abandoning Cibber) and to fashion an image of respectability for Clive that would help his own. See Berta Joncus, *Kitty Clive, or the Fair Songster* (Woodbridge: Boydell Press, 2019), 105–57. I believe, however, that such an account overstates the degree to which Fielding threw Clive under the bus to save himself. Fielding was never on good terms with the Cibber men, and he openly made fun of them whenever possible. The notion that the openly sexual roles that Fielding crafted for Clive were meant to poke fun at her comes from the (unproblematized) assumption that Fielding was a misogynist who considered clever and sexually desiring women to be morally blamable. This is, to put it mildly, imprecise. My view is that in the vehicles that Fielding created for Clive in the early 1730s, the playwright exploited her comedic talents (which generated a good response from audiences), and later, as the tide of public opinion turned, he helped her fashion a new non-scandalous image that was more attuned to the sensibilities of the time.

45. For details of these performances see Scouten, *The London Stage,* 3.2:1223, 1204. *The Miser* was Fielding's free adaptation—or in Thomas Lockwood's words, full "revision and rethinking"—of Molière's *L'avare*. It is worth noting that among the major changes that Fielding introduced were precisely those applied to the role of Lappet, conceived as a vehicle for Clive. For an illuminating examination of these alterations see Lockwood's introduction to this play in Fielding, *Plays*, ed. Thomas Lockwood, 3 vols. (Oxford: Clarendon Press, 2003–2011), 2:464–69.

46. For a discussion of the content and implications of Clive's epilogues, see Felicity Nussbaum, *Rival Queens: Actresses, Performance, and the Eighteenth-Century British Theatre* (Philadelphia: University of Pennsylvania Press, 2010), 174–77.

47. About Clive's "militant chastity" in the 1730s and her determination to "disappoint predatory beaus and managers for the rest of her life, see her entry in Philip H. Highfill Jr., Kalman A. Burnim, and Edward A. Langhans, *A Biographical Dictionary of Actors, Actresses, Musicians, Dancers, Managers, and Other Stage Personnel in London (1660–1800),* 16 vols. (Carbondale: Southern Illinois University Press, 1973–1993), 3:344–45.

48. JoAllen Bradham, "A Good Country Gentlewoman: Catherine Clive's Epistolary Autobiography," *Biography* 19, no. 3 (1996): 259–82, 260–61.

49. Fielding, "An Epistle to Mrs Clive," *The Intriguing Chambermaid,* in Fielding, *Plays,* 2:582.

50. Lisa Freeman, *Character's Theatre: Genre and Identity on the Eighteenth-Century English Stage* (Philadelphia: University of Pennsylvania Press, 2002), 18.

51. Nussbaum, *Rival Queens,* 16, 19.

52. Nussbaum, *Rival Queens,* 6.

53. Nussbaum, *Rival Queens,* 153.

54. Joncus, "Handel at Drury Lane," 195. Elsewhere, Joncus narrates the gradual demise of Clive's positive reputation after a broadside entitled "The Green Room Scuffle" (29 January 1746) satirized the actress as conceited and belligerent. See Joncus, *Kitty Clive, or the Fair Songster,* 324.

55. On the tangled relationship of sexuality and politics as exemplified by Fielding's muff jokes in *Tom Jones,* see Fleming, "The Politics of Sophia Western's Muff."

56. In its collection of "Jacobite prints and broadsides," the National Library of Scotland has two portraits of Clive. They are available for perusal in the NLS digital database (items 140-Blaikie.NPG.15.9-A and 141-Blaikie.NPG.15.9-B) *https://digital.nls.uk/75241184* and *https://digital.nls.uk/75241187.* The first item is labelled "Jenny Cameron, c. 1700–1790. Adventuress, supporter of Charles Edward Stuart as Kitty Clive, the actress. Portrait of Mrs Clive outdoors." The second is also said to be "Jenny Cameron … as Kitty Clive," to which is added that the sitter is "standing outside, holding a shepherd's crook in her hand." No details are provided regarding the original painter, engraver, date, or place of composition. Below the first image, a text written in pencil on the left-hand side reads "J. Faber" and on the right "W. John Alastair." The National Portrait Gallery has in its digital catalogue an image that is the same as item 140. This is listed as an illustration of Kitty Clive as Phillida (in Cibber's farce *Damon and Phillida*), a nineteenth-century engraving by William John Alais, after a 1734 print by John Faber, after Peter van Bleeck, in which Phillida is accompanied by Damon. *https://www.npg.org.uk/collections/search/portrait/mw200202/.* The association of the first NLS image with Jenny Cameron is, thus, a case of mistaken identity. The pencil caption for the second NLS image (item 141) simply reads "Kitty Clive." I have not been able to find the print in any other database, nor is it recorded in the list of likenesses of Clive included in her entries in the *Oxford Dictionary of National Biography,* in Highfill, Kalman, and Langhans's *Biographical Dictionary,* and in the thorough discussions of Clive's portraits in Joncus's *Kitty Clive, or the Fair Songster.* In the anti-Jacobite and anti-Scottish atmosphere of post-Culloden England, it makes sense that if an illustration of Clive as Cameron was ever made, it was not preserved or listed in official records, which would explain its preservation only in a collection of Jacobite broadsides kept by a Scottish connoisseur. Symbols of Jacobitism had to be discreet. Some such motifs can potentially be read in the elegant shepherdess dress worn by the woman in item 141, with her white petticoats and what appears to be a plaid skirt, with what could be oak trees in the distance. The ermine trimming in her cape and stomacher is an ambiguous symbol, in that ermine is used for "the garment of kings, and [is] symbolic of rightful monarchy" (Pittock, *Material Culture and Sedition,*

162). The image would thus seem to be made to suit the interpretation of either side. It could be that it indeed represented Clive as Cameron but only circulated in Jacobite paraphernalia. More details about the composition and circulation of this print would be very useful to clarify the matter. The important point to note here is that Clive was (and still is) associated with Cameron, by Jacobite sympathizers at least—a link that probably came from her acting in the pantomime.

57. On Clive's family history see Highfill, Kalman, and Langhans, *Biographical Dictionary*, 3:341.

58. Sophia is likewise said to possess a melodious voice (226). Its power is exemplified when the heroine is unable to convince her guide to change direction, but the horse "is reported to have been so charmed by Sophia's voice that he made a full Stop, and exprest an Unwillingness to proceed any farther" (561).

59. For this point I am indebted to Campbell, who examines this episode in relation to the way that Fielding "begins to suggest how public identity is structured by role-playing and spectacle outside the theatre as well," given that Booth enjoyed behaving like a king offstage (*Natural Masques*, 167).

60. This appellation occurs throughout the story as a cue for readers to be more alert about the information presented. As Henry Powell persuasively argues, by invoking the work of the classical scholar Richard Bentley with the phrase "sagacious reader," Fielding signals his awareness that readers always interpret texts according to their personal expectations and prejudices and that, no matter how much the writer attempts to guide them, they tend to misconstrue the text. "Henry Fielding, Richard Bentley and the 'Sagacious Reader' of *Tom Jones*," *The Review of English Studies* 61, no. 252 (2010): 749–72.

61. In the pantomime it is Harlequin who betrays his bosses; in Fielding's pamphlet it is the Devil who sees through the Pope's intentions of cheating him of his soul and withdraws his offer to help.

62. O'Brien, *Harlequin Britain*, 5.

63. Examples of pantomimes in which the silent action described in the libretto far surpassed the lines to be spoken (or sung) include *Harlequin Dr. Faustus: With the Masque of the Deities* (1724), *Harlequin a Sorcerer: With the Loves of Pluto and Proserpine* (1725), *Perseus and Andromeda: Or the Devil upon Two Sticks* (1729)—the one employed by O'Brien as an illustration of the genre at the height of its popularity, *Cupid and Psyche: or Colombine-Courtezan* (1734), and *The Tricks of Harlequin: Or, the Spaniard Outwitted* (1739).

64. O'Brien notes how in his last seasons as a dramatist, Fielding "eschew[ed] dance, special effects and elaborate scenery … [thus] avoiding the more objectionable components of pantomimic spectacles à la John Rich" and signalling his "fealty to a conception of literature that he identifies with the word, a conception that is threatened by the modern theatre's reliance on spectacle" (*Harlequin Britain*, 195).

65. Elaine McGirr, *Heroic Mode and Political Crisis, 1660–1745* (Newark: University of Delaware Press, 2009), 12, 24.

66. McGirr, *Heroic Mode and Political Crisis*, 24.

67. Deidre Shauna Lynch, *The Economy of Character: Novels, Market Culture, and the Business of Inner Meaning* (Chicago: University of Chicago Press, 1998), 28.

68. Samuel Johnson, *A Dictionary of the English Language: In Which the Words Are Deduced from Their Originals,* 2nd ed. (London: W. Strahan, J. and P. Knapton; T. and T. Longman; C. Hitch and L. Hawes; A. Millar; and R. and J. Dodsley, 1755–56), 2:851. On the concept of sympathy in this period see Jonathan Lamb, *The Evolution of Sympathy in the Eighteenth Century* (London: Pickering & Chatto, 2009); Michael Frazer, *The Enlightenment of Sympathy: Justice and the Moral Sentiments in the Eighteenth Century and Today* (Oxford: Oxford University Press, 2010); and Ildiko Csengei, *Sympathy, Sensibility and the Literature of Feeling in the Eighteenth Century* (Basingstoke: Palgrave Macmillan, 2012).

69. When prompted to express her views on whether Square or Thwackum is right in an epistemological argument, Sophia refuses to answer (882–83). Ironically, what Allworthy reads as an instance of, from his standpoint, commendable submissiveness stems from her desire to halt further quarrel and her awareness that both educators are equally wrong.

70. Memorable examples of the errors of interpretation that populate *Tom Jones* include Allworthy's believing that Partridge is Tom's father; his general blind trust in the duplicitous Blifil; the episode in which Tom is mistaken for "Banquo's ghost"; the scene in which Partridge takes Tom for a Jacobite supporter; and the night the hero spends in misery believing he has committed incest.

CONSUMPTION AND REMEDIATION

Cluster: Teaching Tough Texts

Introduction: Teaching Tough Texts

ANNE GREENFIELD

In this era of attacks on the humanities and dwindling numbers of liberal arts majors, many faculty have had to market their courses aggressively and pique student interest by highlighting the sexiest qualities of the eras and genres we teach. Courses like "Jane Austen and Zombies" or "Sex, the City, and Restoration Comedy" will likely drum up easy interest, but what are the other effects of syllabi and reading lists that are redesigned chiefly to increase enrollments? And what of the other important authors and texts that may be omitted for their archaic language, their unfamiliar subject matter, or even their length? In other words, what is lost in excluding texts that now seem laborious to students and that no longer carry immediate appeal?

Indeed, how do we respond to the tension between 1) the need to attract students to our courses, programs, and disciplines; 2) the need to remain rigorous, to include texts and course content that are not simple or tidy, and to help students gain knowledge and skills that do not come easily; and 3) the particular problem that arises in our field (and others) that some of the most valuable texts we have are also *tough*—that is, complicated, ambiguous, and unfamiliar. The pressure to resolve this tension gains force as administrative pressures for recruitment and retention rise. And things get messier and more interesting when we ask *why* we should include "tough texts" at all, what their value is (aesthetic, political, etc.), and where our values should lie.

The two essays that follow emerged out of a March 2019 panel at the Annual Meeting of the American Society for Eighteenth-Century Studies in Denver, Colorado. Titled "Teaching Tough Texts," the panel asked its participants to "examine the opportunities, drawbacks, and ideas associated with teaching 'difficult' long eighteenth-century texts in the university classroom." While the scope of the papers solicited was not limited to any particular discipline within long eighteenth-century studies, both of these presentations focused on teaching literature within English departments. Despite the disciplinary continuity, the two essays featured here take very different approaches.

In the first essay of this cluster, "Balancing Relatability and Alterity in Teaching Scottish Restoration Literature: A Case Study," Holly Faith Nelson and Sharon Alker describe the successful strategies they have employed when teaching a notoriously difficult group of texts: Restoration Scottish works in Scots dialect. Using the poem "Maggie Lauder" as an example, Nelson and Alker explain how one may use a lively performative reading to pique interest and make the dialect less intimidating—and how connecting it to modern-day texts may imbue "Maggie Lauder" with relevance and relatability for students. Equally, however, Nelson and Alker emphasize for students the *differences* that make a poem like this one so alien and unfamiliar today, a task of particular importance when studying works of the past that were shaped by cultural, political, linguistic, and rhetorical contexts other than those that our students experience today as readers. Ultimately, Nelson and Alker remind us that fruitful engagement with tough texts can involve not only discovering the relatable elements, but also encountering the "foreign and the strange."

In the second essay, "Teaching *Paradise Lost*: Radical Contingency, Comparative Studies, and Community Engagement," W. Scott Howard highlights the ways in which great and difficult texts can be dynamic, ungraspable, collaborative, and ever-open to new strategies for engaging them. Using Milton's great poem as an example, Howard points out the ways that its many layers of discontinuity and complexity—which include the textual, the rhetorical, the historical, the formal, and the political—resist reification and ready explanation for scholars and students. Ultimately, *Paradise Lost* offers a fitting example of the reasons to embrace what Howard calls the "radical contingencies" of the poem that lie "beyond our interpretive control" and the opportunities therein for new forms of interpretation and engagement with new voices.

While offering very different approaches to teaching tough texts, what these essays share is an earnest desire to meet the needs of students, to challenge them, and to honor and improve our field in the process.

Balancing Relatability and Alterity in Teaching Scottish Restoration Literature: A Case Study

HOLLY FAITH NELSON AND SHARON ALKER

A s those in the field well know, teaching Restoration literature poses significant challenges. Renegade writers like Margaret Cavendish, Aphra Behn, and the Earl of Rochester can appeal to students who enjoy their more nonconforming or titillating works, but much of the literature published between 1660 and 1689 is decidedly occasional, highly intertextual, and often generically novel, leading many students to perceive it as irrelevant, inexplicable, or dull. One of our students passionately exclaimed during a class discussion that "reading Dryden was like smashing his head against a desk," an experience intensified by what he and some others perceive as the exasperatingly monotonous heroic couplet. Teaching literature from the period that is written in Scottish dialect poses even more challenges, especially for students who have had no prior exposure to it. Many North American students equate reading works of literature in the Scots vernacular (from any historic period) with trying to acquire a second language on the fly. Making matters worse, a great many students approach such texts with an inaccurate sense of the Scot and Scotland, (mis)informed, for instance, by such television series as *Outlander*, with its stereotypical vision of the romantic Highlander.[1]

Adding to these pedagogical challenges is the common desire of students to be assigned works they consider "relatable"—literary texts that speak to their lived experience. For many students, Restoration Scottish works, especially those in Scots dialect, seem alien in the extreme, at least at first glance.[2] This is certainly the case when students first confront, for example, poems like "Blythsome Bridal," attributed to the Scots poet Francis Sempill of Beltrees (*c.* 1616–1682), whose jaunty description of guests at a wedding is more likely to inspire in students a sense of estrangement than relatability:

> And there will be *Judan Maclawrie,*
> And blinking daft *Barbara Macleg,*
> Wi' flae-lugged sharny-fac'd *Lawrie,*
> And shangy-mou'd halucket *Meg.*
> And there will be happer-ars'd *Nansy,*
> And fairy-fac'd *Flowrie* by name;
> Muck *Madie,* and fat-hippit *Grisy,*
> The lass wi' the gowden wame.
>
> And there will be *Girn-again-Gibbie,*
> With his glakit wife *Jenny Bell,*
> And misle-shinn'd *Mungo Macapie,*
> The lad that was skipper himsel.
> There lads and lasses in pearlings
> Will feast in the heart o' the ha';
> On sybows, and rifarts, and carlings,
> That are baith sodden and raw.[3]

How then can we deeply engage students with little-known Restoration Scottish works, particularly given that many are not available in print editions and a significant number, such as George Mackenzie's prose romance, *Aretina; Or, The Serious Romance. Written originally in English* (1660), or William Clarke's *The grand Tryal, or Poetical Exercitations upon the Book of Job* (1685), are substantial in length, employ florid language, and center on subject matter that initially feels impenetrable to most students?

In this article, we will share several tactics for inspiring students to attend closely to and embrace works of Scottish Restoration literature that may initially elude them. These tactics are part of a wider pedagogical strategy: the application of a hermeneutic of alterity to texts that complements and complicates rather than wholly abandons or replaces the hermeneutic of relatability that appeals to students, but is often denigrated by university teachers. In adopting this hybrid interpretive method in the classroom, we are indebted to the layered reading practice outlined by Rita Felski in *Uses of Literature,* which involves a fusion of "modes of textual engagement," most notably "historical and phenomenological" approaches to works of literature.[4] Felski contends that teaching literature should involve a significant dose of reader "recognition": readers should feel themselves "addressed, summoned, called to account" "in the pages" they read and find "traces" of themselves mirrored in them.[5] However, she explains that during moments of recognition readers still experience a sense of profound difference or alterity that creates in them "a revised or altered sense" of self: "Recognition is about knowing, but also about the limits of knowing and knowability, and about how self-perception is mediated by the other, and the perception of otherness by the self."[6] Felski attributes the tension between recognition and alterity in English Studies to the success of critical theories of alterity rooted in the philosophy of Emmanuel Levinas, which sidelined theories of recognition in interpretive practice in the English classroom.[7]

While the terms recognition and relatability are not identical in definition and meaning in the context of textual interpretation, they both gesture toward the value of seeing, knowing, and understanding oneself in and through a work of literature. Therefore, the concept of the relatability of literature has, like recognition, suffered a loss of reputation in many English departments, while alterity is still in the ascendant, theoretically speaking. However, in practice most post-secondary English lecturers look for a host of resources and employ a range of techniques to make pre-modern literature more familiar and thus accessible, hence, for example, the regular inclusion in the classroom of modern productions of Restoration drama or the setting of assignments that require students to respond creatively to works of the long eighteenth century in ways that bridge the past and present, the early modern and the (post)modern. In our defense of the benefits of engaging in a hybrid interpretive practice when introducing Scottish Restoration literature to students, we make use of a case study: the ballad "Maggie Lauder," written in Scots dialect. We consider this work a gateway text given its libidinal energy, spirited dialogue, engaging subject matter, and less alienating language.

One of the initial difficulties of teaching Restoration literature in Scots dialect is finding examples of it. During the Restoration, most Scots authors worked to attract the attention of Charles II in the London court and, therefore, chose to anglicize their writings.[8] Many of their literary works are, for the most part, difficult to distinguish from those authored by their English counterparts, unless they reference, say, Scottish history, geography, or culture. This lesson is itself invaluable in the classroom, demonstrating the way in which language and dialect shifts with political circumstance in the long eighteenth century. Despite the difficulty of locating literature in the Scots vernacular, it is nevertheless important to provide extant examples of it to help chronicle the evolution of a Scottish aesthetic.

"Maggie Lauder," which opens with the lines "Wha wadna be in love / Wi' bonnie Maggie Lauder?" is one of a limited number of extant songs or poems in Scots dialect identified as a Restoration work. Francis Sempill is typically named as its author, though the attribution is not settled. The dating of the work is also open to debate. While most scholars in the field of Scottish Studies believe the ballad is a product of the Restoration (or that it circulated during that time), some have assigned it a date as early as 1642; others believe it (or the version of it that has come down to us) was first composed during the mid-eighteenth century.[9] There is a record of accusations against one Robert Rae, minister at Kirkbride, for printing "the obscene ballad of Maggie Lauder" in 1713, suggesting an earlier composition than the mid-eighteenth century.[10] However, since another ballad, "The Scotch Lass's Lamentation for the Loss of her Maiden Head," which begins "There liv'd a Lass in our Town, / her Name was Moggy Lauder," was also, at times, identified as "Moggy Lauder" or "Moggy Lawder" in collections of Scottish or British songs and poems, it is difficult to discern which version of the poem is being referred to by Rae's adversaries.[11] Conversations on such puzzles over attribution and dating in the classroom, however, can be very fruitful, especially when considering how aspects of oral, manuscript, and print culture intersect in the production and transmission of ballads in the Restoration. For the purpose of this essay, we will accept the attribution of the ballad to Sempill and read it in the context of Restoration Scotland.[12]

In order to communicate to students the vitality and comic force of "Maggie Lauder," reproduced in full below, it is best for the instructor to read it aloud in class:

Wha wadna be in love
Wi' bonnie Maggie Lauder?
A piper met her gaun to Fife,
And spier'd what was't they ca'd her:
Richt scornfully she answered him,
Begone, you hallanshaker!
Jog on your gate, you bladderskate!
My name is Maggie Lauder.

Maggie! quoth he; and, by my bags,
I'm fidgin' fain to see thee!
Sit doun by me, my bonnie bird;
In troth I winna steer thee;
For I'm a piper to my trade;
My name is Rob the Ranter:
The lasses loup as they were daft,
When I blaw up my chanter.

> Piper, quo Meg, hae ye your bags,
> Or is your drone in order?
> If ye be Rob, I've heard o' you;
> Live you upo' the Border?
> The lasses a', baith far and near,
> Have heard o' Rob the Ranter;
> I'll shake my foot wi' richt gude will,
> Gif ye'll blaw up your chanter.
>
> Then to his bags he flew wi' speed;
> About the drone he twisted:
> Meg up and wallop'd ower the green;
> For brawly could she frisk it!
> Weel done! quo he. Play up! quo she.
> Weel bobb'd! quo Rob the Ranter;
> It's worth my while to play, indeed,
> When I hae sic a dancer!
>
> Weel hae ye play'd your part! quo Meg;
> Your cheeks are like the crimson!
> There's nane in Scotland plays sae weel,
> Sin' we lost Habbie Simson.
> I've lived in Fife, baith maid and wife,
> This ten years and a quarter:
> Gin ye should come to Anster Fair,
> Spier ye for Maggie Lauder.[13]

An animated oral performance of the ballad should immediately demonstrate to students that it is possible to find texts from Restoration Scotland that are distant but not dull, even by their standards. It will also reveal that deciphering the Scottish dialect is not, in fact, an insuperable task.

Even if the core meaning of "Maggie Lauder" is fairly clear to students, the ballad is probably not going to be immediately *relatable* to our students, at least as Laura Salisbury defines relatable: that which gives "a strong, undefined feeling of relation in the present." Salisbury further explains that for contemporary students, the use of relatable implies they may "find recognition in" the text and that it could somehow meet their "needs."[14] Rebecca Mead earlier defined *relatability*, as our students use the word, as "accommodating to, or reflective of, the experience of the reader or viewer." It is, she continues, "a flattering confirmation of an individual's solipsism," analogous to "a selfie."[15] Mead differentiates this negative term from identification, the positive term in her idiom, which involves students "thinking" themselves "into the experience of the characters on the page or screen or stage."[16]

Despite the attitude of disdain taken by a number of scholars toward the notion of relatability—which Joanna Luloff connects to the sins of "likability" or "fondness" for—often our first impulse as teachers is to try to make a work such as "Maggie Lauder" as relatable to our students as possible, at least to some extent. This is only natural since we are making every effort to connect to a sometimes bored, distracted, or frustrated audience.[17] We see such efforts described very insightfully, for example, by Jeanine Casler in her "Satire as Gateway: Introducing Undergraduates to Eighteenth-Century Literature." Casler shares how she integrates eighteenth-century satirical texts of an occasional nature in a first-year course on "Uses of Satire," teaching works by Swift, Pope, Montagu, and Collier (among others) alongside "selected excerpts from the work of Jon Stewart, Stephen Colbert, Lewis Black and Tina Fey," in addition to having students "attend … a show put on by the players of Second City." Satire, she explains, is "a literary mode that they already know (or think that they know) and enjoy." "Familiarizing students with" eighteenth-century satirists "through the lens of [relatable] satire helps them to feel as if they have an entrée into the sometimes strange world of the long eighteenth century." In Casler's case, however, relatability is simply the first step toward helping her students improve "critical thinking skills," develop "a greater interest in the literature and history of the eighteenth century," and "become more adept at the skills of interpretation and evaluation that are necessary parts of the satirist's (and critic's) arsenal."[18]

Casler shows that relatability as a pedagogical concept may not be all bad: it can be used as an interpretive stepping-stone. In the case of "Maggie Lauder," if we elected to gesture toward relatability, even if we assign the concept an inferior place on the great epistemological chain, we might associate the ballad with contemporary songs that explore men's sexual attraction to a particular woman and the musical performance that helps them win over a desired female. We could point to and even play, for example, the YouTube video of Walk the Moon's 2014 song, "Shut up and Dance," in which a self-possessed female would-be dancer tells a male approaching her on the dance floor to "shut up and dance with" her. We could then read the song as a modern-day ballad reminiscent of early modern ballads like "Maggie Lauder." Both, after all, are songs in which music is shown to intensify sexual attraction and expression. Both are highly suggestive, especially since "Maggie Lauder" was often read allegorically to suggest that Maggie's energetic dance with Rob was far more than that, hence its identification as "an obscene ballad" and a "bawdy folksong."[19]

The connection between "Shut up and Dance" and "Maggie Lauder" would certainly provide some levity to the class and perhaps help students to relate the ballad to their own experiences of music, dancing, and dating. It could, as Salisbury defines relatability (albeit negatively), help students recognize themselves in the text and find some of their own needs met through the reading process; or it could, as Mead laments, provide them with the "flattering confirmation of" their own "solipsism."[20] However, relatability in such a context would not necessarily result in a narcissistic, history-flattening *worm-hole* effect, that is, an ahistorical "interconnection between widely separated regions of space-time."[21] In fact, this moment of relatability early on in the student engagement process might be more about relevance-making: "Connection with the subject or point at issue; relation *to* the matter in hand" or "pertinence to current or important issues, interests, [or] needs."[22] In making the Restoration Scottish work relatable and/or relevant, students, both as individuals and as a group, will likely become more emotionally invested in it, and relatability can thereby become a means of teaching them that both affect and cognition—feeling and thinking—are acceptable in reading and interpreting literature.

This is not to say, however, that a hermeneutic of relatability would be a sufficient framework through which to teach "Maggie Lauder." To the contrary, the alterity of the work is transparent and should be both acknowledged and embraced in the classroom. As Marcus Bull argues in relation to medieval literature, the alterity of early literature is what makes it valuable. He asks, in *Thinking Medieval*, "What is medieval history actually for? What does it do? Why should we be bothered with it?" One of his arguments is that we cannot "anchor ourselves in the present and … project ourselves into hoped-for futures" if we do not have knowledge of our past, leaving us akin to those who suffer "amnesia."[23] With respect to the crusades in particular, Bull concludes that their "true relevance" has "nothing to do with how they may or may not help to explain the modern world," since what matters is "the mental adjustments that we must make if we want to understand the crusaders and their world without importing anachronistic value judgements."[24] That is, exposure to the past allows us "to unthink a raft of modern assumptions and values."[25] Bull, therefore, privileges the ways in which past people, events, and artifacts differ "from our own experience," because such "differences … impress themselves upon us far more than" do any "superficial" resemblances.[26] Mead and Salisbury would likely concur.

While we accept Bull's argument in some respects, we believe there is value in drawing attention to some of these resemblances, superficial or otherwise, for two main reasons: first, to help students find a measure of personal relevance in reading an early work, thereby investing themselves in it emotionally and cognitively; and second, to teach students that apparent similarities among texts can often hide radical differences. Therefore, while we may begin by making some preliminary connections between aesthetic artifacts from the 1660s and contemporary times, we would then move on to the alterity of the Restoration Scottish song, with the first line of L. P. Hartley's novel, *The Go-Between,* in mind: "The past is a foreign country: they do things differently there."[27] We can, that is, begin with a measure of familiarization only to embrace the defamiliarization, or even alienation, that goes with travelling back in time and immersing oneself in the strangeness of otherness.

To accomplish this end in the case of "Maggie Lauder," we would need to unpack the Scottish song tradition, particularly as it manifests in mid- to late seventeenth-century Scotland, in order to demonstrate how that tradition differs significantly from the musical scene out of which "Shut Up and Dance" emerged. We might, for example, consider the political roots of many ballads of the period, associating the song of the royalist Sempill with a desire to help rebuild and stabilize Scottish culture during and after the civil war. We might point out that Sempill is indirectly conceptualizing Scotland in the ballad as a spirited country with a distinct identity and culture, but one that also reflects the values—particularly the secular hedonism—of the three kingdoms as a whole under Charles II.[28] "Maggie Lauder" certainly resonates with the excess and libertinism associated with the Caroline court.

After situating "Maggie Lauder" in the wider political context of the Restoration, we might then explore how Sempill embeds his sexually suggestive song in Scottish landscapes and oral as well as written traditions. He maps the encounter of Maggie Lauder and Rob the Ranter onto the geography of Scotland with references to Fife and Anster Fair and refers to the famed bagpiper Habbie Simpson of Kilbarchan, Renfrewshire. Francis's father, Robert Sempill, was the author of the much admired poem, "The Life and Death of the Piper of Kilbarchan, or the Epitaph of Habbie Simpson," which played a major role in the development of Scottish poetic form.[29] Francis may also be attempting, therefore, to follow in his father's footsteps by trying to carve out an ongoing cultural space for the figure of the Scottish minstrel in the restored Stuart regime. We might have students consider if this is why Sempill also chose to write in the Scottish vernacular at a time when there was a movement away from indigenous dialects, and we might also ask students how this poem participates in inspiring the "renaissance in the Scots vernacular" by the end of the seventeenth and the beginning of the eighteenth centuries.[30]

This type of analysis will reveal how much more complex the cultural significance of "Maggie Lauder" might be in comparison to that of "Shut up and Dance," whose composition Walk the Moon's lead singer Nicholas Petricca describes in an interview thus: "I went to this awesome party they have at The Echo in Echo Park, Los Angeles, called Funky Soul Saturday. The story of 'Shut Up and Dance' is based on a true story of hanging out there with my friends ... this girl actually told me to shut up and dance with her. We took it back to the studio and it spun out very quickly after that."[31] To be fair, if we are engaging in a sensible comparison between the two songs with the goal of revealing both a Scottish Restoration work's relatability and alterity, it would also be critical to have students thoughtfully situate "Shut Up and Dance" in its cultural context, taking into account, for example, its production in a California studio in 2014 and the song's (perhaps unconscious) echoes of 1980s dance music.

Having students unpack the politics and poetics of space, tradition, language, and dialect in the case of a mid- to late seventeenth-century Scots song also paradoxically helps to reveal the relevance of its alterity in light of, for instance, contemporary theories of nationalism, indigeneity, and postcolonialism, while still keeping the text rooted in its distinct and strange cultural moment. To pursue these possibilities, students might also be asked to read and analyze "Maggie Lauder" side-by-side with contemporary Scots political poems, such as Christine de Luca's "The Morning After," written in light of the vote for Scottish independence.[32] Such an activity would require students to recreate the historical and aesthetic traditions of both works to make sense of the way Scottish cultural artifacts from different periods reflect the beliefs and values of their own time and place. This task involves careful reconstruction of historical and cultural conditions in both the past and the present.

Of course, it is essential to remind students when we are teaching works like "Maggie Lauder" that we can never fully reconstruct such conditions in an objective fashion. Philosophers of interpretation are helpful here. We could, for example, turn to the works of Georg Hegel, who wrote that it is impossible for anyone to "escape the substance of his time any more than he can jump out of his skin" since the "essence" of "an individual" is composed of the "substance" of the times.[33] The same is as true of texts as it is of people and ideas. In writing of the practice of interpretation, Gerald L. Bruns observes that one must "reinvest" the "dead letter" of a past text "with one's own spirit." For Bruns, interpretation requires the reader to "appropriate ... it, not merely as a preserved artifact but as something internalized, that is, essential to one's self-reflection and self-identity."[34] Bruns appears to be saying that in interpreting and commenting on a past text—despite its alterity—we must make it relevant, even relatable, to ourselves, although in this case the relatability in question is not the kind of superficial "selfie" censured by Mead.

Hans-Georg Gadamer's theory of "horizons" is also helpful here for students, and it is relatively hopeful. Gadamer argues that we always bring our own horizon to the past, defining horizon as "the range of vision that includes everything that can be seen from a particular vantage point."[35] We bring our own evolving, historically informed views and values with us in encounters with past texts like "Maggie Lauder," which has its own horizon. However, for Gadamer, neither horizon is "entirely distinct" and "reified," and these horizons fuse to allow for new "understanding."[36]

It is useful to give students concrete examples of such philosophical musings by considering, for instance, how a work like "Maggie Lauder" was assigned different meanings by readers well after it first appeared but before our own time (involving a fusion of historically rooted horizons). We might consider, as a case in point, how the Scots Bard Robert Burns brought his own horizon to this song as he anthologized it when working with James Johnson on *The Scots Musical Museum*.[37] In an introductory note to the song as it appeared in *Select Scotish Songs, Ancient and Modern*, Burns writes, "THIS old song, so pregnant with Scottish *naivieté* and energy, is much relished by all ranks, notwithstanding its broad wit and palpable allusions.—Its language is a precious model of imitation: sly, sprightly, and forcibly expressive.—Maggie's tongue wags out the nicknames of Rob the Piper with all the careless lightsomeness of unrestrained gaiety."[38] We would work with students to identify Burns's emphasis on rank and class in this commentary, linking it to the late eighteenth-century working-class perspective that shapes his horizon, and to show how his commentary highlights the aesthetic value of the Scottish voice at a time when Burns was striving to cement and continue "the Scottish vernacular tradition" of Allan Ramsay and Robert Fergusson.[39] In this way, we would encourage students to describe how Burns's present horizon informs his reading of "Maggie Lauder" while still retaining the alterity of the song's "own historical horizon," which he indirectly points to when he mentions the song's "broad wit and palpable allusions."[40]

Along the way, we hope to guide students to experience and accept the tension between the past and the present, the distant and the immediate, the alien and the familiar. As Gadamer explains, "Every encounter with tradition that takes place within historical consciousness involves the experience of a tension between the [historic] text and the present. The hermeneutic task consists not in covering up this tension by attempting a naïve assimilation of the two but in consciously bringing it out."[41] Such an encounter will no doubt make students (as it sometimes does teachers) feel uncomfortable. It may even thrust them into the world of the uncanny, given that this mode of interpretation can lead readers to experience a sense of "that which is unfamiliar—or more literally, un-homely—in the familiar or homely."[42] However, the encounter will also strengthen their critical thinking and interpretive skills as they move back and forth between horizons of understanding.

In conclusion, we recommend that teachers of Scottish Restoration literature, and Scottish literature of the long eighteenth century more broadly, initially apply texts like "Maggie Lauder" to our own relatable world and selves, but then decidedly and firmly turn to the parts of such works that are foreign and strange. This two-stage approach to reading enlarges both our historical horizon and the horizon of the original text along the way. This may involve situating the text alongside a range of other imaginative works and commentaries across time and space as we strive, in the words of Paul Ricoeur, "to communicate at a distance" with Scottish vernacular texts.[43]

Notes

1. Many students, and their teachers, are also unaware of the significant number of works of literature published in Scotland in this period. We have worked to address this knowledge gap in our recent article "Literary Print Culture in Restoration Scotland," in *The International Companion to Scottish Literature of the Long Eighteenth Century, 1650–1800*, ed. Leith Davis, Janet Sorenson, and Dòmhnall William Stiùbhart, forthcoming from the Association of Scottish Literary Studies, 2021.

2. Gaelic literature poses even more significant difficulties for modern students and is, therefore, often overlooked in the university classroom. However, some modern editions of early modern Scottish poetry in Gaelic include English translations, bridging the gap for students unable to take language courses in Gaelic; see, for example, *An Anthology of Scottish Women Poets*, ed. Catherine Kerrigan (Edinburgh: Edinburgh University Press, 1991).

3. "Blythsome Bridal," in *The Tea-Table Miscellany: Or, A Collection of Choice Songs, Scots and English*, ed. Allan Ramsay, 11th ed., 4 vols. (London: Printed for and Sold by A. Millar, 1740), 1:83–84 (stanzas 5 and 6).

4. Rita Felski, *Uses of Literature* (Malden: Blackwell, 2008), 14, 18.

5. Felski, *Uses of Literature,* 23

6. Felski, *Uses of Literature,* 25, 49.

7. Felski, *Uses of Literature,* 26–27.

8. The Scots had already firmly moved in the direction of anglicizing their writing earlier in the Renaissance, especially when James I moved his court to London in 1603 to assume the English throne. On this subject, see, for example, Sarah Dunnigan's "Reformation and Renaissance," in *The Cambridge Companion to Scottish Literature*, ed. Gerard Carruthers and Liam McIlvanney (Cambridge:

228 / NELSON & ALKER

Cambridge University Press, 2012), 41–54, in which she notes: "With the Union of the Crowns in 1603, and the absorption of king and court within London … the pressures of Anglicization … were now more or less absolute" (50). For a discussion of Scottish Restoration literature, including the issue of language/dialect use, see Nelson and Alker, "Literary Print Culture in Restoration Scotland."

9. This mid-century dating relates to the print history of the ballad. The first extant printed version of "Maggie Lauder" appears to be the version in William Hunter's anthology *The Black Bird: A Choice Collection of the Most Celebrated Songs. Few of Which Are to be Found in Any Other Collection* (Edinburgh: Printed by J. Bruce and Company, 1764). Five years later, it was included in *The Ancient and Modern Scots Songs, Heroic Ballads, &c.* (Edinburgh: Printed by and for Martin & Wotherspoon, 1769).

10. Quoted in Anette Hagan, "The Spread of Printing," in *The Edinburgh History of the Book in Scotland, Vol 2: Enlightenment and Expansion, 1707–1800*, ed. Stephen W. Brown and Warren McDougall (Edinburgh: Edinburgh University Press, 2012), 114.

11. Versions of "The Scotch Lass's Lamentation for the Loss of her Maiden Head" appear, for example, in *A Collection of Old Ballads*, vol. 2 (London: Printed for J. Roberts and D. Leach, 1723), 258–60, and in the eighth edition of *The Triumph of Wit: or, Ingenuity Display'd in its Perfection* (London: Printed by A. W. for J. Clark, 1724), 96. The poem is identified as "A New Song" in the latter volume.

12. If "Maggie Lauder" were first composed during the civil wars or in the early to mid-eighteenth century it would not change the substance of our thesis regarding the need to balance relatability with alterity when interpreting Scottish literature in the classroom. It would, however, change the historical and cultural contexts in which students read the ballad. If the earlier dating is correct, the ballad should be considered as a Scottish contribution to the tradition of Cavalier poetry and song, as discussed by Alan Rudrum in "Royalist Lyric," in *The Cambridge Companion to Writing of the English Revolution*, ed. N. H. Keeble (Cambridge: Cambridge University Press, 2001), 181–97. A later dating would suggest that the ballad should be read as part of the project to uncover (and in the case of Allan Ramsey, among others, also manufacture) the Scottish literary tradition, a project related to "eighteenth-century literary antiquarianism" more broadly; Valentina Bold, "Eighteenth-Century Antiquarianism," in *The Edinburgh Companion to Scottish Traditional Literatures*, ed. Sarah Dunnigan and Suzanne Gilbert (Edinburgh: Edinburgh University Press, 2013), 85.

13. [Francis Sempill], "Maggie Lauder," in *The New Penguin Book of Scottish Verse*, ed. Robert Crawford and Mick Imlah (London: Allen Lane, 2000), 207–8. For a defense of Sempill as the author of "Maggie Lauder," see James Paterson, *The Poems of the Sempills of Beltrees* (Edinburgh: Thomas George Stevenson, 1849), 114–19, and J. Cuthbert Hadden, "The Songs of Scotland Before Burns," *The Scottish Review* 25 (April 1895): 204–7.

14. Laura Salisbury, "Relatable," in P. Boxall, Michael Jonik, et al, "30@30: The Future of Literary Thinking," *Textual Practice*, 30, no. 7 (2016): 1156–57.

15. Rebecca Mead, "The 'Scourge' of Relatability," *The New Yorker*, 1 August 2014, *https://www.newyorker.com/culture/cultural-comment/scourge-relatability*.

16. Mead, "The 'Scourge' of Relatability."

17. Joanna Luloff, "Why I Struggle to Relate to Relatability," *Literary Hub*, 25 June 2018, *https://lithub.com/why-i-struggle-to-relate-to-relatability/*.

18. Jeanine Casler, "Satire as Gateway: Introducing Undergraduates to Eighteenth-Century Literature," *Digital Defoe: Studies in Defoe & His Contemporaries* 3 (2011), *https://english.illinoisstate.edu/digitaldefoe/archive/fall11/teaching/casler.html*.

19. Quoted in Hagan, "The Spread of Printing," 114; Allan H. MacLeane, *The Christis Kirk Tradition: Scots Poems of Folk Festivity* (Glasgow: Association for Scottish Literary Studies, 1996), ix.

20. Mead, "The 'Scourge' of Relatability."

21. *Oxford English Dictionary,* s.v. "worm-hole, *n*.2."

22. *Oxford English Dictionary,* s.v. "relevance, *n*.2a and 2b."

23. Marcus Bull, *Thinking Medieval: An Introduction to the Study of the Middle Ages* (Basingstoke: Palgrave Macmillan, 2005), 99.

24. Bull, *Thinking Medieval*, 131.

25. Bull, *Thinking Medieval*, 131.

26. Bull, *Thinking Medieval*, 131.

27. L. P. Hartley, *The Go-Between* (London: Hamish Hamilton, 1953), quoted in J. A. Burrow, "'Alterity' and Middle English Literature," *Review of English Studies* 50, no. 200 (1999): 483.

28. James G. Turner, for example, writes about "the displacement of religious sensibility in the hastily assembled secular-hedonist culture of Restoration England" in "The Libertine Sublime: Love and Death in Restoration England," *Studies in Eighteenth-Century Culture* 19 (1989): 112.

29. Robert Crawford, *Scotland's Books: The Penguin History of Scottish Literature* (London: Penguin Books, 2007), 225.

30. Adam Fox, "The Emergence of the Scottish Broadside Ballad in the Late Seventeenth and Early Eighteenth Centuries," *Journal of Scottish Historical Studies* 31, no. 2 (2001): 188.

31. Rob LeDonne, "'Inside Shut Up and Dance,' WALK THE MOON's Number One Hit," March 5, 2015, *https://americansongwriter.com/inside-shut-up-and-dance-walk-the-moons-number-one-hit/*.

32. Christine De Luca, "The Morning After" (Scotland, 19 September 2014), *Scottish Poetry Library*, *https://www.scottishpoetrylibrary.org.uk/poem/morning-after/*.

33. Georg Hegel, *Introduction to the Lectures on the History of Philosophy*, trans. T. M. Knox and A. V. Miller (Oxford: Clarendon Press, 1985), 112.

34. Gerald L. Bruns, *Hermeneutics: Ancient & Modern* (New Haven: Yale University Press, 1992), 150. In this chapter, Bruns is focusing on biblical interpretation, but the principle applies to any form of textual interpretation.

35. Hans-Georg Gadamer, *Truth and Method*, trans. Joel Weinsheimer and Donald G. Marshall, 2nd rev. ed. (New York: Continuum, 1989), 302.

36. Lauren Swayne Barthold, "Hans-Georg Gadamer," *Internet Encyclopedia of Philosophy*, *https://iep.utm.edu/gadamer/#SH3b*.

37. The poem appeared as Song 544 in the sixth and final volume of *The Scots Musical Museum,* ed. James Johnson, 6 vols. (Edinburgh, 1787–1803). It was assigned the title "Wha wadna be in love &c."

38. R. H. Cromek, ed., *Select Scotish Songs, Ancient and Modern; with Critical Observations and Biographical Notices, by Robert Burns,* 2 vols. (London: T. Cadell and W. Davies, 1810), 1:93. For a discussion of Burns's likely authorship of the note on "Maggie Lauder," see Gerard Carruthers, "Robert Burns's Interleaved *Scots Musical Museum*: A Case-Study in the Vagaries of Editors and Owners," in *British Literature and Print Culture,* ed. Sandro Jung (Cambridge: D. S. Brewer, 2013), 86–87.

39. Douglas Mack, "James Hogg in 2000 and Beyond," *Romanticism on the Net* 19 (2000), *https://www.erudit.org/en/journals/ron/2000-n19-ron431/005934ar/*.

40. Gadamer, *Truth and Method,* 302–3.

41. Gadamer, *Truth and Method,* 306.

42. Ian Buchanan, *A Dictionary of Critical Theory* (Oxford: Oxford University Press, 2010), s.v. "uncanny."

43. Paul Ricoeur, *From Text to Action: Essays in Hermeneutics, II,* trans. Kathleen Blamey and John B. Thompson (Evanston: Northwestern University Press, 1991), 74.

Teaching *Paradise Lost*: Radical Contingency, Comparative Studies, and Community Engagement

W. SCOTT HOWARD

This essay connects a reading of *Paradise Lost* to an exhortation for the field of Milton studies, reflects upon my recent pedagogic activities at the University of Denver, and offers suggestions for teaching that emphasize comparative studies and community engagement.[1] My work here derives from my teaching at all levels (from first-year undergraduates to doctoral students) at the dynamic intersections of my community's contiguous cohorts.

My argument is this: *Paradise Lost* is a work of radical contingency beyond Milton's control that likewise exceeds our best efforts to grasp the whole poem, thereby engendering an open work in a vital field of endless variations upon the text's history of adaptation, interpretation, and production. Milton scholars and early modernists should therefore subordinate their desires to control the text (via established critical methods) to the work's generative legacy of artistic collaborations (among authors, editors, musicians, painters and printers, translators and typographers, et al.). Comparative studies across disciplines may be energized in meaningful ways for twenty-first-century students through community-engaged practices that amplify the poem's inherent openness to diversity, multimodality, and transferrable skills. We should celebrate the epic's living legacy through spontaneous acts of open-access knowledge sharing and experiential learning that could be transformational for the path forward for literary studies. Within the limited scope of this essay's appearance in this cluster, my focus for comparative studies and community engagement will concern literary adaptations of *Paradise Lost* with particular emphasis given to the multimedia fields of book arts and letterpress printing.

∽

Great works of literary art are so much greater than any individual or collective work of scholarship. Indeed, such classics are more than the sum of their parts at every moment in their journeys through time: from their engagements with their source materials and historical moments to their processes of inspiration, composition, revision, production, distribution, exchange, adaptation, interpretation, remediation, and translation.[2] Such texts are beyond the control of their authors and audiences because their complexities escape capture and conversion; such classics are vibrant, open works that "display an intrinsic mobility, a kaleidoscopic capacity to suggest themselves in constantly renewed aspects."[3] We should embrace this vital spirit of the open work's radical contingency. By *radical*, I mean a fundamental concern for and critique of the linguistic roots of reality; by *contingency*, I mean chance affinities among materials and methods that are neither designed nor foreseen—yet still possible due to either present or absent accidents, conditions, or forces. *Paradise Lost* is certainly intricate, but it is not "designed like a complex clock."[4] *Paradise Lost* is a poem of baroque asymmetrical structures and signal escapes engendered by numerous discontinuities within and across the work's individual books as well as among the many paratexts added to the poem after the first three issues of the 1667 ten-book first edition.[5] Considering these countless edits, revisions, and chance variables involved in the epic's journey from the 1667 edition to the 1674 twelve-book second edition, we should read, discuss, and teach *Paradise Lost* as a work of radical contingency that emerges from collaborative and collective efforts, including the text's dictation, transcription, revision, and preparation for printing and distribution, as William Poole's *Milton and the Making of Paradise Lost* (2017) thoroughly demonstrates. We should celebrate the work's multimodal legacy in the spirit of Blake's illuminated poem that strives to correct Milton's vision by breaking apart his overdetermined selfhood.[6] Numerous kindred literary adaptations of *Paradise Lost* reimagine and refashion the poem's materials and methods for modern audiences, such as Erin Shields's *Paradise Lost* (2018); Danny Snelson's *RADIOS* (2016); Pablo Auladell's *Paradise Lost*

(2014); Ronald Johnson's *RADI OS* (1977); and John Collier's *Milton's Paradise Lost: Screenplay for Cinema of the Mind* (1973), just to name a few.[7]

Milton's paradoxical refrain, "know to know no more," underscores these principles and reflections in ways that exceed ready explanations—notwithstanding the best efforts of countless editors and scholars to define (and thus stabilize) numerous complexities in the poem in terms of established methodologies and lines of argument that ultimately reify the apparatus of knowledge for specialists in ways that are no longer sustainable in our current precarious times.[8] Of course, we need specialists and scholarly publications. However, the field of early modern studies (and Milton studies, especially) desperately needs specialists working in collaboration with colleagues and community partners: more diversity and public engagement; more cross-disciplinary and multimodal work that celebrates great (and greatly difficult) literary texts, *not* primarily through established literary critical methods but through comparative studies and transferrable worldly skills, thereby preparing our students for a variety of careers within and beyond academia.

The poem's interdiction, "know to know no more," teaches us this fundamental lesson of radical contingency that exceeds interpretation, calling us back to our existential grounding in shared experiential learning and collaborative making (*PL*, bk. 4, line 775). For example, we have familiar glosses that echo Genesis 2:16–17 and describe the line as "one of many warnings to abstain from desiring to know too much" and to "be wise enough to seek no more knowledge (i.e., of good and evil)."[9] Such reductive readings take an apodictic stance: *know // to know no more*. We should remember, and we should help our students understand, that *Paradise Lost* is *not* a strict doctrinal work but a poem that relentlessly amplifies complexities beyond our control (and beyond Milton's as well). As a first step and in addition to the abovementioned glosses, we should simultaneously read this line as *know to know // no more*. That is, we should understand that true wisdom exceeds discursive reasoning (knowing to know) and embraces the intuitive reasoning that Raphael discusses with Adam and Eve in Book 5 (lines 469–505).[10] Furthermore, we should also amplify the embedded dialogue between *apophatic* and *cataphatic* modes of inquiry in Book 4 (line 775) and related passages by hearing the co-presence of *no* within *know* that instantly inflects a redoubled litotes (*know to know*) beyond the negative dialectics of subversion and containment (*know // to know no more*).[11] Emily Dickinson once expressed a similarly incisive admonition in a letter to Otis P. Lord: "dont you know that 'No' is the wildest word we consign to Language?"[12]

And then, of course, we should read these provocative words in Book 4 (line 775) within and against the contrary and contiguous contexts of their immediate verse paragraph (*PL*, bk. 4, lines 736–775), the whole of Book

4, and other variations upon this key theme throughout *Paradise Lost* (in both the 1667 ten-book and the 1674 twelve-book editions). Indeed, this variable motif of "knowing" appears in so many shapes throughout the poem—each nuanced articulation uniquely placed within charged contexts among characters and settings, plots and counter-plots, figurative expressions and rhetorical discourses, micro-poetic forms (within individual books) and macro-poetic structures (across and between books)—that this so-called interdiction readily invites a proliferation of desires for, questions about, and contrasting perspectives concerning human experience and cosmological wisdom. In all of these ways, "know to know no more" affirms Julia Kristeva's argument that "there is within poetic language ... a *heterogeneousness* to meaning and signification."[13] Such complexity moves readers and writers to ask profound questions about themselves and their worlds, questions that require critically reflective effort when faced with profoundly generative ambiguities that embrace differences and diversities of all kinds. In this regard, Milton's poetics and praxis in *Paradise Lost* echo Richard Rorty's resilient belief in poetry: "To see one's language, one's conscience, one's morality, and one's highest hopes as contingent products, as literalizations of what once were accidentally produced metaphors, is to adopt a self-identity which suits one for citizenship in ... an ideally liberal state."[14]

∞

I've offered this discussion of a minute particular in *Paradise Lost* in order to exaggerate the crux of my argument: that the epic's radical contingency was beyond Milton's control and that that radical contingency exceeds our best efforts to grasp the whole poem and engenders an open work in a rich field of endless variations upon the text's legacy. For the field of early modern studies (and especially for Milton studies), I would also propose these corollaries: that we should subordinate our expertise as literary critics, scholars, and theorists to the poem's inherent complexities; amplify those dynamics through renewed attention to the work's cross-disciplinary and multimodal, multilingual, and transnational histories; and collaborate with colleagues, students, and community partners in open-access celebrations of *Paradise Lost* through the public sharing of transferrable skills. Indeed, the robust legacy of *Paradise Lost*—when encountered as a manuscript via the sole scribal copy in the Morgan Library, as a text via the 1667 and 1674 editions, as a published work via any of the subsequent editions, and as an adaptation via any of the innumerable reconfigurations of the poem in various media throughout the centuries—abundantly shows us that Milton's great poem has always emerged from collaborative and collective efforts to move the material in new directions for new audiences.[15] We should encourage our colleagues and students to become co-creators in that shared legacy within, across, and, most important, beyond our fields of expertise.

∞

The field of Milton studies is ready for new energy and new voices, more diversity of all kinds and in all forms. We need more work that represents students and faculty of color, more work that represents the LGBTQ community, more work from women, and more collaborative, transnational comparative work.

I've been teaching Milton's poetry and prose in a wide range of undergraduate and graduate courses since the years of my doctoral training (1993–98) at the University of Washington, Seattle, and I know that I still have much to learn from a field that has been richly elaborating itself since the late seventeenth century.[16] My perspective on Milton's life, works, and legacy has been formatively shaped by that past work, and I'm grateful for all of it. And my scholarly work continues, as Sara van den Berg and I are returning to our collaborative research and writing for the second of our volumes investigating the legacy of Milton's divorce tracts from 1643 to the Divorce Reform Act of 1969 and beyond.[17]

As I write these paragraphs, though, I'm struggling to reconcile my abiding care and concern for *Paradise Lost* with acute worries about our world today and our future. One of my recurring questions since at least 2016 has been how we might reconfigure the epic's inherent business of providential nationalism (of colonialism, racism, and sexism) into the work of repair.[18] (I recall Regina Schwartz expressing a similar worry, during one of the Milton Society of America dinners in the late 1990s, that the poem's ideology could be co-opted by fascist agendas. As it happens, that concern was prescient: the Assad regime tried to use a 2011 Arabic translation of *Paradise Lost* as propaganda.)[19] Once upon a time in Charlestown State Prison, Malcolm Little read *Paradise Lost* and perceived Milton and Elijah Muhammad as kindred liberators: as political, religious, and social reformers.[20]

As I see it, the "Remaines" of a "higher Argument" in *Paradise Lost* are the ideological principles of racial, religious, sexual, and social prejudices that inform the work's teleological and transcendental matters of critique. Milton's poem is "sufficient of it self to raise / That name," lines in which I hear simultaneously the multiplicity of transitive and intransitive meanings for *raise* (*PL*, bk. 9, lines 43–44).[21] Books 10, 11, and 12 struggle to accommodate and reconfigure those intransigent ideological values within and against the infinitely complex and richly imbricated, swerving contexts of Books 1 through 9. Every moment of violence in the poem illustrates such tensions between contrary and convoluted worldviews of prelapsarian possibilities, fallen problems, and ongoing struggles for racial equity, individual freedom, and social justice. The poem's radical contingency, which manifests itself through bewildering forms and figures of discontinuity, difference, and diversity throughout all twelve books, challenges and escapes the epic's late Medieval, Renaissance, and early modern ideological frameworks. In this regard, I agree with Catherine Martin that *Paradise Lost* epitomizes as well as explodes "the hieratic remnants of its own fragmentation" because no culture "can end and at the same time be reborn without reference to such monumental conceits or their surrogates, which fundamentally derive from the arrogance of the human mind patiently submitting the universe, both its beginnings and its ends, to its own self-justifying means."[22] The poem ultimately releases all of those factors and forces into an increasingly secular world.

The editorial, critical, and scholarly histories of *Paradise Lost* have been dominated by countless endeavors to control the text and to subordinate the poem's radical contingency to the patient work of humanist syncretism and learned arguments for the work's unified and stabilized structure, all of which begins with fantastical notions about Milton's solitary authorial genius, as if the poem were not also shaped by many other hands and voices.[23] That said, and just to be clear, I am *not* recapitulating the vexed hypothesis of Richard Bentley's 1732 edition of *Paradise Lost* that portrays Milton's great poem as the result of a deceptive amanuensis "who rewrote the text of the dictated poem before sending it to the printer."[24] Poole's scrupulous research cogently shows us how as well as why Milton's poems and prose works emerged from fluid, asynchronous contexts of collaboration, editing, revision, transcription, and translation punctuated by countless chance variables.

We have thus been trained by specialists to construct arguments for specialists; those elitist methods have overdetermined our priorities to make our work relevant for a "fit audience ... though few" (*PL*, bk. 7, line 31). In this regard, we find a critical difference between the field of Milton Studies compared with that of Shakespeare Studies.[25]

When I was a graduate student, the ethos of Milton Studies—an ethos of private inspiration, "A Paradise within," characterized by patient, often painful work in isolation—struck me like lightning (*PL*, bk. 12, line 587). All these years later, I'm still confronting the consequences. How many of my colleagues completed their dissertations? How many were successful in their pursuits of academic jobs?

Those are also the worries today of someone who has served as Director of Graduate Studies in my department. How may we do a better job of being mindful of the communities we build together each quarter/semester? How may we build more inclusive communities that support our students and colleagues in their search for employment within and beyond academia?

∞

How shall we work within, against, and through such a tough text as *Paradise Lost* with such urgent matters at stake? How shall we work with a text that chastens and challenges us so often and so variously, *know to know no more?*

Well, we should begin by returning to key elements that animate the inherent radical contingencies in *Paradise Lost*: materials and methods from Milton's time that make the poem wonderfully available to many hands and voices today, especially for our students who need to learn transferrable twenty-first-century analog and digital skills, such as editing, translation, and publishing; book design, typography, and graphic design; literary adaptation and performance; data visualization, marketing, and public communications—all of which may be deftly energized by old-fashioned scholarly practices dedicated to close studies of early modern difficult texts, especially Milton's. We should return to these elements in *Paradise Lost*, however, *not* in order to reaffirm the work's unchanging transcendent values but in order to enrich dialogue and comparative studies across centuries and fields so that our forms of knowing and making—our poetics and praxis— may shape new forms of action that will engender positive social change.

In the space remaining in this essay, I'll offer a selection of electronic and print resources that I've found to be very useful when teaching *Paradise Lost*, and then I'll close by describing some of the activities and methods that have been successful in my recent courses.

During my years of graduate training, I joined the Milton Society of America, which is a truly remarkable community of dedicated scholars.[26] I would also recommend a companion cohort, The John Milton Discussion List.[27] And, of course, there's The Milton Reading Room, which is an invaluable resource. Edited and published by Thomas H. Luxon, in collaboration with his colleagues and students, The Milton Reading Room provides open access to reliable, richly annotated hypertexts of Milton's works and accompanying scholarly essays. The field's two leading journals, *Milton Quarterly* and *Milton Studies*, will amplify these paths of study for your students.

Electronic editions of *Paradise Lost* are just as valuable as printed editions, especially when both are engaged side-by-side for comparison. Whichever edition you may choose, help your students understand how and why that text has been assembled and published: which editorial choices were made (and which were not); which text of the poem and which of the paratexts have been included; how the notes have been written to amplify which lines of argument in the field; how and why the introduction and any other accompanying documents have been written; which illustrations have been chosen; which blurbs have been included, and how the overall work has been designed to compete in the marketplace. This sort of critical attention to your edition of *Paradise Lost* is just as important as your close analysis of the text itself because, as Marshall McCluhan would remind us, "the medium is the message," and this poem in particular has always emerged from dynamically mediated and remediated collaborative processes.[28] You might also consider encouraging your students to produce their own editions of one book, or of selected passages; or you could encourage your students to create their own adaptations of *Paradise Lost* in the media of their choice, including reflective statements on how those reconfigurations embody the story in new ways.[29]

My community, the Department of English and Literary Arts at the University of Denver, values the integration of creative writing and literary studies with cross-disciplinary and multimodal work that connects our faculty and students to a vibrant cohort of artists and makers of all kinds. Our website articulates these priorities: "We believe writers are enriched by great literature in conjunction with philosophy, history, critical and aesthetic theory, anthropology, art history, and the history of science. ... Such a curriculum encourages students to cross genre boundaries in their writing, to relate theory to practice, and to work creatively with scholarly projects."[30] In that spirit, I have shaped many of my courses following the theme of adaptation, emphasizing with *Paradise Lost* the poem's rich history of book arts illustrations from William Blake (1807–22), John Martin (1823), and Gustave Doré (1866) to Carlotta Petrina (1933), Mary Elizabeth Groom (1937), and Pablo Auladell (2016), among others.[31] Most recently, I worked with my library faculty colleague, Katherine Crowe, to host an event featuring adaptations of *Paradise Lost* from our fine press and artists' books collection, including Jan Owen's *Milton Marginalia* (2016), Maureen Cummins's *In the minute before / In the Minute After* (2013), and Fred Hagstrom's *Paradise Lost* (2012).[32] For that event, we collaborated with two local letterpress artists, Jason Wedekind and Jeff Shepherd, from Genghis Kern Letterpress and Design. Their presentation about printing practices during Milton's times and concerning contemporary book arts methods brought new life to *Paradise Lost* for all of us. We invited each of my students to bring one word to class for a collaborative activity. Following Jason's and Jeff's guidance and working with their materials—a desktop poster press, at least five trays of different typefaces, furniture, magnets, spacers, inks, brayers, papers, etc.—we set our words into a letterpress form and pulled broadsides, engendering anew the poem's vital complexities through our shared experience.

Notes

1. Those points of emphasis are in sync with my work during 2018–2020 in collaboration with the Center for Community Engagement (CCESL), *https://www. du.edu/ccesl/*, and the John Madden Center for Innovation in the Liberal and Creative Arts, *https://liberalarts.du.edu/about/strategic-plan/madden-center/current-projects*.

2. Attentive readers will note, in my methodology, the strategic placement of source materials and historical moments before poetic inspiration, composition & etc. Such emphasis echoes the agency, in *Paradise Lost*, of pre-existing cosmic raw materials—"embryon Atoms" (bk. 2, line 900), "dark materials" (*PL*, bk. 2, line 916), and "the vast immeasurable Abyss / Outrageous as a Sea, dark, wasteful, wilde, / Up from the bottom turn'd by furious windes / And surging waves" (*PL*, bk. 7, lines 211–214)—not created by Milton's God, but radically contingent in their vital (if chaotic) co-presence. See Dennis Richard Danielson, ed., *The Book of the Cosmos: Imagining the Universe from Heraclitus to Hawking* (New York: Perseus, 2000); and Stephen M. Fallon, *Milton among the Philosophers: Poetry and Materialism in Seventeenth-Century England* (Ithaca: Cornell University Press, 1991).

3. Umberto Eco, *The Role of the Reader: Explorations in the Semiotics of Texts* (Bloomington: Indiana University Press, 1979), 56.

4. William Poole, *Milton and the Making of Paradise Lost* (Cambridge: Harvard University Press, 2017), 161. However, I do agree with the rest of Poole's observation that "changes in the motion in one part [of the poem] set in motion changes in the others."

5. See Murray Roston, *Milton and the Baroque* (New York: Palgrave, 1980). For rich discussions of the variables specific to the six issues of the ten-book first edition, see John T. Shawcross and Michael Lieb, eds., *Paradise Lost: A Poem Written in Ten Books: An Authoritative Text of the 1667 First Edition* (Pittsburgh: Duquesne University Press, 2007), and their accompanying edited collection of essays, *Paradise*

Lost: A Poem Written in Ten Books: Essays on the 1667 First Edition (Pittsburgh: Duquesne University Press, 2007).

6. "I in my Selfhood am that Satan: I am that Evil one ! / He is my Spectre! in my obedience to loose him from my Hells / To claim the Hells, my Furnaces, I go to Eternal Death." William Blake, *MILTON: A Poem*, ed. Robert N. Essick and Joseph Viscomi (Princeton: Princeton University Press, 1993), plate 12, lines 30-32.

7. Erin Shields, *Paradise Lost* (Toronto: Playwrights Canada Press, 2018); Danny Snelson, *RADIOS* (Make Now Press, 2016); Pablo Auladell, *Paradise Lost*, trans. Ángel Gurria (London: Jonathan Cape, 2014); Ronald Johnson, *RADI OS* (Chicago: Flood Editions, 2005; Berkeley: Sand Dollar, 1977); John Collier, *Milton's Paradise Lost: Screenplay for Cinema of the Mind* (New York: Knopf, 1973).

8. John Milton, *Paradise Lost* (bk. 4, line 775), The John Milton Reading Room, *https://milton.host.dartmouth.edu/reading_room/pl/book_4/text.shtml*. All quotations from *Paradise Lost* will correspond with this open-access electronic text from *The John Milton Reading Room*: the complete poetry and selected prose of John Milton, with introductions, research guides, and hyperlinked annotations; Thomas H. Luxon, General Editor © Trustees of Dartmouth College, 1997–2019; henceforth cited parenthetically in the text as *PL*.

9. "And the Lord God commanded the man, saying, Of every tree of the garden thou mayest freely eat: / But of the tree of the knowledge of good and evil, thou shalt not eat of it: for in the day that thou eatest thereof thou shalt surely die." The Holy Bible: King James Version (New York: Meridian, 1974), 10. The John Milton Reading Room, *https://milton.host.dartmouth.edu/reading_room/pl/book_4/text.shtml*; David Scott Kastan and Merritt Y. Hughes, eds., *Paradise Lost* (Indianapolis: Hackett Publishing Company, 2005), 136, note 775; and Merritt Y. Hughes, ed., *John Milton Complete Poems and Major Prose* (New York: The Odyssey Press, 1957), 296, note 775.

10. Alastair Fowler's note on Book 4 (line 775) offers a kindred yet contrasting view: "either 'know that it is best not to seek new knowledge (by eating forbidden fruit)' or 'know ... how to limit your experience to the state of innocence.'" Alastair Fowler, ed., *Paradise Lost* (New York: Longman, 1971), 242, note iv, 775. Scott Elledge offers a useful discussion in his edition; see John Milton, *Paradise Lost*, ed. Scott Elledge (New York: Norton, 1975), 470. See especially Leonard's discussions of knowledge in the poem: John Leonard, "Introduction" to John Milton, *Paradise Lost* (New York: Penguin, 2000), xxxi-xxxiv; and "Language and Knowledge in *Paradise Lost*," *The Cambridge Companion to Milton*, ed. Dennis Danielson (Cambridge: Cambridge University Press, 1999), 130–43.

11. Apophatic: "Applied to knowledge of God obtained by way of negation." Cataphatic: "Defining God positively or by positive statements." Oxford English Dictionary, *https://www.oed.com/*. See James Dougal Fleming, *Milton's Secrecy and Philosophical Hermeneutics* (Aldershot: Ashgate, 2008). Whereas "most Milton scholars ... argue or assume, implicitly or explicitly, that studying [or editing] the poet's work entails a search for hidden meaning" (4)—hence, the plurality of interpretive methodologies throughout the twentieth century predicated upon esotericism—Fleming aims to correct that bias for secrecy and discovery by returning

to Milton's textuality (ix–x) and the apt placement of his works within a nearly forgotten tradition of early-modern exotericism (6–25).

12. "Letter 562," *Emily Dickinson: Selected Letters*, ed. Thomas H. Johnson (Cambridge: Harvard University Press, 1986), 246. See also W. Scott Howard, *Archive and Artifact: Susan Howe's Factual Telepathy* (Northfield: Talisman House, 2019), 232.

13. Julia Kristeva, *Desire in Language: A Semiotic Approach to Literature and Art*, ed. Leon S. Roudiez, trans. Thomas Gora, Alice Jardine, and Leon S. Roudiez (New York: Columbia University Press, 1980), 133.

14. Richard Rorty, *Contingency, Irony, and Solidarity* (Cambridge: Cambridge University Press, 1989), 61.

15. See "John Milton's *Paradise Lost*," The Morgan Library and Museum, *https://www.themorgan.org/collection/John-Miltons-Paradise-Lost*. "The only surviving manuscript of *Paradise Lost* is this thirty-three-page fair copy [of Book One], written in secretary script by a professional scribe, who probably transcribed patchwork pages of text Milton had dictated to several different amanuenses. This fair copy was corrected by at least five different hands under Milton's personal direction and became the printer's copy, used to set the type for the first edition of the book." We still do not know the identities of these "five different hands." For detailed studies of this manuscript, see Poole, *Milton and the Making of Paradise Lost*; Shawcross and Lieb, eds., *"Paradise Lost: A Poem Written in Ten Books"*; and Helen Darbishire, ed., *The Manuscript of Milton's "Paradise Lost," Book I* (Oxford: Clarendon Press, 1931).

16. See Calvin Huckabay and David V. Urban, *John Milton: An Annotated Bibliography, 1989–1999*, ed. David V. Urban and Paul J. Klemp (Pittsburgh: Duquesne University Press, 2011); John T. Shawcross, *Milton: A Bibliography for the Years 1624–1700 (Revised) and for the Years 1701–1799* (Toronto: ITER, 2009), *https://www.itergateway.org/resources/milton-bibliography*; Calvin Huckabay, *John Milton: An Annotated Bibliography, 1968–1988*, ed. Paul J. Klemp (Pittsburgh: Duquesne University Press, 1996); and Calvin Huckabay, *John Milton: An Annotated Bibliography, 1929–1968* (Pittsburgh: Duquesne University Press, 1969).

17. Sara J. van den Berg and W. Scott Howard, eds., *The Divorce Tracts of John Milton: Texts and Contexts* (Pittsburgh: Duquesne University Press / University Press of New England, 2010).

18. These concerns are widely shared among scholars in the Milton community as well as by other eminent writers. See, for example, Mary Nyquist, *Arbitrary Rule: Slavery, Tyranny, and the Power of Life and Death* (Chicago: University of Chicago Press, 2013); Mary C. Fenton and Louis Schwartz, eds., *To Repair the Ruins: Reading Milton* (Pittsburgh: Duquesne University Press, 2012); Debra Johanyak and Walter S. H. Lim, eds., *The English Renaissance, Orientalism, and the Idea of Asia* (New York: Palgrave, 2009); Mary C. Fenton, *Milton's Places of Hope: Spiritual and Political Connections of Hope with Land* (Aldershot: Ashgate, 2006); Balachandra Rajan, *Under Western Eyes: India from Milton to Macaulay* (Durham: Duke University Press, 1999); and J. Martin Evans, *Milton's Imperial Epic: Paradise Lost and the Discourse of Colonialism* (Ithaca: Cornell University Press, 1996).

19. Islam Issa, *Milton in the Arab-Muslim World* (New York: Routledge, 2017), 41. Issa observes that Hanna Aboud's 2011 translation of *Paradise Lost* "was funded and published by the [Syrian] government during an uprising against it that has since escalated into an ongoing civil war." In their endorsement of Aboud's translation, the Syrian government asserted that "Milton lived through contexts of personal loss and countrywide tension, and in theory, these similarities suggest that this would be a suitable time for Syrians to read and understand the epic" (41). See also Eid Abdallah Dahiyat, *Once Upon the Orient Wave: Milton and the Arab-Muslim World* (London: Hesperus Press, 2012).

20. "In either volume 43 or 44 of The Harvard Classics, I read Milton's *Paradise Lost*. The devil, kicked out of Paradise, was trying to regain possession. He was using the forces of Europe, personified by the Popes, Charlemagne, Richard the Lionhearted, and other knights. I interpreted this to show that the Europeans were motivated and led by the devil, or the personification of the devil. So Milton and Mr. Elijah Muhammad were actually saying the same thing." Alex Haley and Malcolm X, *The Autobiography of Malcolm X* (New York: Random House, 1964), 214.

21. Stanley Fish contends "the question of the 'status of his own discourse' is not one [Milton] evades or dodges or misses, but one he raises and raises with all of the rigor to which a deconstructionist might lay claim." Stanley Fish, "Wanting a Supplement," *Politics, Poetics, and Hermeneutics in Milton's Prose*, ed. James Turner and David Loewenstein (Cambridge: Cambridge University Press, 1990), 44.

22. Catherine Gimelli Martin, *The Ruins of Allegory: Paradise Lost and the Metamorphosis of Epic Convention* (Durham: Duke University Press, 1998), 4, 342.

23. See Poole's discussion of Milton's amanuenses. "Did Milton actually dictate his lines in near-perfect form? We do not know" (*Milton and the Making of Paradise Lost,* 132–33). The sole scribal copy (discussed above in note 15) "was not itself taken down from dictation but copied from a prior written text" (154).

24. Poole, *Milton and the Making of Paradise Lost,* 285.

25. See Nigel Smith, *Is Milton Better Than Shakespeare?* (Cambridge: Harvard University Press, 2008).

26. The Milton Society of America, *https://miltonsociety.commons.gc.cuny.edu/*.

27. Milton-L—John Milton Discussion List, *https://lists.richmond.edu/mailman/listinfo/milton-l*.

28. Marshall McCluhan, *Understanding Media: The Extensions of Man* (Cambridge: MIT, 1964), *http://web.mit.edu/allanmc/www/mcluhan.mediummessage.pdf*. "In a culture like ours, long accustomed to splitting and dividing all things as a means of control, it is sometimes a bit of a shock to be reminded that, in operational and practical fact, the medium is the message. This is merely to say that the personal and social consequences of any medium—that is, of any extension of ourselves—result from the new scale that is introduced into our affairs by each extension of ourselves, or by any new technology" (1).

29. In addition to the selected materials already cited in this essay, I would like to recommend a few more electronic and print resources.

Electronic: *ABO: Interactive Journal for Women in the Arts, 1640–1830, https://scholarcommons.usf.edu/abo/; Appositions: Studies in Renaissance / Early Modern Literature & Culture, http://appositions.blogspot.com/; Early Modern Literary Studies, https://extra.shu.ac.uk/emls/journal/index.php/emls; The Hare: An Online Journal of Untimely Reviews in Early Modern Theater, http://thehareonline.com/; Journal of the Northern Renaissance, http://www.northernrenaissance.org/.*

Print: Heidi Brayman Hackel and Ian Frederick Moulton, eds., *Teaching Early Modern English Literature from the Archives* (New York: MLA, 2015); Sharon Achinstein, *Milton and the Revolutionary Reader* (Princeton: Princeton University Press, 2014); Peggy Keeran and Jennifer Bowers, *Literary Research and the British Eighteenth Century: Strategies and Sources* (Lanham: Scarecrow Press, 2013); Peter Herman, ed., *Approaches to Teaching Milton's Paradise Lost*, 2nd ed. (New York: MLA, 2012); Jennifer Bowers and Peggy Keeran, *Literary Research and the British Renaissance and Early Modern Period: Strategies and Sources* (Lanham: Scarecrow Press, 2010); Nicholas McDowell and Nigel Smith, eds., *The Oxford Handbook of Milton* (Oxford: Oxford University Press, 2009); Laura Lunger Knoppers and Gregory M. Colón Semenza, eds., *Milton in Popular Culture* (New York: Palgrave, 2006); Thomas N. Corns, *A Companion to Milton* (Oxford: Blackwell, 2001); and Barbara K. Lewalski, *The Life of John Milton: A Critical Biography* (Oxford: Blackwell, 2000).

30. University of Denver, Department of English and Literary Arts, *http://www.du.edu/ahss/english/*.

31. See W. Scott Howard, "Milton and Blake: The Poetics & Praxis of Adaptation," *Romantic Textualities: Literature & Print Culture, 1780–1840, Miltonic Legacies*, ed. Daniel Cook, Tess Somervell, and Brian Bates (Cardiff University, February, 2017), *http://www.romtext.org.uk/teaching-romanticism-xviii-miltonic-legacies/*. See also Wendy Furman-Adams, "The Fate of Place in *Paradise Lost*: Three Artists Reading Milton," *To Repair the Ruins: Reading Milton* (Pittsburgh: Duquesne University Press, 2012), 283–338.

32. Jan Owen, *Milton Marginalia* (Belfast: Jan Owen, 2016); Maureen Cummins, *In the Minute before / In the Minute After* (High Falls: Maureen Cummins, 2013); Fred Hagstrom, *Paradise Lost* (Northfield: Strong Silent Type Press, 2012).

EIGHTEENTH-CENTURY BODIES

"Rendered Remarkable": Reading Race and Desire in *The Woman of Colour*

OLIVIA CARPENTER

"My colour, you know, renders me remarkable," writes Olivia, the titular heroine of the 1808 novel *The Woman of Colour*.[1] Olivia's story is indeed remarkable: she journeys from Jamaica to England to follow the wishes in her late father's will and marry her distant cousin to secure her father's fortune. The white English characters she encounters gossip about the racially distinct presence in their midst, and this gossip only worsens once it is revealed that Olivia and Augustus have accidentally committed bigamy. Early nineteenth-century readers would likewise have remarked upon the rare phenomenon of a novel with a mixed-race Black protagonist, especially one who narrates her own story and actively rewrites the traditional marriage plot.[2] In this essay, I examine another aspect of Olivia's remarkable nature: the reactions she inspires in twenty-first-century readers grappling with this character's complexities and ambiguities. Today's reader finds a real paradox in Olivia, who apparently critiques racism on the one hand and idealizes the plantation on the other. Olivia becomes particularly remarkable to the twenty-first-century reader when she ostensibly espouses abolitionist politics but apparently takes possession of a benevolent plantation at the novel's end. I contend that we can untangle this paradox by recognizing the ways that *The Woman of Colour* remains committed to a colonial project. Olivia pairs her firmest anti-racist politics with calls for more malleable racial hierarchies. She apparently seeks to improve the existing system without demanding its disintegration. This becomes clear when we examine how and why Olivia perpetuates as well as enacts colonial authority from her particular position as a mixed-race elite woman who becomes a Jamaican planter.

The paradox of a novel that both condemns racist prejudice and dreams of a brighter future on the plantation makes sense in the context of its own colonial logic—a logic with real historical referents. I want to move beyond that logic, though, and demand something else from *The Woman of Colour*, a novel that in many ways fails to offer a successful challenge to eighteenth-century hegemonic discourse. In addition to remarking upon the crucial ways Olivia's narrative succeeds or fails to satisfy the desires of today's readers, I want to turn also to the ways this novel sheds light on the origins of those desires.

England provides many opportunities for Olivia to respond to racism. George Merton, Jr., the young son of Olivia's racist brother- and sister-in-law, refers to Olivia's enslaved maid Dido as "that nasty black woman," claiming she "has been kissing me, and dirtying my face all over!" (*WC*, 78). At first, the Mertons assume that young George refers to Olivia, but George quickly explains that he refers to someone "much, *much* dirtier" (78). Even located safely off-page, Dido remains a threat in this scene. She ostensibly maintains the power to frighten a child with the darkness of her skin, a darkness that George imagines could transfer to his own skin. Without explicitly knowing it, George depends on racism grounded in biological commitments to feel safe. The threat of the Other, according to this model of racism, can be contained by containing Dido's body, which is always marked as inferior by a set of fixed, phenotypical traits. In such a context, Dido's kiss, her physical demonstration of giving and receiving affection, is transgressive. The final decades of the eighteenth century mark a shift in understandings of race in Britain from a model that took skin color into account along with factors such as religion, clothing, and customs to a model that prioritized skin color as a primary marker of difference.[3] As a result, racist discourse justifying slavery turned more virulently towards the body as a site of restriction, punishment, or disempowerment. The rise of the sugar plantation across the long eighteenth century encouraged an understanding of Black bodies in utilitarian terms. Bodies matter in this discourse according to their ability to perform labor, to survive hardship, and to obey orders.[4] Raised in slavery on the Fairfield plantation, Dido brings to this scene with George a lifetime of servitude in which meeting the domestic needs of white families involves both the physical and emotional labor of childcare. The scene traps her in a doubly precarious dynamic. On the one hand, her position demands that she meet a child's needs by providing emotional labor, caring for a child with her body even to the point of showing physical affection. On the other hand, racist strictures demand her to limit and contain her body, keeping it from making too much contact with white bodies. The adult Dido is thus vulnerable to the child George's perception of how well she walks this fine line. With this scene taking place on English soil, George's displeasure towards Dido will not end in the corporal punishment she might receive on a Caribbean plantation. However, while the geographical difference renders this a scene more of uncomfortable amusement than of impending physical violence towards Dido, the plantation contexts still haunt this scene of English domesticity.

Olivia intervenes by making her own claims to blackness, insisting that she too carries the same unmistakable and immutable markers that leave Dido vulnerable. She insists that George, and by extension readers, consider the visual markers of blackness on her body by comparing her complexion both to Dido's and to George's skin tones. She confronts the discourse that darker skin is dirty head on when she tells George: "I am glad [my skin] does not look so *very* dirty ... but you will be surprised when I tell you that mine is quite as clean as your own, and that the black woman's below, is as clean as either of them" (*WC*, 78–79). When Olivia insists that she and Dido are both sufficiently clean, she unsettles the racist notion that negative qualities remain inextricably wedded to permanent external characteristics. The visual nature of this scene reinforces this point when Olivia invites George to attempt to rub her blackness away with a handkerchief. When George tells Olivia that he can "make [his skin] black by rubbing myself with coals," Olivia replies "And so can I make mine white by rubbing myself with *chalk* ... but both the coal and the chalk would be soon rubbed off again" unlike the natural colors of their respective skins (79).

David Dabydeen in *Hogarth's Blacks* describes two distinct modes at the heart of eighteenth-century visual art depicting Black subjects. One mode, present in paintings such as Joseph Wright's *Two Girls with Their Black Servant* (1770), glorifies whiteness through the use of visual racial stereotyping. Such paintings, in depictions of posture, gaze, and perspective, imply the superiority of white subjects, frequently young women, via the inferiority of Black servants; interior or mental qualities follow from external appearances.[5] Dabydeen finds a different mode of representation in Hogarth's paintings. According to Dabydeen, Hogarth depicts Black subjects who critique white British culture, exposing rudeness and vulgarity in the latter's hypocritical claims to politeness and normativity. When Olivia discusses skin tone with George and invites him to compare their appearances, she moves towards Hogarth's dynamic. Her visual juxtaposition with George makes room for an implicit indictment of his white family for raising him to follow in the footsteps of their own vulgar racism. Her pleasant but firm defiance asserts that her blackness is something she cannot change and something she should not want or need to discard.

This moment presents Olivia in her most revolutionary attitude. Lyndon Dominique reads this scene as one in which Olivia patently resists nineteenth-century ideology surrounding "amalgamation" or "whitewashing," the idea that through racial intermixing there would emerge "a superior race of mulattos who understand that their superiority is in service of upholding a racial hierarchy that white British men have been actively involved in establishing."[6] For Dominique, Olivia becomes "a specific symbol of *'failed whitening'*—a free, literate, mulatto heiress—using her own body to do the work of not confirming the little boy's superiority but improving his attitude."[7] The novel invites its readers to celebrate and respect its protagonist in her moment of gaining "conquest over prejudice" (79). *The Woman of Colour* thus implicitly calls on readers to reject any notion that blackness should disappear and posits Olivia as a powerful champion of anti-racism.

In this brief exchange engaging George and Dido, Olivia momentarily fulfills the promise she makes in her very first letter of taking pride in her blackness, the stance twenty-first-century readers most desire her to defend. In her first letter to Mrs. Milbanke, Olivia writes: "*We* are considered, my dear Mrs. Milbanke, as an inferior race, but little removed from the brutes, because the Almighty Maker of all created beings has tinged our skins with jet instead of ivory" (*WC*, 53). This early moment in the novel ostensibly promises a polemical, passionate, anti-racist heroine in Olivia. Note the italics employed for Olivia's use of "we" here. Even down to the choice of typeface, this letter urges readers to situate Olivia proudly and firmly in a pan-African understanding of blackness. This mixed-race heroine willingly embraces the blackness that extends to all people of African descent, even when that means that she too will occupy a category divorced from power, linked more to animals than human beings in a racist white imaginary. We see in this first letter the promise of a heroine who can rewrite the "already read text" of stereotypes about Black women.[8] Literate and erudite, Olivia opens the novel with the assurance that she can write her own story and use the tools of pen, ink, and narrative on behalf of other Black people. After all, Olivia provides a miniature seduction plot in her earliest letter, making her own mother, Marcia, its protagonist. She indulges in a meditation on her mother's merits, detailing how she "learned to venerate the memory of this sable heroine (for a heroine I *must* call her) from the time that my mind has been enabled to distinguish between vice and virtue!" (*WC*, 55). Olivia willingly criticizes her own conception here. Emphasizing her mother's heroine status within this seduction narrative implicitly casts her father as seducer and villain. The novel thus opens with a forceful critique of the sexual exploitation of Black women by white men within the institution of slavery. This unabashed move towards taboo racial and gendered themes promises, as Dominique points out, fiction that deconstructs both race and gender.[9] With a dismal scarcity of Black heroines haunting eighteenth-century British novels across the period, a novel that lauds the merits of multiple Black women, our main protagonist as well as her mother, seemingly promises a profound challenge to this lack of representation in the canon.

Olivia's story arguably remains twenty-first-century readers' best hope of encountering intersectional feminism in a novel from this period, but her relationship with anti-racism is ultimately far too troubled to satisfy our contemporary desires. These disappointments led Tricia Matthew to tweet on 20 September 2019, for example, that many of her students were: "DONE with Olivia. I had to remind them her last name is Fairfield NOT Pope."[10] Olivia frustrates the twenty-first-century reader who is hungry for the kind of passionate condemnation of racism Olivia offers in one moment in the novel but snatches away in the next. Twenty-first-century readers, especially those of us who smile contentedly at the sight of Kerry Washington in a power suit, want a Black woman protagonist who can challenge the status quo, transcend limitations, and fight for other Black women who never get the chance to access Olivia's socioeconomic privilege. When, at last, the early nineteenth century offers a Black heroine to close out the long eighteenth century, we want to rest assured that this period in literary history finally offers readers a character of color with the kind of admirable self-determination and radical sociopolitical stakes we see at work in white female characters throughout the period, from Moll Flanders to Elizabeth Bennet. Olivia certainly deserves credit for the many instances in the novel in which she provides just that. She frequently calls out racist culture in England, even when that means risking the ire of people with more power, money, and privilege than she has. She dares to fall in love with a white man across the increasingly strict color line operating in the early nineteenth century, and she foreswears marriage to another white man because the match would potentially hinder her independence and ability to pursue her goals. She becomes all the more disappointing, then, when she upholds the very racism she purports to combat and shores up the institution of slavery she supposedly abhors. As much as Olivia supposedly extends kinship to Dido, she repeatedly stresses all the ways she is unlike Dido, claiming for herself freedom and privileges that she denies to her darker-skinned, enslaved servant.

Though this novel often places Olivia in the civilizing position of one of Hogarth's Black figures, it just as frequently places her, paradoxically, in the position Dabydeen ascribes to white women in the opposite mode. Dido, gazing adoringly at Olivia, provides a contrast in which Olivia appears more like the typical white female subjects of eighteenth-century portraiture. Dido's position as an object and Other makes Olivia's virtue, status, and comparative proximity to whiteness more visible. For example, when Olivia and Dido cross the Atlantic together on their journey from Jamaica to England, Olivia describes a scene in which she draws while Dido, "ever officiously happy and busy about her 'Missee,' was standing behind the sofa (which she had drawn towards the table), and very assiduously watching for the colours I wanted." Olivia goes on: "At intervals, I felt her removing and replacing the combs of my hair ... marking the progress of my pencil, and exclaiming, 'Ah, my goody Heaven! If my dear Missee be not making the own good Massee's plantation, and all of dis little bit of brush, and dis bit of paper!" (*WC*, 57). In this deeply metafictional moment, the novel presents Olivia creating a visual rendering of the plantation on fictional paper while she re-creates plantation dynamics in the scene she narrates in her letter to Mrs. Milbanke. When Olivia takes up the ladylike pastime of drawing, she flaunts her possession of years of education and training unavailable to Dido. Olivia's father, the master of the Fairfield plantation, was clearly invested in his mixed-race daughter's education, ensuring that she possessed at least the basic accomplishments of a lady. Dido, handing Olivia her colored pencils, becomes like one more of Olivia's artistic implements, a tool that indicates her status as a lady and, therefore, a worthy heroine of a novel. In fact, Olivia's pointed separation from Dido enables the positions that Olivia must occupy in the rest of the novel, from white man's wife to benevolent slave mistress. The novel thus makes this contrast highly visible from the beginning. Olivia sits while Dido stands. Olivia engages in a leisure activity while Dido is always at work. Olivia writes and speaks in only the most polished English, while the illiterate Dido speaks in dialect.

The Olivia we see in this example apparently betrays the ideals put forward in the scene in which she debunks the Mertons' racism in her conversation with their young son. In her moment with young George, Olivia promises, as Dominique points out, to champion "racial equality for *all* people of African descent, not just the appealing light-skinned ones."[11] While this is indeed Olivia's function in much of the novel, her relationship to blackness in this scene onboard the ship to England undermines her supposedly subversive role. When Olivia chooses to represent the plantation in her visual art, she simultaneously represents the power dynamics of the plantation even after she and Dido are physically removed from it. Holding its image on her drawing paper, she holds the power to invoke its hierarchies.

Bound for England sometime in the first decade of the nineteenth century, Olivia and Dido have left the colonial soil in which Dido's enslaved status would remain uncontested. However, once they set foot on English soil some three decades after the 1772 Mansfield decision, they have technically entered territory in which Olivia cannot compel Dido to return to life in plantation slavery. As Edlie Wong reminds us, the Mansfield decision, contrary to its often mythic status in both the eighteenth century and our own time, did not actually end slavery on English soil. It merely made the act of forcing enslaved persons to return to colonial soil illegal. A slave owner would have to leave behind any enslaved people brought to England, effectively freeing them, if the owner in question wanted to return to the colony.[12] Olivia and Dido, in the liminal space of the sea, move towards soil that can potentially remove Dido from plantation life forever, yet Olivia pointedly reintroduces an aestheticized image of the plantation. Dido's telling response, one of admiration for this image of "good massee's plantation" and Olivia's skill in recreating it, in turn meets with Olivia's implicit approval. She displays Dido's quaint loyalty for Mrs. Milbanke and readers alike as a reminder that Dido, enslaved to benevolent owners, is happy with her status.

Furthermore, Olivia appears particularly proud of Dido when Dido appears most committed to plantation slavery. Olivia fondly notes that Dido cannot wait to leave London for the English countryside, recounting how Dido told her: "we shall be there again, as if we were at the dear Fairfield plantation, only that Dido won't see the dear little creatures of her own colour running about:—but no matter ... it be very, *very* hard, if poor Dido cannot find some little babies and their mammies to care after, and to doctor, and to feed with goodee things, from her goodee Missee, go where she will!" (*WC*, 99). In Olivia's imagination, Dido longs for a return to the plantation and actively seeks its approximation on English soil. The plantation is reimagined here as a space of Olivia's benevolent charity in which Dido, on Olivia's behalf, happily cares for poor enslaved families on the plantation in much the same way the maid of a benevolent nineteenth-century matriarch might extend her charity to poor families in rural communities. When Olivia insists that the colonial space of the plantation shares British countryside virtues, she lays claim to the traits of a normative British heroine at the expense of Dido's freedom. In order for the comparison to work, the plantation must include happy enslaved people who willingly accept improvements to their situation via their owner's generosity—a group of people who call for an amelioration of the status quo rather than a radical restructuring of the racist institution that keeps them in bondage.

When Dido longs for a space that more closely mimics plantation life than she can find in English cities, she implicitly accepts and even celebrates her own place in Olivia's vision of benevolent slavery. Olivia further emphasizes Dido's commitment to slavery just a few sentences later, when she describes Dido's response to white English servants' racism. According to Olivia, Dido declares: "But Mrs. Merton's maid treats me, as if me was her slave; and Dido was never slave but to her own dear Missee, and she was *proud* of that" (*WC*, 100). Dominique notes Dido's use of the past tense in this sentence as an indication that Dido considers herself a former rather than a current slave.[13] However, Dido's status in England is actually more precarious. She is still legally bound to Olivia, even if the latter cannot technically return her to Jamaica. Dido seems to reassure Olivia and readers alike that even though her status has been brought into question, her desires always rest with the beloved Fairfield plantation. Olivia insists that Dido can and does take pride in slavery. By extension, Olivia puts forward the idea that plantation life, managed with sufficient virtue, can provide a healthy and affirmative basis for Dido's identity.

Olivia maintains a troubled relationship to the trope of the grateful slave. George Boulukos theorizes this literary trope in terms of affect, citing the responses of enslaved people on fictional plantations. According to Boulukos, their happiness and gratitude in response to a reformed plantation, managed with the kindness of "a sentimental planter or overseer," rests on the idea "first that plantation slavery will continue in a brutal form that makes the humane reformers' efforts remarkable and, second, that Africans can be induced not just to accept slavery but to embrace it, to be overwhelmed by ecstatic gratitude toward someone who continues to claim mastery over them."[14] Julie Murray cites Boulukos in her analysis of Olivia's tendency to inhabit this affective position, noting that Olivia primarily situates her father in the role of sentimental planter.[15] For Murray, though, Olivia's story glorifies the plantation for different reasons, arguing that this dynamic allows Olivia to cast the plantation as a site of country virtue. Murray resolves the seeming contradiction between the novel's anti-slavery politics and its idealized representations of plantation life by examining the novel's rejection of commerce, especially commerce in human beings.[16] I agree that *The Woman of Colour* rejects commerce and insists on defending the humanity of enslaved persons for largely anti-slavery ends. The novel still, however, disappoints readers looking for a progressive heroine, because, even with these features, it fails both to renounce its commitments to racism fully and to upend plantation hierarchies sufficiently. The echoes of the grateful slave that Murray identifies reverberate too loudly throughout *The Woman of Colour*, not just in Olivia's warm feelings towards a slave-owning patriarch but, more inescapably, in Dido's warm feelings towards Olivia's slave-owning father and even towards Olivia herself.

Published just one year after the 1807 British abolition of the transatlantic slave trade, the novel points straight to contemporary discourse surrounding the kidnap, transportation, and selling of human beings as a major economic enterprise. Both humanitarian and economic reasoning increasingly supported the abolition of this traffic in African bodies.[17] Olivia makes no scruple of condemning the transatlantic slave trade and pushing for its abolition, calling it "this disgraceful traffic" (*WC*, 81). However, condemnation of the slave trade crucially diverges from a condemnation of the institution of slavery itself. Like many pieces of public discourse from the period taking up the problem of the transatlantic slave trade, the institution of slavery, and the broader problem of race, this novel must pick a side on the most immediate political issue—that of the trade—and address its broader implications for the other issues in their turn. *The Woman of Colour* does just that when it joins other early nineteenth-century discourses insisting that the abolition of the slave trade could, in fact, be a good thing for the plantation. According to Daniel Livesay's research, a particular strain of early nineteenth-century reformist thought posited the abolition of the slave trade as a moralizing impetus on plantations. It argued that the end of the trade would mean the growth of Black family life for slaves on plantations. Now that the slave trade would no longer supply laboring bodies by importing them from abroad, the institution could only continue through the self-sustaining reproduction of people who were already enslaved. In theory, this would prompt slave owners to treat their slaves with more care, lengthening the life expectancy of enslaved people long enough to allow them to reproduce. This more humane treatment would simultaneously improve the morals of enslaved people, such discourse argued, because enslaved people could then be encouraged to marry and start families, producing stable generations of people who could thrive under the institution.[18] A congruent paradox of anti-slavery sentiment married to dreams of a stable, happy plantation permeates *The Woman of Colour*.

Even when the novel is most overtly and directly committed to abolition, the problem of race ultimately destabilizes the certainty of Olivia's position on the issue. When Mrs. Merton presses Olivia for her thoughts on abolition, Olivia responds in apparently unequivocal terms: "Mine will, I hope, be immediately understood; the feelings of humanity, the principles of my religion, would lead me, as a Christian, I trust, to pray for the extermination of this disgraceful traffic, while *kindred claims* (for such I must term them) would likewise impel me to be anxious for the emancipation of *my* more immediate brethren!" (*WC*, 81). With the italicized "my," Olivia owns her identity as the multi-ethnic daughter of an enslaved African woman and claims closer kinship ties to enslaved Black people than Mrs. Merton can claim. In this example of Olivia placing her own blackness front and center, readers can feel most convinced that she truly desires a radical alteration to existing structures of power, one that sufficiently topples plantation hierarchies and their violent suppression of Black slaves. These wishes crucially depart from her earlier wish that she could stay in Jamaica, "happily and usefully employed in meliorating the sorrows of the poor slaves who came within my reach, and in pouring into their bruised souls the sweet consolation of religious hope!" (6). Does Olivia want to abolish the trade and the institution it supports immediately, or does she dream of making the existing institution better?

It is easy to imagine that limited options prompt Olivia to support amelioration when she would rather see total abolition. Without securely possessing her father's fortune, Olivia is not, after all, in a position to make such radical demands throughout most of her narrative. However, at the novel's ending, when both Olivia's fortune and the Fairfield plantation are firmly in her hands, Olivia ultimately returns to her earliest aspirations: "I shall come back to the scenes of my infantine happiness. I shall again zealously engage myself in ameliorating the situation, in instructing the minds—in mending the morals of our poor blacks" (188). Invoking nostalgia for plantation life, Olivia recommits herself to the project she could only consider in abstract, imaginary terms at the beginning of the novel. Her marriage plot shattered, Olivia becomes a sentimental planter, the hero of a grateful slave narrative, when she cannot become the heroine of a marriage plot.

Of course, as much as Olivia's ameliorative aspirations disappoint twenty-first-century readers hoping for a more unequivocal rejection of slavery, her actions maintain a deep commitment to the most progressive politics available to her at the time, in all their nuances and limitations. In many ways, Olivia continues the legacy of her father's failures. According to Olivia's first letter: "his wishes, and his principles, would have led him to reform abuses, but his health was daily declining, and he could not give the tone of morals to an island; he could not adopt a line of conduct which would draw on him the odium of all his countrymen: he contented himself, therefore, with seeing that slaves on his estate were well kept and fed, and treated with humanity—but their minds were suffered to remain in the dormant state in which he found them!" (*WC*, 55). Likewise, Olivia's inclinations, wishes, and principles might urge her to free all the enslaved people on the Fairfield plantation and fight for the abolition of plantation slavery altogether, but she too risks the wrath of the entire Jamaican planter class. Such actions would fly too severely in the face of the most powerful community in Jamaica, a group Olivia willingly critiques throughout the novel and openly challenges at its end when she makes ready to implement her plan of offering religion and mass education to her own slaves. This group could—and did according to Livesay's research—accept an elite mixed-race planter as one of their own.[19] It would not, however, accept too extensive a challenge to plantation economies as a way of life, particularly in the sensitive sociopolitical climate of the earliest decades of the nineteenth century as debates surrounding the abolition of the slave trade and the institution of slavery itself more forcefully threatened the stability of this small, powerful group of mostly white men. Just as her father contented himself with humane treatment without providing education and religion, Olivia contents herself with the latter two improvements without offering the enslaved people on the Fairfield plantation any real freedom. Indeed, her reference to their minds in a "dormant state" rests on the racist assumption that enslaved people represent fundamentally unenlightened subjects waiting for a savior. According to her thought, enslaved people most particularly need and desire the education and the Christian morals supposedly exemplified by British Protestant values rather than freedom and self-determination.

Occupying the role of civilizing, Christian master means negotiating an uneasy relationship with anti-racist and anti-slavery ideas. In a strange way, Olivia must first occupy the subject position of someone who critiques racism so that she can later occupy the subject position of slave master by the novel's end. She adopts a racial hierarchy in which enslaved Black subjects, while still recognizably human, occupy a lower level than she occupies as a mixed-race Black member of elite society. This model, which gestures towards the Great Chain of Being, treats humanity as an unevenly distributed property, to which those at the top can more fully lay claim than those beneath them.

Sylvia Wynter's theorization of what she terms "the coloniality of being" is particularly helpful in unpacking the fraught racial hierarchy in *The Woman of Colour*. Wynter contends that the western European colonization of the Caribbean saw the rise of a "new mode of being human," one that prioritized "the political subject of the state Man."[20] Wynter charts how the European Enlightenment's ideal political subject replaced the medieval period's model Christian as the normative ideal. These ideas about what a human being should be follow directly, Wynter argues, from "realizing of the modern state's own secular goals of imperial territorial expansion."[21] In this project, Man, always gendered male and racialized as white, becomes the only "normal" human being, while people who do not fit within this gendered and racialized category become human Others. In particular, "in the wake of the West's second wave of imperial expansion, *pari passu* with its reinvention of Man in now purely biologized terms, it was to be the peoples of Black African descent who would be constructed as the ultimate referent of the 'racially inferior' Human Other." Black people thus become "the ostensible embodiment of the non-evolved backward Others—if to varying degrees, and, as such, the negation of 'normal humanness,' ostensibly expressed by and embodied in the peoples of the West."[22]

When Olivia insists "I do consider myself as more than *half* an English woman and it has always been my ardent wish to prove myself worthy of the *title*," she claims a place in these racially defined hierarchies with Man at the top and inferior human Others at the bottom (*WC*, 111). Olivia's race and gender already exclude her from the category of Man as such. Olivia will never be a normal human in this sense, but her quest for belonging in England demonstrates the ways in which she can still make claims to the category of Man. When she becomes a wealthy planter at the novel's end, she ultimately assumes a role overwhelmingly dominated by wealthy white men, persons who much more closely embody Man as Wynter describes him. Despite only having one English parent, Olivia becomes more than half English, and thereby less than half African, as she strives to inhabit the category of the human ostensibly only available to Man.

Olivia's participation in eighteenth-century British colonialism makes this possible. When Mrs. Merton requests that her servants bring Olivia rice to eat, Olivia responds: "I eat just as you do, I believe: and though, in Jamaica, our poor slaves (*my brothers and sisters*, smiling) are kept upon rice as their chief food, yet they would be glad to exchange it for a piece of your nice wheaten bread here" (*WC*, 77–78). Reflecting on Mrs. Merton's gesture, Olivia explains to Mrs. Milbanke, "this was evidently meant to mortify your Olivia; it was blending *her* with the poor negro slaves of the West Indies! It was meant to show her, that, in Mrs. Merton's idea, there was no distinction between us—you will believe that I *could not* be wounded at being classed with my brethren" (77). Here, Olivia, through her performance at the dining table, asserts her connection to Man and insists that enslaved Black people, though relegated to the Other in Mrs. Merton's eyes, nonetheless deserve a reconsideration of their place in the human hierarchy. She insists that their eating habits, a set of behaviors that contribute to their status as Other, are imposed by outside forces. They are not nearly as far removed from Man as Mrs. Merton believes.

Olivia's relationship to blackness is characteristically ambiguous, though. Readers must untangle the complicated dynamic. Olivia takes offense that Mrs. Merton wants her to be offended. On the one hand, we can read her as making the claim that she is proud to be Black and offended that Mrs. Merton would assume otherwise. On the other hand, however, another viable reading would suggest that Olivia actually wants Mrs. Merton to distinguish between Olivia and the slaves on the Fairfield plantation. That is, Olivia does not object to the distinction—she just wishes that Mrs. Merton would make it in a different way.

Olivia wants people like the Mertons to accept a mixed-race elite Black woman as an equal, despite her inability to meet all the race and gender requirements of Man. At the same time, she also hopes to extend the habits and cultural practices of white English people, such as their eating of bread, to enslaved Black people. She does not ask for enslaved Black people to embody the category of Man in the same way as she hopes to do but rather reminds Mrs. Merton that even human Others explicitly belong, as she does, to the category of the human. She troubles the idea that the Other must always remain so fundamentally antithetical to Man when all people are human.[23] This is not, however, the same as collapsing distinctions altogether. When Olivia uses the possessive pronoun "our" in reference to the "poor slaves" in Jamaica, she reminds Mrs. Merton and readers alike of her position of power and privilege in comparison to other Black people in the Caribbean plantation economy. Mrs. Merton's problem lies in treating Olivia and enslaved Black people as equally the antithesis of Man. Olivia rebuts that they are both just as human as white English people, though she attempts to maintain a higher sociopolitical position in this racial hierarchy than her slaves can ever occupy.

Humanity thus becomes fundamental to the ways *The Woman of Colour* fetishizes whiteness. Unable to access whiteness herself, Olivia can still lay claim to the cultural practices and knowledge available to Man. In making herself more like the normative human, she makes herself more like a white person, implicitly granting herself more power. When she extends that humanity to Black people from whom she otherwise remains markedly separate, she wields Man's power to declare who and who does not constitute the Other. She certainly reorganizes racist hierarchies, calling for more privileges to be extended towards Black people at every level and demanding the reduction of abuse. However, she remains committed to leaving a race-based hierarchy in place in which proximity to whiteness denotes a higher status. Her commitment to such a hierarchy also allows her to lay claim to white femininity. As Felicity Nussbaum argues, eighteenth-century discourse dictated that "to be truly feminine (white, heterosexual, passive, domestic, chaste, and of a certain status) is to possess tender feelings for the oppressed (the black, the enslaved, the laboring classes) and yet to remain distinct from them and superior to them."[24] Olivia's purported identification with enslaved Black people even while keeping herself markedly separate from them actually aligns her more closely with the period's conception of normative femininity. Her contradictory behavior points straight to the performed patterns of identification expected of ideal white women at the time.

Twenty-first-century readers thus cannot escape feelings of frustration and disappointment when they look for profound radicalism in the titular heroine of *The Woman of Colour*. In some scenes, the narrative provides a version of Olivia who actively takes a stand against racism. Then, in other scenes it pivots to a stance that idealizes the plantation. Twenty-first-century readers cannot trust their protagonist to commit to the radical anti-colonial project we desire from a heroine who appears otherwise endowed with independence, wit, and self-proclaimed agency. When Olivia realizes her true calling of becoming a benevolent planter at the end of the novel, her vested belief in positive plantation slavery shocks twenty-first-century readers. Olivia's dream of a reformed plantation imagines ways that the project of colonialism can be made more stable because it will be made more enduring. By extension, she imagines ways racist hierarchies can be perpetuated when more room for Black elites and fewer abuses for the Black majority create healthier, happier plantations. With an ending poised to make Olivia's dreams a fictional reality in the off-page space of a quasi-utopian plantation, early nineteenth-century readers could rest assured that existing structures of power might ultimately remain stable with the collapse of the transatlantic slave trade. The plantation could and would continue with or without the trade and possibly with or without slavery so long as benevolent planters created environments that were sufficiently hospitable and hierarchical. Making room for mixed-race elites would solve more problems than their inclusion would create, especially since those mixed-race elites would remain safely contained in faraway colonial spaces and would not mix too profoundly with white Britons—especially not via miscegenation. All these ideas could soothe nineteenth-century British conservatives worried about the destabilizing effects of abolition on empire. They also enrage, disenchant, and disillusion twenty-first-century readers looking for unequivocal commitment to progressive politics. The promise of a heroine of color in a literary canon that often excludes Black women becomes a devastating letdown when this protagonist cloaks colonialism in fashionable attire. What should today's readers do with all their bad feelings?

Perhaps we can best begin answering this question by addressing its core issue: what did we hope to find within the pages of *The Woman of Colour*? Why were we looking for a revolutionary in Olivia in the first place? Inadvertently, in that desire we might have just made the same mistake with novels that Ann Laura Stoler and Anjali Arondekar urge us not to make with imperial archives. Stoler explores how imperial archives, records of colonial projects, become "sites of the expectant and the conjured—about dreams of comforting futures and forebodings of future failures."[25] According to Stoler, one would expect to find emotionless matter at the heart of imperial archives replete with legislative documentation, facts, and figures. However, Stoler asks us to turn our attention to all the affective content there as well: the traces left by colonial hopes, dreams, and fears—and all the emotions that go with them. When we find these spaces unexpectedly replete with affect, the stuff we might more reasonably expect to find in novels, we are forced to reevaluate what we wanted from colonial archives in the first place.

I contend that *The Woman of Colour* poses a similar challenge to our thinking. In the archives, we expect to find records of colonial power and get a kind of affective discourse for which we did not bargain. In *The Woman of Colour,* we expect the privileging of affective discourse as a means of resisting the kind of power we find in colonial archives, but we actually get that power shored up and reinforced. Olivia's collected letters, compiled by an editor who insists that their fictionality is irrelevant, would seem to offer an alternative to the records that Stoler describes. Once we get a set of documents authored by a Black woman who can openly champion emotional experience, we are ready for the antithesis of the power dynamics at work in the colonial archive. The sentimental novel is, after all, required to supply empathy where much of the documentation preserved in the colonial archive is required to withhold it. We want to see colonial objects become speaking subjects, and we want to see longings for sustainable empire replaced by visions of revolutionary futures. When *The Woman of Colour* offers us both what we want and what we most assuredly do not want, we find ourselves mired in readerly frustration in the midst of the novel's colonial optimism.

I propose that *The Woman of Colour* offers twenty-first-century readers an opportunity to investigate our own political commitments with respect to novels and what we hope to find within them. I follow the line of thinking that Anjali Arondekar calls for in archives, which "mandates a theory of reading that moves away not from the nature of the object, but from the notion of an object that would somehow lead to a formulation of subjectivity: the presumption that if a body is found, then a subject can be recovered."[26] *The Woman of Colour* demonstrates the many ways fictional space can mimic and reproduce the archive. It can also teach us about the ways we might reorient ourselves with respect to novels in a way similar to how Arondekar asks us to reorient ourselves to archives. If for readers of archives the problem is a desire for subjectivity when the documents in question offer only objects, then the novel reader's problem in *The Woman of Colour* is a desire for radical, empowered politics in a text that offers a much more fraught Black female political subject. Olivia's story puts enormous and uncomfortable pressure on the idea that recovering Black female representation in the literary canon offers an alternative to the hegemonic discourses we primarily encounter both inside and outside the realm of fiction. When it exposes the political limitations of a fictional subject, this novel simultaneously reminds us that we do not actually need Olivia to give us what we want. We can make a readerly turn away from the assumption that Olivia's subjectivity will give us the politics we seek. Instead, we can remember that eighteenth-century novels, even those that include Black characters, often remained crucial perpetrators of the colonial apparatus even when they could resist it. We can remember, too, that we do not actually need Olivia's subjectivity to translate into resistance. We may not glean from Olivia's story a powerful example of a woman who overturns hegemonic regimes, but we do learn a lot about our own desires.

Notes

1. Lyndon Dominique, ed. *The Woman of Colour* (Ontario: Broadview Press, 2008), 84, henceforth cited parenthetically in the text as *WC*.

2. See Melissa Adams-Campbell, *New World Courtships: Transatlantic Alternatives to Companionate Marriage* (Lebanon: Dartmouth College Press, 2015).

3. Roxann Wheeler, *The Complexion of Race: Categories of Difference in Eighteenth-Century British Culture* (Philadelphia: University of Pennsylvania Press, 2000), 9.

4. Andrew Curran, *The Anatomy of Blackness: Science and Slavery in the Age of Enlightenment* (Baltimore: Johns Hopkins University Press, 2011), 53.

5. David Dabydeen, *Hogarth's Blacks: Images of Blacks in Eighteenth Century English Art* (Manchester: Manchester University Press, 1987), 32.

6. Lyndon Dominique, *Imoinda's Shade: Marriage and the African Woman in Eighteenth-Century British Literature, 1759–1808* (Columbus: Ohio State University Press, 2012), 226.

7. Dominique, *Imoinda's Shade*, 226.

8. Barbara Johnson, *The Critical Difference: Essays in the Contemporary Rhetoric of Reading* (Baltimore: Johns Hopkins University Press, 1980), 3.

9. Dominique, introduction to *The Woman of Colour*, 34.

10. Matthew, Tricia. Twitter Post. September 20, 2019, 12:14 PM. *https://twitter.com/triciamatthew/status/1175080847306821634.*

11. Dominique, introduction to *The Woman of Colour*, 31.

12. Edlie Wong, *Neither Fugitive nor Free: Atlantic Slavery, Freedom Suits, and the Legal Culture of Travel* (New York: New York University Press, 2009), 21.

13. Dominique, introduction to *The Woman of Colour*, 31.

14. George Boulukos, *The Grateful Slave: The Emergence of Race in Eighteenth-Century British and American Culture* (Cambridge: Cambridge University Press, 2008), 3.

15. Julie Murray, "The Country, the City, and the Colony in *The Woman of Colour*," *Lumen* 33 (2014): 93.

16. Murray, "Country, the City, and the Colony," 99.

17. Murray, "Country, the City, and the Colony," 98. For further discussion, see Christopher Leslie Brown, *Moral Capital: Foundations of British Abolitionism* (Chapel Hill: University of North Carolina Press, 2006).

18. Daniel Livesay, *Children of Uncertain Fortune, Mixed-Race Jamaicans in Britain and the Atlantic Family, 1733–1833* (Chapel Hill: University of North Carolina Press, 2018), 202, 325–26.

19. Livesay, *Children of Uncertain Fortune*, 330. Livesay's study of the history of elite mixed-race Jamaicans during the long eighteenth century presents real individuals who often found themselves, like the fictional Olivia, migrating to England and navigating a complicated set of family and sociopolitical dynamics. Livesay notes that the turn of the nineteenth century, marked by abolitionist politics, saw a rise in debates about the role of mixed-race elites in sustaining a viable British colony in Jamaica. For example, Livesay describes the period's increased willingness to accept wealthy mixed-race Jamaicans among the elite white governing class: "If establishing a permanent and self-regenerating white population in the Caribbean was an impossible dream, then allowing an elite cohort of color to supplement, if not replace, that population might be the only viable alternative" (330).

20. Sylvia Wynter, "Unsettling the Coloniality of Being/Power/Truth/Freedom: Towards the Human, After Man, Its Overrepresentation—An Argument," *CR: The New Centennial Review* 3, no. 3 (2003): 265.

21. Wynter, "Unsettling the Coloniality of Being," 265.

22. Wynter, "Unsettling the Coloniality of Being," 266.

23. Olivia's insistence that all are human locates her understanding of race in a monogenesis tradition, i.e., the belief that human beings of all different races are the descendants of a common ancestor. Curran explains that during the early nineteenth century in Europe, proponents of abolition typically adopted a monogenesis account of race, citing shared ancestry between different races as a valid reason to extend liberty to all. Proponents of slavery, by contrast, typically adopted a polygenesis account of race that denied humanity to people of African descent based on the idea that they came from different, non-human ancestral bloodlines than white Europeans. However, adopting a monogenesis account did not necessarily mean adopting a patently anti-racist account of human difference. For a detailed discussion of these politics, see Curran, *The Anatomy of Blackness*, 130.

24. Felicity Nussbaum, *The Limits of the Human: Fictions of Anomaly, Race, and Gender in the Long Eighteenth Century* (Cambridge: Cambridge University Press, 2003), 176.

25. Ann Laura Stoler, *Along the Archival Grain: Epistemic Anxieties and Colonial Common Sense* (Princeton: Princeton University Press, 2009), 1.

26. Anjali Arondekar, *For the Record: On Sexuality and the Colonial Archive in India* (Durham: Duke University Press, 2009), 3.

The Habit of Habits: Material Culture and the Eighteenth-Century London Masquerade

MEGHAN KOBZA

> I hear, I am to see you in town on Monday. Lady Grace informed me, she believes, you would have lent me a clean Domino for the Masquerade at Richmond House. I wish I had known it sooner, for I am to pay 2 Guineas for the Hire of a Domino, which I have *already* bespoke; I should have been pleased to have spared that sum, for it is better than giving 4 Guineas & ½ to have it entirely to myself: I shall be extreamly *beautiful*, a straw colour trimed with Purple; what say you to that. I understand, you are to be in a *Harlequin dress*, & that [Fat?] Ward with his *great Guts* is to play the part of *Pierot.*[1]

In this 1763 letter to his brother Thomas, James Brudenell shared the dilemma he faced in obtaining a habit for the upcoming masquerade at Richmond House: should he have hired or purchased his domino? Though he decided on hiring, Brudenell also mentioned borrowing a habit from his brother as a third form of acquisition. The letter continued to include details regarding what his brother would be wearing, as well as the habit choice of a shared acquaintance. This letter draws attention to consumer practices associated with the masquerade, which have been overlooked in the existing scholarship on this form of eighteenth-century leisure.[2] The process of habit acquisition is not the only aspect of the masquerade that has been understudied. As Brudenell mentioned, his choice of which sort of habit to wear—a domino cloak or to dress in character—was an additional component, as was the physical aspect of wearing the habit and mask themselves. While both types of dress provided some level of disguise, the simple nature of the domino did not require the wearer to adopt a character role, which was expected to accompany character dress (e.g., acting as Harlequin when dressed as Harlequin). In this article, I argue that the material objects of the masquerade, the processes of consumption, and the context in which the objects were used deserve more attention than they have been given. Each component presents new perspectives on the experience of the masquerade, revealing it to be a space of elite sociability and differentiation.

While there has been some significant work done on the eighteenth-century masquerade in England, its use as a cultural trope in literature has left an incomplete representation of the entertainment's social history. Previous research has presented the masquerade as a space that predominately enabled individuals to transcend social norms and behavioral constraints. In her foundational work, Terry Castle proposed that "the presence of masks and costumes, not surprisingly, was responsible for this collective sense of increased liberty."[3] This may have been the case in literary representations and some first-hand experiences of the masquerade; however, Castle's work, and those following her example—including Catherine Craft-Fairchild and Dror Wahrman—relied primarily on fictional accounts of masquerades, often overlooking the significance of other textual and material sources such as correspondence and masquerade habits themselves. Beyond literary studies, dress historian Aileen Ribeiro has examined the appearance and function of masquerade dress in portraiture. Although Ribeiro's research engages with important aspects of visual culture, it focuses on artistic representations and newspaper accounts, leaving a gap between the individual habit, its relationship to the masquerade, and how it informed the social function of the entertainment.[4]

Drawing from manuscripts, business records, and objects provides new insight into the social history of the masquerade and revises the existing scholarship on this leisure activity. This article uses these sources and employs material culture methodologies to examine the social biography of the masquerade habit and how it contributed to the masquerade's reputation within leisure culture. The term *material culture* itself has received increasing attention in recent years and has influenced the work of many eighteenth-century historians. Amanda Vickery, Giorgio Riello, and other scholars have subsequently established that material culture refers to the use of objects to inform historical inquiry.[5] This involves examining the physical attributes of an object (history from things) and drawing upon written and material sources to find further evidence of an object's function and meaning within society (history of things). Igor Kopytoff has shown that engaging with an object and analyzing its movements through society can produce essential contextual information, forming connections between the object and user as well as the object and society.[6] The work of Vickery, Zara Anishanslan, and Jennifer Van Horn, among others, has skillfully pursued these methods in order to create object biographies, presenting more complete understandings of objects' significance in social and cultural contexts.[7] In addition to Kopytoff's approach, this article draws upon Riello's description of how historians approach the history of things, drawing meaning from the material artifact, especially when written texts are lacking.[8] These methodologies will aid in the construction of a new narrative for the masquerade and will further contribute to understanding the relationship between masquerade objects and people, as well as exploring the relationship between masquerade habits and the social role of the masquerade.

While objects themselves can provide new historical narratives, theoretical approaches to understanding the significance of objects in representing individual taste and character can contribute additional perspectives.[9] Colin Campbell argues that consumer choices could reflect and indicate an individual's desire to be perceived in a certain way. This "character confirming conduct," part of Campbell's character-action theory, can be applied in some instances to the study of masquerade habits. The eighteenth-century character ideals of the aristocrats, dandies, and romantics that Campbell describes help explain the motivations behind a range of masquerade habits that do not obviously advance the self-inversion, transgression, or debauchery that has been the focus of previous scholarship. Combining Campbell's character theory with Riello's history of things reveals that the choice of habit, when examined within the social and spatial context of fashionable display, can supply a variety of new avenues for understanding the decision-making process. Though there is never a single universal consumer motivation, examining costume choice in relation to the physicality of the pieces involved, the method of acquisition, and the presence of an audience can show how masquerade participants may have selected their dress to signify any number of things: taste, creativity, social connections, wealth, and/ or worldliness. Costume and conduct were responsible for reflecting the wearer's cultural sensibilities and were seldom used to actively betray his or her rightful social rank for the sake of transgression. Ultimately, the habit was a reflection on the participant's ability to fit within fashionable society rather than break from it.

Using Campbell's and Riello's methodologies, this article constructs a social biography of the masquerade habit. It begins with an explanation of contemporary terms and the various types of costume available to consumers. It then moves to examine the physical nature of the habit, how it was worn, and how this impacted the function and reputation of the masquerade. Tracing the various forms of acquisition and the habit's subsequent movement through society provides additional insight into where and how habits were sourced, how they could be representative of socio-economic status, and how their use could change over time. The article concludes with an examination of the habit within the context of the masquerade, highlighting the significance of audience in validating the ritual of cultural self-presentation. The analysis therefore engages with images and objects while also using manuscripts and other texts as supplementary sources to further clarify and substantiate the analysis. Key objects include the mask, the classic Italian domino, and the character habit, all of which are recognizable and consistent physical components of the masquerade. This work will also draw upon previously unused forms of evidence regarding the commercial aspect of masquerade habits, including bills of sale, trade cards, and the auction records of James Spilsbury's masquerade warehouse inventory. These sources contribute a new perspective on the relationship between masquerade objects and masquerade participants, the sensory qualities of the masquerade, and the methods of acquisition associated with the entertainment, ultimately challenging the existing scholarship on the masquerade and revealing it to be a space of fashionable sociability, display, and recognition.

The costume and mask were essential components of the London masquerade experience in the eighteenth century and, as such, helped to define the term *masquerade*. The term masquerade, when used as a noun, was defined in its most basic sense as "an assembly of maskers," that is, a gathering of people wearing masks. This definition changed only slightly throughout the century, sometimes including mentions of dancing, music, or gaming.[10] While other forms of social assemblies also included dancing and music, such as balls and ridottos, the prerequisite of wearing a mask highlighted the mask's formative role in establishing the masquerade as a distinct form of leisure in fashionable society.

The term *masquerade habit* and its related vocabulary deserves equal clarification. Masquerade habit was used loosely throughout eighteenth-century London, sometimes referring solely to the garment worn on the body and other times referring to the masquerade costume in its entirety—mask, garment, and accessories. The latter of these definitions was the more commonplace and was interchangeable with the term *masquerade dress*, both of which appeared in masquerade warehouse advertisements, trade cards, bills of sale, and manuscripts. These commercial sources indicate that "habit" and "dress" typically referred to the garment and mask as a unit. In his diaries, William Byrd II—a frequent masquerade attendee and wealthy plantation owner—interchanged the words "habit" and "dress" as well, using them to describe his costume as a whole. For instance, while preparing for a masquerade, Byrd "sent to borrow of Mr. Jeffreys his Marquis dress for the masquerade," later preparing "myself in the habit of the Marquis. ... And about ten went to the masquerade, where I was well diverted."[11] This interchange of habit and dress continues throughout Byrd's diaries, signaling that the words were larger terms of categorization, which could be applied to many types of masquerade costume.

While dress and habit were applied to all forms of masquerade garments, bills of sale and Spilsbury's auction book provided a more comprehensive look into the types of costumes that were available. These sources contain descriptive, itemized lists of habits and indicate if the costume fell under the category of generic domino, character, or masquerade dress. The domino was the cheapest costume option, consisting of a hooded cloak and mask. Character dress entailed a more complex costume, requiring the wearer to act the part of the costume he or she chose. If dressing as an old lady, the participant was expected to act the part of an old lady. This was commonly referred to as "supporting one's dress."[12] While the category of "masquerade dress" could be applied in a broad sense, it also filled the gap between character and domino dress. Masquerade dress, therefore, sometimes referred to a generic range of garments designed specifically for a masquerade but that did not align with the character or the domino styles. Dressing in Vandyke style or as Rubens's wife fell under this categorization, as they were considered fancy masquerade dress but did not require a character to support.

Masks

The first piece of the masquerade habit under examination is the mask. Though this object was apparently mandatory, according to textual definitions and contemporary images the mere requirement of a mask did not guarantee it would be worn for the duration of the entertainment, nor did it promise the wearer absolute anonymity. The extent to which the wearer's identity was concealed was relative. This was determined by several material and physical factors and also, of course, whether the wearer intended to be recognized.

Masquerade-goers, hereafter referred to as maskers, were presented with a range of options when it came to selecting and purchasing a mask. Masquerade warehouses had a constant presence in London throughout the fashionable season and offered maskers a variety of choices: masks in the

Venetian style and masks made from papier-mâché, leather, silk, or wax. The materials that formed the mask are worth considering themselves. Venetian and silk masks were lighter, considered to be higher quality, and were more comfortable, allowing maskers to wear their masks for longer periods of time. In 1750, masquerade warehouseman Mr. Hussey advertised "Masques, of a new Invention, made of Silk, which are free from the Inconveniencies of those made of Wax."[13] Mask-maker Conrad Rishman, who imitated the Venetian style, similarly promised:

> I do not doubt but those Gentlemen and Ladies, who shall use [these masks], will find them much more convenient than any other Masks, as they do not stick to the Face, and are not only much lighter and cooler, but are intirely free from any offensive Smell and Sticking, as also exceeding commodious for eating and drinking without the Trouble and Inconvenience of taking off.[14]

As materials, silk and papier-mâché were preferable to wax and leather due to their relative ease of wearing. Eighteenth-century wax was unrefined, odorous, rather hot and unbreathable, and tended to melt, causing the mask to lose its original shape and stick to the wearer's face. Although leather masks did not melt, they were heavier in construction and did not breathe well in warm masquerade rooms, resulting in their being removed early in the evening (see fig. 1). The inherent physicality of the materials and the ways in which the mask engaged with the senses of touch and smell mark a shift in praxis, changing the mask from a fixed form of disguise to a temporary accessory that could be discarded as necessary.

Similar to having a range in choice of material, prospective wearers of masks could select from four different mask shapes (see fig. 2). The variety of styles—*bauta, columbina, volto*, and character—allowed maskers to decide how much of their face they wanted to hide (or reveal) when wearing their masks. The *columbina* and *bauta* offered partial coverage, while the *volto* and character masks hid the majority of the face from sight. These masks were held in place either by string or with an attached holding stick. Those tied with string offered a more robust and semi-permanent form of attachment, while the nature of the holding stick indicated the mask would probably not be worn for the entirety of the evening. This design was not ambidextrous and so demanded the masker spend the evening with the mask occupying one hand, leaving the other available for limited activity (including eating, drinking, and dancing)—unless they wished to reveal their identity. The stick style does not often appear in images of masquerades, though there are

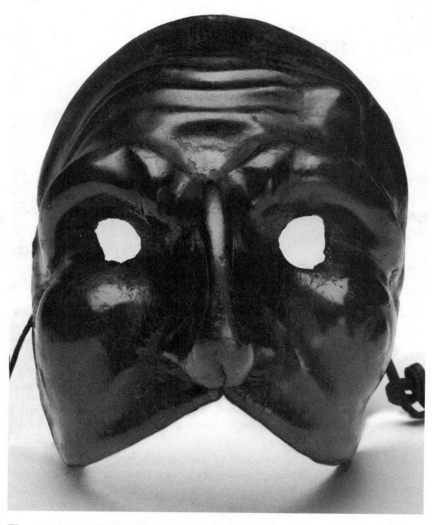

Figure 1. molded leather mask; upper portion of a man's face with hooked nose, probably Pulcinella from the *commedia dell'arte*, Italy, early eighteenth century. ©Victoria and Albert Museum, London.

Figure 2. Venetian papier-mâché masks. Private collection. Objects from top to bottom: character mask in shape of cat is complete; grey mask (*columbina*) has just been dried and molded—it needs further steps to be complete; full face white mask (*volto*) is almost complete—it requires glazing and painting; the object on the right is the mold used to set the shape of the layers of paper used to construct the mask.

frequent depictions of the mask being held away from the face. This points to the mask being a necessary requirement of the evening but not a fixture once inside the masquerade.

Apart from the material nature of the mask and the limitations it presented, be it breathability, the vision of the wearer, or dexterity, there were additional features of the masquerade that caused individuals to take off their masks. The first, which also impacted costume selection, was the heat of the rooms. Masquerades were consistently held indoors in London. The spaces of the King's Theatre, Carlisle House, and the Pantheon—and even the rotundas of Vauxhall and Ranelagh pleasure gardens—were described as stuffy and exceedingly warm spaces. Lady Coke noted that at one masquerade, Miss Irby "with the heat & the crowd grew so sick" that she removed her mask and relieved herself in a neglected turban. Agneta Yorke, who attended a masquerade at the King's Theatre in 1768, likewise commented on the temperature of the room: "Most of the Company unmasked as soon as they got into the Room the Heat was so great."[15] A letter published in the *General Evening Post* perhaps best explained the common experience: "I perceived that the people of consequence knew each other almost in the moment of their entrance; and as for those who had objections to relieving their features from the heat and inconvenience of their vizors, they were pronounced the people not worth knowing."[16] As the newspaper noted, inconvenience and identity could play equal parts in motivating an individual to remove their mask early in the evening. While those of the upper ranks would lose little in the way of status upon unmasking, those of aspiring upper-middling and mercantile backgrounds would become obscure and irrelevant once unmasked due to a lack of recognition. The complaint issued in the *General Evening Post* indicated that those of higher status spoiled mingling and networking opportunities for those below them by unmasking—the very act of keeping the mask on could identify an individual as someone inconsequential.

This is further shown through the many instances of unmasking motivated by those seeking recognition rather than, or in addition to, ending their physical discomfort. At a masquerade in 1776, "Lord Lyttelton seemed determined that all present should know that *one* Lord was in company, and therefore walked about unmasked very early in the evening."[17] The popular actress Sophia Baddeley similarly sought recognition at masquerades. One of her acquaintances recalled: "Before we entered the Ballroom, I begged the favour of Mrs. Baddeley not to unmask, and for some time she obliged me. Our dresses were much admired, but no sooner had she her mask off, than she attracted the attention of the whole room."[18] Whether or not someone unmasked early in the evening, a ceremonial unmasking usually concluded a masquerade. Individuals were expected to reveal themselves and ultimately become accountable for their actions. Taken together, the material nature of the masks, the ways in which they were worn or not worn, and the unmasking ritual all indicate that the mask was not required nor was it expected to be worn for the duration of the entertainment, despite the fact that it was a crucial and defining feature of the masquerade. The physical nature of the mask and its relationship with the wearer suggests a new form of praxis that changes the ways we think about and construct the masquerade as a social entertainment. Though the mask may have allowed the wearer to disguise herself, the practicalities and physical experience of wearing a mask suggest that concealment and protection of one's reputation were not the highest priority. Recognition was arguably as much a part of the masquerade as disguise.[19]

Domino

We now move from face to body with an examination of the classic domino costume. This garment came from *carnavale* in Venice and was made up of a cloak and a hood, which were worn over existing clothing and accompanied by a hat and *bauta* mask (see fig. 3 and fig. 4).[20] The domino's versatility made it a staple costume choice at masquerade warehouses, where it was available to let, purchase, and customize. Like the mask, the domino offered varying levels of concealment and could be made from an assortment of materials, such as silk or velvet. This resulted in the price ranging from seven shillings to four pounds (and higher), presenting buyers with a relatively affordable costume option. Warehouse owner D. Moore advertised having "a great variety of fancy dresses, and Dominos, at half a guinea for the night (mask included) also a great choice of beautiful fancy masks."[21] It is important to note that even at the lowest prices, renting a domino for half a guinea or purchasing one for fifteen shillings (masks at an average of 5s and dominos at 10s 6d) was a significant financial investment for the middling sort. This expense, when combined with the purchase of a two guinea ticket, was far from affordable and would have limited 96 percent of London's population from attending the masquerade, however infrequently.[22] The opportunity to rent, rather than purchase, this disguise made the costume more accessible to lower-income maskers, while customization and embellishments allowed the *beau monde* to display their personal, if not lavish, tastes. As an advertisement in the *General Advertiser* put it: "Mr. Hussey begs Leave to acquaint the Nobility and Gentry, That he has provided an entire New Assortment of Masquerade Habits; particularly Venetian Dominos, of all Sizes and Colours, trimm'd and embellish'd in a polite Taste."[23] Warehouseman James Spilsbury's bill of sale provides an additional point of reference, listing the cost of a domino at £3.3s. His auction list at Christie's includes additional details about dominos, ranging from color to material used to type of embellishment. Unlike the traditional Venetian domino, which was predominately black, masquerade dominos came in a range of colors, including white, lilac, green, and pink, and were often trimmed with contrasting colors or pinked along the edges as a form of embellishment. These details reveal that dominos were not all the same and that they contributed to a colorful visual landscape.[24] Here is another way in which the evidence provided by surviving costumes can usefully supplement the sources on which most previous scholars have relied. Dominos hardly ever appear in contemporary images of the masquerade, and, when they do, their popularity is significantly underrepresented. Additionally, on the relatively rare occasions when dominos are visible, they tend to be depicted as black rather than shown in the array of colors that were available and worn.

Figures 3 and 4 offer two examples of dominos, which substantiate the variations listed in Spilsbury's auction: color, material, and embellishments. They are identified as being made in the latter half of the eighteenth century, making them close contemporaries of the items in Spilsbury's bill of sale and auction list. As Spilsbury's list indicated, pink (or rose) and black were recurring color options for the domino habit. Although this is perhaps the most obvious characteristic of each domino, there are other important components to consider. While both dominos are made of silk and have hoods, they are of different shapes and feature distinct embellishments. The front opening and wide sleeves of the black domino (see fig. 3) would have revealed the clothing underneath. The Museum of London's choice to dress the mannequin in a contemporary silk and linen dress, a customary under-domino garment, suggests the wearer of the domino would have been a female member of the *beau monde*. If worn similarly in the eighteenth century, this disguise would have offered limited concealment, suggesting the wearer was keen to use the exposed under-clothing as a means of social display or perhaps recognition.

The pink domino offered the wearer a higher level of cover, extending into the buttoned cuffs of the sleeves (see fig. 4). This domino could have obscured both the social status and gender of the wearer. However, as Hussey implied in his advertisement and as later seen in Spilsbury's auction, the embellishments, such as the material (silk) and the pinking along the edges would have been points of recognition, giving away at least the wearer's social rank. Upon closer examination, the pink domino reveals the ephemerality of the masquerade habit. The style of stitching throughout the object suggests ease of adjustment and the rental potential of the garment. The large stiches and pleats in the shoulders would have allowed the maker to adjust the size of the shoulders and length of the sleeves quickly. When viewed from behind, the collar appears to have been altered, as does the hood, again suggesting that the domino had multiple wearers, either from the same family or social network, or as it passed in and out of a warehouse. Brudenell's letter to his brother was a case in point, mentioning both renting a domino from a warehouse and borrowing one from a family member.

The domino was both the most accessible and the most popular costume, ranging in price from seven shillings to six pounds, and occasionally more. A quick glance through Spilsbury's auction book supports this, with the domino making up 37.7 percent of his available inventory and selling for 8s 6d to £2 18s. Newspapers and personal accounts were also frequently overrun with references to maskers dressed in dominos. After attending a masquerade at Wargrave, Lybbe Powys recalled there were "numbers of fancy dresses and many good masques, and a great many black dominoes;

Figure 3. masquerade costume, c. 1760. ©Museum of London.

Figure 4. a domino for a man or a woman, 1765–70, English; pink silk lustring with cape and hood; altered c. 1775. ©Victoria and Albert Museum, London.

my lord [Barrymore] and all his party in these, and unmasqued … Mr. Powys, myself, and our two sons [also] in black dominoes."[25] The *General Evening Post* reported that the dominos at a King's Theatre masquerade "were about three to one in proportion to all the rest, and exceeded them in dullness as much as in number."[26] This was echoed in the *St. James's Chronicle*: the "Masquerade at Carlisle House on Monday Night opened for the Reception of Masks at Half past Nine, and the Rooms were remarkably elegant; but a certain Indolence, perhaps peculiar to this Country, induced the greatest Part of the Company to appear in Dominos. All seemed desirous to receive, but few took any Pains to give Pleasure."[27] As the papers noted, the domino was considered a dull choice of habit because it did not require its wearer to adopt a character persona. Unlike a character habit, which required the wearer to play the part of their costume and actively contribute to the entertainment of the evening, the domino's lack of a performative role resulted in it being banned from a handful of masquerades in the 1770s and 1780s. Masquerade hosts placed notices in their advertisements and on the tickets, serving as reminders of the ban. In 1782, an advertisement for the upcoming masquerade at the Pantheon warned: "No Masques will be admitted but such as are dressed in a character; and no domino on any pretence whatever, to appear in the rooms any time of the night."[28] True to its advertisement, the guards overseeing admittance to the masquerade did not hesitate in denying Lord Peterborough entrance despite his having a ticket. The *Morning Herald and Daily Advertiser* reported:

> The door-keepers refused him admittance, because he wore a black domino. After expostulating with them for a considerable time in vain, his Lordship asked, what he should do to gain admission? "Why, sir, you must come in a character." "Oh, very well," says his Lordship, "that I'll do in a minute;" —on which he took off his domino, rolled it up, and put it in his pocket;— "There, gentlemen," adds his Lordship, "I think I appear now in a character that will pass muster— the character of a gentleman."— "Very true, sir," replied one of the Cerberuses rather archly, "you have now a right to walk in; for it is no business of ours whether you are able to support your character, or not!"[29]

Despite his rank, Lord Peterborough's access was restricted until he met the criteria of dressing in character. As the guard satirically pointed out, it was no matter if Lord Peterborough could act the part of a gentleman so long as he arrived as a character. The preference for drawing character dress to the masquerade and the subsequent banning of domino costume indicated the presence of an audience and the significance of the entertainment as one of display and recognition.

Character and Fancy Dress

Though popular, the domino was not the only form of masquerade habit worn to the entertainment. Character and fancy dress allowed maskers the opportunity to display their wealth, social connections, and ingenuity among the *beau monde*. Character dress presented maskers with a substantial variety of garment options, including costumes falling under the themes of exoticism and empire (nabob, sultana, Native American), pastoral and mythological (shepherd, Athena), historical and political (Henry VIII, John Wilkes, a Highlander), and *commedia dell'arte* (Harlequin, Pierrot, Columbina), among others. Character choices and performance received equal approbation and censure in the papers. *The London Evening Post* reported on the successful dress of a political bedlamite "run mad for Wilkes and Liberty; he was covered with an old tattered blanket, with No. 45 on his shoulder; a whisp of straw in his hand; and his continual cry was 'Wilkes and Liberty:' this masque was not ill performed, and occasioned much mirth," while the *General Evening Post* criticized maskers' lack of ambition in supporting their character choices at a Pantheon masquerade: "Few of the characters were well supported, it being the modern custom of masquerade frequenters to consult the richness and grotesqueness of their habits, rather than attempt preparing themselves with that sort of dialogue their characters require."[30]

Fancy or masquerade dress was not as clearly defined as character dress or dominos and bridged the gap between the two, encompassing all the habits that were not dominos or did not require performative support. Costumes of this nature were therefore more intricate than a domino but far less entertaining than a character costume. Vandyke dress, Rubens's wife, and other forms of ambiguous but conspicuous dress fell under this classification and were often the most expensive masquerade habits.[31] In her preparation for a masquerade, Frances Burney differentiated between character and fancy dress, detailing the pains of decision-making in selecting her own masquerade apparel:

> I could think of no character I liked much, and could obtain; as to Nuns, Quakers, &c. (which I was much advised to) I cannot help thinking there is a gravity and extreme reserve required to support them well, which would have made me necessarily so dull and stupid, that I could not have met with much entertainment, and being unable to fix on a *character*, I resolved at length to go in meer *fancy dress*. ... My dress was, a close pink Persian *vest*, ... covered with gauze, in loose pleats, and with flowers &c. &c. ... a little garland or wreath of flowers on the left side of my head.[32]

Burney's choice to avoid dressing as a nun or Quaker was influenced by the dullness of their characters, being grave and reserved and therefore quite different from herself. These choices did not represent a character with which she wanted to be associated, thus illustrating Campbell's ideal of sensibility. Campbell contends that through conduct and consumption, and, by extension, dress, individuals were able to exhibit their particular characters and express certain ideals. In his explanation of the ideal of sensibility, Campbell argues that the choice "to manifest sensibility was crucial because it was tantamount to manifesting virtue."[33] This ideal therefore closely aligns with Burney's actions and internal debate about her choice of habit. In avoiding the nun and selecting a neutral option ("meer fancy dress"), she indicated that her selection would not only advertise her taste but also represent her moral and social standing. Rather than cast aspersions on her own self-perception and the public's perceptions of her through the dress of a nun, Burney remained characterless in her non-descript Persian garment.

Like the domino, these habits were available through various forms of acquisition; however, the prices of character and fancy dress costumes were more varied than the domino, ranging from one guinea to forty-eight pounds to as high as several thousands pounds. This, of course, was dependent whether the habit was a rental or purchase, as well as the materials used and the financial situation of the wearer. Both character dress and fancy dress provided maskers with further opportunities to display their rank, creativity, and social connections through their choice of dress, indicating that the masquerade functioned as a space for display and differentiation. Hannah Greig's work on the *beau monde* provides further support for this analysis, as she argues leisure spaces operated "as contexts for the performance of social separation and distinction. Far from encouraging a widespread 'mixing' of society, such commercial venues supported a system of fashionable differentiation."[34] While the lack of surviving examples of this style of dress presents an obstacle to recreating and understanding the physical nature of character and fancy dress habits, bills of sale, contemporary prints, and manuscripts provide supplementary, qualitative information that fills in some gaps and answers questions about the experience of dressing in these garments.[35]

Consider the habit depicted in the far-left corner of a 1771 print, *The Remarkable Characters at Mrs. Cornely's Masquerade* (see fig. 5). This character habit undeniably fulfilled all the criteria associated with dressing in character: it provided entertainment, exhibited social connections, and displayed a sense of humor and creativity—it also created a spectacle. Perhaps overlooked at first glance, the costume in question was none other than a coffin. To be clear: this was an actual habit (there is an extant bill of sale for it that was paid in 1772), not the invention of a printmaker. The feet appearing at the bottom of the structure belonged to the wearer who remained unidentified according to reports of the night, but was subsequently recognized as Colonel Luttrell. The image is brought to life through the related bill of sale and various accounts that circulated in the press in the days following the masquerade. The transcription of the bill of sale holds several keys to unlocking a more complete understanding of the complex nature of this costume (see Appendix 1). The first involves the maker, who was noted as being an undertaker rather than a masquerade warehouseman or woman, indicating the lengths to which maskers might go in procuring their costumes. The itemized list further reveals that there were three costumes ordered: the coffin itself and two additional supporting figures whose cooperation was essential to the execution of the habit. The cost of these costumes was rather high, totalling £6 6s. The bill of sale also provided missing information concerning the engraving on the front of the coffin, which is not legible in the print. The message consisted of two quotations from the Bible, presenting a play on words and acting as a conversation piece—thus providing entertainment for the other maskers in attendance. The *General Evening Post* supplied additional details regarding the way in which this habit was worn, reporting that "the most remarkable character last night was A gentleman in a coffin: the back part exactly a form resembled a coffin covered with black, and with white nails; the middle of the front was open, when there appeared a corpse in a shroud."[36]

Character costumes that transgressed social rank or nationality did not excuse individuals from contemporary expectations of politeness and decorum. Highlanders were responsible for performing ballads, harlequins for mischievous and comedic behavior, nuns for wisdom and gravity, and so on. This was no different for those who opted to dress below their station, as evidenced in the case of a law student:

> About two o'clock a very extraordinary fracas happened from the following odd circumstance: a student of the Temple who had obtained a habit similar to that in which the waiters were dressed, and standing as an attendant behind a few of his own friends, was observed to drink very freely and behave with uncommon freedom to some of the company; upon which a person was sent to order him out of the room ... for however a gentleman may be free to wear the dress of a waiter he had no right to assume the office, or set the example of too much freedom to the other attendants, who were unacquainted with his quality.[37]

The character of a waiter should act as a waiter—subservient, respectful, sober—so as not to give dangerous or radical ideas to the real waiters who

Figure 5. *The Remarkable Characters at Mrs Cornely's Masquerade*, engraving, c. 1770. Harry Beard Collection, ©Victoria and Albert Museum, London.

were present at the event. It is apparent that regardless of their choice of costume, participants were still confined to the expectations of civility and pre-existing societal conceptions of order.

While a waiter or peasant might offer a representational opportunity to act below one's social rank, costumes such as sultanas and nabobs allowed maskers the opportunity to lace their habits with ostentatious amounts of jewels and exhibit their connections and wealth. This was highlighted at the King of Denmark's masquerade in 1768, when many of the persons of quality in attendance dressed in eastern costume to represent the strength of empire and their associations with trade.[38] The Duchess of Northumberland recalled: "The Dutchess of Grafton was a magnificent Sultana in purple Velvet and Ermin & the Diamonds she wore that night were valued at a hundred & fifty thousand pounds."[39] Using the masquerade as a means to display social connections and reinforce status was particularly popular among the upper ranks of society and those wishing to solidify their place within it. Luke Scrafton, also in attendance, appeared in the finest nabob costume and wore the borrowed jewels of Lord Clive.[40] An early servant of the East India Company, Scrafton represented Lord Clive within the Court of Directors and later served as Director of the Company for three years.[41] His wearing of Lord Clive's jewels visually reinforced Scrafton's connection to persons of status, while his choice of dress, the nabob, directly referenced his professional role within the empire. Scrafton's display of his social connections helps identify self-exhibition as a main component of the masquerade. At least in his case, "oriental" dress was motivated by the wish to represent a fashionable character rather than any sort of desire for transgression.

Acquisition

Examining the material culture of masquerade habits themselves provides original and substantial information about the experience of the eighteenth-century British masquerade; however, as many accounts and reports have noted, the process of acquiring these items was an equally significant part of preparing for and attending the masquerade. Maskers were presented with four main types of acquisition: purchasing, renting, borrowing, or repurposing. The decision to use one form or another was dependent on many factors, though it is important to note that these methods were not independent from each other, and multiple methods could be used to assemble a single habit. Sophia Baddeley employed both purchasing and renting when preparing her costume:

> She had made up a very handsome masquerade dress, but the diamonds were wanting to complete it; these I consented to her having, and the following articles were hired for her, by me; Of Mr. Drury ... a pair of brilliant ear-rings. Of Mr. Bellas, Pall-Mall — a large diamond bow and pins. Of Mr. Dingwell ... three diamond necklaces. For her design was to put the three necklaces together, and make a belt of them, from her shoulder to her waste, with the bow at the end.[42]

Likewise, finding a dress for one masquerade might lead to renting a domino, while obtaining a costume for another might result in commissioning and purchasing the habit of a running footman. This shifting between methods of acquisition and constant alternating of habit choice from one masquerade to another indicated the ephemerality of the habit itself. Analyzing the ways in which masquerade habits were obtained, through singular or multiple forms of acquisition, gives perspective on the lifespan of the habit, its material and emotional value, and its social significance. Exploring these forms of acquisition and the ways habits flowed through society further contributes to a new narrative about the eighteenth-century masquerade and the significance of its material culture in establishing it as a leisure space used for display and social differentiation.

The option to purchase a masquerade habit was not unfamiliar to maskers, though it could, and often did, require a financial commitment, as noted in Brudenell's letter to his brother. Tracing purchasing practices through existing bills of sale has provided information about the life span of the habit, the cost of owning such a garment, and the objects that made up a masquerade dress. Using bills of sale from the Prince of Wales, the future George IV, reveals more than just his keen interest in attending masquerades. For example, a bill of sale from H. Wayte provides an itemized list of costume pieces, recording the Prince of Wales's selections as a friar and an old lady. His purchase of two "Rich Old Ladys Dresses," additional accessories, masks, and fake noses suggested that these costumes were for his and possibly another's use.[43] It was not uncommon for the Prince of Wales to attend the masquerade with his uncle, the Duke of Cumberland, or a coterie of nobility in complementary costumes. Other masquerade bills of sale show similar signs of group purchases, with multiple masks and fake noses appearing on each. The reoccurring purchases of masks and noses, regardless of their being used for a group, points to the need for a new mask at each masquerade. If we think back to the material nature of the mask, its limitations, and the warmth of any given masquerade room, it becomes apparent that these objects could either melt, become soaked in sweat, or be lost upon unmasking, making their physicality short-lived.

The chronology of these purchases gives additional insight regarding the lifespan of the masquerade habit and the consumer experience. The running list of purchases in Wayte's bill of sale showed the Prince of Wales acquiring a "Black Bumbaset Friars Dress" and domino on 14 May, followed by two new "Old Ladys Dresses" less than two weeks later. The recurring purchases of dominos and character costumes, specifically the old lady habit (bought again in 1803), suggests that the masquerade habit was a transient item that was not to be worn repeatedly by the same individual.[44] Newspaper reports and supplementary manuscript accounts reveal comparable practices among the *beau monde,* showing that the habit of wearing a different habit to each masquerade was not exclusive to royalty. However, the cumulative cost of purchasing multiple masquerade habits would have made ownership limited, even among the upper ranks of society who could afford to buy new costumes for each ensuing masquerade.

Renting and borrowing appear to have been the two most common and affordable forms of acquisition. Renting a habit entailed hiring a costume for temporary use from a masquerade warehouse, while borrowing was done within one's family or social network and did not require a commercial transaction. Both methods further highlight the ephemerality of the habit, as the garment lost its purpose for the masker once worn to a masquerade. The practice of renting a habit alone allowed maskers to change their dress for a significantly lower price—as Brudenell recalled, paying two guineas to rent was far better than spending four and a half guineas to purchase. The Duchess of Northumberland similarly rented masquerade habits in 1744, hiring "a Gown for the Masquerade" for five shillings in February and again in May "a Black Domino & use of a Cloak" for £4 6s 6d with the purchase of a "Venetian Black Slk Mask" for 7s 6d.[45] The very nature of hiring costumes indicates there were limited emotional attachments made to the habit, as it was returned at the end of the evening after having served its singular function.

Borrowing within one's social circle had even fewer financial repercussions, as it was free and served the additional purpose of displaying the wearer's social connections. It was common for maskers within the same social circles to lend each other costumes and/or accessories, which served as visual reinforcements of their social ties and rank. As Greig explains, "the display of an item given or lent by a fashionable figure broadcast the wearer's fashionable contacts."[46] William Byrd II and Horace Walpole both recorded borrowing and lending habits to and from friends. Byrd recalled, "I sent to borrow of Mr. Jeffreys his Marquis dress for the masquerade," while Walpole similarly related, "I had a large trunk of dresses by me, I dressed out a thousand young Conways and Cholmondeleys" for the ensuing masquerade.[47] Borrowing a habit not only displayed one's social connections, it also ensured that maskers did not wear their own habits too frequently, which was a faux pas. As his brief but meticulous diaries note, Byrd only ever wore one type of costume twice and never within the same year.

As with the case of Baddeley's diamonds, renting and borrowing did not solely apply to habits. Maskers also rented and borrowed jewels with which to bedazzle their costumes. In 1757 *Lloyd's Evening Post* remarked, "The number of jewels lent out on account of the ensuing Masquerade at the Opera-house [was] really amazing. One Jeweller [had] alone furnished to upwards of the value of two hundred thousand pounds."[48] Wearing rented diamonds was not the only form of jewellery acquisition available to the upper ranks, as evidenced in Scrafton's wearing of Lord Clive's jewels. Using the masquerade as a space for self-representation and physical displays of social connections encouraged borrowing within social networks. New York born social climber Stephen Sayre also saw benefit in lending items to exhibit his ties to the elite. His attendance at a masquerade in the 1770s was noted in Elizabeth Steele's memoirs. She mentioned Sayre's relationship with Lady Townshend, the wealthy widow of the prominent Whig politician Charles Townshend, and recalled Lady Townshend "took the liberty to send to Mr. Sayer, to request the use of his gold chain, to go to a masquerade in, as her dress required such an ornament, and he lent it to her."[49] This seemingly casual statement was loaded with allusions to Sayre's social status. Vickery and Styles's analysis of objects serving as visual representations of social networks highlights the significance of Sayre's loaning his chain. They argue: "Outrageous ostentation was *the* defining feature of London's *beau monde*. Lords shared diamonds with their ladies to ensure the necessary glitter."[50] Lady Townshend's wearing of Sayre's chain advertised their connection and points to the masquerade as a fashionable space for social display.

The remaining option to acquire a dress was to repurpose one style of masquerade habit as another. In a letter describing her attendance at a masquerade, Agneta Yorke ended with a brief anecdote on her own habit:

> it occasioned me no little vexation, my fine nabob dress was cut to pieces to make the vest I wore, and when I came to put it on at seven oclock I could not get my Hands thro the sleeves it was made so much too small in every part, I had nothing else to do but to pull it all to pieces and new make it myself, and it was very ill finished about nine oclock, but I think it will be impossible to make any thing out of the remnants of this beautiful dress it was so spoiled by Mrs Spilsburys People.[51]

This account revealed not only the wearer's involvement in the making of her own costume, but it also referred to Mrs Spilsbury, the wife of James Spilsbury, both of whom were associated with habit production at Pritchard's Masquerade Warehouse.

Masquerade garments were also repurposed in other ways. Sophia Baddeley "once bought a whole piece of very fine muslin, plated with silver leaves, for which she paid forty-eight pounds. Of this she made a masquerade dress, and wore it only one night; the next day she cut it out, to make up in nonsensical things to give away to children."[52] Like the stitching of the domino and Mrs. Yorke's own experience with repurposing her habit, this recollection indicated the ephemerality and adaptability of the masquerade habit, challenging Castle's argument that "costume ideally represented an inversion of one's nature."[53] In these instances, costume choice and acquisition were not so much about inversion as they were practicality.

Spectacle

The choice of masquerade habit may have offered participants the opportunity to engage with conceptions of the Other in gender, ethnicity, or religion, but they did not eclipse contemporary expectations of decorum. Rather, they reinforced the importance of conduct and dress in signifying social rank. The presence of an audience, both within the walls of the masquerade and lining the streets to the entertainment, further added to the costume's need to embody a curated character of self-representation and further highlighted the importance of good behavior. The work of John Brewer and Hannah Greig has identified cultural sites, like the masquerade, as spaces where participants displayed their wealth, status, and social charms to the wider world.[54] In her work on the *beau monde* and leisure Greig argues: "The world of fashion harnessed urban sociability to consolidate and advertise their prestigious rank. In this regard, the social practices of London's beau monde were less about mingling and more about parading distinction."[55] These visual cues of rank and taste would be meaningless without an audience of peers and subordinates to show off to. While the obstacles of obtaining a habit and the often costly nature of acquisition designated the masquerade as a luxury experience designed for those of the upper ranks, it was the ensuing spectacle presented to an audience that solidified the unique role of the masquerade in acting as an exclusive space for character and socio-economic display. Differing from other contemporary entertainments, including assemblies, concerts, and theatre, the masquerade was split into varying degrees of participation and access. The availability of a five shilling *viewing* ticket allowed middling and lower sorts to access the masquerade from the galleries; however, they were limited to visual access only. These tickets did not permit viewers the opportunity to dress in masquerade habits or to mingle with their social betters. Likewise, the crowds who gathered in the streets to watch carriages pass could access the masquerade through observation of the spectacular costumes guarded within the boundaries of the vehicles. The masqueraders were aware of this component of the masquerade and the opportunity it provided to reinforce their social positions through visual cues of wealth and taste.

The ritual of watching maskers arrive in their boxes and carriages was a regular feature of the masquerade evening in London. In a letter to a friend, Walpole described the spectacle of a 1763 masquerade, noting both the spectators and the brilliance of dress: "Whitehall [was] crowded with spectators to see the dresses pass ... composed the gayest and richest scene imaginable; not to mention the diamonds and sumptuousness of the habits."[56] In 1770, *The Independent Chronicle* reported that the route to Carlisle House was "lined with thousands of people, whose curiosity led them to get a sight of the persons going to the masquerade; nor was any coach or chair to go unreviewed, the windows being obliged to be let down, and lights held up to display the figures to more advantage."[57] Walpole recalled the crowd "was beyond all belief; they held flambeaux to the windows of every coach, and demanded to have the masks pulled off and put on at their pleasure, but with extreme good humour and civility."[58]

The consistent theme of spectacle, the prominent public display of wealth, and the subtle significance of recognition corresponds with E. P. Thompson's work on plebeian and patrician culture in the eighteenth century. The appearances of the maskers, like those of the gentry and nobility, had "much of the studied self-consciousness of public theatre ... the elaboration of the wig and powder, ornamented clothing and canes, ... all were designed to exhibit authority to the plebs and to exact from them deference."[59] This parading of distinction challenges the existing research on the masquerade and provides new meaning to the role of the masquerade habit, suggesting that while costume may have afforded the temporary obscuring of identity, the London masquerade operated as an elite space of sociability in which the gentry and nobility could exhibit authority in a public space.

Examining the social biography of the masquerade habit through the lenses of material culture and supplementary texts has revealed a series of new perspectives on the practice of wearing a costume and attending the masquerade. The physicality of the habit, including the mask and garment, has changed the ways in which we understand the function of the costume and the practicalities of being or remaining in disguise. This provides an alternative to the existing scholarship on the masquerade, as the action of unmasking and seeking recognition defines the space as one of display and sociability. The forms of acquisition and the need for continued consumption of different habits further contributes to this new perspective, presenting the masquerade dress as an ephemeral object that held little emotional meaning for the wearer. The habit served as a temporary means of displaying one's social status and network, indicating taste and character ideals, and so calls into question Castle's argument concerning transgression and the carnivalesque.[60] The spectacle of maskers en route to the entertainment draws attention to the importance of the audience in establishing a social context for differentiation and display. The significance of being seen and recognized in one's habit, when combined with the material culture of the habit, the processes of acquisition, and the praxis of wearing masquerade dress, ultimately reshape the ways in which we think about the eighteenth-century masquerade. Engaging with objects, images, and texts associated with the masquerade has therefore resulted in the construction of a new narrative surrounding this popular form of entertainment, transforming it from a space of anonymity and debauchery into a space of fashionability, recognition, and social differentiation for the upper ranks of society.

APPENDIX 1

Transcription of a Bill of Sale from the Fillinham Collection at the British Library
[pasted onto page 22 of the collection]

1772	To Walbank.
March	Undertaker, Corner of
	Rathbone Place.

To a Masquerade-dress as a Coffin,   }
covered with fine black cloth,   }
with a printed inscription* on   }
the lid of the Coffin.   }

To a superfine Ruffle (crape) neatly   }
Pink'd, the whole properly orna-   }
mented, with Handles, Nails, and   }
Dropd (?), complete.   }

To a superfine Crape Shroud and   }
Case, made like a shirt, neatly   }
pink'd, complete.   }

To Two Men bearing in ditto, to fitt
To Two Men bearing in ditto, and fitting   }
The night of the Masquerade   }

£6..6....

*The inscription referred was as follows.
[picture of crown, five points with stars on top]
"The Grave is my House." (Job XVII.13.)
"The House is appointed for all Living." (Job XXX.23.)

Notes

1.   James Brudenell, later Lord Brudenell and Lord Cardigan, to Thomas Brudenell, 4th Earl of Ailesbury, 26 May 1763, letter, MSS 9/35/316, Wiltshire and Swindon Archives, Chippenham, England.

2.   Terry Castle, *Masquerade and Civilization: The Carnivalesque in Eighteenth-Century English Culture and Fiction* (Stanford: Stanford University Press, 1986); Catherine Craft-Fairchild, *Masquerade and Gender: Disguise and Female Identity in Eighteenth-Century Fictions by Women* (Pennsylvania: Pennsylvania State University Press, 1993); Dror Wahrman, *The Making of the Modern Self: Identity and Culture in Eighteenth-Century England* (New Haven: Yale University Press, 2006); Gillian Russell, *Women, Sociability and Theatre in Georgian London* (Cambridge: Cambridge University Press, 2007).

3.   Castle, *Masquerade and Civilization,* 34.

4.   Aileen Ribeiro, *The Dress Worn at Masquerades in England, 1730 to 1790, and Its Relation to Fancy Dress in Portraiture* (London: Garland Publishing, Inc., 1984).

5.   Igor Kopytoff, "The Cultural Biography of Things: Commoditization as Process," in *The Social Life of Things: Commodities in Cultural Perspective,* ed. Arjun Appadurai (Cambridge: Cambridge University Press, 1986), 66–68; Daniel Miller, *Material Culture and Mass Consumption* (Oxford: Basil Blackwell Ltd, 1987); Colin Campbell, "Understanding Traditional and Modern Patterns of Consumption in Eighteenth-Century England: A Character-Action Approach," in *Consumption and the World of Goods,* ed. Roy Porter and John Brewer (London: Routledge, 1993), 45–48; Maxine Berg, *Luxury and Pleasure in Eighteenth-Century Britain* (Oxford: Oxford University Press, 2005); John Styles and Amanda Vickery, eds., *Gender, Taste, and Material Culture in Britain and North America, 1700–1830* (New Haven: Yale University Press, 2006); Karen Harvey, ed., *History and Material Culture: A Student's Guide to Approaching Alternative Sources* (New York: Routledge, 2009); Giorgio Riello and Anne Gerritsen, eds., *Writing Material*

Culture History (London: Bloomsbury Academic, 2015); Zara Anishanslin, *Portrait of a Woman in Silk: Hidden Histories of the British Atlantic World* (New Haven: Yale University Press, 2016); Jennifer Van Horn, *The Power of Objects in Eighteenth-Century British America* (Chapel Hill: University of North Carolina Press, 2017).

6. See Kopytoff, "Cultural Biography of Things."

7. Amanda Vickery, introduction to *Gender, Taste, and Material Culture in Britain and North America, 1700–1830*, ed. John Styles and Amanda Vickery (New Haven: Yale University Press, 2006); Amanda Vickery, *Behind Closed Doors: At Home in Georgian England* (London: Yale University Press, 2009); Giorgio Riello, "Things That Shape History: Material Culture and Historical Narratives," in *History and Material Culture: A Student's Guide to Approaching Alternative Sources*, ed. Karen Harvey (Routledge, 2009), 24–26.

8. Kopytoff, "Cultural Biography of Things," 66–68; Riello, "Things That Shape History," 25.

9. Campbell, "Understanding Traditional and Modern Patterns," 46–48; Lorna Weatherill, *Consumer Behaviour and Material Culture in Britain, 1660–1760*, 2nd ed. (London: Routledge, 1996), 5.

10. John Kersey, in *A New English Dictionary* (London: Robert Knaplock, 1713); Nathan Bailey, in *Dictionarium Britannicum* (London: T. Cox, 1730); Samuel Johnson, in *Johnson's Dictionary of the English Language in Miniature* (London: Lee and Hurst, 1797).

11. William Byrd, *The London Diary (1717–1721) and Other Writings*, ed. Marion Tinling and Louis B. Wright (Oxford: Oxford University Press, 1958), 76.

12. See, for example, the *General Evening Post*, 12–14 September 1771: "the rooms were finely illuminated, and some of the characters well supported"; and the *Morning Post and Daily Advertiser*, 19 May 1784: "Dominos predominated as usual, though there were a good number of characters, or rather of persons who put on dresses indicating their intention to support a character."

13. This advertisement is taken from the *Daily Advertiser*, 16 January 1752, with the original, though abbreviated, advertisement appearing in the *General Advertiser*, 7 February 1750.

14. *Covent-Garden Journal*, 25 January 1752.

15. Lady Mary Campbell Coke, *The Letters and Journal of Lady Mary Coke*, vol. 2 (Edinburgh: David Douglas, 1899), 392–93; Agneta Yorke, letter to Lady Hardwicke, MSS L30/9/97/159, The Wrest Park Papers, Bedfordshire Archives, Bedford, England.

16. *General Evening Post*, 17–19 September 1771.

17. *Morning Chronicle and London Advertiser*, 10 January 1776.

18. Elizabeth Steele, *The Memoirs of Mrs. Sophia Baddeley, Late of Drury Lane Theatre*, 6 vols. (London, 1787), 3:2.

19. Castle, *Masquerade and Civilization*, 33.

20. Ribeiro, *The Dress Worn*, 33–39.

21. *Morning Herald and Daily Advertiser*, 3 March 1783.

22. Peter Earle, "The Middling Sort in London," in *The Middling Sort of People: Culture, Society, and Politics in England, 1550–1800*, ed. Christopher Brooks and

Jonathan Barry (London: Macmillan Press Ltd., 1994), 144–45; Neil McKendrick, "The Commercialization of Fashion," in *The Birth of a Consumer Society: The Commercialization of Eighteenth-Century England*, ed. Neil McKendrick, John Brewer, and J. H. Plumb (London: Europa Publications Limited, 1982), 29.

23. *General Advertiser*, 7 February 1750.

24. *A Catalogue of the Genuine, Rich and Very Expensive Wardrobe Consisting of a Great Variety of Masquerade Dresses, the Property of Mr. Spilsbury, Auction by Mess. Christie and Ansel* (London: Christie and Ansell's, 4 and 5 Feb 1779).

25. Lybbe Powys, *Passages from the Diaries of Mrs. Phillip Lybbe Powys,* ed. Emily J Climenson (London: Longmans, Green, and Co., 1899), 249.

26. *General Evening Post,* 13–15 January 1773.

27. *St. James's Chronicle or the British Evening Post,* 19–21 December 1775; see also reports in the *Gazetteer and New Daily Advertiser*, 29 May 1772; *Morning Chronicle and London Advertiser,* 23 January 1781; *Morning Post and Daily Advertiser*, 9 February 1785.

28. *Morning Herald and Daily Advertiser*, 13 April 1782.

29. *Morning Herald*, 13 April 1782.

30. *London Evening Post,* 3–6 March 1770; *General Evening Post,* 18–20 February 1773.

31. Further references to Vandyke and portraiture-influenced dress are mentioned in *The Yale Edition of Horace Walpole's Correspondence*, 48 vols. (New Haven: Yale University Press), 17:338; and the diaries of Elizabeth Percy, Duchess of Northumberland, DNP: MS 121/31a, 28–30, The Archives of the Duke of Northumberland at Alnwick Castle, England.

32. Frances Burney, *The Early Diary of Frances Burney, 1768–1778: With a Selection from Her Correspondence, and from the Journals of Her Sisters Susan and Charlotte Burney*, ed. Annie Raine Ellis, vol. 1 (London: G. Bell and Sons, 1889), 64–65.

33. Campbell, "Understanding Traditional and Modern Patterns of Consumption," 49.

34. Hannah Greig, *The Beau Monde: Fashionable Society in Georgian London* (Oxford: Oxford University Press, 2013), 234.

35. Riello and Gerritsen, eds., *Writing Material Culture History*, 3.

36. *General Evening Post*, 5–7 February 1771.

37. *Middlesex Journal and Evening Advertiser,* 25–27 April 1776.

38. Gillian Russell, *Women, Sociability and Theatre in Georgian London* (Cambridge: Cambridge University Press, 2007), 40.

39. Elizabeth Percy, Duchess of Northumberland, DNP: MS 121/5a, 25, The Archives of the Duke of Northumberland at Alnwick Castle, England.

40. Yorke, letter to Lady Hardwicke.

41. D. L. Prior, "Scrafton, Luke (1732–1770?)," in *Oxford Dictionary of National Biography* (Oxford: Oxford University Press, 2008).

42. Steele, *Memoirs of Mrs. Sophia Baddeley,* 5:222.

43. C. Wayte to the Prince of Wales, Royal Archives at Windsor Castle, GEO/MAIN/29315. The bill was begun on 8 February 1802, but also contains purchases from 14 and 26 May of that year.

44. C. Wayte to the Prince of Wales, Royal Archives at Windsor Castle, GEO/ MAIN/29414. The bill was initiated on 25 May 1803 and includes purchases made up through June 1806. It was finally paid in 1808.

45. Elizabeth Percy, Duchess of Northumberland, "1744 Cloaths Account," DNP: MS 121/174, The Archives of the Duke of Northumberland at Alnwick Castle, England.

46. Hannah Greig, "Beau Monde," in *Gender, Taste, and Material Culture in Britain and North America 1700–1830*, ed. John Styles and Amanda Vickery (New Haven: Yale University Press, 2006), 307.

47. William Byrd, *The London Diary*, 76; Horace Walpole, letter to Horace Man, 27 February 1770, *The Yale Edition of Horace Walpole's Correspondence* 23:193–94.

48. *Lloyd's Evening Post*, 7–10 October 1757.

49. Steele, *Memoirs of Mrs. Sophia Baddeley*, 6:115.

50. Vickery, introduction to *Gender, Taste, and Material Culture*, 5.

51. Yorke, letter to Lady Hardwicke.

52. Steele, *Memoirs of Mrs. Sophia Baddeley*, 2:147–48.

53. Castle, *Masquerade and Civilization*, 4.

54. John Brewer, "'The Most Polite Age and the Most Vicious': Attitudes towards Culture as a Commodity, 1660–1800," in *The Consumption of Culture 1600–1800: Image, Object, Text*, ed. John Brewer and Ann Bermingham (London: Routledge, 1995), 346.

55. Greig, *The Beau Monde*, 66.

56. Walpole, letter to Horace Mann, 5 June 1763, *Yale Edition of Horace Walpole's Correspondence*, 22:149.

57. *Independent Chronicle*, 26–28 February 1770.

58. Walpole, letter to Horace Mann, 27 February 1770, *Yale Edition of Horace Walpole's Correspondence*, 23:194.

59. E. P. Thompson, "Patrician Society, Plebeian Culture," *Journal of Social History* 7, no. 4 (1974): 389.

60. Castle, *Masquerade and Civilization*, 4–9, 27–34, 160.

EIGHTEENTH-CENTURY BODIES

Cluster: Disability in the Eighteenth Century

Introduction: Disability in the Eighteenth Century

TRAVIS CHI WING LAU AND
MADELINE SUTHERLAND-MEIER

D isability studies emerged out of the rights-based activism of the 1970s and 1980s to become an interdisciplinary field invested in challenging stigmatizing notions of disability as individual impairment, pitiful tragedy, or human lack. Critical both to the disability civil rights movement and to the academic field is the social model of disability, which understands environments, institutions, cultures, and attitudes to be disabling, rather than locating those disabilities within individuals, who are then subject to curative intervention or even elimination. For disability scholars, the medical model's reduction of disability to pathology is symptomatic of a more pervasive cultural preference for able-bodiedness—what Tobin Siebers has called "the ideology of ability."[1] Foundational scholarship in disability studies, such as Lennard Davis's *Enforcing Normalcy: Disability, Deafness, and the Body* and Rosemarie Garland-Thomson's *Extraordinary Bodies: Figuring Physical Disability in American Culture and Literature,* have worked to historicize the ways in which able-bodiedness has been normalized through not only state policies and statistical thinking, but also literary and artistic production.[2] Since the late 1990s, literary and cultural disability studies have responded to the legacy of representations that depict disabled people as infirm, infantile, or inhuman. David Mitchell and Sharon Snyder critique this deployment of disability as a *crutch* used to shore up narratives of progress or recovery.[3] Disability, invoked only for its transgressive or symbolic potential through typically flat, minor characters, is then promptly cast away through curative resolution. The ubiquity and stereotypicality of these narratives, Mitchell and Snyder suggest, enable the normativizing of able-bodiedness. Disability thereby becomes "the master trope of human disqualification."[4]

The "tyranny of the norm" and disability as "the master trope of human disqualification" have become ur-narratives in disability scholarship. Yet, attention to historical periods prior to the development of what Rosemarie Garland-Thomson has called the "normate"—a composite identity unmarked by bodily difference and defined by and against other bodies coded as "deviant" or "defective"—radically unsettles an otherwise deterministic model of disability as ever-moving toward oppression and pathology.[5] As scholars like Helen Deutsch, Felicity Nussbaum, Chris Mounsey, and David Turner have demonstrated, disability as a concept was in flux and was frequently "subsumed under other categories, notably deformity and monstrosity" in the eighteenth century.[6] Before the rise of the hard sciences and the professionalization of medicine, the eighteenth century witnessed intense debates over the definition of the human, a category which radically shifted how bodies were understood and ultimately valued. Embodied concepts of deformity and debility attached to race, gender, class, and sexuality preceded the eugenic thinking of the nineteenth century that reified the binary of normal and abnormal. Yet, during this transformative period, disabled people also survived, resisted, and even flourished. Scholarship in eighteenth-century studies, as exemplified by the essays in this cluster, has not only powerfully contributed to more historically nuanced interpretations of disability, but also to a larger shift toward more intersectional disability studies informed by other minority fields like queer studies and critical race studies.

The Disability Studies Caucus is a relatively young caucus of the American Society for Eighteenth-Century Studies compared to the Race and Empire Caucus and the Women's Caucus. Its beginnings can be traced back to 2004, when Lennard Davis and D. Christopher Gabbard organized a panel titled "Defect, Deformity, and Disfigurement in the Long Eighteenth Century." There would not be another panel on the topic of disability until 2011, when Chris Mounsey organized two panels under the title "Looking at Disability in the Eighteenth Century." These would be followed by collaborations with Stan Booth, George Haggerty, Paul Kelleher, Jared Richman, and Jason Farr that resulted in panels and roundtables like the "History of Disability (Studies)," "Eighteenth-Century Disability Studies: Past, Present, and Future," "Disability, War, and Violence," and "Disability in the Long Eighteenth Century." By 2014, the Disability Studies Caucus had become formally recognized by ASECS and has since held sessions on topics like crip theory, disability and aging, and crip approaches to eighteenth-century narratives.

The essays composing this cluster stem from two roundtables organized for the 2019 Annual Meeting in Denver: one on the topic of "Disability as Metaphor / Lived Experience" and another on the topic of "Disability, Impairment, and Improvement." Responding to critics who perceive disability theory to be increasingly removed from the actual lived experiences of disability, "Disability as Metaphor / Lived Experience" asked, in the disability activist spirit of "nothing about us, without us," how disability theory could more ethically witness the lives from which it derives. In order to answer this question, D. Christopher Gabbard turns, in "Deformity, Life Writing, and the Overcoming Narrative," to three eighteenth-century writers—William Hay, George Colman the Elder, and Josef Boruwlaski—who composed early forms of disability life-writing that countered ableist assumptions about bodily form and function drawn from aesthetic theory and natural history. Autobiographical works like Hay's *Deformity, an Essay* (1754) challenged negative stereotypes by advocating for the value and even advantage of disabled experience. For Gabbard, centering the lived experiences of disability in the eighteenth century is an urgent ethical project that challenges the often anachronistic bent of disability studies by attending to the ways that disabled people have long imagined and narrated their own bodyminds.

In "Disability as Metaphor and Lived Experience in Samuel Richardson's *Pamela* and Sarah Scott's *Millenium Hall*," Jason Farr shares Gabbard's investment in the lived experience of disability but advocates for a synthetic method that "juxtapos[es] literary representations of ableist metaphor with dynamic, three-dimensional portrayals of disability." In his reading of Mrs. Jewkes from *Pamela* (1740) and the queer and disabled utopia imagined in *Millenium Hall* (1762), Farr makes the case that corporeal metaphor constructs ableist ideology through language that is then lived out through bodies marked as nonnormative or monstrous. These novels expose how able-bodiedness and heterosexuality are connected through arbitrary bodily norms and how both texts radically gesture toward social and political reform.

Like Farr, Hannah Chaskin adopts an intersectional approach to the social nature of illness and debility. Focusing on "Heterosexual Plots and Ill Narratives in Jane Austen's *Pride and Prejudice*," Chaskin argues that the juxtaposition of Elizabeth and Anne affirms a heteronormative ideology defined by companionate marriage. If suitability is characterized by able-bodiedness, Anne's "sickly and cross" nature excludes her from the marriage plot that is antithetical to her pathologized gender expression.

The consequences of pathology and its potentially irredeemable nature emerged in the second roundtable on the concept of improvement in the eighteenth century. If improvement was crucial to the Enlightenment progress narrative, how did disability undermine this project of human improvement that continues to animate eugenic practices like prenatal testing and gene-editing technologies? Declan Kavanagh provides a preliminary answer in his "Rochester's Libertinism and the Pleasures of Debility" by recasting the Earl of Rochester's libertinism as an explicit poetics of impairment that revels in impotence and refuses improvement and recovery. Together, these essays offer provocative new ways of reading disability in the archive against the normative grain. They show how an intersectional approach can also be richly historicist and grounded in the complexly embodied experiences of disabled people.

Notes

1. Tobin Siebers, *Disability Theory* (Ann Arbor: University of Michigan Press, 2008), 8.

2. Lennard Davis, *Enforcing Normalcy: Disability, Deafness, and the Body* (Ann Arbor: University of Michigan Press, 1995); Rosemarie Garland-Thomson, *Extraordinary Bodies: Figuring Physical Disability in American Culture and Literature* (New York: Columbia University Press, 1996).

3. David T. Mitchell and Sharon L. Snyder, *Narrative Prosthesis: Disability and the Dependencies of Discourse* (Ann Arbor: University of Michigan Press, 2000), 49.

4. Mitchell and Snyder, *Narrative Prosthesis*, 3.

5. See Rosemarie Garland-Thomson, *Extraordinary Bodies*.

6. David M. Turner, "Introduction: Approaching Anomalous Bodies," in *Social Histories of Disability and Deformity: Bodies, Images, and Experiences*, ed. David M. Turner and Kevin Stagg (New York: Routledge, 2006), 4. See also Helen Deutsch and Felicity Nussbaum, eds., *Defects: Engendering the Modern Body* (Ann Arbor: University of Michigan Press, 2000); Chris Mounsey, ed., *The Idea of Disability in the Eighteenth Century* (Lewisburg: Bucknell University Press, 2014).

Deformity, Life Writing, and the Overcoming Narrative

D. CHRISTOPHER GABBARD

A significant development in publishing over the last fifty years has been the explosion of disability memoirs. This phenomenon is attested to by the two-volume *Disability Experiences: Memoirs, Autobiographies, and Other Personal Narratives* published in 2019, a massive reference work containing entries for hundreds of first-person accounts of disability and illness.[1] While disability has figured prominently in all genres of literature dating back to Sophocles's *Oedipus Rex,* representations of it, according to G. Thomas Couser, have often functioned to the detriment of disabled people, who "have rarely controlled their own images."[2] Couser states that in the 1970s disabled people started initiating and controlling "their own narratives in unprecedented ways and to an extraordinary degree," and he points out that the rise "in personal narratives of disability ... roughly coincided with the disability rights movement."[3] The campaign for civil rights generated both a need and an opportunity for disabled people to tell their life stories in order to make their demands for justice intelligible to the nondisabled population.

Conditions were not favorable for such life writing in the eighteenth century, making that of three men with uncommon builds—William Hay, George Colman, and Josef Boruwlaski—all the more remarkable. The reasons why conditions were unfavorable for those with such bodies will be of chief concern in this essay, as will be the question of why these three men took up the pen. The fact that they published accounts including extensive references to their own physical anomalies during such an uninviting period is something worth exploring. This essay will contend that these three writers saw an opportunity to leverage the discourse of sympathy in order to help the reading public distinguish, in Helen Deutsch's words, "between disability as sign and disability as experience. …between disability as stigma and disability as impairment."[4] The means of persuasion Hay, Colman, and Boruwlaski employed included the overcoming narrative: an embryonic rhetorical trope at the time, and one that is undoubtedly problematic.[5] Problematic or not, though, the trope gained ground over time and persists into the present era.

My investigation begins with the concept of the norm. Lennard Davis has demonstrated that the concept as we understand it today did not come into formation until the first half of the nineteenth century and that words such as *normal* and *normative* would have been unintelligible to the people living in the eighteenth.[6] In speaking about the world before normal, we must inquire into what communal standards for typical or socially acceptable bodily form predominated in that earlier time. The short answer is that a paradigm of what Edmund Burke termed "the complete common" physical "form" prevailed. In his work exploring the anti-sentimental eighteenth century, Simon Dickie convincingly establishes that sensibility did not impede the practice of ridiculing "cripples"—those whose bodies deviated from the complete common form.[7] Responding to Dickie, Roger Lund asserts that such behavior did not spring from wanton cruelty but from an "argument from design": the supposedly symmetrical, harmonious, and beautifully functioning universe that the Creator designed did not allow for corporeal defect.[8] In a world where order supposedly reigned supreme, those with deformed bodies were perceived to be ludicrous aberrations, "God's little jokes."[9]

Lund's "argument from design" summons forth a pair of concepts—the natural and the beautiful. With regard to the natural, Newtonian physics established a template for understanding how the material world ordinarily, or "naturally," operated according to mechanical and mathematical models. With regard to the beautiful, the discourse of aesthetics emerged centrally in the eighteenth century and became its own discipline—the "science" of the beautiful. Various theorists wrestled with the undeniably subjective nature of perception, but they did agree, in Martin Battestin's terms, that "beauty was objectively founded in a principle of Nature as firmly fixed as the law of gravity: namely, the principle of symmetry and proportion."[10] This is to say that the beautiful was natural, and that the natural was beautiful, in a sort of endless feedback loop.

The ideas to be found in eighteenth-century theoretical writing on the subject of beauty, as well as those in scientific texts focused on determining what was natural, coalesced into an ideology of "the complete common form," one promoting a minimum standard of acceptance for human bodies. In his 1757 *A Philosophical Enquiry into the Origins of Our Ideas of the Sublime and Beautiful,* Edmund Burke states, "for *deformity* is opposed not to beauty, but to the *compleat, common form.* If one of the legs of a man be found shorter than the other, the man is deformed; because there is something wanting to complete the whole idea we form of a man."[11] This ideology would have profound implications for people with somatic impairments. Naomi Baker finds that the Newtonian vision "insist[ed] that the beauty of the universe lay in its rigid conformity to natural laws, [so that] all instances of apparent deviation became repellent."[12] In Enlightenment thinking, the world was harmonious and rule-bound, and because people with physical deformities deviated in a conspicuous way from this decorous, balanced, and systematic natural order, no legitimacy remained for them. In fact, their presence in the visual field was disturbing precisely because it was interpreted to be a perverse and irrational challenge to the overall rightness of creation.

The major thinkers in aesthetics frequently invoked deformity, but they did not treat it as a formal category; rather, it was a litmus test used to determine which forms were aesthetically pleasing. While beauty was gratifying to the eye, deformity—characterizing as it did the disproportionate, disharmonious, and/or peculiar—caused uneasiness, discomfort, disgust, and/or disappointment. Spectacles eliciting these unpleasant emotional effects were deemed ugly. Helen Deutsch argues that during this period the term *deformity,* when applied to the human figure, encompassed just about every kind of physical deviation from the status quo.[13] Those individuals exhibiting defects represented the quintessence of the entwined concepts of the ugly and unnatural, with the two becoming virtually interchangeable. Together, they stood for that which was loathsome. As such, *beauty* and *deformity* became coupled in a commonly recognized binary opposition, one which underwrote the antipathy of the able-bodied public with regard to those displaying corporeal difference.

Moreover, the linkage of corporeal difference with an underdeveloped mind became customary, and this connection was a central tenet of the complete common form. Jason Farr makes the case that the relationship between defective outward form and mental dullness can be found in the writings of John Locke. Summarizing one aspect of Lockean thought, Farr explains: "To be *un*sound—to be found lacking in either mind or body—is to want the necessary conditions for cultivation of the intellect—depriving the individual of 'a happy state in this world.'"[14] A mutual resemblance of mind and body was an animating principle of the ancient pseudo-science of physiognomy, and almost a century following Locke, Johann Kaspar Lavater published *Essays on Physiognomy* (1775–79) that posited a correlation between bodily appearance and moral standing. À la Locke, Lavater, and others in-between, eighteenth-century novelists increasingly relied upon physiognomy, employing visual physical descriptions to depict characters' inner status, with deformity frequently being deployed to signal moral depravity.[15]

The resurgence of physiognomic thinking may have contributed to the jarring disconnect between sensibility and hilarity at the expense of the deformed, but such amusement may also have generated a reaction. David Turner maintains that, in the early eighteenth century, moderate Anglican religious authorities began promoting the notion that deformity—one's own and that of others—could provide an opportunity to achieve a virtuous state.[16] Stemming from this teaching, narratives from the mid-eighteenth century onward also portrayed the deformed with the intent of eliciting compassion, with novelists depicting them as objects of pity and charity. Turner states "these sympathetic portrayals were to some extent reliant on more negative images in order to achieve their impact. 'Sentimental' representations ... required the production of 'innocent' disabled characters deemed worthy of compassion, in contrast to 'guilty' figures that were deserving of derision, fear, or contempt."[17] Callous laughter at the deformed itself became a vehicle for eliciting pity for the victims of that laughter. In other words, the fact that innocent "cripples" were ridiculed became sufficient reason to shed tears of sympathy on their behalf.

Along similar lines, Davis has forcefully argued that over the course of the century the signifier of deformity began to shift from apparent vice to seeming virtue, with the degree of that virtue being measured in terms of the extent to which the individual sufferer triumphed over his or her affliction.[18] Davis further contends that the notion of the triumphant sufferer contributes to the development of the overcoming narrative. The eighteenth century is famously the period when the genre of life writing (autobiography, memoir, and personal essay) gained popularity, and it is against this backdrop that Hay, Colman, and Boruwlaski seized the moment by taking up their pens to engage in a common endeavor of self-exposure. In Deutsch's words, the act of "writing from the body allows its author to question appearances, to challenge the constraints of a body already written upon by common wisdom."[19] Specifically, their self-representations were meant to counteract physiognomic presumptions and the Lockean notion of unsoundness. In the process of telling their life stories, Hay, Colman, and Boruwlaski described the challenges they had been forced to overcome.

William Hay was a member of the British parliament and a man with a hunchback. In his 1754 *Deformity, an Essay*, Hay touts the benefits of his unique corporeal shape, arguing powerfully against the ideology of the complete common form and its facile correspondence between outer irregularity and inner malice, stressing instead deformity's incentive to virtuous living.[20] Kathleen James-Cavan notes that Hay demonstrates "that his deformed body produces precisely the upright mind so valorized by his culture."[21] Indeed, Hay observes that a deformed body "tends to the Improvement of the Mind."[22]

While Hay has received considerable attention from disability studies scholars, Sara van den Berg has recently shed light on the writings of two other eighteenth-century figures, one a person of short stature, the other a dwarf.[23] Both men wrote autobiographical works to reshape how the public understood them, and both attempted to draw attention to their inner lives and the impediments associated with their size that they had to rise above. The first, the short-statured playwright and theater manager George Colman the Elder, develops his argument about the difference between the body as exterior and character as interior in an essay published in 1761 in *The Guardian*.[24] Whereas Hay accepted his lot stoically, Colman was unapologetically "galled" by the way people mistreated him due to his height and judged him solely in terms of it.[25] Overall, however, Colman stresses his achievements and successes. The other, Josef Boruwlaski, began his career as a court dwarf, but when court dwarfs went out of fashion and he lost his position, he transitioned to earning his living as a public entertainer. Published over a number of years in the 1780s and 1790s, the four editions of Boruwlaski's *Memoirs* offer complex self-representations and commentary on his size. As van den Berg writes, Boruwlaski's self-representation entails "assertions of his manly desires, and his persistent claims to full social and manly status."[26] Overall, Boruwlaski's and Colman's self-descriptions insist upon their rich inner lives and the hurdles they have surmounted.

Hay, Colman, and Boruwlaski used life writing as a vehicle to validate their inner worth and to cast the obstacles posed by their deformities as oppositions heroically conquered. These three distinguished "between disability as sign and disability as experience. ... between disability as stigma and disability as impairment."[27] They strove to present liberatory narratives to counter the reigning ideology of the complete common form and to move the public beyond its preoccupation with size and shape to affirm the primacy of character. In so doing, they helped inaugurate the subgenre of disability memoir so prominent today.

Notes

1. G. Thomas Couser and Susannah B. Mintz, eds. *Disability Experiences: Memoirs, Autobiographies, and Other Personal Narratives*, 2 vols (New York: Macmillan Reference USA, 2019).

2. G. Thomas Couser, "Disability, Life Narrative, and Representation," in *The Disability Studies Reader*, ed. Lennard Davis, 3rd ed. (New York: Routledge, 2010): 531–34.

3. Couser, "Disability, Life Narrative, and Representation," 531, 532.

4. Helen Deutsch, "The Body's Moments: Visible Disability, the Essay, and the Limits of Sympathy," *Prose Studies*, 27, no. 1–2 (2005): 11–26, 9.

5. For the reasons why it is problematic, see Couser and Mintz, *Disability*, xxxix.

6. Lennard Davis, "Constructing Normalcy," in *The Disability Studies Reader*, ed. Lennard Davis, 3rd ed. (New York: Routledge, 2010): 3–19.

7. Simon Dickie, "Hilarity and Pitilessness in the Mid-Eighteenth Century: English Jestbook Humor," *Eighteenth-Century Studies* 37, no. 1 (2003): 1–22.

8. Roger Lund, "Laughing at Cripples: Ridicule, Deformity, and the Argument from Design," *Eighteenth-Century Studies* 39, no. 1 (2005): 91–114.

9. Lund, "Laughing at Cripples," 92.

10. Martin C. Battestin, *The Providence of Wit: Aspects of Form in Augustan Literature and the Arts* (Oxford: Clarendon Press, 1974), 23.

11. Edmund Burke, *A Philosophical Inquiry into the Origin of our Ideas of the Sublime and Beautiful,* ed. Adam Phillips, 2nd ed. (Oxford University Press, 1990), 93.

12. Naomi Baker, *Plain Ugly: The Unattractive Body in Early Modern Culture* (Manchester: Manchester University Press, 2015), 40.

13. Helen Deutsch, "The Author as Monster: The Case of Dr. Johnson," in *"Defects": Engendering the Modern Body,* ed. Helen Deutsch and Felicity Nussbaum (Ann Arbor: University of Michigan Press, 2000), 177–209.

14. Jason Farr, *Novel Bodies: Disability and Sexuality in Eighteenth-Century British Literature* (Lewisburg: Bucknell University Press, 2019), 6.

15. Robert W. Jones, "Obedient Faces: The Virtue of Deformity in Sarah Scott's Fiction," in *"Defects"*, 280–302.

16. David Turner, *Disability in Eighteenth-Century England: Imagining Physical Impairment* (London: Routledge, 2012), 33.

17. Turner, *Disability,* 73.

18. Lennard Davis, "Dr. Johnson, Amelia, and the Discourse of Disability in the Eighteenth Century," in *"Defects"*, 54–74.

19. Deutsch, "Body's Moments," 11.

20. William Hay, *Deformity: An Essay*, ed. Kathleen James-Cavan (Victoria: University of Victoria Press, 2004).

21. Kathleen James-Cavan, Introduction to *Deformity: An Essay*, 12.

22. Hay, *Deformity,* 42.

23. Sara van den Berg, "Atypical Bodies in the Long Eighteenth Century," in *The Cultural History of Disability in the Long Eighteenth Century*, ed. D. Christopher Gabbard and Susannah B. Mintz (London: Bloomsbury 2020), 19–37.

24. George Colman the Elder, "*The Genius*, Number II" (from *The Guardian*, 1761), in *Prose on Several Occasions, Accompanied by Some Pieces in Verse*, vol. 1 (London: T. Cadel, 1787).

25. Van den Berg, "Atypical Bodies," 27.

26. Van den Berg, "Atypical Bodies," 28.

27. Deutsch, "The Body's Moments," 19.

Disability as Metaphor and Lived Experience in Samuel Richardson's *Pamela* and Sarah Scott's *Millenium Hall*

JASON S. FARR

Disability studies scholars often champion the investigation of the lived experiences of disability over metaphor. In *Disability Theory*, for instance, Tobin Siebers historicizes disabled bodies in part because metaphor often converts disability into something else.[1] Given the exclusionary nature of ableist metaphors, Siebers adopts this approach for good reason. I would argue, however, that we are at a point now in eighteenth-century literary disability studies in which we can do both; that is, we can uncover lived experiences of disability in the eighteenth century *and* we can take metaphor seriously. By juxtaposing literary representations of ableist metaphor with dynamic, three-dimensional portrayals of disability, we may conceptualize how disability was often imagined as deprivation but also how it could serve personally and socially transformative ends in narrative. To show how such a method works, I examine Samuel Richardson's *Pamela* (1740) and Sarah Scott's *Millenium Hall* (1762): two novels that portray physical disability in starkly different terms. *Pamela* conceives of deformity as a plot device while *Millenium Hall* reveals how socially constructed bodily standards subjugate disabled people.[2] Despite their differences, these novels depict disability and queerness as transformative narrative devices for imagining social and sexual reform.

In *Pamela*, Richardson shores up the able-bodied, heterosexual romance between Pamela and Mr. B. through Mrs. Jewkes, who is portrayed as monstrous in her embodiment and queer desire. In its plot development, *Pamela* adheres to the tenets of what David T. Mitchell and Sharon L. Snyder call "narrative prosthesis," or a transhistorical representational model in which disability serves as a "crutch" for generating plot conflict and resolution.[3] According to the tenets of narrative prosthesis, "the materiality of metaphor" is the tendency of narrative to make abstract concepts visible in the disabled body, which are first uncovered and then explained and justified. As a result, disability is brought from the margins to the heart of the narrative before it is finally rehabilitated, fixed, or eradicated.[4] In *Pamela*, Mrs. Jewkes's disability and queerness work together as narrative prostheses to ground Richardson's conceptions of libertinism, female virtue, and sentiment. For example, upon first meeting Mrs. Jewkes, Pamela describes her in these terms: "She is a broad, squat, pursy, fat Thing, quite ugly. ... She has a huge Hand, and an Arm as thick as my waist. ... Her nose is flat and crooked, and her Brows grow over her Eyes; a dead, spiteful, grey, goggling Eye, to be sure, she has. And her Face is flat and broad."[5] Mrs. Jewkes is also said "to waddle" when she walks, indicating a mobility impairment that would appear to supplement her monstrous body and intentions (*PA*, 114). Pamela's portrayal of Mrs. Jewkes reveals physiognomic thought, in which an unconventional appearance mirrors inward depravity. Pamela's caricature of Mrs. Jewkes's facial features—the sustained attention to her "flat and crooked" nose and eyebrows—is supposed to reveal her inner wickedness (114). Pamela construes Mrs. Jewkes's face as a metaphorical repository of uncouthness that threatens young women's virtue.

Mrs. Jewkes's character also symbolizes the libertine sexuality that Richardson hopes to expunge from British society. Mrs. Jewkes pursues Pamela aggressively, just as Mr. B. does. In these characters' alignment, Mrs. Jewkes's deformity becomes a metaphor for Mr. B.'s sexual excess. Pamela describes her first meeting with Mrs. Jewkes in these terms: "The naughty Woman came up to me with an Air of Confidence, and kiss'd me, See Sister, said she, here's a charming Creature! would not she tempt the best Lord in the Land to run away with her!" (*PA*, 107). Mrs. Jewkes justifies Mr. B.'s ignominious actions by calling attention to Pamela's desirability. Later, in the carriage ride to Lincolnshire, Pamela reports that Mrs. Jewkes sat next to her, "squeezing my Hand, and saying, Why you are very pretty, my silent Dear! and once she offer'd to kiss me. But I said, I don't like this Sort of Carriage, Mrs. Jewkes; it is not like two Persons of one Sex" (108). In this and in other passages, Mrs. Jewkes becomes a grotesque, queer symbol of tyranny, conflated with the power and violence that Mr. B. asserts over Pamela. Her advances on Pamela's person are reminiscent of Mr. B., whom she eventually assists in an attempted rape of Pamela. Mrs. Jewkes absorbs much of the blame for Mr. B.'s actions, making his conversion to a man of feeling seem plausible as she can be dispensed with handily in the narrative. Once Pamela and Mr. B. are in a good place to marry, Pamela's description of Mrs. Jewkes's peculiar bodily features falls out of view. Mrs. Jewkes at last becomes virtuously disembodied, even as the details of a novel heteronormative order get established around Pamela's virtue and Mr. B.'s newly acquired sentiment. We might say that *Pamela* indicates a hetero-abled future and that Pamela's imprisonment at the hands of a crip/queer character serves as a threat to that future. Richardson asserts a hetero-abled temporality in large part by imagining Mrs. Jewkes's body as material metaphor.

In its portrayal of queer and disabled bonds as viable alternatives to heterosexual, able-bodied union, Scott's *Millenium Hall* offers a vastly different account of corporeality from that of *Pamela*. Through her criticism of the "common standard" that stigmatizes and isolates so many individuals, Scott imagines physical disability as inevitable and therefore as that which ought to be accommodated in any community.[6] In *Millenium Hall,* disability is what Tobin Siebers would call "complexly embodied"—that is, Scott represents impaired bodies as "possessing both social and physical form."[7] Impairment, in other words, is not merely a metaphor for Scott as it is for Richardson; rather, it is a source of both social *and* physical pain, and it serves as the basis for her restructuring of British society. Scott achieves this in *Millenium Hall* through various means, but I focus here on her critique of the socially driven nature of bodily norms.

When showing George Ellison and Lamont around the estate's enclosure, Mrs. Mancel shares her thoughts about Procrustes, the figure from Greek mythology whose metal bed served a violent purpose. After inviting unwitting guests into his home, Procrustes would tie them to his bed and either stretch their limbs if they were too short or amputate their legs if they were too tall. Mrs. Mancel reflects upon the impact of such subjective standards on disabled people: "But is not every man a Procrustes? We have not the power of shewing our cruelty exactly in the same method, but actuated by the like spirit, we abridge of their liberty, and torment by scorn, all who either fall short, or exceed the usual standard" (*MH*, 72). In using qualifiers like "usual" and, as she does shortly thereafter, "common," Mrs. Mancel draws attention to the violence of arbitrary corporeal ideals on the bodies and minds of individuals in British society (72–73). As rejoinder to such a model, Scott represents the various characters who populate the novel's titular estate as complexly embodied. Their appearance unsettles those standards; it also indicates a future in which personal fulfillment is reliant upon the building of robust communities that diminish individualism in the service of a communal living that is class-stratified.

Metaphors can function as a screen. That is why we cannot only consider examples like Mrs. Jewkes. But metaphors are also illuminating. They shed light on disability in different historical and cultural moments. We can recognize Scott as an extraordinary theorist of the body by understanding the metaphorical grain against which she wrote. We should take disability metaphor seriously because it constructs ableist ideology through language that disavows disability. By attending to disability as metaphor, we can examine the ways in which a canonical literary text like *Pamela* adheres to ableist tropes that shore up the primacy of heterosexuality. And we can also conceptualize how narratives from the eighteenth century that represent impairment as complexly embodied imagine social reform. Together, Richardson's use of corporeal metaphor in *Pamela* and Scott's rendering of complex embodiment in *Millenium Hall* allow for an expansive understanding of how physical disability was socially constituted and lived during the eighteenth century.

Notes

1. Tobin Siebers, *Disability Theory* (Ann Arbor: University of Michigan Press, 2008).

2. David T. Mitchell and Sharon L. Snyder, *Narrative Prosthesis: Disability and the Dependencies of Discourse* (Ann Arbor: University of Michigan Press, 1997), 47.

3. Mitchell and Snyder, *Narrative Prosthesis*, 49.

4. Mitchell and Snyder, *Narrative Prosthesis*, 61–64.

5. Samuel Richardson, *Pamela,* ed. Thomas Keymer and Alice Wakely (Oxford: Oxford University Press), 114, henceforth cited parenthetically in the text as *PA*.

6. Sarah Scott, *Millenium Hall,* ed. Gary Kelly (Peterborough: Broadview Press, 1995), 73, henceforth cited parenthetically in the text as *MH*.

7. Siebers, *Disability Theory*, 30.

Heterosexual Plots and Ill Narratives in Jane Austen's *Pride and Prejudice*

HANNAH CHASKIN

Angry at Fitzwilliam Darcy for his role in disrupting her sister's courtship, Elizabeth Bennet of *Pride and Prejudice* (1813) looks on his alleged intended with a sarcastic bite in her voice: "I like her appearance. ... She looks sickly and cross.—Yes, she will do for him very well. She will make him a proper wife."[1] The "sickly and cross" woman is Anne de Bourgh, cousin of Darcy and daughter of the overbearing Lady Catherine de Bourgh. In the context of *Pride and Prejudice*'s primary marriage plot, Anne is Elizabeth's most direct structural foil: both are imagined as potential future wives for Darcy. Yet Anne is not a real obstacle to Elizabeth's ultimate success; she exists in the narrative primarily to delineate the difference between the marriage of interest (in which Darcy marries Anne to consolidate his wealth) and the companionate marriage, or marriage for love (in which Darcy and Elizabeth enter into a partnership based on mutual esteem and compatible personalities). The novel's critique of aristocratic greed and the marriage of interest is figured through Anne's under-defined illness; her elitism and her illness are conflated, as though "sickly" and "cross" are synonymous. This essay concerns the roles of sickness and health in the construction of *Pride and Prejudice*'s heterosexual marriage plot. My title pays homage to Marilyn Farwell's work of queer feminist narratology, *Heterosexual Plots and Lesbian Narratives*, in which Farwell argues that normative narrative structure "encode[s] heterosexuality … in its very mechanics."[2] I will suggest that the *mechanics* of Austen's most influential marriage plot operate by deploying an idealized femininity that is essentially healthy and by defining ill femininity as narratively unviable.

We are generally accustomed to a gendered ideology that understands dependency, passivity, and femininity to be interlocking terms that are set against self-sufficiency, agency, and masculinity. It is not, therefore, surprising that a propensity towards illness has often been conceived of as a feminine trait. Symptoms of specific illnesses, like consumption, intersect with norms of feminine beauty, and sentimental literature often represents acute or fatal illness in the wake of trauma as indicative of feminine virtue.[3] However, by the end of the eighteenth century, feminist critiques of sentimental femininity were becoming prevalent, and these critiques were often framed in terms of illness and illness's effect on companionate heterosexuality. Mary Wollstonecraft, for example, indicted a system of sentimental education designed to keep upper-class white women weak, beautiful, and essentially ill. In *A Vindication of the Rights of Woman* (1792), Wollstonecraft argues that due to "inattention to health during infancy … dependence of body naturally produces dependence of mind; and how can she be a good wife or mother, the greater part of whose time is employed to guard against or endure sickliness?"[4] Wollstonecraft and Austen are often cast as political foils, but *Pride and Prejudice* manifests *Vindication*'s pathologizing strategy to critique sentimental, aristocratic femininity, with the result that it paints healthy and resilient femininity as essential to the companionate marriage plot.

All of Austen's novels are invested in exploring the lines between health and illness, and between illness and character flaw.[5] I focus on *Pride and Prejudice* in this essay because the relationship between the healthy heroine and the ill foil is so stark and so central to the plot itself and because it is perhaps the most influential of Austen's novels, insofar as it provided both plot and character types that have become ubiquitous in Anglo-American culture. If we accept that *Pride and Prejudice* has had an outsized role in the replication of what we now call the romantic comedy, the fact that Austen understood narrative structure through the lens of health and illness matters. While Austen's novels do not evince uncomplicated relationships to their own marriage plots, it is the narrative and characterological structures—often flattened out or simplified—that have made their way through the centuries in many forms. These structures have impacted our modern assumptions about the role of health and wellness in happy (usually heterosexual) plots and lives.[6]

Elizabeth Bennet's status as the heroine of *Pride and Prejudice* is built on a foundation of her good health, often expressed through her mobility. Elizabeth's particular marriage plot depends on her ability to travel to wherever Darcy is, whether that means walking three miles through the mud to Netherfield, making the twenty-four-mile journey to Rosings, or traveling to Derbyshire with her aunt and uncle, which results in a tour of Pemberley and the crucial reconciliation between Elizabeth and Darcy.[7] Before this last trip, the narrator tells us that "one enjoyment was certain—that of suitableness of companions; a suitableness which comprehended health and temper to bear inconveniencies" (*PP*, 231). The conflation of "[good] health and [good] temper" demonstrates how health and sickness are not simply bodily states but character traits. While not quite a physiognomic schema, where internal traits manifest visibly (and usually permanently) on the body, good temper is nonetheless realized through bodily health. Seemingly a straightforward comment on the immediate companions, the crucial role this journey plays in the marriage plot retroactively draws our attention to the importance of "health and temper" to companionable relationships more broadly, especially conjugal love and companionate marriage, where women were expected to be partners to their husbands, rather than dependent on them.[8]

In contrast to Elizabeth's literal and narrative mobility, Anne de Bourgh's chronic sickliness exists in a kind of narrative dead space. Anne's illness is not a narrative event, nor does it incite any. Anne's illness never materially manifests in the action of the text. Her speech is never reported, either directly or indirectly, by the narrator. As a result, she never complains of pain, and we never hear about her symptoms. Anne's lack of movement is noted; her refusal to leave her phaeton to enter the Collins's house is interpreted by Elizabeth as snobbishness, and by Mr. Collins as the sign of her importance (*PP*, 156). Both conflate a potential marker of illness with one of class. But just as we never hear Anne speak, we also never see Anne move, and so we do not know if—or to what extent, or with what assistance—she can. Instead, we are given the constant refrain of the descriptor "sickly": her "sickly constitution" (66), her "sickly and cross" demeanor, her "pale and sickly" body (159). When the narrator moves to describe Anne beyond these terms, all that is said is that "her features, though not plain, were insignificant" (159). The same can be said of Anne's character. Anne has no "features" beyond her illness; her illness is all that signifies. Far from acting as a real rival, Anne produces only a shadow narrative in which Darcy marries Anne in spite of her illness and because of her money. Yet even in this spectral alternative, Anne is positioned not as a character, but as a narrative punishment for Darcy's greed—as Elizabeth makes clear when she calls the "sickly and cross" Anne a "proper wife" for the ill-natured (so to speak) Darcy. In a novel that depends so heavily on character mobility and flexibility to further the plot, Anne is essentially excluded from the narrative itself.

Indeed, given the limits of her characterization, we might say that Anne is entirely constituted by her sickness, which operates almost solely on the level of metaphor. David Mitchell and Sharon Snyder have identified the "perpetual discursive dependency on disability" as a "narrative prosthesis," designed to provide a "metaphorical signifier of social and individual collapse."[9] Anne certainly operates as a social critique in this way. Her illness, we are told, prevents her from being presented at court; this—alongside Lady Catherine's desire to marry her to her cousin Darcy in order to join their obscenely large fortunes—signifies the antisocial, insular nature of those who put their pride above all sentiment. As the consequence of Lady Catherine's overbearing aristocratic greed, Anne's illness implies that treating your daughter only as a means of consolidating interest leads to a daughter who has no substance but her femininity and her class status—pathologized as "sickly" languorousness and "cross" antisociability. Austen's recourse to illness as metaphor accords with Mitchell and Snyder's observation of narrative's "discursive dependence" on disability. However, while Anne is Elizabeth's most direct structural foil because both are potential wives for Darcy, she neither furthers nor obstructs the marriage plot. Her illness is not the "object of [narrative] fascination" that Mitchell and Snyder identify in disability, nor does it operate as a "textual obstacle" to "narrative open-endedness."[10] On the level of the plot, Anne's illness does not operate at all. While an acute illness like Jane's fever acts as a stimulant to Elizabeth's marriage plot, the chronically ill Anne is nearly, if not entirely, irrelevant. One can imagine a version of Anne who is freed from the constraints of heterosexuality by her exclusion from it, but it is perhaps easier to imagine a version of *Pride and Prejudice* without Anne.

Austen constructs Elizabeth as a kind of proto-feminist who offers a class-conscious critique of idealized white femininity as passive, inactive, and non-agential. Reading *Pride and Prejudice* through a disability studies lens, however, forces us to consider how to engage substantively with legitimate social critiques that make illness a figure for social ills—that pathologize, in other words, the object of the critique. How does health function as a prerequisite to serving as a protagonist in certain genres and for certain women? What are the consequences of these narrative structures for the lived experience of illness and disability, where women wait an average of four years for diagnoses initially brushed off as domestic or professional frailty—whose illness, in other words, signifies only metaphorically?[11] Further research will hopefully continue to complicate our understanding of the role of health and strength in representations of normative and heterosexual femininities.[12]

Notes

1. Jane Austen, *Pride and Prejudice,* ed. Vivien Jones (London: Penguin, 2014), henceforth cited parenthetically in the text as *PP.*

2. Marilynn Farwell, *Heterosexual Plots and Lesbian Narratives* (New York: New York University Press, 1996), 31.

3. Rosemarie Garland-Thomson, *Extraordinary Bodies: Figuring Physical Disability in American Literature and Culture* (New York: Columbia University Press, 1997), 27, 38–43.

4. Mary Wollstonecraft, *A Vindication of the Rights of Woman* and *A Vindication of the Rights of Man*, ed. Janet Todd (Oxford: Oxford University Press, 1993), 111.

5. See John Wiltshire, *Jane Austen and the Body: "The Picture of Health"* (Cambridge: Cambridge University Press, 1992). Wiltshire's analysis provides perspective on the persistent theme of bodily health across Austen's oeuvre, though when attention is given to *Pride and Prejudice*, Wiltshire's primary focus is on the nervous Mrs. Bennet and the acutely ill Jane Bennet, not on Anne de Bourgh.

6. For example, while Austen's novels are not unambiguous in their understanding of health and illness, Bryan Kozlowski's *The Jane Austen Diet* (Nashville: Turner Publishing, 2019) builds on the idea that Austen had a particular insight into health and wellness. Laura Mechling's review of Kozlowski's book in *Vogue* operates on the same assumption, calling Austen "something of a health-and-happiness guru." Lauren Mechling, "What Jane Austen Can Teach Us about Wellness," *Vogue*, 4 March 2019; *https://www.vogue.com/article/what-jane-austen-can-teach-us-about-wellness.*

7. Wiltshire notes that, in the first case, Austen's narrative plotting acts as a commentary on the ill Mrs. Bennet's attempt to effect Jane's marriage plot: Jane's subsequent illness leads to Elizabeth showcasing her health and vibrancy, bringing her into contact with Darcy, who is smitten by those marks of good health (Wiltshire, *Jane Austen and the Body*, 5).

8. This was an ideological and narratological norm rather than a reflection of lived experience. See Ruth Perry, *Novel Relations: The Transformation of Kinship in English Literature and Culture, 1748–1818* (Cambridge: Cambridge University Press, 2004), 192–96. Perry prefers not to use the term "companionate marriage," instead using "privatized marriage." I use "companionate" because I am interested in the narrative norm as an ideology and expectation.

9. David Mitchell and Sharon Snyder, *Narrative Prosthesis: Disability and the Dependency of Discourse* (Ann Arbor: University of Michigan Press, 2000), 47.

10. Mitchell and Snyder, *Narrative Prosthesis,* 57, 50.

11. "Women and Autoimmunity," American Autoimmune Related Diseases, Inc, *https://www.aarda.org/who-we-help/patients/women-and-autoimmunity/.*

12. The question of how mainstream feminism's focus on independence and resilience has affected the inclusion of ill and disabled women has been discussed in feminist theory. See, for example, Susan Wendell, *The Rejected Body: Feminist Philosophical Reflections on Disability* (New York: Routledge, 1996), esp. 144–50.

Rochester's Libertinism and the Pleasure of Debility

DECLAN KAVANAGH

In "The Maimed Debauchee"—a poem written c. 1675 and attributed to John Wilmot, Earl of Rochester—the speaker laments the onset of "days of impotence," which are caused "by pox and wine's unlucky chance."[1] Suffering from the aggregated symptoms of years of libertine overindulgence in sex and wine (namely, syphilis and cirrhosis of the liver), the debilitated libertine, who is now "deprived of force but pressed with courage still," reflects upon his former exploits (line 2). The speaker addresses himself to "new-listed soldiers," younger would-be male libertines, who might "meanly shrink" at the prospect of pursuing such pleasure (line 23). In literal and metaphorical terms, the speaker is militant about sexual pleasure, both physical and imaginative:

> Nor shall the sight of honourable scars,
> Which my too forward valour did procure,
> Frighten new-listed soldiers from the wars:
> Past joys have more than paid what I endure. (lines 21–22)

Although now physically impaired and "On the dull shore of lazy temperance" (line 16), the speaker does not recall his own impairment in terms of past or future treatments. The androcentric narrative fantasy conjured in this poem does not imagine improvement in terms of the treatment of the libertine's debilitated embodiment. Instead, the narrative focuses upon the pleasure that can be reached through bodily impairment. For the maimed debauchee of the poem's title, the memory of past pleasures more than compensates for his present sufferings. However, aside from the recollection of past pleasure, impairment itself is given an erotic valence in "The Maimed Debauchee," insofar as debility emerges as a crucial part of libertine praxis.

Scholars in disability studies have recently begun to theorize the politics of debility with decisive consequences for readings in the field. In *The Right to Maim*, Jasbir K. Puar mobilizes "the term 'debility' as a needed disruption … of the category of disability and as a triangulation of the ability/disability binary."[2] Puar argues that "while some bodies may not be recognized as disabled, they may well be debilitated, in part by being foreclosed access to legibility and resources as disabled."[3] Although Puar focuses on twenty-first-century liberal politics, she contends that "disability is not a fixed state … but exists in relation to assemblages of capacity and debility, modulated across historical time."[4] Debility in its current historical modulation registers as bodily injury and social exclusion engendered by economic and political forces, with entire populations debilitated and denied access to the distribution of privilege afforded through disability rights discourse. In late seventeenth-century England, debility took on a different valence within a libertine imaginary in which incapacitation was a sign of privilege, not disadvantage. Indeed, the very historicity of disability and debility are interwoven into the transmissional record of poems like "The Maimed Debauchee." Some versions are entitled "The Disabled Debauchee," and this textual variation teasingly hints at an ontological oscillation between the state of being "disabled" and that of being "maimed." While all versions of the poem present crip embodiment as erotically charged, they do not all present this eroticism as queer. As Harold Love notes, seven manuscripts omit the stanza that refers to the speaker's sex with the linkboy.[5] States of debility, disability, and queerness are variously present or absent across the different versions of this poem. While the age of the linkboy is not stated, the speaker does refer to him engaging in sexual intercourse with Cloris. Therefore, the kind of queerness that I attribute to this passage reads the linkboy firmly as a young man and not as a "boy" (at least, insofar as we presently conceive of that category). The reading that follows also focuses upon the "Maimed" version, which includes lines 37–40, in order to attend to the specific register that *maimedness* invokes as a privileged kind of debility in queer libertine discourse. In historicizing Puar's reading of contemporary debility, I argue that in Restoration aristocratic male culture, debility is rendered as bodily injury endured and *sustained* through social and political privilege.

Debility confers access to pleasure for the elite man at a historical juncture long before disability had coalesced into a rights-based discourse. In thinking through libertine experience and what we today would call disability, I argue that the debility arising from sexually acquired infections offered a prized opportunity for male libertines to imaginatively experience pleasure. In *Itch, Clap, Pox*, Noelle Gallagher argues that "a good many eighteenth-century writers and artists" did not consider sexually transmitted infections to be "serious."[6] Sexual infections, like gonorrhoea and syphilis, were widely believed to be "curable," if not "treatable."[7] As an erotic discourse that foregrounds the capacity of the sensory body, libertine writing is deeply invested in representations of the (white and male) body and its pleasures. Yet, the body that is erotically emplaced in libertine discourse is rarely ever an able one. Pleasure and infection merge. From Rochester's self-described cankered phallus to Charles Churchill's syphilitic sores to James Boswell's burning infection, readers consistently find that sexual disease imaginatively infects libertine language just as it also, in a more material sense, courses through libertine practices. Gallagher is interested in the cultural representations of disease as well as in showing how "satirists used the accusation of venereal disease to attack public figures ... [and] to scrutinize the larger social, political and legal systems that allowed powerful men to stay in power."[8] Like Gallagher, I am interested in tracing the connections between masculinity and sexual infection. However, I argue that libertine accounts of venereal disease function not only at the level of discourse, but also operate at the level of experience. Whilst these accounts are undoubtedly satirical, on a more immediate level they also offer up a space for readers to confront the pleasures of impairment. Poems like the "Maimed Debauchee" paradoxically valorize *maimedness* as a powerfully disempowering white, male experience.

As presented by Rochester, venereal disease is not only not "serious," but the physical impairment that stems from it is actually rendered imaginatively pleasurable. Infection and its consequences mark out a specific register of libertine experience that is, in fact, desirable. As David M. Turner remarks, "Scholars of the eighteenth century ... face the problem of writing disability history before 'disability' existed in its modern sense."[9] While modern understandings of disability cannot loosely be applied to Restoration culture, Turner has shown that the "term 'disabled' was most often used in relation to fitness for military or naval service."[10] In gesturing toward impairment, libertine literature often employs this militaristic use of *disabled* in its symbolic comparison of military wounds with (the more amorously arrived at) chancres and sores. Susan Sontag argues in *Illness as Metaphor* that the "military metaphor [in accounts of illness] first came into wide use in the

1880s, with the identification of bacteria as agents of disease."[11] Attending to erotic libertine writing as illness narrative helps us to complicate Sontag's reading of the military metaphor in medicine. In the context of disability's prehistory, militaristic imagery serves to encode debility as pleasurable and empowering. The aged libertine is the distinguished army general who enjoys a privileged kind of safety. Gallagher argues that in Rochester's poetry, specifically, "venereal disease is not dismissed but glorified."[12] Yet what is actually glorified in these accounts is not venereal disease *per se,* but rather the pleasurable debility that this disease engenders. The figuring of male libertine debility as pleasure is a crucial, albeit overlooked, trope in disability's gendered prehistory. Too often, the erotic valences of debility get overlooked due, in part, to our own contemporary cultural and political de-eroticizing of impaired bodies.

In thinking about the discourse of male libertinage and debility, I am reminded of what Rosemarie Garland-Thomson describes as the: "*normate* [body] ... the veiled subject position of the cultural self ... outlined by the array of deviant others whose marked bodies shore up the normate's boundaries."[13] How might the normate white, male body, at particular historical moments, shore up its boundaries by incorporating the debilitating experience of *maimedness*? In libertine literature, sexual infection is necessary as a route to an experience of pleasure that is only ever possible through debilitated embodiment. Jason S. Farr has persuasively argued that Restoration and early eighteenth-century Anglophone literatures depict people with physical disabilities as incapable of heterosexual sex, whilst also positioning libertine sexuality as the apotheosis of manhood.[14] Complicating Farr's prehistory, I view libertines like Rochester as privileging the experience of debility as a stimulus for heightened erotic pleasure. If debility is a limit, then it is a prized one that offers valued possibilities for the erotic imagination.

In "The Maimed Debauchee," the speaker is clear that his debility now prevents him from engaging in sexual activity: "I'll fire his blood by telling what I did / When I was strong and able to bear arms" (lines 31–32). According to Farr, the "spectre of corporeal failure permeates" libertine poetry.[15] Although the libertine speaker is no longer capable, his erotic authority is actually leveraged from his debilitated embodiment. Corporeal failure is recast as privileged debility; it is the speaker's *ability* to inspire sex acts through narrative description that is successfully foregrounded. Rochester's inspiration porn aims then to imaginatively conjure an erotic community in which debility is not abject, but rather confers privilege, status, and descriptive power upon propertied white men:

Or should some cold-complexioned sot forbid,
With his dull morals, our bold night alarms,
I'll fire his blood by telling what I did
When I was strong and able to bear arms.

I'll tell of whores attacked (their lords at home),
Bawds' quarters beaten up and fortress won,
Windows demolished, watches overcome,
And handsome ills by my contrivance done.
With tales like these I will such heat inspire (lines 29–36; 41).

From violent scouring (the libertine practice of vandalizing property and abusing people) to sexual intercourse with Cloris and the linkboy (lines 37–40), the poem's concluding lines bristle with libertine physicality. Erotic inability in this part of the poem gets attributed to the phlegmatic inaction of the young man, whose cold constitution, in humoral terms, requires the "heat" of the speaker's narrative power to warm him into pleasurable action. Far from shoring up the normate body, the speaker of the "Maimed Debauchee" eschews physical ability in favour of the more elevated pleasures that are solely reached through the lived experience of embodied debility. While the history of sexuality has done much to denaturalize conceptions of the sexually normal across time and space, such work—despite its care and attention in other ways—has failed to account for the ways in which diseased or impaired bodies shaped, and ultimately dictated, the period's dominant narratives of sex and gender. Accounting for the pleasurableness of experiential debility in libertine writing offers us one crucial way of addressing this ellipsis. Reading debility in Rochester invites us to trace how impaired bodies are also pleasurable bodies. Crucially, however, such male crip embodiment emerges in Restoration culture as only ever pleasurable for the few, not the many.

Notes

1. John Wilmot, Earl of Rochester (attributed), "The Maimed Debauchee," lines 13–14, in *John Wilmot, Earl of Rochester: The Complete Works*, ed. Frank H. Ellis (London: Penguin Books, 1994), 87, henceforth cited parenthetically in the text by line number.

2. Jasbir K. Puar, *The Right to Maim: Debility, Capacity, Disability* (Durham: Duke University Press, 2017), xv.

3. Puar, *The Right to Maim*, xv.

4. Puar, *The Right to Maim*, xiv.

5. Harold Love, ed. *The Works of John Wilmot, Earl of Rochester* (Oxford: Oxford University Press, 1999), 370.

6. Noelle Gallagher, *Itch, Clap, Pox: Venereal Disease in the Eighteenth-Century Imagination* (New Haven: Yale University Press, 2018), 14.

7. Gallagher, *Itch, Clap, Pox,* 14.

8. Gallagher, *Itch, Clap, Pox,* 14.

9. David M. Turner, *Disability in Eighteenth-Century England: Imagining Physical Impairment* (London: Routledge, 2012), 11.

10. Turner, *Disability*, 33.

11. Susan Sontag, *Illness as Metaphor* (London: Allen Lane, 1979), 65–66.

12. Gallagher, *Itch, Clap, Pox,* 23.

13. Rosemarie Garland-Thomson, *Extraordinary Bodies: Figuring Physical Disability in American Culture and Literature* (New York: Columbia University Press, 1997), 8.

14. Jason S. Farr, "Libertine Sexuality and Queer-Crip Embodiment in Eighteenth-Century Britain." *Journal for Early Modern Cultural Studies*, 4, no. 16 (2016): 96–118.

15. Farr, "Libertine Sexuality," 103, 114.

Contributors to Volume 50

Sharon Alker is the Chair of Humanities and Fine Arts and the Mary A. Denny Professor of English and General Studies at Whitman College in Washington State. She has co-edited *James Hogg and the Literary Marketplace: Scottish Romanticism and the Working-Class Author* (Ashgate, 2009) and *Robert Burns and Transatlantic Culture* (Ashgate, 2012) and published articles on such authors as Margaret Cavendish, Daniel Defoe, John Galt, Maria Edgeworth, Aphra Behn, Mary Brunton, and James Hogg. Her co-authored monograph on the literary representation of siege warfare, *Besieged: Early Modern British Siege Literature, 1642–1722*, has just been published by McGill-Queen's University Press.

Olivia Carpenter is a doctoral candidate in the English department at Harvard University. Her dissertation examines the relationship between racialized marriage plots and colonial archives in the long eighteenth century. A version of this essay won the 2019 ASECS Race and Empire Caucus Graduate Student Essay Prize.

Anaclara Castro-Santana is a Lecturer in the English Department at the School of Philosophy and Letters of the National Autonomous University of Mexico (UNAM). She took her PhD in English at the University of York, sponsored by a scholarship from the Mexican National Council of Science and Technology (CONACyT). She is the author of *Errors and Reconciliations: Marriage in the Plays and Novels of Henry Fielding* (Routledge, 2018), as well as various articles and book chapters about Laurence Sterne, William Hogarth, Jonathan Swift, Eliza Haywood, and Daniel Defoe.

Hannah Chaskin recently received her PhD in English from Northwestern University. Her research focuses on queer theory and narrative form, and her current book project explores the representation and construction of femininity in the eighteenth-century epistolary novel. Her work can be found in *Modern Philology* and *Women's Writing*.

Logan J. Connors is Associate Professor of Modern Languages and Literatures at the University of Miami. He is the author of *Dramatic Battles in Eighteenth-Century France* (Voltaire Foundation, 2012) and *The Emergence of a Theatrical Science of Man in France,*

1660–1740 (Voltaire Foundation, 2020). His new project explores the relationships between theater and the military in France and its colonial empire from 1650–1815.

Alison DeSimone is Assistant Professor of Musicology at the University of Missouri–Kansas City. She has a forthcoming monograph entitled *The Power of Pastiche: Musical Miscellany and Cultural Identity in Early Eighteenth-Century England* (Clemson University Press) and, with Matthew Gardner, she edited *Music and the Benefit Performance in Eighteenth-Century Britain* (Cambridge University Press, 2020). Her articles appear in the *A-R Online Anthology*, *Händel-Jahrbuch*, and *Early Modern Women*. In 2018, she won the Ruth Solie Prize for an Outstanding Article on British Music from the North American British Music Studies Association.

Laurent Dubois is Professor of Romance Studies and History and the Faculty Director of the Forum for Scholars and Publics at Duke University. He is the author of eight books, including *The Banjo: America's African Instrument* (Harvard University Press, 2016) and, with Richard Turits, *Freedom Roots: Histories from the Caribbean* (University of North Carolina Press, 2019).

Amy Dunagin is an assistant professor of history at Kennesaw State University, where she specializes in the cultural and political history of Britain and its empire. Recent publications include "A Nova Scotia Scheme and the Imperial Politics of Ulster Emigration" in the *Journal of British Studies* and "Tory Defenses of English Music: Thomas Tudway and Roger North" in *Eighteenth-Century Life*. She is currently completing a book manuscript entitled "The Land without Music: English Identity and the Italian Other." Following a doctorate in history and musicology from Yale University, Dunagin served as Managing Editor of *Eighteenth-Century Studies* between 2015 and 2017.

Michael Edson is associate professor of English at the University of Wyoming and associate editor for *Eighteenth-Century Life*. His articles have appeared in or are forthcoming in the *Journal for Eighteenth-Century Studies*, *The Eighteenth Century*, *Textual Cultures*, and *1650–1850: Ideas, Aesthetics, and Inquiries in the Early Modern Era*. His edited volume, *Annotation in Eighteenth-Century Poetry* (Lehigh University Press), appeared in 2017.

Jason S. Farr is assistant professor of English at Marquette University. His book, *Novel Bodies: Disability and Sexuality in Eighteenth-Century Britain*, was published by Bucknell University Press in 2019.

D. Christopher Gabbard is Professor of English at the University of North Florida, where he teaches courses in British Enlightenment literature, Disability Studies in the Humanities, and creative nonfiction. He is the author of *A Life beyond Reason: A Father's Memoir* (Beacon, 2019) and co-editor of *A Cultural History of Disability in the Long Eighteenth Century* (Bloomsbury, 2020). His work has appeared in numerous journals, including *PMLA* and *Eighteenth-Century Studies,* and he serves on the editorial board of the *Journal of Literary and Cultural Disability Studies*.

Anne Greenfield is Associate Professor of English at Valdosta State University. She is editor of the book collections *Interpreting Sexual Violence: 1660–1800* (Pickering and Chatto, 2013) and *Castration, Impotence, and Emasculation in the Long Eighteenth Century* (Routledge, 2019) and she has published articles on Restoration and eighteenth-century literature, especially drama. She is Editor-in-Chief of *Restoration and Eighteenth-Century Theatre Research*.

Julia Hamilton is a PhD candidate in Historical Musicology at Columbia University, where she is writing a dissertation, "Political Songs in Polite Society: Singing about Africans in the Time of the British Abolition Movement." Her work explores the intersections of antislavery politics, masquerade culture, and women's domestic music-making practices in the late eighteenth and early nineteenth centuries.

W. Scott Howard received his Ph.D. (1998) in English and Critical Theory from the University of Washington, Seattle. His teaching, research, and publications engage the fields of Renaissance and early modern literature and culture, modern and postmodern American poetry, literary and cultural theory, and book arts and digital humanities. He is founding editor of *Appositions: Studies in Renaissance / Early Modern Literature and Culture*; co-editor, with Sara van den Berg, of *The Divorce Tracts of John Milton: Texts & Contexts* (Duquesne University Press, 2010); and editor of *An Collins and the Historical Imagination* (Ashgate, 2014). His most recent book, *Archive and Artifact: Susan Howe's Factual Telepathy*, was published by Talisman House in 2019. Scott's work has received support from the Modern Language Association; the Pew Charitable Trusts; the National Endowment for the Humanities; the Beinecke Library, Yale University; and the Andrew W. Mellon Foundation. At the University of Denver, he is Professor of English and Literary Arts, and Editor of *Denver Quarterly*.

Melissa Hyde is Professor of Art History and Distinguished Teaching Scholar in the School of Art and Art History at the University of Florida. Her books include *Making Up the Rococo: François Boucher and His Critics* (Getty Research Institute, 2006) and several co-edited volumes of essays: *Women, Art, and the Politics of Identity in Eighteenth-Century Europe* (Ashgate, 2003), *Rethinking Boucher* (Getty Research Institute, 2006), *Plumes et pinceaux: l'art français vue par les Européenes* (Les Presses du réel, 2012), and *Rococo Echo: Art, Theory, and Historiography* (Voltaire Foundation, 2014). In fall 2019, she co-edited a special issue of *Journal 18* entitled "Self/Portrait." Hyde co-curated with the late Mary Sheriff the exhibition, *Becoming a Woman in the Age of Enlightenment: French Art from the Horvitz Collection* (Ackland Art Museum, University of North Carolina, 2017). She holds an honorary doctorate from her alma mater, Colorado College. In 2018–19, she served as president of ASECS.

Declan Kavanagh is Senior Lecturer in Eighteenth-Century Studies in the School of English, University of Kent, United Kingdom. He is the author of *Effeminate Years: Literature, Politics, and Aesthetics in Mid-Eighteenth-Century Britain* (Bucknell University Press, 2017).

Meghan Kobza recently completed her PhD at Newcastle University. Her dissertation and published work focus on the masquerade as an elite space of sociability where fashionable display, recognition, and conspicuous consumption were used to reinforce, rather than transgress, social identities and status hierarchies in Britain and its North American colonies. She has received several prizes for her conference papers, including the BSECS Presidential Prize (2018) and the Midwest Conference on British Studies prize for the best postgraduate paper (2019). Kobza was also awarded the Omohundro Institute of Early American History and Culture's Georgian Papers Programme Fellowship in 2018.

Travis Chi Wing Lau is Assistant Professor of English at Kenyon College. He researches and teaches eighteenth- and nineteenth-century British literature, health humanities, and disability studies.

Erica Levenson is Assistant Professor of Music History at the Crane School of Music, SUNY Potsdam. She has published on Anglo-French translation and cultural adaptation, including in *Music, Myth, and Story in Medieval and Early Modern Culture* (Boydell and Brewer, 2019). The research for the present article was supported by the American Musicological Society's Jan LaRue Travel Fund and a Cornell University Society for the Humanities Dissertation Research Travel Grant. She holds a PhD in musicology from Cornell University.

Heather McPherson is Professor of Art History at the University of Alabama at Birmingham. She is the author of *Art and Celebrity in the Age of Reynolds and Siddons* (Pennsylvania State University Press, 2017). Her research focuses on portraiture, caricature, and cultural politics, and the intersections between the visual and performing arts. She served as President of ASECS in 2010–11.

Rebecca Messbarger is Professor of Italian and a cultural historian of medicine at Washington University, where she was founding director of the Medical Humanities Program. Her book *The Lady Anatomist: The Life and Work of Anna Morandi Manzolini* (University of Chicago Press, 2010) was a finalist for the College Art Association's 2012 Charles Rufus Morey Book Award, and is the inspiration for a German feature film, directed by Iris Fegerl, to be released in Italy and the United States in 2021. She is also the author of *The Century of Women: Representations of Women in Eighteenth-Century Italian Public Discourse* (University of Toronto Press, 2002) and co-edited, with Christopher Johns and Philip Gavitt, *Benedict XIV and the Enlightenment: Art, Science, and Spirituality* (University of Toronto Press, 2016). Among her articles is "The Re-Birth of Venus in Florence's Royal Museum of Physics and Natural History" in *The Journal of the History of Collections*, which won the 2012–13 James L. Clifford Prize from the American Society for Eighteenth-Century Studies and the 2014 Percy G. Adams Prize from the Southeastern Society for Eighteenth-Century Studies.

Holly Faith Nelson is Professor and Chair of English, and Co-Director of the Gender Studies Institute, at Trinity Western University in Langley, British Columbia, Canada. She has co-edited nine volumes, most recently *Games and War in Early Modern English Literature: From Shakespeare to Swift* (Amsterdam University Press, 2019), and her co-authored study, *Besieged: Early Modern British Siege Literature, 1642–1722,* has just been published by McGill-Queen's University Press. She has published widely on the literature of the seventeenth and long eighteenth centuries, often examining Scottish literature composed during the Renaissance, Restoration, or Romantic periods.

Felicity A. Nussbaum, Distinguished Research Professor at the University of California, Los Angeles, is author most recently of *Rival Queens: Actresses, Performance, and the Eighteenth-Century British Theatre* (University of Pennsylvania Press, 2010). Among her other books are *The Arabian Nights in Historical Context* (Oxford University Press, 2008) with Saree Makdisi; *The Limits of the Human: Fictions of Anomaly, Race, and Gender* (Cambridge University Press, 2003); and *Torrid Zones: Maternity, Sexuality and Empire* (Johns Hopkins University Press, 1995). Her most recent essay is "Racial Intimacies: Indian Ayahs, British Mothers" in a special issue of *1650–1850: Ideas, Aesthetics, and Inquiries*; and she has just completed a play on Hester Thrale Piozzi.

Jason H. Pearl is Associate Professor of English at Florida International University. He is the author of *Utopian Geographies and the Early English Novel* (University of Virginia Press, 2014) and Book Reviews Editor at *Digital Defoe*. His current project investigates balloon flight and the view from above in late eighteenth- and early nineteenth-century Britain.

Adam Schoene received a Ph.D. in Romance Studies from Cornell University. He is currently at work on a project that interrogates the politics of silence in literary depictions of despotism. His work has previously appeared in journals such as *Eighteenth-Century Studies, The French Review, George Sand Studies, The Journal of North African Studies,* and *Law and Humanities,* and in a range of edited volumes. He served on the editorial board of *Diacritics,* and as Managing Editor of *Eighteenth-Century Studies.*

Madeline Sutherland-Meier specializes in Spanish literature, particularly the Spanish Ballad or *Romancero* and Spanish periodicals. She is the author of *Mass Culture in the Age of Enlightenment: The Blindman's Ballads of Eighteenth-Century Spain* (Peter Lang, 1991) and co-editor of *Leo Spitzer: Representative Essays* (Stanford University Press, 1988). Her current research focuses on the *Semanario Erudito,* a late eighteenth-century periodical, and on the history of disability in Spain.

Morgan Vanek is Assistant Professor in the Department of English at the University of Calgary, where her research and teaching focus on transatlantic literature, environmental writing, and the history and philosophy of science. Her work has appeared in *Eighteenth-Century Fiction,* the *Journal for Eighteenth-Century Studies, Literature Compass,* and as part of *Climate and Literature,* a new volume for the Cambridge Critical Concepts series. She is currently at work on a book about the politics of weather in eighteenth-century British literature.

Howard D. Weinbrot (1936–2021) was Ricardo Quintana Professor of English, Emeritus, and William Freeman Vilas Research Professor, Emeritus, at the University of Wisconsin, Madison. After retiring from the classroom, he spent a number of years as a reader at the Huntington Library. Its friendly confines helped him write numerous essays on Swift, Johnson, Fielding, Richardson, historical criticism, sermons, and satire. As of the time of this volume's release, his most recent books were *Literature, Religion, and the Evolution of Culture, 1660–1780* (Johns Hopkins University Press, 2013) and the edited collection, *Samuel Johnson: New Contexts for a New Century* (Huntington Library, 2014). He was also working on a long study of how Pierre-Antoine de la Place and Samuel Johnson helped Shakespeare to become accepted in eighteenth-century France. Voltaire was not amused.

Jessica Zimble is a doctoral student in the Department of English Literature and Linguistics at Bar Ilan University in Ramat Gan, Israel. Zimble is a recipient of the Presidential Fellowship and the Rector Prize. Her dissertation, "Entrapped by Ideology: Confinement and Flight in *Clarissa*," explores the motif of entrapment and release in relation to contemporary debates about filial duty, female choice in marriage, chastity, and suicide in the eighteenth century. Jessica received her B.A. and M.A. from the University of Pennsylvania.

ASECS Executive Board 2018–2019

For information about the
American Society for Eighteenth-Century Studies, please contact:
ASECS
Buffalo State College
1300 Elmwood Avenue, KH213
Buffalo, NY 14222
Telephone: (716) 878-3405
Fax: (716) 878-4939
E-mail: asecsoffice@gmail.com
Website: http://ASECS.press.jhu.edu

331

American Society for Eighteenth-Century Studies